Knowledge, Scale and Transactions in the Theory of the Firm

Firms in market economies vary enormously in size, nature and competitiveness. In this important contribution to the literature on the theory of the firm, Mario Morroni provides a new analytical framework which improves our understanding of the causes of this diversity in organisational design and performance. The relations between internal and external basic conditions, decision-making mechanisms and organisational coordination are addressed, as are the circumstances in which capabilities, transactions and scale-scope considerations interact. With the emergence of the knowledge-based economy and the increasing pressure of global competition, the development of capabilities is acquiring ever-greater importance in boosting competitiveness. Morroni shows that long-term relational agreements enhance learning processes and offer powerful tools for improving competitiveness in a context of conflicting interests, incomplete knowledge and uncertainty.

MARIO MORRONI is Professor of Economics in the Department of Economics of the University of Pisa, Italy.

T0328793

Knowledge, Scale and Transactions in the Theory of the Firm

MARIO MORRONI

CAMBRIDGE
UNIVERSITY PRESS

CAMBRIDGE UNIVERSITY PRESS
Cambridge, New York, Melbourne, Madrid, Cape Town, Singapore,
São Paulo, Delhi, Dubai, Tokyo

Cambridge University Press
The Edinburgh Building, Cambridge CB2 8RU, UK

Published in the United States of America by Cambridge University Press, New York

www.cambridge.org
Information on this title: www.cambridge.org/9780521123181

First published 2006
This digitally printed version 2009

A catalogue record for this publication is available from the British Library

ISBN 978-0-521-86243-1 Hardback
ISBN 978-0-521-12318-1 Paperback

To Giorgia, Rossana and Lorenzo – with love

Contents

Figures

Tables

Acknowledgements

I started this book seven years ago during a visit to the Institute of Management, Innovation and Organisation, Hass School of Business, University of California, Berkeley. I continued in the subsequent months at Clare Hall, Cambridge University, where I was a visiting fellow. I am grateful to both these institutions for providing an ideal research setting during my sabbatical leave in 1998 and to Oliver Williamson and Elizabeth Garnsey for interesting discussions on the early project of the book. Special thanks are due to Nicolò De Vecchi, Geoffrey Harcourt and Paolo Mariti for insightful help and warm encouragement over the long time span of the book's preparation.

Two preliminary drafts of the book were completed in May 2000 (*Edizioni Il Campano*, Pisa) and in January 2001 (Department of Economics, Working Paper, no. 77, University of Pisa). I have greatly benefited from the reactions of students who used my materials in class. Colleagues who read the work in progress or participated in seminars and conferences where I presented some parts of the book have furnished useful criticisms and suggestions. This has led me to radically revise the original structure of the book, to reformulate many of my ideas and to introduce numerous substantial improvements. In particular, I owe a debt to Cristiano Antonelli, Pier Luigi Barrotta, Markus Becker, Marina Bianchi, Adriano Birolo, Carlo Borzaga, Carlo Casarosa, Sergio Cesaratto, Alfred Chandler, Roberto Ciccone, Giovanni Dosi, Stephen Dunn, Massimo Egidi, Davide Fiaschi, Francesco Filippi, Giuseppe Fontana, Nicolai Foss, Jetta Frost, Alfonso Gambardella, Paola Giuri, Henrich Greve, Neil Kay, Roger Koppl, Brian Loasby, Mauro Lombardi, Tommaso Luzzati, Andrea Mangàni, Roberto Marchionatti, Maria Cristina Marcuzzo, Nicola Meccheri, Pere Mir, Vittorio Moriggia, Bart Nooteboom, Paolo Ramazzotti, Nathan Rosenberg, Andrea Salanti, Christian Schmidt and Alberto Vannucci. I would also like to thank Chris Harrison, Lynn Dunlop and Barbara Docherty for editorial assistance and the anonymous reviewers of Cambridge University Press for thoughtful comments.

I received financial support from the Italian National Research Council (CNR) and from the University of Pisa. Finally, my thanks to Rachel Costa for her skilful language revision that has made the text both fluent and accurate.

Introduction and summary

I.1 Purpose and scope

THIS book addresses the properties, behaviour and growth of the firm. A 'firm' is defined here as a social organisation and an autonomous legal entity that produces and sells goods or services by means of a set of human, physical and financial resources that are coordinated, combined and monitored under an administrative structure. Although the focus of this book is on business organisations, its main conclusions largely concern the 'economic reasons' for all social organisations. Organisations undeniably represent a ubiquitous and dominant presence in what is usually called the 'market economy'. The efficiency of the 'market economy' depends to a very considerable extent on how social organisations operate.[1]

Since the 1980s, the literature on the theory of the firm has expanded, following numerous lines of research and offering differing interpretations of the nature of the firm. I do not propose here to provide a survey of this fast-growing literature.[2] Rather, this book examines how the relations between basic conditions, decision-making mechanisms and organisational coordination within firms influence their relative performance. The present study pursues the avenue of research started with my *Production Process and Technical Change* (Morroni, 1992), moving from analysis of the temporal, organisational and qualitative dimension of production toward a

---

[1] On the ubiquity of organisations, see Simon (1991, p. 27); on the efficiency of markets and organisations, see Coase (1991, p. 13).

[2] Useful collections of readings which offer an overview through a wide selection of the vast literature on the nature of the firm are, for instance: Barney and Ouchi (1986); Williamson and Winter (1991); Buckley and Michie (1996); Casson (1996); Putterman and Kroszner (1996b); Foss (2000); Langlois, Yu and Robertson (2002); Kay (2003); Ménard (2004a: part II, 2004g).

new analytical framework based on a cognitive perspective that also encompasses transaction and scale considerations. This makes it possible to overcome the traditional disjunction between the capabilities, transaction costs and scale–scope analyses which so far have generally been treated within separate theoretical approaches. Although scrutiny of the interaction between the foregoing three aspects highlights the fact that *some* explanations provided by the different lines of research will appear complementary rather than rival accounts, I do not set myself the task here of either outlining a synthesis of some features of the existing approaches on capabilities, transactions and scale of processes, or suggesting a joint application of these approaches.[3] I wish to stress that the primary objective of this book is, instead, to provide a theoretical perspective that seeks to improve our understanding of *organisational functioning* and *boundaries* through investigation of the basic conditions under which capability, transaction and scale–scope considerations are significant and interact in shaping the boundaries and growth of the firm. I do not dispute that further empirical work is needed, but I judge it to be essential first to make constructive efforts toward a more integrated theory of the firm on which to build additional evidence. Consequently, an application of the conceptual framework presented here is left as a possible future direction for empirical research, though in the following pages illustrative examples will be drawn from historical investigations, case studies, evidence from experimental results or surveys of applied literature. Business history and applied research on cognitive mechanisms, learning processes and innovative activity provide a vast number of case reports, giving empirical results that are consistent with the arguments developed in the present book.

I shall argue that the interplay between capability, transaction and scale–scope aspects in moulding the individual firm's performance

---

[3] A synthesis or joint application of the different existing approaches on the theory of the firm is extremely problematical because of the great heterogeneity of analytical aims, conceptions of the nature of the firm and explicit or implicit assumptions. Holmström and Tirole (1989, pp. 64–5) put it clearly in their now classic survey: 'The theory of the firm addresses a wide range of questions . . . Obviously, no single model or theory will capture all elements of the puzzle . . . Trying to organise these fragments of a theory into a coherent economic framework is difficult.' On this, see the discussion and formal framework in Gibbons (2004, pp. 1ff., 37).

and growth occurs whenever *learning processes, complementarities* and *uncertainty* matter. In particular, this interaction is intense if technical and transactional knowledge are costly, some inputs and processes are indivisible and complementary and some relevant knowledge is tacit, non-transmittable and characterised by set-up processes with high fixed costs. I would like to emphasise that these conditions, which are increasingly important with the spread of the knowledge-based economy, cause interplay among the three aspects of the organisational coordination of the firm even in the presence of perfect rational agents who make decisions under costly information and weak uncertainty.

On the other hand, *the impact* of the foregoing basic conditions on both the relevance of the three aspects of organisational coordination, and also on the interaction among them, is *strongly amplified* in all circumstances where the assumption of perfect rationality has to be abandoned because of the presence of radical uncertainty, which prevents individuals from estimating the probability distribution of future contingencies and pay-offs. Chapters 4, 5 and 6 will show that business organisations provide efficacious instruments to cope with this kind of uncertainty.

This book traces its roots backs to several pioneering works. In particular, it rests on the seminal contributions by Frank Knight and John Maynard Keynes on uncertainty; Ronald Coase on transaction costs and flexibility of the employment relationship within firms; Joseph Schumpeter, Nathan Rosenberg, Richard Nelson and Sidney Winter on the innovation activity and evolution of business organisations; Edith Penrose and Robin Marris on managerial resources and the growth of the firm; Nicholas Georgescu-Roegen and Alfred Chandler on the time profile of production and on the relationship between organisation and efficiency; and, finally, Friedrich von Hayek, Herbert Simon, George Shackle, Kenneth Arrow, Richard Cyert, James March, Brian Loasby, Daniel Kahneman and Amos Tversky on knowledge and decision-making.[4]

My attempt to develop an analytical framework involves a considerable broadening of the focus, with the unavoidable risk of sacrificing

---

[4] See Knight (1921a); Keynes (1936, 1937); Coase (1937); Schumpeter (1912); Rosenberg (1969); Nelson and Winter (1982); Penrose (1959); Marris (1964); Georgescu-Roegen (1969); Chandler (1962, 1977, 1990); Hayek (1937, 1945);

depth and omitting mention of significant works regarding some specific issues. Whenever the analysis appears too concise in relation to the complexity of the subject, I shall suggest surveys and collections of writings that provide the reader with further and more detailed discussion and exhaustive bibliographical references. Sadly, for numerous key concepts utilised in the present conceptual framework there is not yet a common vocabulary. This may cause ambiguities and misunderstandings. In the following pages, an effort is made to relate different taxonomies and clarify the definitions used in this study. At the end of the book, a Glossary gathers together the main definitions adopted.

I.2 The multifarious nature of the firm

In industrial countries, firms exhibit a very wide range of possible property and financial structures, hierarchical set-ups, incentive and control structures, size and market power, arrangement of production processes, degree of vertical integration and organisational features. Alfred Chandler showed in his historical investigation on industrial enterprises that firms have evolved by implementing new management ideas and by inventing new organisational and incentive systems, as well as by introducing new strategies and new business initiatives in the attempt to pursue economies of scale and scope.[5] The organisational structure of the firm is an evolutionary outcome of a combination of several elements, whose specific traits may take very dissimilar forms in different types of firms. In market economies, distinct organisational structures can live side by side. Suffice it to reflect on the dimensional and organisational structure of American high-tech sectors, such as microelectronics, computers, medical technologies and biotechnologies. As Nathan Rosenberg demonstrates, the American high-tech scene is complex because it is characterised by a mixture that includes a great number of start-up and small firms and, at the same time, very large business organisations such as AT&T, INM, Merck, General Electric, Johnson & Johnson, etc. The presence of different technical and organisational structures and the coexistence

Simon (1951, 1972); March and Simon (1958); Shackle (1954, 1955, 1979, 1990); Arrow (1962, 1973, 1994a); Cyert and March (1963); Cyert (1988); Loasby (1976); Tversky and Kahneman (1974); Kahneman and Tversky (1979).
[5] Chandler (1977, 1990). The multiplicity of possible organisational configurations is stressed and analysed in depth by Grandori (1995).

of firms of noticeably different size and function are common features of many industries even in mature sectors of activity.[6]

By the same token, in industrialised countries a considerable variety of ownership structures can be found. Family firms, managerial corporations, public companies, state-owned firms, partnerships, non-profit firms, social enterprises, workers' cooperatives and consumers' cooperatives all represent instances of a rich tapestry of ownership characterising the typology of the firm.

The firm's size may differ greatly even within the same sector of activity. Size ranges from a very small business to very large companies with hundreds of thousands of employees that give rise to a turnover constituting a significant percentage of their country's gross national product (GNP). The huge distinctions in the size of firms yield remarkable disparities in market power among them.

Production processes may be organised in series, in parallel and in line according to the sector of activity, the technology and the different types of equipment used. These various arrangements result in a dissimilar distribution of idle times among inputs and different forms of division of knowledge and labour.

The 1990s saw the emergence of contrasting tendencies with regard to integration and concentration processes. High levels of merger and acquisition (M&A) activity coexist with a trend in the opposite direction towards contracting out. The growth of giant firms has been based on horizontal expansion and diversification, and increasing concentration has been balanced by a tendency toward outsourcing and by new entries.[7]

The firm's organisational form may consist of just one production unit, or several production units.[8] Moreover, there are centralised enterprises (U-form), multidivisional enterprises (M-form) and holdings controlling other firms spread across various countries (H-form structure). A centralised enterprise is composed of a functionally

---

[6] Rosenberg (2002, p. 37). For a historical account of such diversity, see also Rosenberg and Birdzell (1986, pp. 189ff., 269ff.).

[7] Holmström and Roberts (1998, pp. 73, 80, 83–9); Marris (2002, pp. 74, 78).

[8] A production unit, or a business unit, consists of one or more plants situated in one or more departments, within a single establishment or in neighbouring establishments. The production unit is responsible for organising the production of a single commodity (or a range of commodities) and the corresponding production methods.

departmentalised unitary structure. The multidivisional firm is characterised by corporate headquarters whose function is to oversee a number of divisions functioning as independent profit centres organised along product, brand or geographic lines.[9] Many holdings take the form of conglomerates that control a group of subsidiary companies engaged in a variety of dissimilar and unrelated activities.

In the literature on the theory of the firm, many contributions tend to focus on one particular kind of firm – such as a particular ownership form, governance structure, size, production model or organisational form. Alternatively, and more restrictively, they may address only one distinctive aspect or single function of its activity. This has brought about a proliferation of special-purpose models with analytical results built on ad hoc hypotheses.[10] The analysis set out here does not provide a study of a particular kind of firm, nor does it attempt to build formal models that capture certain specific features of the internal behaviour of firms. Rather, this book is offered as a theoretical framework designed to study the *multifarious and changing nature* of the firm as a result of the complex links between basic conditions, organisational structure, efficiency and efficacy of business organisations.

I.3 Basic conditions, decision-making and organisational coordination

Efficiency (in terms of input requirements) and *efficacy* (in terms of matching current or potential market needs) jointly determine the

[9] Since the period between the two world wars, in many US corporations a centralised structure (U-form) has been progressively replaced by a multidivisional structure (M-form). On this, see Chandler (1962, 1977, 1990). The continuous evolution of the M-form over time in the paradigmatic case of General Motors has been analysed by Freeland (1996, 2001), who shows that control has been achieved through significant variations on the original organisational and administrative structure.

[10] Holmström and Roberts (1998, p. 75) cast strong doubts on partial models. Their paper points out, and we cannot but agree, that approaches based on 'a single instrument' result in a 'potentially misleading' explanation of the behaviour and growth of the firm. A similar position is expressed in Milgrom and Roberts (1988, p. 450). Partial models have recently attracted various criticisms from other lines of research as well; see, for instance, Simon (1991, p. 27); Dosi (1994, p. 231); Foss (1996a, pp. 470ff., 1996b, pp. 519ff.); Arena and Longhi (1998a, p. 6); Hodgson (1998b, p. 32); Krafft and Ravix (1998, p. 237).

firm's competitiveness. Both efficiency and efficacy depend on the organisational setting which, in turn, is influenced by basic conditions and internal decision-making. Naturally, the causal chain also runs in the opposite direction: the competitiveness of a firm contributes to creating the basic conditions that shape internal decision-making processes (see figure I.1).[11] This causal chain can be regarded as an adaptive toolbox useful in developing an analysis of the strengths and weaknesses of the firm, so that strategies and policies aiming to increase competitiveness can be devised.

The causal chain

Basic conditions result from the interplay between the environmental conditions that business organisations face and the internal conditions created by business organisations themselves as a result of external constraints and opportunities. The left-hand rectangular block in figure I.1 gives an overview of the basic conditions that will be discussed in depth in chapter 1.

A firm's decision-making is a consequence of the interaction between individuals and organisations created by individuals to achieve their aims. Equally, however, decision-making mechanisms also significantly affect individual aims, which can vary according to each individual's specific role in the firm. Furthermore, basic conditions such as institutional forms and market conditions shape both individual aims and the firm's organisational structure. Since individual motivations, aims and abilities are affected by the basic conditions and the firm's decision-making mechanisms, the individual cannot be treated as an isolated entity. Among important elements that influence decision-making mechanisms within the firm, property structures, control rights, the aims of the firm, incentive structures and the level of rationality occupy a salient position (central square block of figure I.1).

In order to produce and sell goods or services, a firm must:

---

[11] The tables and figures included in this book summarise the main arguments elaborated in the text. They are intended to provide a visual support that may constitute useful material for presentations and lectures. These illustrations are downloadable from the author's personal web page.

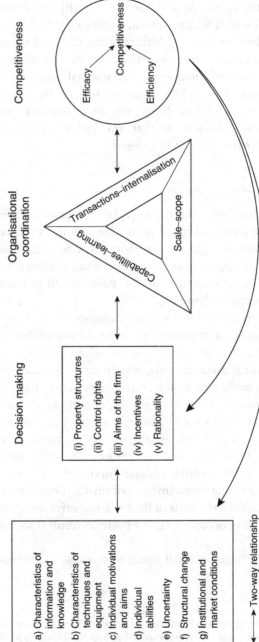

Figure I.1. Basic conditions, decision-making, coordination and competitiveness.

Basic conditions

a) Characteristics of information and knowledge
b) Characteristics of techniques and equipment
c) Individual motivations and aims
d) Individual abilities
e) Uncertainty
f) Structural change
g) Institutional and market conditions

→ Two-way relationship
→ One-way relationship

Decision making

(i) Property structures
(ii) Control rights
(iii) Aims of the firm
(iv) Incentives
(v) Rationality

Organisational coordination

Transactions–internalisation
Capabilities–learning
Scale–scope

Competitiveness

Efficacy
Competitiveness
Efficiency

- develop specific *capabilities* by coordinating and motivating learning processes
- arrange *transactions* with suppliers and customers by establishing the degree of internalisation of processes
- design the operational *scale* by balancing the different productive capacities of *indivisible* and *complementary* inputs and processes.[12]

These three aspects of the organisational coordination of the firm are listed in the central triangle in figure I.1 and extensively examined in chapter 3.

First, developing capabilities means finding, interpreting and using knowledge on both how to plan, organise and perform production processes, and how to arrange transactions with suppliers and customers in order to create and maintain a competitive advantage. Differential capabilities can help to explain the performance of firms, and therefore their boundaries.

Secondly, firms establish the level of internalisation of separable processes and organise transactions with suppliers. The internalisation of external processes eliminates the transaction costs stemming from the costliness of economic exchange. Transaction costs are usually relevant in the presence of measurement and informational problems. In particular, they can could result from insufficient knowledge concerning the characteristics of what is being exchanged and the opposing party's behaviour, and from lack of enforcement. Transaction costs affect the level of vertical integration and the extension of organisational coordination among firms. Cooperative agreements with suppliers aim to reduce transaction costs, favour specialisation and enhance learning processes. Overall, organisational coordination within or among firms encourages the transmission of information and knowledge, the strengthening of enforcement power as well as flexibility in facing unexpected contingencies.

Thirdly, in designing the operational scale of each process the firm has to balance the productive capacities of different indivisible and complementary inputs and intermediate stages. Usually, this balancing is obtained by increasing the scale dimension of individual firms or

---

[12] The financial dimension might be fruitfully added as a fourth aspect of the organisational coordination of the firm. However, the analysis of the financial dimension goes beyond the aims of this book. The integration of this aspect into the present framework could be a subject of future research.

organisations of firms, which makes it possible to reduce idle times or underutilisation of productive capacities of various inputs. Moreover, processes based on information and knowledge have a cost that is completely independent of the scale of the process in which such information and knowledge is used. This involves super-fixed costs and therefore favours remarkable economies of scale and economies of scope. Finally, in facing unpredictable contingencies, an expansion of the boundaries of organisational coordination allows economies of diversification of activities and of holding reserves that are linked to statistical factors.

The growth of the firm: strengths and weaknesses

Basically, growth is a consequence of managerial ability to build on the firm's strengths and to limit the negative consequences of various counteracting forces. A firm's strengths derive mainly from its ability to exploit potential, mutually reinforcing advantages provided by the organisational coordination of competencies, transactions and operational scale of different processes. These advantages help to explain the existence and the growth of the firm. Each of the three aspects of organisational coordination is endowed with a different degree of importance in the growth of all social organisations. In figure I.1, these three aspects are indicated within the central equilateral triangle, but in the organisational coordination of real-world firms the three aspects usually have uneven weight according to the sector of activity and the type of business organisation considered. Nonetheless, it must be stressed that it is quite rare, even though conceivable in some circumstances, for the growth of the firm to be based on advantages deriving exclusively from one aspect.

A firm can expand by hiring new resources and by allocating managerial and administrative tasks to specialist employees. The magnitude of the firm's growth rate may be affected by the need to adapt its organisational capacity, and this requires time. However, while possibly limiting the rate of growth at any moment, this need *does not* represent a limit on the expansion of its size beyond a certain point (Penrose, 1959, p. 55). Even so, there are numerous weaknesses that may result in organisational costs, to the point of hampering the growth of the firm and even precipitating its failure. The weaknesses and internal inefficiencies of firms derive from an inability to seize potential opportunities. If a firm is incapable of anticipating and adapting to environmental changes or countering the negative consequences of morally hazardous behaviour, or does not succeed in developing knowledge or cannot advantageously arrange transactions and exploit economies of scale, then this may compromise its efficiency and efficacy, hamper its growth and even cause its failure.

Many counteracting forces stem from asymmetric information and heterogeneous knowledge, such as the action of moral hazard, or influence activities, or in some cases parochial interests and burdens of bureaucracy. But the underlying cause of these weaknesses is to be sought in the lack of *managerial ability* to create the necessary knowledge, incentive structure and conditions. Several routes to overcome these flaws can be undertaken: (i) vertical communication within the organisation can be enhanced; (ii) organisational loyalties can be enlisted and incentives devised that attenuate the hazards of internal opportunistic behaviour, as well as mitigating internal influence activities and conflicts of interest; (iii) the organisational set-up and power structure can be modified in order to strengthen the competitive advantage.

The upshot is that the management's ability to seize opportunities and contrast countervailing forces is characterised by an unavoidable subjective dimension. This subjective component of managerial choice moulds the firm's evolutionary path and yields a large variety of outcomes. In the presence of limited transmittability or tradability of some bits of information and units of knowledge, the evolutionary path takes shape by means of adjustments that occur day by day and which are cumulative, partially irreversible and specific to one business organisation. The firm's revealed performance, size and boundaries must be regarded as 'time- and path-dependent' (non-path-determined) phenomena constantly influenced by the evolution of the different internal decision-making mechanisms and the various basic conditions.

Interaction of the three aspects of organisational coordination

With weak uncertainty, costly knowledge and perfectly rational agents, the interaction among competence, transaction and scale considerations may be significant. However, this interaction is significantly reinforced in the presence of cognitive limitations that prevent individuals from computing all possible pay-offs of their actions, thus obliging them to operate under radical uncertainty. Radical uncertainty is attributable to the incompleteness of the information set (substantive radical uncertainty) or to cognitive limitations in processing information (procedural radical uncertainty).[13]

The former type of radical uncertainty derives from a lack of information about possible outcomes due to the non-stationary characteristics of the environment – for instance, creative learning may produce an unexpected novelty.[14] Hereafter, the unqualified term 'learning' will be used in the sense of creative learning.[15] The intrinsic characteristics of the innovative activity, which can be regarded essentially as a learning process, are sources of substantive radical uncertainty. If individuals have to face unforeseeable contingencies at the time when the contract is drawn up, enforcement difficulties and high transaction costs arise.

The second type of radical uncertainty – procedural uncertainty – depends on personal capacities to process information in relation to the complexity of the situation that individuals find themselves facing.

Farsightedness, uncertainty and multiple decision strategies

Arguably, in many circumstances when the problem at hand is well specified and when individuals possess the relevant information and knowledge as well as sufficient information-processing ability, the hypothesis that they are able to foresee all possible pay-offs is plausible and useful for an analysis of the interaction among the various

[13] These two types of uncertainties have been analysed in depth in an insightful paper by Dosi and Egidi (1991, pp. 165ff.). These two authors have proposed to call them 'substantive' and 'procedural' uncertainty in analogy with Simon's (1972) distinction between 'substantive' and 'procedural' rationality.

[14] The analytical consequences of the transmutable and unknowable nature of the future have been discussed by Davidson (1994, pp. 87, 89–90, 1996, p. 482); Dunn (1999, pp. 204–5, 212); Slater and Spencer (2000, pp. 61ff.); Loasby (2004a, pp. 265–6).

[15] On the distinction between *acquisitional* learning, in the sense of the 'acquisition of information from a prespecified set', and *creative* learning, understood as the generation of new knowledge that broadens the set of available alternatives, see Loasby (1999, p. 3).

aspects of organisational coordination and functioning.[16] However, as stressed by the economic literature based on a cognitive perspective, in some circumstances – that are significant for decision-making within the firm – individuals lack relevant information and knowledge and do not have sufficient information-processing ability. As a consequence, they are unable to predict all possible pay-offs and operate in conditions of radical uncertainty. Within a comprehensive theory of the firm both the perspective which assumes farsightedness and that encompassing radical uncertainty must be considered, according to the particular problem under consideration. These two perspectives can coexist because they address diverse decision strategies. The analytical framework presented in this book is thus characterised by a broad generality because it can take into account different degrees of rationality and uncertainty according to the level of agents' abilities in relation to the specific problem they are facing.

Wrestling with uncertainty

If not all information and knowledge is fully transmittable and tradable and radical uncertainty is present, then market failures may occur or markets may be missing as a consequence of informational problems.[17] Most ways of contrasting radical uncertainty and its consequent market failures or missing markets imply the creation and development of organisations that have suitable instruments for mediating between conflicting interests, enforcing and regulating market contracts and limiting adverse selection and moral hazard by substituting market exchange with relational agreements. Possible responses to these problems may be found by reducing informational asymmetries and knowledge heterogeneities and restraining conflicts of interest and opportunistic behaviour through: (i) special contracts

---

[16] On how perfectly rational and self-interested organisation members might produce sub-optimal results due to inefficient, informal and institutionalised organisational behaviour, see Gibbons (2000, pp. 1, 8) who provides a comprehensive survey; other bibliographical references will be indicated later in the text.

[17] Market failure means that markets fail to achieve efficient allocation. Markets for certain commodities are missing when these markets do not exist and therefore trade does not take place even if some agents would be willing to buy or to sell these commodities. On these definitions, see Newbery (1989, pp. 212ff.) and Akerlof (1970, pp. 488ff.).

that imply screening, signalling, monitoring, incentives and safe-guards; (ii) organisations that regulate markets and enforce contracts which are not self-enforcing; and (iii) organisational coordination within and among firms.

Whenever information and enforcement are not costless, organisations have a crucial role. Contracts, which increase information and protect a given party from the other party's potential opportunistic behaviour, generally need the action of organisations that ensure enforcement and market functioning. These organisations, in turn, require expressly designed institutions that regulate contracts.

Organisational coordination may operate *within firms*, through management direction, and *among firms*, through the creation of interfirm networks.[18] Organisations foster learning by activating the exchange of information and knowledge on the market, favouring non-traded internal transmission of information and knowledge and facilitating the internal creation of tacit knowledge through experience. The substitution of market coordination by organisational coordination limits uncertainty, curtails opportunistic behaviour, assures protection for specific investment, provides incentives and increases flexibility. In so doing, organisations transform the cost of radical uncertainty into a source of superior efficiency and efficacy. Organisational coordination within and among firms is a tool to cope with uncertainty because it rests on long-term relational agreements and usually implies the existence of some reserves constituted by the asset of the firms.

As far as individual firms are concerned, their assets – such as equipment, warehouses, capabilities and competencies – represent reserves in case of unanticipated events. Moreover, firms establish relational agreements *over time* that involve adaptive decision-making in facing unanticipated changes. Long-term relational agreements provide the opportunity for managing conflicts of interests among the firm's stakeholders through mutual obligations, but also through identification of common aims and the design of incentives and rules that ensure enforcement and foster trust. With dispersed knowledge and interdependence, as is unavoidable under division of labour, *trust*

[18] See Penrose (1995, pp. xvi, xix), according to whom Richardson (1972) challenged 'the whole notion of a firm/market dichotomy', pointing out that there are three means of coordination: market coordination, direction within firms and interfirm networking.

becomes essential because work cannot proceed without recourse to knowledge possessed by others (Loasby, 1999, p. 87). The employment relationship, which is an important example among the myriad of possible relational agreements that may be established by a firm, entails the employer's authority in terms of capacity to decide on the employee's activity. The assets of the firm, which represent reserves, and the employment contracts, which include the right to specify what the employee is expected to do, both allow decisions to be postponed to 'a later and better-informed time' – that is, the possibility of *adaptive behaviour*. In this respect, the firm plays a role analogous to money, which is a purchasing power that 'can be deployed at will' and permits 'the choice to be deferred'.[19]

Rights of control within the firm ensure flexibility and reduce the degree of uncertainty in that they permit *simplification* and *learning processes*. Simplification and learning mitigate uncertainty because they diminish the gap between the abilities required and the abilities possessed. In fact, simplification – which is achieved mainly by routinised operating procedures, technical division of labour and adaptive behaviour – decreases the abilities required, while learning processes increase the abilities possessed. Simplification and learning are closely related because simplification facilitates learning by making limited cognitive resources available.

In complex and uncertain situations, cognitive and behavioural routinisation save on the abilities required and enhance coordination and predictability. Technical division of labour and knowledge transforms individual incomplete abilities into a firm's specific capabilities in producing goods and services. Division of labour requires intentional coordination, which is characterised by increasing returns because division of labour and knowledge allows managerial economies of scale – and, even more significantly, saves on the selection and transmission of information. Such a saving appears to be of overwhelming importance today, in the wake of the emergence of the new knowledge-based economy.

---

[19] Loasby (1999, pp. 90, 118). These considerations are drawn from Shackle's (1972, p. 160) analysis of money that 'allows the deferment of choice'. On this, see also the discussion in Davidson (1991a, p. 130, 1994, pp. 86ff., 1996, pp. 482, 492–3). Early important contributions on the role of power and coordination in the employment relationship come from Coase (1937, p. 38) and Simon (1951, pp. 11ff.).

Adaptive behaviour or sequential aiming is a dynamic mechanism that adjusts intermediate goals on the basis of new information concerning the environment. It also involves the ability to plan and form mental images of possible future events. This 'memory of the future', which opens up the potential for innovation and creation of new opportunities, is a specifically human ability.

Last but not least, firms facilitate internal learning by virtue of their ability to select useful information and develop communication codes, trust and knowledge based on experience. The coordination of individual learning and production activities within teams makes it possible to cope with the complexity of routines required in many processes and to mitigate the problem of the incompleteness of individual abilities deriving from dispersed personal knowledge and limited information-processing ability.

The entrepreneur–manager may be an individual or collective agent.[20] In facing uncertainty, the entrepreneur–manager's judgement and role are essential not only to design the business strategy and build a 'business conception', but also to perform a number of essential tasks. These include discovering or creating opportunities, devising markets, formulating conjectures about the future, developing interaction between the environment and the internal organisation, ensuring coordination, creating corporate culture, managing informal relational agreements with suppliers and employees, evaluating techniques and products, mediating between multiple conflicting interests, identifying the necessary capabilities to maintain the competitive advantage and balancing the productive capacities of different processes.

The complementary relationship between markets and organisations

This description of the different ways of coping with uncertainty shows that the traditional dichotomy between business organisations and markets may be misleading. This dichotomy has frequently been seen as a reflection of the long-lasting traditional contraposition between *centralisation*, through planning and intentional organisation,

---

[20] On the collective nature of the entrepreneur, see Schumpeter (1949, pp. 71–2); and the discussion in Hagedoorn (1996, p. 891); Cohendet, Llerena and Marengo (2000, p. 107); and Shane (2003, pp. 8–9).

and *decentralisation*, through the self-regulatory properties of markets associated with the action of the 'invisible hand'.[21] Moreover, business organisations and markets are viewed, by some authors, as substitutes because of the emphasis on alternative ways of coordinating the use of resources. However, as rightly argued by Demsetz (1995, p. 9), markets and organisations are *not* substitutes – rather, they are complementary and interdependent: 'Markets do not produce goods for others, because they do not produce . . . Prices do not coordinate; they supply information.' Organisations need the pressure of market competition to pursue increasing efficiency and efficacy. On the other hand, market functioning requires substantial transactional investment in capabilities, organisations and institutions by the major transactors, whose investments often create externalities:[22] 'Without the appropriate institutions no market economy of any significance is possible.'[23]

Both the market and organisations are subject to conflicts of interest, opportunistic behaviour, swindling, cheating, fraud, influence activities and lobbying. Both need the agency of organisations that ensure enforcement. Firms defend themselves against external opportunistic behaviour by direct monitoring activity and by means of other organisations which offer information and control services, such as business organisations operating within markets, or organisations that operate outside of the market and can ensure enforcement of contracts (courts or state organisations).

Both the market and organisations are *knowledge generators*: they channel learning processes but also provide a setting for the development and selection of new ideas. Innovative activity and creative learning are favoured by the presence within the market of a myriad

---

[21] For an intriguing critical reconstruction of the debate begun in the early decades of the twentieth century on the dichotomy between planning and market equilibrium, see Egidi and Rizzello (2003, pp. 6–9) and Sylos-Labini (1992, pp. 55ff.).

[22] Loasby (1999, pp. 115–124). On market making, see Casson (1982, pp. 163–4, 1997, pp. 5–6, 90–2).

[23] Coase (1991, p. 13). On this, Coase cites the example of the transition toward a market economy in Eastern European countries. The negative microeconomic and macroeconomic effects of recent cases of fiddling accounts in the United States and Europe, and the consequent revision of rules that regulate auditing and set book-keeping standards, are further evident examples of the paramount importance of institutional conditions for the growth of firms and the economic system as a whole.

of small organisations that can generate diverse options: 'A consider-able virtue of the market place' is that 'when uncertainties are very high, as is inevitably the case with new technologies', it encourages exploration 'along a wide variety of alternative paths' (Rosenberg, 1996, p. 353, 2002, p. 36, *passim*). The marketplace provides strong incentives to terminate 'directions of research whose once-rosy pro-spects have been unexpectedly dimmed' by changes in the conditions in which firms operate (Rosenberg, 1996, p. 353). However, selection processes cannot operate in perfectly competitive markets because they require a certain degree of variety on which to work.[24]

There is a multiplicity of relationships intermediate between the market and the firm, such as networks of firms and various long-term forms of collaboration among firms. In many sectors of activity, business organisations have increasingly superseded the market. This has made the executives of giant firms the most influential group of economic decision-makers.[25]

An adequate system of cross-checks within and among organisa-tions is the only possible and ultimate defence against moral hazard within both markets and organisations. In this context, organisational coordination can carry out a *mediation activity* that involves manage-ment of the conflict of interests between parties, with the aim of achieving mutual benefits. Searching for mutual advantage is itself a process of learning, one that can provide opposing parties operating within firms and markets with new opportunities for growth.

---

[24] Loasby (1999, pp. 23–4, 127). Loasby warns against the ill-considered analogy with biological selection arguments and rightly argues that since selection requires pre-existing variety, 'the selection argument which is invoked [by Alchian (1950), Friedman (1953a) and Becker (1962)] is incompatible with the assumptions of product and factor homogeneity and a common knowledge of production functions' (1999, p. 23). On a fruitful application of Darwinian principles of selection in economics, see Nelson and Winter's (1982) seminal work and the more recent discussion in Hodgson (2004b); Hodgson and Knudsen (2004); Niman (2004); Witt (2004). An interesting analysis on the meanings of evolutionary theory and its philosophical implications is in Dennett's classic book (1995). For a overview on technological innovation as an evolutionary process, see the collections of papers in Martin and Nightingale (2000: part III, IV, V); Ziman (2000); Foster and Metcalfe (2001).
[25] This historical process is vividly described in Chandler's *The Visible Hand* (1977).

I.4 Constraints and opportunities in the knowledge-based economy

With the upsurge of the knowledge-based economy, learning inevitably becomes a central issue in the theory of the firm because intelligence-related assets and the ability to learn are playing a more and more prominent role in determining production and transaction costs, and consequently in shaping the competitiveness of enterprises and the growth of economic systems. The emergence of a knowledge-based economy provides increasing scope for firms, and organisations of firms, that favour learning within markets.

Since the 1970s, the transformation of basic conditions has led to two interconnected phenomena: an *increasing need for knowledge* and *rising uncertainty*. On the one hand, learning processes lead to innovations that change the environment in which firms operate and augment the degree of radical uncertainty. On the other, growing radical uncertainty and mounting pressure for innovation in processes and products call for an increase in knowledge.

The expansion of the knowledge-based economy has resulted in an increase in the abilities required in all economic processes. Technical innovations have called for the acquisition, on the part of the *consumer*, of learning capacities in order to execute a sometimes complex sequence of operations. Increasing knowledge is also required for *exchange activities* due to the growing difficulty of evaluating the technical and service characteristics of similar commodities. In production activities, the increased need for knowledge is mainly due to: (i) the intensification of competitive pressure, which results in continual introduction of new processes and new products; (ii) the spread of new technologies, which requires new skills; (iii) the saturation of mass markets, leading to the spread of more and more differentiated and personalised commodities; and (iv) the expansion of service industries which demand a high level of knowledge (such as health care, education, research and development (R&D), software programming, planning, organisation and design).

Learning processes are linked to the possibility of discovering unexploited opportunities (Kirzner, 1997, p. 5). Firms not only seek to identify existing opportunities as yet unperceived by others, but they also attempt to broaden the set of available alternatives and to create new opportunities. Learning is seen in this study as a process of expansion of the set of possible of choices.[26] New opportunities may consist in incremental changes, which are generally predictable, and in radical changes which bring genuine novelties that are, by definition, unforeseeable. The discovery and exploitation of opportunities is not limited to the innovative 'Schumpeterian entrepreneurs', or the executives of a corporation, or the members of an R&D department. Rather, unexploited opportunities are potentially open to all individuals operating in market processes under radical uncertainty, including consumers, traders, employees and, more generally, members of organisations.

When all possible alternatives are known, the decision-making process consists in considering the cost of alternative courses of action under specific *constraints*. With a given and perfectly known set of alternatives, constraints appear to be the major analytical element in decision-making. On the other hand, in a learning framework characterised by the creation of real options, constraints still play an important role, but the ability to look for and create opportunities then becomes a crucial factor.

According to Kenneth Arrow, 'it is probably not entirely accidental, though a little unfair', that economists have been referred to 'as the practitioners of the dismal science'. 'We frequently have to say, "This or that, not both"' (1974a, p. 17). This is due to the existence of inescapable trade-offs and the centrality of the opportunity cost concept in economics.[27] However, with the possibility of

---

[26] Penrose (1959, pp. 52–3) was one of the first economists to emphasise and elaborate the link between learning processes and 'productive opportunities'. She argued that the experience gained by the members of the firm 'develops an increasing knowledge of the possibilities for action . . . This increase in knowledge not only causes the productive opportunity of a firm to change . . ., but also contributes to the uniqueness of the opportunity of each individual firm' (1959, pp. 52–3). On sources of new entrepreneurial opportunities, see Shane (2003: chapter 2).

[27] This modern meaning of the adjective 'dismal', which is nowadays generally accepted, greatly differs from the original given by Thomas Carlyle, who coined this expression in 1849 in his attack on classical economics. Carlyle strongly criticised classical political economy on the basis of a vile and odd 'jumble of romanticism, reaction', racism and apology for slavery (Persky, 1990, pp. 165–6) that was a legacy of the feudal age. For an interesting discussion on the origin of this expression, see also Olson and Kähkönen (2000, pp. 7–8); Levy (2001, pp. 5ff.); and Mäki (2002a, pp. 3ff.).

learning and the creation of new opportunities, the options available are not merely trade-offs, so that to 'get both' might be possible. New knowledge and technical change shift the frontier of technical possibilities.

The potential gains derived from diffusion of the knowledge-based economy are enormous, as the use of a bit of information or a unit of knowledge does not in general preclude its utilisation by others. For example, in contrast to hard assets, the number of people who can use a given piece of software is potentially infinite and knowledge is characterised by strongly increasing returns due to the insignificant marginal cost. As has been noticed, this is very different from the economics of the oil barrel and opens up a much more optimistic perspective on economic growth (Romer, 1998, pp. 12–13; cf. Arrow, 1994a, pp. 4–5). However, even if it is true that some units of knowledge can be reproduced at very low cost, as in the case of a piece of software, 'to extend the use of existing knowledge in time and space is not at all the trivial matter it is often made out to be' (Winter, 2005, pp. 249–50). Transferability of knowledge across time and space requires learning processes and absorptive abilities that take place in communities, markets and organisations, and which may be developed only if some specific favourable conditions are present.

Within business organisations, learning processes imply *effective communication* and *active participation*. Participation by the members of the firm means that they are considered as effective agents in the process of knowledge growth and not as mere inputs that passively adjust to external parameters. The focus on learning and opportunities enriches the theory of the firm and also provides a crucial insight into other important related issues (such as industrial relations, labour economics, market structures, technical change, and development).

To recapitulate, a move from the 'dismal science' of constraints to the new economics of opportunities simply means widening the field of research to include analysis of the economic effects of learning in organisations and market processes. The focus on learning implies consideration of the temporal dimension since this dimension becomes essential whenever knowledge changes (Loasby, 2001, p. 393). In other words, taking into account learning processes entails a shift from an analysis of the properties of states of equilibrium toward a study of the processes by which firms acquire or lose their competitive strength. The intrinsic nature of firms is closely linked to the temporal dimension of production and market processes. In this book, we shall be concerned with processes rather than states of equilibrium. *Entrepreneurship is about processes.*

I.5 Outline of the box

The book is structured as follows. Chapter 1 discusses basic conditions. Chapter 2 addresses decision-making mechanisms within the firm. Chapter 3 analyses the organisational coordination of the firm. In this chapter, the interaction between capability, transaction and scale–scope aspects is moved centre-stage. Chapter 4 seeks to elucidate in which contexts and by what means uncertainty and its costs can be mitigated. Special market contracts, organisations regulating markets, organisations of firms and firms are seen in this chapter as responses to uncertainty in a world characterised by privately held information and heterogeneous knowledge. In general, organisational coordination through relational agreements, both *within* firms and *among* firms, is more likely to be preferred, the more uncertain are the conditions in which firms operate. This is mainly because organisational coordination fosters flexibility, the management of conflicting interests, routinised operating procedures and division of labour, as well as sequential aiming and learning. Chapter 5 examines in detail how control rights deriving from the employment contract allow firms to shape the organisational setting in such a manner as to cope with uncertainty. Chapter 6 focuses on the growth of the firm as the interplay between capabilities, transaction and scale–scope under uncertainty and some particular characteristics of the production elements, information and knowledge (e.g. indivisibilities, complementarities, appropriability, etc.). Here, particular attention is dedicated to diversification and flexibility. Section 6.4 puts forward some concluding remarks on the strengths and weaknesses in the process of the growth of the firm. Each chapter ends with a list of key concepts so that the reader may recap the main topics covered in the chapter. All key concepts are included in the Glossary (p. 264).

Key concepts

conglomerate firm
corporation
entrepreneurship
firm
H-form (holding form)
holdings
market
M-form (multidivisional form)
opportunities
opportunity cost
organisation
U-form (unitary form)

1 | *Basic conditions*

T HIS chapter is about the external and internal basic conditions that affect the decision-making mechanisms, organisational co-ordination and competitiveness of the firm. The basic conditions are listed in the left-hand rectangular box in figure 1.1, which also indicates the section number in which each basic condition is discussed. Basic conditions are mainly composed of the following interrelated features: (i) attributes of information and knowledge, (ii) techniques and equipment available, (iii) individual motivations and aims, (iv) individual abilities, (v) degree of uncertainty, (vi) structural change and (vii) institutional and market conditions. The basic conditions are two-fold: they have an *external* face given by the characteristics of the environment and an *internal* face which emerges from the organisational setting of the firm. For instance, a given enterprise may acquire external knowledge characterised by specific features (e.g. low cost of reproducibility) and may produce internal knowledge that is highly tacit. The former is an external environmental condition while the latter is an internal condition. Analogously, firms mainly rest on the labour supply characteristics of the local market. The abilities of the members of firms largely derive from the abilities of labour forces available on the market. However, firms have the option of training their employees. This changes the abilities possessed by their employees and moulds the characteristics of the labour force actually utilised by the firm. Hence, internal training and the development of experiences by the employees tends to influence the level and kind of abilities available on the market. The same may be said for the equipment in use, the characteristics of technological change and the market conditions.

Basic environmental conditions influence the firm's decision-making processes in two ways. First, external basic conditions create the 'objective' set of opportunities and constraints for the firm. Secondly,

24

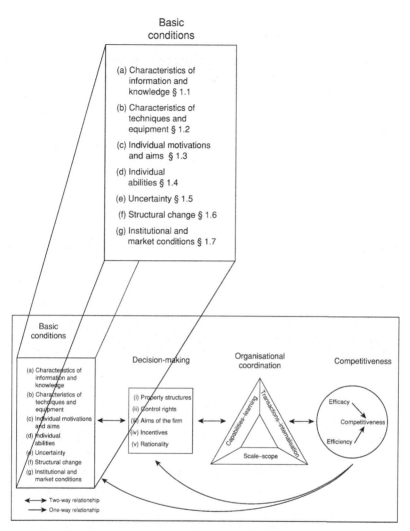

Figure 1.1. Basic conditions.

§ = Section in the text where the topic is discussed.

decision-making mechanisms are shaped according to the subjective 'image' of the environmental conditions that have developed in the mind of entrepreneurs and managers.[1]

---

[1] On the environment treated not as an 'objective fact' but rather as an 'image' in the entrepreneur's mind, see Penrose (1959, p. 215).

1.1 Information and knowledge

Among the basic conditions, let us start by addressing the characteristics of *information* and *knowledge*. The ways in which information and knowledge are created, transmitted and exchanged outside and inside the firms greatly affect their decision-making mechanisms and their organisational structure. These processes of creation, transmission and exchange are, in turn, shaped by the characteristics of information and knowledge that clearly set them apart from other commodities.

Data, information and knowledge

First and foremost it is useful for the purpose of our analysis to distinguish between data, information and knowledge.[2] Data derive from the senses, either directly or as reported by others, and consist in various *signals* that reach the brain from the outside world. Information is an *organised set of data*. A flow of information from one individual to another consists in the one-way transmission of organised data. By definition, a bit of information is an indivisible set of data. Information is not self-interpreting; rather, its interpretation is mediated by individual knowledge. Knowledge is acquired by elaborating bits of information, and derives from the ability to search, select, memorise, store, retrieve, structure, compute, embody and use bits of relevant information within a *cognitive system*. Knowledge helps to correlate and interpret events and information, as it is based on beliefs, skills and emotional attitudes, and depends on individual interests and roles within organisations. Individual knowledge consists of

---

[2] The relevance of the characteristics of knowledge for economic analysis is increasingly recognised. See, for instance, Fransman (1994, pp. 715–16, 753–6); Grandori (1995, pp. 21ff.); Nonaka and Takeuchi (1995, pp. 57ff.); Grant (1996, pp. 110ff.); Hodgson (1997, pp. 673–6); Antonelli (1999, pp. 44–5, 2004: chapters IV, VII); Saviotti (1999, pp. 125ff.); Screpanti (2001, pp. 230–2) Lombardi (2003b, pp. 121–5); Boisot and Canals (2004, pp. 43ff.). In addition, see the collection of essays on this issue in Jussawalla and Ebenfield (1984), Dow and Hillard (1995), Neef (1998), Dierkes *et al.* (2001), Lazaric and Lorenz (2003a: part I). This rapidly expanding body of literature derives from the pioneering works of Hayek (1937, 1945), Arrow (1962, 1973), Polanyi (1966) and Grossman and Stiglitz (1980).

different units of knowledge pertaining to different aspects. A unit of knowledge is a piece of knowledge that cannot be further divided: for instance, a belief or a specific skill may be seen as a unit of knowledge.

An example may help to clarify the difference between data, information and knowledge. For instance, a casual list of professions, names and telephone numbers represents data. Information consists, instead, in a list in which the previous messy data are reorganised so that each name is associated with its corresponding telephone number and all names are gathered under the various professions listed in alphabetical order as in the Yellow Pages directory, online or in hard copy. Finally, in order to utilise this kind of information, knowledge is needed concerning what type of service the listed professions actually provide. The opposite process - from information to data – is obviously likewise conceivable: thanks to cryptography, which requires special knowledge in developing algorithms, it is possible to convert information (present, for example, in the Yellow Pages directory) into data.

Transmittability

Knowledge is transmittable from one person to another not only if it is explicit and replicable, but also if there is a common code or language, the mutual recognition and compatibility of the respective cognitive maps that makes its receipt possible. Explicit and replicable knowledge can be expressed in an articulated, codified and formal language such as mathematical formulae, software, journals, manuals, books, compact disks, data bases, blueprints, codified procedures and so on (see table 1.1). Transmittability is, of course, a matter of degree. There are units of knowledge that are fully transmittable, others for which transmittability is only partial, while in other cases some units of knowledge may be non-transmittable because they are tacit and non-codifiable. Information is instead by definition explicit; nevertheless, for information to be transmittable, a common code or language is required.

Transmission of information and knowledge may take place on the market or outside the market. Let us first examine *traded* transmission. An important characteristic of traded transmission is that knowledge, when sold, still remains in the hands of the seller.

Table 1.1. Transmittability and tradability of information and knowledge (I&K)

Transmittability of I&K	Tradability of I&K		Type of learning
Transmittable (explicit and replicable knowledge, common language and cognitive map)	**Traded transmission** (appropriability and trust)	Market transmission	Learning based on: – exchange of I&K as commodities (direct purchase) – information incorporated in the goods or services – information acquired during the exchange activity
	Non-traded transmission (non-appropriability, no interest in exchanging I&K or lack of trust)	Free transmission within communities and social networks	Learning by imitation, replication, emulation and informal contacts
		Coordinated transmission within organisation	Organisational learning (learning based on organisational coordination through the identification of common interests and creation of mutual trust)
Non-transmittable (tacit knowledge, different languages, heterogeneous cognitive maps)	**Non-tradable transmission**		Learning based on personal experience (learning-by-doing and learning-by-using) within organisations, communities and social networks

Traded transmission

The transmission of information and knowledge takes place on the market (traded transmission) when information and knowledge are appropriable and when the potential buyer of the information and knowledge in question has trust in the seller. Information and knowledge are appropriable if the holder can capture and protect the advantages deriving from possessing certain information and knowledge. A high level of appropriability involves exclusivity and makes knowledge tradable.[3] It useful to distinguish between appropriability seen from the perspective of the producers of information and knowledge, which involves *tradability*, and appropriability from the perspective of its potential users, which involves *absorptive capacity*. For the producer, appropriability consists in the possibility of either retaining private possession of the information and knowledge or selling it on the market, while for the recipient of information and knowledge, appropriability implies absorptive capacities in order to identify, understand, interpret, appraise, assimilate from the environment, retain, process and utilise the information and knowledge in question.[4] Absorptive capacities are built up through specific learning processes. Appropriability for the potential user thus depends on previously acquired knowledge. Recent changes in production and market processes have led to an increase in the amount of knowledge required to adopt new techniques and to use new products.

Patents and copyrights make information and knowledge appropriable for their producers. They are also regarded as 'devices to increase transparency in the knowledge markets and hence facilitate market transactions' (Antonelli, 2004, p. 152). Patents represent an incentive that favours private investment in innovative activity, but they tend to reduce the diffusion of valuable information and knowledge that has already been produced; this renders information and knowledge artificially scarce. Therefore, the need to provide incentives for innovative activity, such as patents and copyrights, generates a contradiction between the production of information and its diffusion and adoption among consumers.[5]

---

[3] On knowledge as a quasi-private good see Antonelli (2004, p. 54).
[4] The notion of 'absorptive capacity' was introduced by Cohen and Levinthal (1989, pp. 458ff.).
[5] Arrow (1994a, p. 5); see also Rosenberg (1990, p. 166).

A bit of information and a unit of knowledge are measurable whenever it is possible to ascertain their value and nature. Informational asymmetries, inherent in this kind of exchange, raise the problem of the purchaser's inability to make an advance judgement on the value of the information or knowledge to be purchased. This leads to the famous paradox, envisaged by Arrow (1962, p. 615) over forty years ago, whereby the 'value for the purchaser' of information 'is not known until he has the information', but once the buyer knows the information he has in effect 'acquired it without cost' and then has no incentive to pay for it. If the potential purchaser cannot measure the value of information before the exchange occurs, the marginal utility of different units of information cannot be assessed and hence it is impossible to ascertain the benefits of any further information acquisitions. Difficulties in measuring information and knowledge may culminate in their scarcity, as individuals could be induced to buy a greater amount of knowledge if they knew more about its value before purchasing. The inevitable presence of informational asymmetries in exchange on the market of information and knowledge make trust an essential element. *Trust* is understood here as the buyer's confidence in the value and in the absence of contradictions affecting the information and knowledge to be purchased. Without this kind of trust, communication – and, hence, the transmission of information and knowledge – do not take place.

Markets could not work without trust. Trust is particularly important in all market exchanges of 'experience goods', i.e. of those commodities whose value for the buyer can generally be ascertained only after that transaction has taken place. Commodities with a high content of information and knowledge are, by their very nature, experience goods.

Trust is characterised by two components. The first component is *calculative*. This is generated as a result of experience: it is a consequence of a credible commitment on the basis of knowledge of the opposing party's interest, and derives from membership in the family, community, culture and religion (characteristic-based trust), or in organisations that ensure respect for rules, ethics and professional standards (institution-based trust). The second component of trust is *non-calculative* in the sense that it rests on the *a priori* belief that the opposing party will behave in an honest and correct manner. In certain circumstances, correctness and loyalty may imply a behaviour that goes against one's (direct or short-term) interest.[6] As Denzau and North (1994, p. 20) remark: 'a market economy is based on the existence of a set of shared values such that trust can exist.' The fact of belonging to a community with law, rules, moral codes and enforcement mechanisms enhances trust which is often a precondition that makes the market exchange possible.[7]

Market transmission of information and knowledge may derive from direct purchase (for example, buying a book or a data base) or from information incorporated in the goods or services exchanged. Alternatively, information may be acquired during the exchange activity (for instance, the specifics of an exchanged commodity may be ascertained during the bargaining process and may be mentioned in detail in the contract).[8]

Recent studies have documented an increase in licensing revenues and, more generally, in the market transmission of information and knowledge and the emergence of new markets for technology in several industries.[9] Moreover, new communication technology tends to favour easier access to information and knowledge that yields

---

[6] For a taxonomy of the various kinds of trust see Nooteboom (2002, pp. 74–88). Other authors who have analysed the issue include Dasgupta (1988); Sako (1992: part I); Casson (1995a, 1995b, 1997, pp. 118ff.); Kay (1996, pp. 93ff.); FitzRoy, Acs and Gerlowski (1998: pp. 376–8); Lazaric and Lorenz (1998); Bolle (1999, pp. 575ff.); de Jong and Nooteboom (2000, pp. 21–2); Allsopp (2002); Silverman (2002); Khalil (2003). Empirical evidence on the determinants and the process of trust development can be found in Sako (1992: part II); Burchell and Wilkinson (1997); Nooteboom (2002: chapter 6); Nooteboom and Six (2003).

[7] Laws and ethical behavioural codes are important for economic performances, 'as there exist gains from trade and production that require coordination' (Denzau and North, 1994, pp. 15, 20–1, *passim*). An ethical behavioural code is a set of rules governing an organisation. Unlike the law, a code of ethics is not enforced by legally binding sanctions, even though, in some cases, legal incentives for the adoption of a corporate ethical code have been introduced. On this subject, see the theoretical investigation in Benson (1989, pp. 305ff.), and Sacconi (1997, pp. vii ff.). Among empirical analyses, see Center for Business Ethics (1986) and Langlois and Schlegelmilch (1990).

[8] The role of the ceaseless motion of the market process in revealing information and in recomposing fragments of knowledge distributed among individuals was stressed by Hayek (1937, 1945); cf. Kirzner (1997, p. 20).

[9] Discussion and extensive bibliographical references on the increase in licensing revenues and the upsurge of patenting activities can be found in Arora, Fosfuri and Gambardella (2001, pp. 419, 424ff.).

shrinkage in search costs and augments transparency, accessibility and, in some cases, the degree of competition. However, new technology considerably heightens the quantity of available information. As a consequence, decision-makers may be overwhelmed by the massive flow of data and information that may generate difficulties in ordering and interpreting information and requires costly selection processes.

Non-traded transmission
Transmittable information and knowledge are not traded when information and knowledge are not appropriable, or there is no interest in the exchange, or there is a lack of trust.

Consider first the case of lack of interest in exchange of the relevant information and knowledge. The case of the second-hand car market, illustrated by Akerlof (1970, pp. 488ff.), is a famous highly stylised example of a market that is driven out of existence due to initial asymmetric information reinforced by lack of interest in exchanging the relevant information. Initial asymmetric information derives from the fact that: (i) the owner who sells the used car knows the quality of the car much better than the potential buyer; (ii) the potential purchaser knows the overall percentage of good cars on the market, but lacks knowledge about the actual condition of the individual car for sale. This *informational asymmetry* between seller and buyer tends to persist because those who are seeking to sell a low-quality used car have a strong interest in withholding information that may devalue it. Since it is impossible for the buyer to tell the difference between a good car and a 'lemon', good cars and bad cars tend to be sold at the same price, that reflects the average quality on the market on the basis of the shares of good and bad cars. At this average price it is profitable to sell 'lemons' but it is not worth selling good-quality cars. Apart from cases when a good-quality car has to be sold even at a price that does not reflect its real condition, the owners of cars in good condition who are not forced to sell have a strong incentive to hold onto them because they cannot obtain the vehicle's real worth. If there is no way to ascertain the quality of traded cars, the result is that there is a reduction in the average quality of second-hand cars offered on the market and a decrease in the size of the market, because good-quality second-hand cars tend to disappear from the market even if there might be customers interested in paying a higher price for a good vehicle. In short, bad cars tend to drive out the good.[10] This phenomenon is called *adverse selection* and essentially stems from the presence of *pre-contractual* informational asymmetries.

Akerlof's example is an illustrative caricature of the real used-car market, which has been chosen because it 'captures the essence of the problem' (Akerlof, 1970, p. 489). In real second-hand car markets, as well as in other markets with similar problems, there are many devices that counteract the effect of quality uncertainty, such as warranties that transfer the risk from the buyer to the seller, the brand-name that indicates quality, licensing practices, quality certification by independent organisations and rules that establish sanctions against dishonest practices and thereby increase the welfare of both parties. Screening, signalling, information activities, monitoring, incentives and organisational coordination are responses to informational asymmetries, market failures and missing markets.

In general, when participants in a potential exchange are not equally informed about the commodity that is offered for sale, the contracting party that possesses the relevant private information may have no interest in exchanging this information but may instead have an interest in internalising information as a source of quasi-rent. This surplus, which represents an excess return received by virtue of the individual's private information, is termed *informational rent*. Informational asymmetries can prevent any agreement from being reached, even if the agreement would be efficient under complete information.[11] Although the problem of informational asymmetries can be serious even in a bilateral relationship,

it becomes much more serious when the numbers of people who must agree begin to grow . . . In theory, with a large enough set of participants [with a diversity of interests], it can be a virtual certainty that there are gains to be realized from an agreement, and yet there may be no agreement that meets the incentive and participation constraints, making it impossible to realize the potential gains. (Milgrom and Roberts, 1992, p. 145)

Simply put, with informational asymmetries, the market exchange may not take place and a market equilibrium may not be reached.

---

[10] Akerlof (1970, pp. 488–9, 495). A concise but complete illustration with very clear numerical examples of how the market price converges toward the price of low-quality used cars is in Baron and Kreps (1999, pp. 577ff.).

[11] On this point see Milgrom and Roberts (1992, pp. 140–1 and n. 7).

Some bits of information and units of knowledge have the characteristics of *quasi-public goods*, and are therefore not appropriable for their producer. The transmission of this kind of information and knowledge takes place outside of the market. A public good is by definition non-rival and non-excludable because its use by one individual does not preclude its use by another *(non-rivalry)* as the stock of information and knowledge is not reduced by use, and its owner cannot prevent others from using it or the cost of enforcing excludability is too high *(non-excludability)*. Non-rivalry is a purely technological attribute mainly linked to the low cost of replication of information and knowledge, while non-excludability depends on technological characteristics and on the institutional context (Arrow, 1973, p. 142, 1994a, p. 5; Romer, 1990, pp. 73–4). Non-rivalry and non-excludability render knowledge non-appropriable by its producer, in the sense that it cannot be made into private property, but is appropriable for its potential adopters. Difficulties faced by record companies in enforcing the copyright payment for music downloadable with negligible replication costs from the web provide a good example of this kind of information and knowledge. A rather different case is when appropriability is hampered not so much by non-rivalry and non-excludability as by excessively high transmission costs that make the information and knowledge non-worthy of being traded.

By virtue of their non-rivalry and non-excludability characteristics, information and knowledge can be regarded as *merit goods* because they imply significant external economies (Screpanti, 2001, pp. 241–2). Whenever poorly appropriable new information and knowledge create positive externalities and cause productivity to increase, the social returns of this new information and knowledge tend to be higher than the private returns. Furthermore, if it is difficult to prevent others from gaining access to relevant elements, the market for information and knowledge fails because there are no incentives to produce new information and knowledge. This creates scope for government funding of activities that leads to the creation of such information and knowledge. In fact, most basic research, which has no 'specific commercial objectives', and often displays the characteristics of a quasi-public good, is financed by governments. For instance, in the United States since the Second World War the federal government has provided the majority of funds devoted to basic research and poured huge sums of money into private and public university and research laboratories.[12]

Non-traded transmission of information and knowledge comes about through free transmission within communities and social networks or coordinated intentional transmission within organisations.

First, free transmission within communities and social networks is obtained through imitation, replication, emulation and informal contacts between individuals who belong to the same community or social network. Within communities or social networks, individuals learn from others through joint contributions to the understanding of problems they find themselves facing (Teece, Pisano and Shuen, 1997, p. 208). This accounts for *agglomeration economies* in industrial districts or local production systems.[13] Non-traded transmission of information and knowledge within communities and social networks favours the reduction of asymmetric information and heterogeneous knowledge.

A second form of non-traded transmission is obtained by the co-ordinated intentional transmission of information and knowledge within organisations. Lack of interest in revealing and exchanging information and knowledge on the market or lack of trust in the person who supplies the market with information may be conditions that favour the emergence of organisational transmission because organisations identify potential common interests, design appropriate incentive structures, select the relevant information when the decision-maker is overwhelmed by redundant information, generate common behavioural codes, engender shared values, build enforcement mechanisms and create mutual trust among their members (see sections 4.3, 5.4).

---

[12] See Rosenberg (1990, pp. 165ff., 2002, pp. 6ff.) for evidence and discussion on basic research in the United States. Rosenberg observes that 'although the federal share [of funds devoted to basic research] has been declining in recent years . . ., it still constitutes about two thirds of the total' (*ibid.*).

[13] On importance of non-market mediated social interactions in developing knowledge and creating externalities, see Arrow (1994b, pp. 5–8). In particular, on industrial districts, see: Becattini (1979, pp. 123ff.); cf. Brusco (1982, pp. 223–240); Goodman and Bamford (1989); Foss and Eriksen (1995, pp. 48ff.); Belussi and Gottardi (2000); Lombardi (2003a, pp. 1445–6, 2003b, pp. 121ff.); Belussi, Gottardi and Rullani (2003); Becattini *et al.* (2003).

Non-transmittability of information and knowledge

Let us now consider the case of non-transmittable information and knowledge due to the existence of tacit knowledge, different languages and contradictions in the cognitive maps that hamper communication between people.

Knowledge is *tacit* when it cannot be expressed directly. For example, we usually cannot explain how we are able to walk, ride a bicycle or recognise a face we know. Tacit knowledge derives from 'the fact that we can know more than we can tell'.[14] Tacit knowledge is accumulated by experience and hence is inextricably embedded in the individual who possesses it. It is the fruit of learning-by-doing processes and is deeply rooted in an individual's action, ideals, feelings and emotions. Even the intuition and anticipation of a discovery largely consists in tacit knowledge. The concept of tacit knowledge breaks down the traditional dichotomy between mind and body, reason and emotion, cognitive and technical elements (Nonaka and Takeuchi, 1995, p. 60). Tacit knowledge implies a degree of 'knowledge stickiness' in the sense that with tacit knowledge it is difficult to separate the new knowledge from the human capital in which that knowledge has been generated (Antonelli, 2004, p. 122). All knowledge concerning a particular production technique has a tacit dimension that can never been made completely explicit.

Scientific knowledge is mostly, but not entirely and not in all circumstances, explicit and therefore potentially transmittable. Quite often, knowledge developed in research laboratories is largely tacit because it involves experience, methods and procedures that are specific to the

---

[14] Polanyi (1966, p. 4). In order to explain the difference between tacit and explicit knowledge, Polanyi quotes the example of the identikit: police identikits are attempts to transform tacit knowledge into explicit knowledge (Polanyi, 1966, pp. 23–5). Nonaka and Takeuchi (1995, pp. 8, 59–60) focus on the relationship between tacit and explicit knowledge within organisational knowledge creation. Knight (1921a, pp. 211, 251) and Penrose (1959, p. 53) anticipated and elaborated some themes on the tacit, non-tradable and operational nature of entrepreneurial and managerial knowledge. See Best (1990, p. 127); Foss (1996c, pp. 78, 81–2); Hodgson (1998b, p. 40). On tacit knowledge, see also Nelson and Winter (1982, pp. 76–82); Dosi (1988, p. 74); Grandori (1995, pp. 26–7).

laboratories where it has been developed and are not communicated through professional journals.[15]

Tacit knowledge can be acquired through imitation and practice within interpersonal relationships, school, families, firms, communities, associations, social networks, districts and local production systems. Tacit knowledge can be purchased through lessons and therefore can be acquired on the market as long as there is guided copying behaviour. For example, one can buy lessons to learn how to use a computer software program, ski or drive a car. Firms and other organisations, such as families and associations, play an important role in enhancing imitation, learning-by-doing and learning-by-using. The tacit dimension of most knowledge makes the social nature of learning evident. In business organisations, productive knowledge is partially in explicit form, such as written information, data bases, patents and copyrights, in which case it is possessed by the owner of the firm. However, the most productive knowledge and entrepreneurial knowledge is tacit or firm-/sector-specific and embedded in managers and workers, because it is the fruit of on-the-job experiences which consist in learning processes over time based on personal interaction, learning-by-doing, learning-by-using and face-to-face contact with skilled and experienced people.[16] Therefore a large part of these experiences developed by the firm's members gives rise to untransmittable knowledge. This is particularly true as far as entrepreneurial conjectures and judgement are concerned.

Overall, whenever information and knowledge are non-traded or untradable, information and knowledge markets may not exist – or, among those that do exist, some may work in a distorted manner (Egidi, 1992a, p. 8). The consequence will be an underinvestment in knowledge, market failures or missing markets. 'Firms replace the missing markets in which future contracts might . . . have been made' (Loasby, 1999, p. 76). In other words, organisations may arise as responses to the difficulties markets encounter in handling and

---

[15] On the tacit dimension of knowledge, method and procedures developed within laboratories in innovative sectors, such as in the biotechnology industry, see Rosenberg (2002, p. 35).

[16] On the relationship between learning and socialisation within business organisations see Nonaka and Takeuchi (1995, pp. 70–3).

transmitting information and knowledge that subjects are unwilling to disclose, or which cannot be exchanged at all.

1.2 Techniques and equipment

Among the various basic conditions, the characteristics of production processes and elements have a striking influence on the organisation of the firm. In particular, indivisibility, non-saturability and complementarity play a central role in shaping organisational settings.

Indivisibility

As proposed by Georgescu-Roegen (1970, pp. 63–5, 1971, p. 226), production elements can be divided into *flows* and *funds*. Flows can enter one process as inputs, such as raw materials or energy, or can emerge as outputs, such as the finished product and waste, whereas funds provide their services in many processes, entering and leaving each process, such as a loom, a computer, or a worker. Flows are measured in their specific unit of measurement (kilos, metres, units produced, etc.), while services provided by funds are measured by time. The distinction between flow and fund elements is based on their specific use within production processes. As a consequence, the same commodity may be a flow in one process and a fund in another according to the productive services that it provides. For instance, a computer is a flow in its production and is measured by the number of units produced, but it is a fund in a process in which it provides its services, when it is measured by hours (or days) according to its service time.

Apart from agricultural land, most fund elements are indivisible (e.g. ovens, pipes, containers, most tools and equipment). Flow elements are instead mostly divisible (with the important exceptions of components needing to be assembled). A production element is defined as indivisible when it is impossible to divide it for exchange, production or consumption purposes. A process is indivisible if it is characterised by a particular size above and below which it cannot take place: in other words, if it is impossible to activate processes that have the same proportions of inputs and outputs, but on a smaller scale. This is the case, for instance, whenever the process is characterised by indivisible production elements.

In this respect, it is useful to distinguish between *economic* and *technical* indivisibility (Morroni, 1992, pp. 26–7, 144–5). Economic indivisibility means the impossibility of exchanging and paying for a good in exact correspondence with the quantity used (i.e. economic indivisibility in relation to quantities) and the time strictly necessary for its use (i.e. economic indivisibility in relation to time). Technical indivisibility, on the other hand, consists in the impossibility of dividing a particular good, once it is exchanged, into amounts usable for production or consumption. For instance, a length of cloth is technically divisible but it may be economically indivisible if sold wholesale, while a portable personal computer (PC) or a needle are both technically and economically indivisible. Technical indivisibility always implies economic indivisibility in relation to quantities, and it clearly cannot be confused with the possibility of producing a given fund available in different sizes. For example, it is possible to produce and exchange a series of bread ovens with ever-increasing diameter or portable PCs with increasing speed, but a given bread oven of a given diameter or a portable PC of a given speed is obviously a technically indivisible piece of equipment.

The problem of technical indivisibility of flow elements, such as components to be assembled, is easily overcome if such components are used in large quantities, as is frequently the case.[17] Therefore, the 'economic significance' of indivisibility 'is relatively less when the number of units is large' (Arrow and Hahn, 1971, p. 62). On the other hand, the economic indivisibility of some flow elements may make it necessary to maintain large stocks of goods, with major consequences for production costs. For example, certain raw materials have to be bought in large quantities. Economic indivisibility is not the only reason why firms hold large stocks of flow elements; other frequent reasons are the instability of demand for final products or the need to produce in large batches.

However, the most serious consequences for the organisation of the production process, and thus for the size of the production unit, arise

---

[17] A component is 'a physically distinct portion' of the final product that 'performs a well-defined function' and is linked to other components through a set of interfaces defined by the product architecture. For instance, 'in the fan, a particular motor is a component of the design that delivers power to turn the fan' (Henderson and Clark, 1990, p. 11).

from the indivisibility of fund elements. Most funds are economically indivisible in relation to both quantities and to time. Economic indivisibility in relation to quantities implies that funds may run below their full productive capacity – for instance, a lorry travelling half-empty or below its optimal speed. On the other hand, economic indivisibility in relation to time entails that in certain periods some of the fund elements involved may be unused; in other words, they will have periods of idleness (for instance, a lorry that cannot travel on some days of the week, or an agricultural machine that does not operate during the winter months). Economic indivisibility of funds in relation to time is due to the fact that buying and selling them according to the periods of their actual utilisation would imply an economic loss beyond normal wear and tear due to the presence of sunk costs. There are different routes for organising production processes in such a way as to overcome the consequences of economic indivisibility of funds. One way is to hire funds instead of buying them or to buy less durable equipment. When such options are not feasible, organisational settings can reduce idle times. Within the factory system, sub-contracting production and forms of collaboration among firms represent attempts to overcome the problem of indivisibility of production funds, so as to make full use of their productive capacity.

Set-up processes

A set-up process (for instance, checking proofs or designing a product) is often economically divisible in its production and always technically indivisible when used in some production process. An example of a set-up process that is divisible in its production is proof-checking, which can be divided into economically separable sub-processes, such as checking the proofs of single chapters of a book. The technical indivisibility of a set-up process, when used in some production, implies that this process cannot be reduced when overall production is reduced. Technical indivisibility involves increasing returns at plant level (i.e. 'partial adaptation' or 'short-period' increasing returns). However, the relevant aspect of a set-up process is not so much its technical indivisibility, as rather the fact that a set-up process has no saturation point when used in some production process. This means that it is not necessary to increase its scale when the scale of the overall process increases. Non-saturability gives rise to fixed costs, even in the case of an increasing dimension of scale, and therefore increasing returns to scale. I term these costs, which originate from non-saturability, 'super-fixed costs'. Technical indivisibility and non-saturability are sometimes confused but this misunderstanding should be avoided because they generate completely different types of increasing returns.

Complementarity

The presence of both indivisible funds and limitational flows (i.e. inputs that are transformed in strict proportions during the production process) implies a low possibility of substituting the production elements. If a fund element is indivisible, it combines with the other elements through a relationship of complementarity rather than of substitutability; that is to say, a fixed-coefficient type of production prevails. In certain circumstances, due to the specific technical characteristics of the production process, substitutability is not guaranteed even with perfect divisibility of funds. In general, the various production elements combine in certain determined proportions, and each machine requires a fixed number of workers. In other words, machines and labour tend to be complementary. Complementarity also concerns the organisation of labour services because of the particular characteristics of team production. The usual reasoning has to be reversed so that fixed coefficients should be considered the general case, while variable coefficients should be considered a particular case, or more precisely a *curiosum*. The assertion that variable coefficients are the general case, which includes fixed coefficients as a special case, is theoretically untenable because, as pointed out by Giovanni Dosi, 'reversibility and variable coefficients, on the one hand, and irreversibility and fixed coefficients, on the other, yield radically different properties of the object of inquiry'.[18] Irreversibility involves economic losses in the presence of sunk costs. Moreover, irreversibility has an important analytical consequence: it becomes impossible to move in either direction, unlike the case of logical time

---

[18] Dosi (1984, p. 303); cf. Pasinetti (1981, pp. 203–4).

adopted in the static economic analysis that has been built in analogy to classical mechanics.[19]

The distinction between funds and flows makes it clear that there is no possibility of substitution, for example, between the sewing-machine, which represents a fund, and the fabric used for making shirts, which is a flow element (transformed in the production process thanks to the services of the funds). In fact, it is hard to conceive of a form of textile production in which fabric could be replaced by sewing-machine-hours or worker-hours (though some working arrangements or maintenance operations may reduce fabric waste).[20]

Complementarity may also arise among different productions whenever their processes are less costly if combined, as in the case of economies of scope. One example of this type of complementarity is production of honey and fruit crops. Bees need flowers for producing honey and, at the same time, fruit-growing is enhanced by the presence of bees which, by visiting different blossoms in succession, facilitate pollination and the subsequent production of seeds.

Furthermore, complementarity may concern the processes and activities that give rise to the various components of an individual output or final stand-alone products which are used together, with the result that the demand for each is linked to the demand for others. Product bundling involves additional demand for each product above that which would exist in the other's absence. Positive complementarities between two different processes or activities imply that an increase in the level of one process or activity will raise the profitability of the other.[21]

---

[19] For further discussion and bibliographical references on the contraposition between historical and logical time see: Shackle (1958, pp. 13ff.); Hicks (1976, pp. 282ff.); O'Driscoll and Rizzo (1985, pp. 53–9); Currie and Steedman (1990, pp. 2–3); Faber and Proops (1990, pp. 55–96); Morroni (1992, pp. 31ff.); Davidson (1996, pp. 479ff.); Harper (1996, pp. 103ff.).

[20] Georgescu-Roegen, (1970, pp. 64–5). If in order to measure the marginal productivity of labour the quantity of yarn is kept constant, as well as the quantity of other inputs, while increasing only the quantity of labour, we will obtain no increase in output, 'with the consequence that the marginal productivity of labour would appear to be zero' (Tani, 1986, p. 64).

[21] On complementary processes and activities, the classic *locus* is Richardson (1972). See also the interesting paper by Leijonhufvud (1986, pp. 203ff.). Cf. Milgrom and Roberts (1990b, p. 515) who argue that complementarities and 'non-convexities . . . explain why the successful adoption of modern manufacturing methods may not be a marginal decision'. Moreover, see Spiller and

To recapitulate, complementarity consists in interdependencies among the productive capacities of indivisible inputs, intermediate phases of a single production process, different production processes or activities. Imbalances between these productive capacities exert a crucial influence on the size of the firm. The need to render compatible the different productive capacities of funds and various individual stages of the production process is a factor that helps to explain the existence of increasing returns.[22] More specifically, to avoid using individual machines at sub-optimal levels the overall scale of a production unit must be equal to the lowest common multiple of the productive capacities of the individual machines. In this respect, the flow–fund model can be usefully applied to explore the effects of combining the productive capacities of indivisible and complementary funds or processes on the relationship between organisation and efficiency.[23] Under this perspective, the economic problem in producing a certain commodity is no longer a simple problem of optimal combination of inputs, but involves choosing a combination of processes, or single phases, largely characterised by *indivisibilities* and *complementarities*.

1.3 Individual motivations and aims

Individual motivations and aims are moulded by family background, personal history, education, definition of property rights, institutional environment and self-imposed constraints, as well as the role and responsibilities within the organisations to which the individual belongs and their incentive structure. In the process of formation and development of individual motivations and goals, there is a strong mutual influence between firms and their stakeholders, the latter being defined as all the persons who derive advantages and bear costs resulting from the action of the firm. Organisations are created by

Zelner (1997, pp. 562ff.) on functional product complementarity, Lindbeck and Snower (2004) on technological and informational complementarities, Hart (1995a, pp. 50–1) on complementary assets and Zenger (2002, pp. 81ff.) on human resource practices.

[22] See Milgrom and Roberts (1990b, pp. 515ff., 1995, pp. 179ff.), and Hart (1995a, pp. 54–5).

[23] See, among others, Landesmann (1986); Tani (1988); Morroni (1992, 1999), Scazzieri (1993); Piacentini (1995).

individuals to pursue their own aims. Their motivation and objectives affect the firms' organisation and performance – whereas, conversely, the firms can exert great influence on the individual motivation and aims of their stakeholders.

Economising

Individuals seek to increase economic benefits and reduce costs. *Benefits* include everything that satisfies individual needs and desires, whereas *costs* include everything that causes discomfort and pain. The two-fold process of increasing benefits and reducing costs will henceforth be defined by the term 'economising'. This meaning of the term 'economising' remains close to its Greek etymology and its original meaning in English.[24] It is used here in its broad sense, which is close to Ludwig Mises' concept of 'human action', referring to courses of action taken by a human being 'to remove uneasiness' and to make himself 'better off'.[25] Therefore, cost reduction is just one aspect of economising.

As argued by Tibor Scitovsky, the sources of satisfaction may be subdivided into three categories: personal and social comforts, and stimuli.

Personal comforts cater to biological needs, make one physically comfortable . . .
Social comforts are satisfactions derived from one's membership and standing in society, in professional and social organisations, in one's workplace . . ., as well as from whatever titles, objects, possessions and activities symbolise such membership or standing.
Stimuli are anything the individual values for the novelty, variety, excitement, challenge, surprise, or stimulus interest it provides.

(Scitovsky, 1979, p. 119, *passim*)

Economists have recently begun to investigate the complex role of emotions in the generation of human behaviour.[26] Individual interest

---

[24] The first two meanings of 'economising' provided by the *Oxford English Dictionary* (2nd edn., 1999) are: '(1) to act as the governor of a household; (2) to arrange, constitute, organise'.

[25] Mises (1949, pp. 253–4), quoted in Kirzner (1973, p. 33). This definition is also close to that provided by Day (2002, p. 221).

[26] Elster (1998, p. 48, 1999) singles out various types of emotions, such as anger, hatred, guilt, shame, self-esteem, pride, admiration, regret, disappointment, fear, hope, envy, disgust, jealousy, love, surprise, boredom, sexual desire,

is influenced by emotions, whose significance in terms of their location on the pleasure–pain scale is known to have a crucial impact in the motivational sphere. Thus although emotions are usually experienced passively, individuals seek occasions on which they are likely to experience some satisfying emotions (Elster, 1998, pp. 51, 54).

Every desire 'brings about a wish for the ability to gratify it, and therefore some form of the love of power'. 'Love of power, in its widest sense, is the desire to be able to produce intended effects upon the outer world.'[27] Power over persons is understood as a social relationship between two individuals by which the one has influence on the behaviour of the other. Power derives from a number of factors: endowments possessed (such as wealth, particular abilities, exclusive possession of inputs or information), force (defined as the ability to exert physical coercion over persons), or authority legitimated by rules, originating from accepted social relations or based on influence over opinions. As remarked by Bertrand Russell, 'to revert to the analogy of physics: power, like energy, must be regarded as continually passing from any one of its forms into any other'.[28]

Heterochronia

In following their aims individuals may have heterogeneous time horizons. A *time horizon* is the time span established by an individual in order to pursue a particular aim. It may therefore be seen as *planned time investment*. Time horizon heterogeneity, or heterochronia, can result from the simultaneous presence of various aims within the same individual, each aim having its own time horizons. Furthermore, different individuals may adopt different time horizons when pursuing the same aim. The time span depends on many factors such as expertise, available alternatives, endowments – and, most importantly, the individual's role and function within the organisation.

---

enjoyment, worry and frustration; on emotions see also Hirshleifer (1987); Frank (1988).

[27] Russell (1938, pp. 274–5), who observes that 'the love of power is one of the strongest of human motives' as soon as 'a moderate degree of comfort is assured' (1938, pp. 10–12, *passim*).

[28] Russell (1938). The economic and social implications of the desire for power have been investigated by Young (1995, pp. 48ff.); Screpanti (2001, pp. 157ff., 245–7); and Palermo (2003).

Heterogeneous and conflicting aims

Individuals may have heterogeneous and conflicting aims, with divergencies arising within the same individual or between different individuals.

When *aim dissonance* occurs within the same individual, it results in various well-known phenomena such as indeterminacy and inconsistency of behaviour (the apparently inexplicable switch from one choice to another), multiplicity of selves (separation of different roles and obedience to different 'local rules'), weakness of will (as in the example of the difficulty in sticking to a diet), self-deception, wishful thinking, regret and hesitation.[29] Rapid institutional changes and the fact of belonging to different organisations are two elements that engender aim dissonance within an individual.

Different individuals may be characterised by a multiplicity of motivational drives and aims. Conflicting aims between individuals reflect conflicts of interest, typically deriving from mutually inconsistent preferences and identities. Such conflicts are present in social relationships within organisations between individuals with different roles (for instance between members of different departments within a firm, such as administration, R&D, production, etc., or between union members and the top management) and in the marketplace between the seller and buyer (March, 1997, pp. 24–5).

Firms shape customers' tastes and preferences through advertising, and greatly influence public choices by means of lobbying activities. Firms also follow a strategy designed to align members' behaviour with the main aims of the organisation. They may not only select members on the basis of the motivations and aims of their potential workforce, but they may influence both the motivations and aims of members through human resource (HR) policies by means of specifically designed contractual clauses, monitoring and enforcement activities. Moreover, employees' aims receive feedback from efficacy, efficiency and competitiveness through the firm's margins. Profits are linked to the level of competitiveness and may be distributed as incentives that help to shape individual aims.

---

[29] Screpanti (2001, pp. 53–4, 67, 71–2); see also Elster (1999, pp. 20–1, 94–5, 99–100, 287); Loasby (1999, p. 42).

1.4 Individual abilities

Individual abilities are strongly relational because they are mainly developed and applied in social contexts. The abilities of the workforce available to firms on the labour market greatly influence firms' organisation and competitiveness. Firms' performance is also affected as result of the abilities possessed by trade partners (such as suppliers and contractors). Firms can in turn directly shape their members' abilities through internal training and those of their trade partners by supplying specific instructions and external training. Moreover, in certain cases, the success of an enterprise may also depend on the abilities possessed by consumers, as some products embody technologies that require consumers to acquire mastery of new abilities.

Theoretical knowledge, practical knowledge and information-processing ability

Individual abilities comprise theoretical knowledge, practical knowledge and information-processing ability (figure 1.2). Theoretical knowledge means knowing about things ('knowing what'), while practical knowledge signifies knowing how to do something ('knowing how'). The former involves *being*, while the latter is applied to *doing*.[30]

Theoretical knowledge implies a representation of the world – or, more precisely, a cognitive system that arises from re-elaboration of information deriving from the environment. Theoretical knowledge stems from learning processes that consist in acquiring information with interpretation. It is formed of a complex set of elements, some of which are only apparently simple – for instance, the ability to put stimuli in the right interpretative box – and some involving elaborate mental activity – for instance, knowledge of actual states of the world and outcomes, awareness of rules, capacity to construct mental models, ideologies, or the ability to identify aims, discover opportunities and recognise pay-offs. *Mental models* are representations that individual cognitive systems build to perceive, define and codify

---

[30] On this distinction, see Polanyi (1966, p. 7); Drucker (1993a, p. 15); Loasby (1998, p. 172).

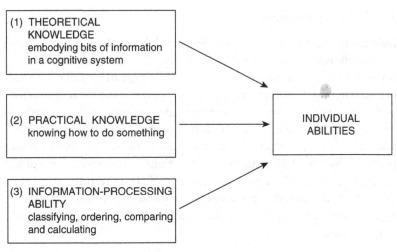

Figure 1.2. Individual abilities.

the information through which individuals make sense out of the environment, design their problem-solving activity and construct their strategy (Egidi, 2002, p. 110).

In contrast, practical knowledge concerns the process of the actual making of individual choices and includes know-how and skills. It consists in applying the appropriate course of action on the basis of a solution obtained through a problem-solving procedure. Practical knowledge is mainly based on adoption of automatic mechanisms of conduct derived from the repetition of routines and from acceptance of traditions and conventions. Practical knowledge has a large tacit component because it is rooted primarily in personal experience. The use of a computer offers a good illustration of the contrast between theoretical and practical knowledge. Computer users are well aware that there is a huge difference between possessing information on the characteristics and capacities of the vast choice of software on the market, and being able to use any of the programs effectively. The latter ability comes only through a process of practice. It is not sufficient to know the sequence of operations to be performed; rather, one must acquire the ability to carry out chains of routines that are not easily deducible from instructions alone (Egidi, 1986). Practical knowledge develops locally and gradually from techniques in use toward the alternatives belonging to the surrounding space.

Finally, information-processing ability is the third element that makes up individual abilities. The expression 'information-processing ability' is used loosely to refer to the complex of abilities that make it possible to handle information. These include assessing probabilities, enumerating, classifying, ordering, comparing bits of information and problem-framing, which consists in 'all those activities leading from the identification of the problem to the selection of possible actions' (Dosi and Egidi, 1991, p. 170). Since information-processing ability requires the formation of mental models, the close link with theoretical knowledge is evident. It also needs logical consistency and acquisition of rules for computation. Information-processing ability must be assessed according to its adequacy in resolving the problems an individual has to face. The larger the bits of information to be handled, the higher the information-processing ability necessary.

Abilities are distributed according to individual specific experiences and different roles in organisations, inasmuch as they are the fruit of personal experience within organisations that operate in a given institutional context. Heterogeneous abilities depend on heterogeneous knowledge among individuals who possess different units of knowledge and mental models. Naturally, this does not imply that individuals may not have some units of knowledge in common. Organisations (such as family, schools and firms) tend to generate common knowledge among their members through transmission of the *culture* elaborated on the basis of past experiences. The cultural heritage provides a means of reducing the divergence in mental models among individuals. The presence of institutions, ideologies,[31] communities, social networks and structures implies the existence of shared mental models. Yet individual knowledge is to some extent heterogeneous because it is linked to individual cognitive abilities and personal experiences that are varied and limited. Knowledge can be increased and created through division of labour, but division of labour augments dispersion. Furthermore, since individuals who possess heterogeneous knowledge may interpret the same bit of information in a different way, heterogeneous knowledge is a self-reinforcing phenomenon and the divergent subjective models

---

[31] Ideologies are shared frameworks of mental models, which groups of individuals possess on the basis of their interests (Denzau and North, 1994, pp. 3–4, 15).

show no tendency to converge.[32] In more general terms, heterogeneous knowledge is due to different processes of acquisition, selection, interpretation and re-elaboration of new bits of information. As a consequence of learning processes, individual knowledge is in constant flux over time and is characterised by strong *path-dependence*.

The absence of uniformity in individual knowledge gives rise to a differential that explains the very nature of all economic processes. The essence of competition, understood as rivalry, is that a certain person can perform some particular tasks better than another.

Individual theoretical and practical knowledge and information processing abilities are intrinsically limited because personal knowledge is fallible and is based on personal cognitive ability and experience, these being by definition limited. However, this does not necessarily imply incomplete abilities in all circumstances. The completeness of abilities depends on the relationship between the abilities *required* and the abilities *possessed*. Even if individual abilities are always limited, they may effectively be complete if they are sufficient to deal with the situation at hand. By the same token, individual abilities are incomplete whenever the abilities possessed are insufficient to cope with the specific situation and, therefore, there is a gap between the abilities *possessed* and the abilities *required* in the given situation. In complex systems individual abilities tend to be unavoidably incomplete because such systems are characterised by non-reducibility and often also by unpredictability. A complex system is constituted by structural linkages and the interactions of ensembles of different elements exhibiting 'a collective behaviour that is very different from that one might have expected from simply scaling up the behaviour of the individual units'.[33]

Increasing need for knowledge

Market and technological transformations have brought a significant increase in the personal abilities required. Admittedly, the tendency

---

[32] Hayek (1937, pp. 62–3), in his seminal article published in the same year and the same journal as Coase's famous article on the nature of the firm drew attention to the role of partial and dispersed knowledge in economic processes. See also North (1990, p. 17); Denzau and North (1994, p. 14); Fransman (1994, p. 716); Loasby (1994, pp. 289–90).

[33] Agliardi (1998, pp. 5–6); see also Hodgson (1997, p. 669) and Loasby (1999, pp. 3–4).

toward an increase in the need for knowledge is not totally new. Since the beginning of the Industrial Revolution, the development of each technological paradigm[34] has led to a jump in the need for knowledge and to the creation of new organisational models that have enhanced new learning mechanisms. The production of useful knowledge concerning the production of artefacts has become increasingly specialised and professionalised, with an incessant emergence of new disciplines and sub-disciplines. 'The range of disciplines' relevant to firms' innovative activities 'is expanding in both breadth, i.e. the number of . . . disciplines increases, and depth, i.e. their sophistication and specialisation increase'.[35]

Since the 1980s the need for knowledge has sharply accelerated, to such an extent that there is now almost unanimous recognition of the essential role of the creation and circulation of information and knowledge as a factor in determining the competitive capacity of firms, the performance of economic systems and thus the rate and the direction of *economic growth*. This phenomenon encompasses all economic processes in production, exchange and consumption. Let me summarise the transformations involved in each of these three areas.

Production

In production, changes in market conditions have led to: (i) an intensification of competitive pressure, (ii) expansion of service industries and (iii) production differentiation. Meanwhile, technical change has brought about: (iv) the spread of new technologies and (v) increasing diffusion of multitechnology products and a rise in the number of technical and service characteristics of many commodities. All these factors, which are listed in figure 1.3, closely interact.

---

[34] A technological paradigm has been defined by Dosi (1988, p. 70) 'as a "pattern" of solution of selected problems based on highly selected principles derived from natural sciences, jointly with specific rules aimed to acquire new knowledge . . . Examples of such technological paradigms include the internal combustion engine, oil-based synthetic chemistry, and semiconductors.'

[35] Brusoni, Prencipe and Pavitt (2001, pp. 597–8). On the implications of the emergence of the knowledge-based economy, see Burton-Jones (1999) and Foss (2005, pp. 1–15), and the numerous papers published in Andersson, Batten and Karlsson (1989); Baets (1998); Macdonald and Nightingale (1999); Buigues, Jacquemin and Marchipont (2000); Archibugi and Lundvall (2001).

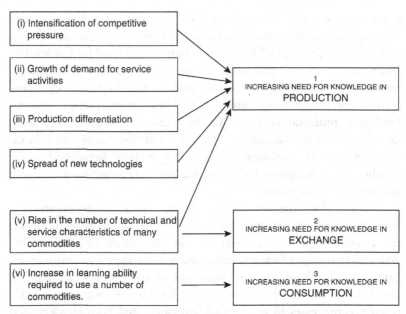

Figure 1.3. Increasing need for knowledge.

1 Intensification of competitive pressure. The boom in international trade, the surge of new high-technology industries[36] and falling communication costs are intensifying competitive pressure. This drives producers into pursuing continuous improvements in methods, processes, goods and services. Innovation processes imply a gradual increase in the knowledge content of commodities, new forms of cooperative interfirm relations oriented to the market and the emergence of what has been called by Best (1990, pp. 2–3) a 'new competition'.

2 Expansion of the service industries. Fast-growing service activities – such as health care, education, R&D, planning, marketing, organisation and design – call for a high level of knowledge in their production. This affects services for final consumers and business services. The recent growth of service activities stems from

[36] Following Chandler's definition, a high-technology industry is 'one in which new learning in science and engineering leads to opportunities to commercialize – to develop and bring into public use – new products based on that new learning' (Chandler, 2003: chapter 1, p. 1).

two phenomena. First, a structural modification in the composition of final demand has led to an increase in the demand for services. Second, as mentioned above, there has been growth in the share of services for manufacturing activity (i.e. in the production of industrial goods); as a consequence, manufactured goods contain an increasing quantity of services. This has brought about a progressive change in the occupation structure: the proportion of the labour force in service activities *within* the manufacturing sector (such as managing, planning, design, R&D, marketing) has shown a constant increase.

3   *Product differentiation.*   The widening of the range of products and the continuous introduction of new differentiated models require an increase in knowledge-intensive activities (R&D, design, marketing, etc.). The spread of more and more differentiated commodities is due partly to the saturation of numerous mass markets and the related evolution of consumption models, but also to increasing international competitiveness (point 1). Standardised production has become less and less competitive in industrialised countries as it has spread among less developed countries, which often have considerably lower direct costs. In these mature sectors international competitiveness is maintained only in those market segments where product differentiation is essential, and where the products have a high service content (point 2).

4   *Spread of new technologies.*   Technological advances have been particularly rapid in the following areas: new materials, new energy sources, environmental engineering, transportation, aerospace technology and information technology (IT) (networked computing and telecommunications). Among these technologies, the spread of IT has played an important role in almost all other sectors of activities. This pervasive presence implies that new skills are needed in almost all industries. The extensive use of new information technologies have stimulated demand for technological knowledge and the emergence of firms specialised in processing and producing knowledge: in short, the creation of new markets for knowledge (Antonelli, 1999, pp. 161, 169, 172). This is bringing about a progressive dematerialisation of commodities and production processes.

5   *Increasing diffusion of multitechnology products and rise in the number of technical and service characteristics of commodities.*
Technical change has brought about an increasing diffusion of multitechnology products that are made up of different components

and embody different technologies. Firms that deliver multitechnology and multicomponent products face the need to develop and maintain technological capabilities in a wider number of fields than those in which they decide to produce in-house; therefore they have to coordinate activities with specialised suppliers of equipment, knowledge and components (Brusoni, Prencipe and Pavitt, 2001, p. 597).

Moreover, technical change has caused an increase in the number of technical and service characteristics of commodities. Commodities increasingly exhibit a complex structure of characteristics, which often conflict with one another, resulting in a series of trade-offs. An example may be useful here to clarify the nature of these trade-offs. A car has a range of characteristics, such as type of engine, power, number of seats and doors, size, type of gears, maximum speed, fuel consumption (per km), safety and reliability, etc. Within these features, the following trade-offs may be cited: compact overall size for easy parking and driving along narrow roads versus spacious interior for passengers and luggage; compact overall size versus safety; energy consumption versus speed; fuel consumption versus safety (which increases weight); spacious interior (because of a higher centre of gravity) versus good stability; short delivery time versus a wide range of choices in accessories, options and colours. Whenever two or more characteristics conflict, multiple trade-offs result. Significantly, most product improvements are introduced in order to overcome these trade-offs.

Exchange

The rapid increase in the number of technical and service characteristics of many commodities affects not only the productive strategies adopted by firms but also the buyer's choice in exchange activities, because it becomes difficult and costly for the consumer to ascertain quality at the time of exchange. Information-processing abilities and knowledge of the specific technical and service characteristics of commodities are required for ordering similar commodities containing a mix of different characteristics on the basis of quality indices. For instance, the individual consumer may find it extremely difficult to ascertain the quality, performance and durability of a car or hi-fi equipment in relation to similar products, even if some knowledge of the characteristics of commodities can be bought on the market. In many cases, a real evaluation by the buyer can be made only after considerable experience. The consumer's evaluation of quality is particularly difficult for educational and health services, which cover a growing proportion of GDP in industrialised countries.

Consumption

Finally, the knowledge requirement in consumption has undergone continuous increase. Product innovations due to technological trans-formations have called for the acquisition, on the part of the con-sumer, of special capacities in order to perform a sometimes complex sequence of operations required for the use of a number of products. In many cases, consumers have to possess considerable learning abil-ity. For instance, several previously existing commodities (such as radios and cameras), which have been improved and transformed with the introduction of microelectronics, and some completely new com-modities (such as videos, mobile phones and computers) require the acquisition and use of particular abilities and information.

In conclusion, the increasing need for knowledge tends to create a gap between the abilities possessed and the abilities required. In com-plex and rapidly changing situations, individuals may be unable to estimate even the 'ability gap' itself. In these cases, understanding what abilities are required becomes part of the learning process itself.

1.5 Uncertainty

Uncertainty and individual abilities are strongly interconnected basic conditions because the degree and kind of uncertainty individuals have to face is linked to forecasting ability, which rests on individual theoretical knowledge of the list of possible outcomes and on information-processing abilities (figure 1.4).

Forecasts are crucial whenever there is a lapse of time between a choice and its outcome - in other words, whenever the outcome of any given choice occurs at a later instant of time than the moment when the decision to act is made. Firms have to face an inevitable lag between the decision to organise production and the availability of output for sale.[37] This time lag between *decision* and *outcome* is unavoidable in all economic processes that involve production of goods and services, as production occurs in chronological or real time.

[37] Davidson (1991c, pp. 35ff., 1996, p. 480), Davidson and Davidson (1984, p. 327).

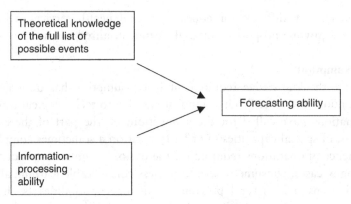

Figure 1.4. Forecasting ability, theoretical knowledge and information-processing ability.

It is first necessary to distinguish between *complete* forecasting ability, which implies certainty or probabilistic risk, and *incomplete* forecasting ability, which involves radical uncertainty (figure 1.5). This distinction – one that plays a crucial role in the theories of John Maynard Keynes, Frank Knight, Joseph Schumpeter and other very influential authors, in spite of significant dissimilarities in analytical goals and methodologies –[38] is fundamental in analysing the relationship between the degree of uncertainty, decision-making mechanisms, learning processes, the characteristics of contracts and the boundaries of firms.

---

[38] In his theory of the firm, Knight (1921a, p. 233) distinguishes between 'measurable uncertainty' (probabilistic risk) and 'immeasurable uncertainty' ('true uncertainty'). An analogous distinction is clear in Keynes (1937, pp. 113–14), who writes:

> By 'uncertain' knowledge . . . I do not mean merely to distinguish what is known for certain from what is only probable. The game of roulette is not subject, in this sense, to uncertainty; . . . Even the weather is only moderately uncertain. The sense in which I am using the term is that in which the prospect of a European war is uncertain, or the price of copper and the rate of interest twenty years hence, or the obsolescence of a new invention . . . About these matters there is no scientific basis on which to form any calculable probability whatever. We simply do not know.

An in-depth discussion on uncertainty in Keynes is developed by Carabelli (1995, pp. 139, 155); Dequech (1999, pp. 415ff.); and Dunn (2004, pp. 65ff.). Differences between the definition of uncertainty found in Knight and that proposed in Keynes

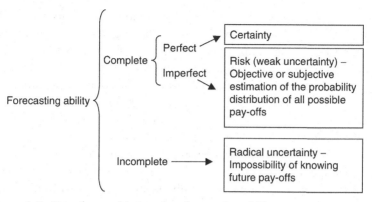

Figure 1.5. Complete and incomplete forecasting ability.

Complete forecasting: nil uncertainty or risk

Complete forecasting requires: (i) complete theoretical knowledge of all possible outcomes; and (ii) complete information-processing ability to frame and resolve problems by choosing the appropriate cognitive categories.

Complete forecasting ability can be divided into *perfect* and *imperfect* forecasting.[39] The former implies perfect knowledge of the actual outcomes among all possible events and is thus characterised by nil uncertainty. The latter stems from knowledge of the probability distribution of possible outcomes under the following conditions: (i) outcomes are unconnected with and independent of the agent's decision, (ii) decision-makers know the full list of possible events and (iii) 'the

---

are examined in Davidson (1996). For an interesting interpretation on the role of uncertainty in the Schumpeterian theory of the entrepreneur, see De Vecchi (1995, pp. xiv, 48, 51–5). Finally, one can mention, for instance, the insightful considerations on the difference between risk and uncertainty in Shackle (1954, p. 7, 1955: chapters I–IV; 1979, pp. 7ff.); and Georgescu-Roegen (1971, pp. 122–3).

[39] Note that in game theory the adjectives 'incomplete' and 'imperfect' are used with a different meaning. There is incomplete information when some players do not know the pay-offs of the others, while there is imperfect information when at some move in the game the player with the move does not know the history of the game (Fudenberg and Tirole, 1991, pp. 209–10; Gibbons, 1992, pp. 55, 143).

process of attribution of consequences to actions and events is procedurally trivial' (for instance, in the case of flipping a coin, if I gamble on tails and heads comes up, I lose; or, in football pools, if I bet on the winning football team I get large winnings).[40]

Imperfect forecasting is characterised by two possible different kinds of probabilistic risk: (a) *objective* risk, when the probability distribution is assumed to be known and (b) *subjective* risk, when individuals do not know the objective probability distribution but can estimate or infer the subjective probability distribution from the complete list of possible outcomes (see table 1.2 and bubbles 1, 2 and 3 in the Venn diagram in figure 1.6). Probabilistic (objective or subjective) risk has also been termed ' weak uncertainty'. A large body of the literature on uncertainty exclusively addresses this type of uncertainty related to probabilistic risk.[41] Table 1.3 provides corresponding definitions of objective and subjective risk.

To use Georgescu-Roegen's (1971, p. 122) words, both objective and subjective risk describe 'the situations where the exact outcome is not known but the outcome does not represent a novelty'. In conditions of objective risk, the probability distribution is reliable – as, for example, in a game of coin-flipping, dice or roulette. Although the final position of the roulette ball is not precisely predictable, we know that there is a one in thirty-seven (thirty-six plus zero) chance that any specified number will come up. Under subjective risk, a reliable objective probability cannot be attached to each outcome and so individuals can estimate only the subjective probability distributions of possible events. This is true in the case of a football match or a horse race.

In the example of second-hand cars mentioned in section 1.1, we have assumed that the buyers are in a situation of objective probabilistic risk because they know the proportion of good and bad cars – i.e. they know the objective probability distribution between cars of good quality and cars of bad quality. If buyers do not know the objective probability, they can nevertheless estimate the subjective probability distribution according to the expected utility theory and therefore they are in a situation of subjective probabilistic risk. In both cases they are

---

[40] Dosi and Egidi (1991, p. 167); see also Hey (1991, p. 253).

[41] See, for example, the survey presented by Machina (1987), and Davidson's (1991a, pp. 129ff.) critical discussion. Large collections of writings are in Hey (1997a, 1997b); and Luini (1999).

Table 1.2. *Forecasting ability and uncertainty*

Forecasting ability	Theoretical knowledge	Information-processing ability (IPA)	Degree of uncertainty	
Complete forecasting — Perfect forecasting	Perfect knowledge about the actual outcome	Complete IPA	Nil uncertainty	
Complete forecasting — Imperfect forecasting	Imperfect knowledge — Knowledge of the objective probability distribution of possible events	Complete IPA	Objective risk (e.g. dice or roulette games)	⎫ Weak uncertainty
	Knowledge of the subjective probability distribution of possible events	Complete IPA	Subjective risk (e.g. horse race or football match)	⎬
	Incomplete knowledge of the list of possible events due to transmutable future	Complete IPA	Substantive uncertainty	⎫ Radical uncertainty
Incomplete forecasting	Complete knowledge of the list of possible events	Incomplete IPA	Procedural uncertainty	⎬

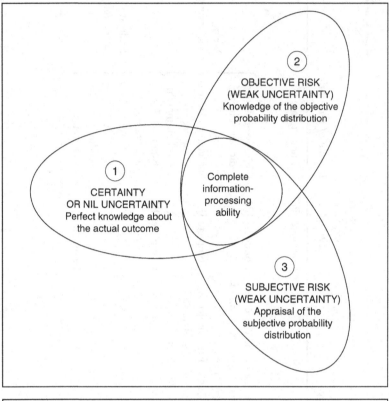

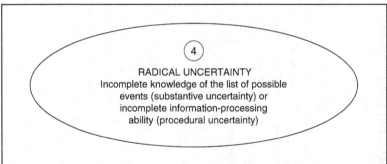

Figure 1.6. Different degrees of uncertainty.

able to ascertain all possible pay-offs and they operate in a situation of weak uncertainty. It should be noted that both these forms of weak uncertainty necessarily require complete information-processing

Table 1.3. Some references on the definitions of risk (weak uncertainty)

	Corresponding expressions	References
Objective risk	Objective risk	Hargreaves Heap *et al.* (1992, pp. 53, 349).
	Risk or measurable unceranity	Knight (1921a, pp. 20, 233).
	Arrovian, measurable uncertainty	Rosenberg (1996, p. 340).
	Risk	Hey (1991, p. 253); Tversky and Fox (1995, p. 93).
	Soft uncertainty	Vercelli (1995, pp. 256–7, 1999, pp. 242ff.).
Subjective risk	Subjective risk	Hargreaves Heap *et al.* (1992, pp. 53, 349).
	Uncertainty	(Tversky and Fox (1995, p. 93); Hey 1997b, p. 258); Fox and Tversky (1998, p. 118f.).

ability to enumerate possible events, in order to ascertain the objective or subjective probability distribution (i.e. procedural certainty).[42]

Incomplete forecasting: Radical uncertainty

Let us now turn to incomplete forecasting ability. Under incomplete forecasting, a decision made at a given moment of time may at a later date turn out to have been wrong. Incomplete forecasting ability implies the possibility of unanticipated consequences and therefore induces *radical uncertainty*.[43] Radical uncertainty corresponds to all

[42] There is so far no shared taxonomy on uncertainty. Williamson (1985, pp. 57–8) calls this kind of weak uncertainty – which 'is attributable to opportunism' and 'arises because of strategic non-disclosure, disguise, or distortions of information' – 'behavioral uncertainty', while Dunn (2001a, pp. 568) uses the expression 'behavioural uncertainty' to designate the type of uncertainty that stems from insufficient information-processing abilities in coping with a given situation.

[43] On uncertainty associated with incomplete forecasting, see the collection of writings in Dow and Hillard (1995).

(objective or subjective) situations in which *incomplete forecasting prevents agents from knowing future pay-offs* (see table 1.2 and bubble 4 in figure 1.6).[44]

Incomplete forecasting ability arises when individuals do not have complete theoretical knowledge of the list of future outcomes or lack sufficient information-processing abilities to select the relevant variables, assess, single out and decompose problems, classify events and compute probabilities and pay-offs.

Incomplete theoretical knowledge of future outcomes involves substantive uncertainty, while incomplete information-processing abilities imply procedural uncertainty (Dosi and Egidi, 1991, p. 165). The former type of radical uncertainty, substantive uncertainty, is independent of personal abilities to process information and refers to a situation that may change in an unexpected manner, while the latter type arises when individual information-processing abilities are insufficient to cope with the situation at hand.[45] In spite of this substantial dissimilarity, both are *per se* a sufficient condition for what I call 'radical uncertainty' in so much as they both lead to incomplete forecasting and thus the impossibility of optimising (see table 1.2).

---

[44] In the economic literature, several adjectives have been used in order to express different forms of uncertainty associated with different types of incomplete forecasting: 'irremediable' (Shackle, 1972, p. 407), 'Keynesian' (Earl and Kay, 1985, p. 57), 'Knightian' (Rosenberg, 1996, p. 340; Loasby, 2004b, p. 132), 'true or immeasurable' (Knight, 1921a, pp. 20, 233; Davidson, 1991a, p. 31; Hoogson, 1993a, p. 84; Rosenberg, 1996, p. 340), 'strong' (Denzau and North, 1994, p. 9), 'epistemic' (Grandori, 1995, pp. 11, 30); 'structural' (Langlois and Robertson, 1995, pp. 18ff.; Harper, 1996, p. 95; Egidi and Rizzello, 2003, p. 2), 'fundamental' (Dequech, 1999, pp. 415ff.; Dunn, 1999, pp. 200–4, 2001a, p. 569; Loasby, 2004a, p. 266; Fontana and Gerrard, 2004, pp. 629ff.), 'genuine' (Heiner, 1983, p. 571; Foss, 1996b, p. 90), 'radical' (Hargreaves Heap *et al*, 1992, pp. 53, 349; Nooteboom, 2002, pp. 5–6, 2003: p. 3), 'pervasive' (Becker and Knudsen, 2005, pp. 746ff.) uncertainty. However it should be noted that the above expressions involve often dissimilar, or even conflicting, conceptions and methodologies.

[45] The opposition between substantive uncertainty and procedural uncertainty is very close to Dunn's (2001a, pp. 568, 571–5) difference between fundamental uncertainty and behavioural uncertainty. As observed by Dunn, the different nature of fundamental and behavioural uncertainty relates to Davidson's (1996) distinction between immutable (ergodic) systems and transmutable (nonergodic) systems, which may be regarded as similar to Lawson's (1997) opposition between open and closed systems; see also Fontana (2000, pp. 29ff.).

As we shall see, firms may be regarded as a response to both of these diverse types of uncertainties.

Incomplete theoretical knowledge: Substantive uncertainty

The possibility of unpredictable contingencies due to the transmutable characteristics of the environment results in incomplete theoretical knowledge of the list of possible outcomes, implying the impossibility of computing any probability distribution of future contingencies and therefore leading to a particular type of radical uncertainty called *substantive uncertainty*.

With a non-stationary environment and creative learning, 'those same capabilities which allow some to generate unforeseeable changes (e.g. developing a new product, opening a new market, etc.) are endogenous sources of uncertainty for other agents' (Dosi and Egidi, 1991, p. 171). Whenever the menu of choices is not fully known *a priori* by the decision-makers but must instead be learned, events are not 'states of nature' but are endogenous to individuals' decision processes, so that events are not independent from actions. Basic conditions (characteristics of production elements, information and knowledge, and techniques, individual aims and tastes, institutional and market conditions) may change either endogenously or through exogenous shocks. This entails '*bi-directional interactions between actions, events and outcomes*'. Substantive uncertainty springs from changes triggered by the effects of creative learning that may modify 'the basis for future actions', yielding unexpected events and heterogeneous individual knowledge.[46] A novelty implies incomplete forecasting ability because, in the case of production of new knowledge, it is impossible to assess the probability distributions of an unknown event. In other words, the outcome cannot be predicted because it represents a novelty for the decision-makers. Forecasting ability

---

[46] Dosi and Egidi (1991, p. 168), Dosi and Metcalfe (1991, p. 144). See also Dosi and Orsenigo (1988, pp. 463ff.). There are numerous empirical studies that analyse the effects of various degrees and kinds of uncertainty on firms' behaviour. See, for instance, Ouchi (1980); Wilson (1980); Anderson and Schmittlein (1984); Masten (1984); Walker and Weber (1984); Anderson (1985); Palay (1985); Balakrishnan and Wernerfelt (1986); Gatignon and Anderson (1988); Klein, Frazier and Roth (1990); Masten, Meehan and Snyder (1991); Shane (1994).

depends on the similarity of the future to the past, 'but our need to predict the future results from our belief that it will be different from the past' (Loasby, 1999, p. 5). If we assume the possibility of creative learning, the future cannot be known before its creation.

An endogenous creation of a novelty causes incomplete theoretical knowledge in that a party may surprised by unexpected actions and contingencies of other agents such as individuals or social organisations (firms, trade unions, cartels, political bodies, etc.). Economic conditions 'can be changed often in ways not completely foreseeable even by the creators of change' (Davidson, 1996, p. 482). Indeterminacy of outcomes is linked to interdependence and subjective reaction. In fact, which action is optimal for one individual depends on the behaviour of the individual's opposite number, but under heterogeneous knowledge it is impossible to predict the behaviour of the opposing party, whose reactions are unavoidably based on subjective interpretation of private information. As argued by Jan Kregel, 'what must be known to decide today will be known only when the effects of those decisions take place'.[47] Since substantive uncertainty derives from the impossibility of predicting future events because of the transmutability of the future, no matter how much information-processing ability we impute to agents, the course of outcomes remains unpredictable. Substantive uncertainty can arise even if individuals can make full use of the present knowledge thanks to complete information-processing abilities (Dunn, 1999, pp. 204, 212, 2001a, p. 568).

Substantive uncertainty corresponds to what the Post Keynesians term 'fundamental uncertainty'. Under substantive uncertainty, individuals are unable to foresee relevant future contingencies because the future is not a mere statistical reflection of the past, as in an ergotic stochastic process, but rather is characterised by an intrinsic transmutability of the environment. In these conditions, the 'existing market information does not, and cannot, provide reliable data for forecasting the future'.[48]

---

[47] Kregel (1980: 37), quoted in Slater and Spencer (2000, p. 76). Concerning the impact of individual decisions on aggregated outcomes see also Simon (1959, p. 296); Dunn (2001a, p. 585); and Minsky (1996, p. 360), who observes that 'uncertainty (or unsureness) is a deep property of decentralized systems in which a myriad of independent agents make decisions whose impacts are aggregated into outcomes that emerge over a range of tomorrows.'

[48] Davidson (1994, p. 87, 89–90, 1996, pp. 482); see also Dequech (1999, pp. 415ff.); Dunn (1999, pp. 204–5, 212, 2000a, pp. 346ff.) and the bibliographical reference therein.

An unpredictable novelty leads to a modification in people's beliefs. The interaction between experience of external facts and other people's actions is a continuous and never-ending process (Hayek, 1937, p. 61). Admittedly, technical change that leads to constant increases in production due to in-firm learning curves may easily be predicted on the basis of past experience. However, as forcefully argued by Rosenberg (1996, p. 334), genuine innovations are characterised by a high degree of uncertainty because of 'the inability to anticipate the future impact of successful innovations, even after their technical feasibility has been established'. Rosenberg cites numerous striking examples of important successful innovations whose economic impact was long overlooked, even for decades, and which have led to completely unexpected utilisations. It suffices to mention here the case of the laser, for which very different uses have been developed than those initially imagined – for instance, in precision measurement, navigational instruments, chemical research, surgery, the textile industry, or laser jet printers. Or take the case of telecommunications: the application of the laser together with fibre optics has dramatically increased the number of conversations carried simultaneously through a telephone cable (from 139 in the mid-1960s, prior to the development of lasers, to 1.5 million in the early 1990s once fibre optic cables were installed). And yet, as reported in 1968 by Charles Townes, who subsequently won a Nobel Prize for his research on the laser, Bells Labs were initially 'unwilling even to apply for a patent on the laser, on the ground that such an invention had no possible relevance to the telephone industry' (Rosenberg, 1996, p. 336).

In brief, the inability to predict the future impact of innovations gives rise to surprise and inconsistency of expectations, which in turn generates radical uncertainty. This kind of radical uncertainty derives from the intrinsic characteristics of creative learning that will be considered further in section 1.6 on structural change.

Incomplete information-processing ability: Procedural uncertainty

Radical uncertainty may also be due to procedural uncertainty caused by an insufficient level of information-processing ability in relation to the degree of complexity of the situation. Procedural uncertainty may be due to an inability to frame problems through selection of the relevant variables, to compute, order or assess phenomena or simply the inability to take into account possible outcomes that are nevertheless known.

Since the early 1970s experimental psychology has provided a considerable body of evidence on human information-processing ability. Laboratory studies have confirmed that our information-gathering and information-processing abilities vary enormously from one person to another and are generally very limited. It has been shown that

For instance, if [one] . . . is subjected to a number of stimuli to his various sense organs, in general he can discriminate and recognize only about seven-eight at once. Again, this is about the number of items that a man can simultaneously bring to mind, out of all those stored in his memory, and take into consideration at one and the same time when coming to a decision about something. (Waddington, 1977, p. 32)

In many complex situations in which there is a very high number of interacting elements, individual information-processing ability is therefore insufficient. Furthermore, experimental findings suggest that the number of cognitive anomalies in the perception of information and in the process of choice is very high.[49] McFadden (1999, pp. 84ff.) enumerates at least twenty-five empirically observed cognitive anomalies that lead to the formulation of choice problems which are inconsistent with perfect rationality. As illustrated in the summary of definitions given in table 1.4, these anomalies can be grouped into six broad categories: context, reference point, availability, superstition,

---

[49] The pioneering works concerning experiments on cognitive anomalies in perception and in the process of choice that prevent full rationality and optimisation were carried out jointly by Daniel Kahneman, who was awarded the Nobel Prize in 2002, and Amos Tversky, who died in 1996. Among the numerous papers by these two authors, see, for instance, Tversky and Kahneman (1974, pp. 3ff., 1992, pp. 44ff.); Kahneman and Tversky (1979, pp. 17ff., 1996, pp. 582ff.); Tversky and Fox (1995, pp. 93ff.); Kahneman (2003, pp. 1449ff.). On experimental evidence, see also Allais (1953, pp. 503); Simon (1976, pp. 426-32); Hargreaves Heap *et al.* 1992, pp. 38–49, 53); Egidi (1996, pp. 303ff., 2002, pp. 109ff.); Egidi and Narduzzo (1997, pp. 678ff.); March (1997, pp. 14–17); Rabin (1998, pp. 11ff.); Rubinstein (1998, p. 8); Bonini and Egidi (1999, pp. 153ff.); Luzzati (1999, pp. 567ff., 2003, pp. 1ff.); McFadden (1999, pp. 73ff.); Williamson (1999a, pp. 10–17); In addition, see the interesting discussion on this issue in North (1990, pp. 18–19); Filippi (2003: pp. 75ff.); Hodgson (2003a, p. 6–8, *passim*); Egidi (2004, pp. 7ff.).

Table 1.4. Cognitive anomalies

Effect	Description
(A) CONTEXT	
Anchoring	Judgements are influenced by quantitative cues contained in the starting statement
Context	History and presentation of the decision task influence perception and motivation
Framing	Equivalent lotteries, presented differently, are evaluated differently
Prominence	The format in which a decision task is stated influences the weight given to different aspects
Saliency	Subjects are inconsistent in selecting and weighting the information judged salient to a decision task
(B) REFERENCE POINT	
Asymmetry	Subjects show risk aversion for gains, risk preference for losses, and weigh losses more heavily
Reference point	Choices are evaluated in terms of changes from a reference point
Status quo/endowment	Current status and history are favoured compared to alternatives not experienced
(C) AVAILABILITY	
Availability	Responses rely too heavily on readily retrieved information, and too little on background information
Certainty	Sure outcomes are given more weight than uncertain outcomes
Focal	Quantitative information is retrieved or reported categorically
Isolation	The elements of a multiple-part or multistage lottery are evaluated separately
Primacy and recency	Initial and recently experienced events are the most easily recalled
Regression	Idiosyncratic causes are attached to past fluctuations, and regression to the mean is underestimated

| Representativeness | High conditional probabilities induce overestimates of unconditional probabilities |
| Segregation | Lotteries are decomposed into a sure outcome and a gamble relative to this sure outcome |

(D) SUPERSTITION

Credulity	Evidence that supports patterns and causal explanations for coincidences is accepted too readily
Disjunctive	Consumers fail to accept the logical consequences of actions
Superstition	Causal structures are attached to coincidences
Suspicion	Consumers mistrust offers particularly in unfamiliar situations

(E) PROCESS

Rule-driven	Behaviour is guided by principles and analogies rather than utilitarian calculus
Process	Evaluation of outcomes is sensitive to process and change
Temporal	Time discontinuity is temporally inconsistent, with short delays discounted too sharply relative to long delays

(F) PROJECTION

| Misrepresentation | Subjects may misrepresent judgements for real or perceived strategic advantage. |
| Projection | Judgements are altered to reinforce a self-image internally or project it to others |

Source: Adapted from McFadden (1999, pp. 84ff., table 1, pp. 85) who provides further explanation and discussion on these definitions.

process and projection effects. In particular, evidence shows that individuals tend to be more sensitive to the way their current situation differs from some reference level than to the absolute level of their current situation (Rabin, 1998, p. 13). Moreover, empirical research demonstrates beyond any doubt that computing ability is usually quite low when probability distributions are involved. Experimental findings suggest that individual assessment of probabilities is often systematically biased by *framing effects*, in the sense that choices are dependent on the description of decision problems – i.e. on the way information is provided. In other words, choice is not invariant to logically equivalent change in descriptions of alternatives. For instance, equivalent lotteries presented differently are evaluated differently.[50]

Empirical findings have shown that statistical innumeracy, which is the inability to think with numbers that represent risk, is widespread even among the highly educated. It has been noticed that the human mind has general difficulties in computing probabilities, but has good computing ability when dealing with frequencies of actual events of which individuals have direct experience. In other words, the human mind tends to represent 'probabilistic information as frequencies' of contingencies that have occurred in past personal experience.[51] Cosmides and Tooby observe that

What *was* available in the environment in which we evolved was the encountered frequencies of actual events – for example, that we were successful 5 out of 20 times we hunted in the north canyon.
During their evolution, humans regularly needed to make decisions whose success could be improved if the probabilistic nature of the world was taken into account.[52]

However, many economic situations are unique, and so decisions are made only once, as non-repeatable experiments. With *non-repetitive choices*, the individual cannot ascertain the frequency of a particular event in order to estimate the individual probability.[53]

On the other hand, knowing the probability does not, of course, make it possible to forecast whether this event will occur or not for

---

[50] For an analysis of the framing effect see, for instance, Machina (1987, pp. 141–7); Johnson *et al.* (1993, pp. 224ff.); Rabin (1998, pp. 11ff.); McFadden (1999, pp. 73ff.).

[51] Cosmides and Tooby (1996, p. 1). For instance, Gigerenzer's experiments on samples of physicians demonstrate their poor diagnostic reasoning in using probabilities in interpreting breast, prostate and colorectal cancer screening tests (Gigerenzer, 2002, pp. 108–9).

[52] Cosmides and Tooby (1996, pp. 15–17, *passim*). See also the comment by Williamson (2002, p. 430). On the human mind as an evolving system, see Raffaelli (2003, p. 50).

[53] North (1990, p. 24); Langlois (1994, p. 119); Hargreaves Heap *et al.* (1992, p. 56); see also Runde (1998, p. 15). Knight (1921a, pp. 20, 233, *passim*) stressed that in the case of risk 'the distribution of the outcomes in a group of instances is known . . . while in the case of [immeasurable or true] uncertainty . . . it is impossible to form a group of instances, because the situation dealt with

any given person. For a large group of individuals, according
to the law of large numbers, the frequency of a given event is very
close to the probability and therefore it is possible to forecast with
precision the number of people who will be affected by this event in a
certain period. However, whenever events are restricted to the experience of a single individual, the probability is associated with
intrinsic uncertainty.

To conclude this section, the conditions in which firms operate
may be characterised by very different degrees of uncertainty depending on the problem at hand and individual abilities (theoretical knowledge and information-processing ability), which differ greatly among
individuals.

1.6 Structural change

Structural change consists in a mutation of the economic system and
of the industrial organisation due to changes in production techniques, market conditions and the composition of demand. Structural
dynamics is linked to the fact that the different elements of the existing
structure change at a different speed and each element is modified over
time.[54] Structural dynamics is characterised by various, sometimes
contrasting, features. It leads to path-dependent changes that generate
variety, complementarities and substantive uncertainty.

Variety stemming from innovative activity

Innovative activity broadens variety. Innovations are produced because firms deliberately seek to differentiate themselves from rivals
and adapt to their external environment. Hence, variety derives from
the purposeful ability to introduce a genuine new idea. Purposefulness
plays a crucial role in the selection processes that take place in a

---

is in a high degree unique.' 'We shall accordingly restrict the term "uncertainty"
to cases of non-quantitative type. It is this "true" uncertainty, and not risk, . . .
which forms the basis of a valid theory of profit.'

[54] Pasinetti (1993, pp. 1, 36ff.) presents a theoretical formulation of the endogenous structural change caused by technical progress and consumer learning. On
this point, see also Landesmann and Scazzieri (1996a, pp. 5ff.).

social context.[55] Variety and diversity constitute a general condition for both the growth of knowledge and profit.[56]

The achievement of technological progress produces, but at the same time requires, a high degree of variety and heterogeneous abilities among individuals. In economic systems, variety springs from the existence of different abilities among individuals and from the fact that individuals are placed in different contexts. This implies potentially different patterns of connections between available bits of information – i.e. individuals and organisations can interpret given information in a variety of ways. As Loasby puts it: 'incompleteness and dispersion of knowledge are a constant source of opportunities for creating new knowledge' (1999, p. 149). The emergence and maintenance of diversity among organisations through innovative activity is favoured by the division of knowledge and is linked to accumulation of different individual abilities and the development of specific capabilities according to specific learning paths. There is thus a *two-way relationship* between innovative activity and heterogeneous abilities. Innovative activity may create asymmetric information and heterogeneous abilities. On the other hand, heterogeneous abilities explain why individuals may have a different propensity or ability to innovate.

Complementary processes, components and products

Innovative processes are marked by complementarity in *production* (among the various inputs, components, intermediate stages and activities) and in *consumption* (among products that are utilised in conjunction with others).

---

[55] As pointed out in Hodgson and Knudsen (2004, pp. 283–4), artificial selection, particularly important in social contexts where purposefulness is important and acquired characters might be inherited, is consistent with Darwinian principles and can be regarded as a special case of natural selection. On the generation of novelty in the economic process see Dopfer (1993, pp. 130ff.).

[56] Loasby (2002b, p. 1234); and Saviotti (1996, pp. 42, 111). As far as the problem of persistent different revealed performances is concerned, Loasby (1967, p. 167) wittily argued in one of his early works that 'all firms do not behave in the same way in similar circumstances and a theory which helps to explain why they do not is perhaps to be preferred to one which asserts that they should' (quoted in Earl, 2002, p. 1).

A technical advance that speeds up one intermediate stage of the production process induces a concentration of innovative forces aimed at speeding up the other stages as well. In this regard, Rosenberg (1969, pp. 111–12) cites the technical evolution that characterises the history of the textile sector: 'Kay's fly shuttle led to the need for speeding up spinning operations; the eventual innovation in spinning in turn created the shortage of weaving capacity which finally culminated in Cartwright's introduction of the power loom.' This creates interdependencies among the single technical changes. To cite an example regarding the various components of a final commodity, the 'improved designs of automobile engines have led - through the achievement of higher speeds - to the invention of improved braking systems'. 'Similarly, to someone constructing a hi-fi system it is obvious that the benefits of a high-quality amplifier are lost if it is attached to a low-quality loudspeaker.'[57] Thus an improvement of a single component of a good may lead to an investment in R&D in order to improve other complementary components. Furthermore, independent advances in a technology may allow improvements in a component of a given commodity that dramatically increase its performance and make its market success possible. For instance, in the mid-1960s Teldix (controlled by Bosch and AEG) produced the first prototypes of an anti-lock braking system (ABS) that helped to maintain steering control in situations that required hard braking. However, its adoption in most models of cars became possible only from the late 1980s onwards thanks to improvements in microelectronics that allowed a considerable reduction in the weight, number of components, volume and cost of this device. Analogously, as we have already seen in section 1.5, laser efficiency, in terms of the number of communications carried on a cable, increased dramatically with the introduction of fibre optics at the end of the 1980s.

Incremental changes, learning-by-doing and learning-by-using

Rosenberg drew attention to the importance of *incremental changes* (or minor innovations) within innovative processes. Incremental changes are the innumerable small improvements and modifications

---

[57] Rosenberg (1965, pp. 111–12). On modularity and complementarity among audio components, see also Robertson and Langlois (1992, pp. 321ff.).

that occur more or less continuously in any industry and which arise from learning-by-doing and learning-by-using. These improvements are 'often individually small but cumulatively very large'. There are numerous empirical studies on the different sectors of manufacturing industry demonstrating that 'the cumulative effects of minor technological changes' which brought an increase in efficiency and cost reduction 'were greater than the effects of major technical changes' (Rosenberg, 1978, pp. 6–8, 1982a, p. 121).

In exploring the role of these cumulative small changes it is helpful to distinguish between *learning-by-doing and learning-by-using*. 'Learning by doing consists in developing increasing skill in production processes'; while learning-by-using is not the result of 'experience involved in producing the product but of its *utilization* by the final user' (Rosenberg, 1982a, pp. 121–2). Learning-by-using is essential in complex productions that imply massive uncertainty in prediction of the output performance. In these cases, the performance of the product may be ascertained by using it over time. Rosenberg provides detailed examples of industries in which gradual learning-by-using plays an essential role, such as aviation, electricity production in steam power plants, software engineering – i.e. above all in productions associated with a high degree of complexity of the output (Rosenberg, 1982a, pp. 122ff.).

Innovation as a source of uncertainty

Innovation is a source of substantive radical uncertainty. The degree of innovativeness of an economic system affects the level of environmental uncertainty because 'when the activity attempted is of a novel kind in itself, judgements about feasibility are subject to hazards and uncertainties'.[58] There can be little doubt that the question as to whether an innovation will actually be workable is the main source of uncertainty. However, as highlighted by Rosenberg (1996), there are other

---

[58] Winter (2005, p. 235). For a similar point of view see Harper (1996, pp. 3–21, 81–93, 295–350), who stresses that innovative activity is in principle unpredictable and open-ended, and develops the neo-Austrian approach in a dynamic and non-subjectivist perspective. The close relationship between innovation and asymmetric information is stressed, for instance, by Dosi and Egidi (1991, pp. 183–5); Metcalfe (1995, p. 26). On uncertainty and technological choices, see Freeman (1974, pp. 149ff.); Kay (1979, pp. 17ff.); Garud, Nayyar and Shapira (1997a, pp. 20ff.).

subtler and overlapping sources of uncertainty that are worth mentioning in detail. Five further sources of uncertainty deriving from the features of innovative processes can be identified:

1. New technologies 'come into the world with properties and characteristics whose usefulness cannot be immediately appreciated' (Rosenberg, 1996, p. 340).
2. 'The impact of an innovation' depends on improvements that take place in ' complementary inventions'. Examples include the impact of the invention of dynamos in the gradual spread of electricity, or the availability of fibre optics in the application of the laser to telecommunications, or the introduction of the transistor, and later integrated circuits, into computers that initially were made with vacuum tubes (Rosenberg, 1996, pp. 342–3).
3. 'Major technological innovations often constitute entirely new technological systems.' In a system, 'improvements in performance in one part are of only limited significance without simultaneous improvements in other parts'– as, for instance, in the case of railways, power generation and distribution. Uncertainty in predicting the economic impact of an innovation depends on difficulties in foreseeing the direction of future complementary innovations and associated investment.[59]
4. Many major inventions had their origins in the attempt to solve specific problems. 'However, it is common that once the solution has been found, it turns out to have significant applications in totally unanticipated contexts.' For instance, the steam engine 'was invented in the eighteenth century specifically as a device for pumping water out of flooded mines. In fact it was, for a long time, regarded as a pump. Only a succession of improvements later rendered it a feasible source of power for many uses such as factories and transport' (Rosenberg, 1996, p. 345).
5. Finally, evaluation of the impact of some innovations requires the identification of certain specific human needs and the means to satisfy them in a novel and cost-effective way (Rosenberg, 1996, p. 347). Thus, Guglielmo Marconi regarded his invention, the radio, as a device to communicate between two points, as in

---

[59] Rosenberg, (1996, pp. 344–5), for further evidence see also Rosenberg (1990, p. 169).

ship-to-ship or ship-to-shore communication, and could never have imagined that this device could become a vehicle for public broadcasting. Understanding the technical basis for wireless communication was 'a very different matter from anticipating how this device might be used to enlarge the human experience' (Rosenberg, 1996 pp. 337, 348).

Basically, then, the specific characteristics of technological change create the possibility of unexpected and unplanned outcomes that make it very difficult to predict the trajectory of future improvements. This generates substantive radical uncertainty.

Path-dependence

Structural-change processes are, at one and the same time, largely unpredictable and path-dependent. A process is *path-dependent* where initial conditions and the subsequent sequence of steps exert strong effects on its development, and on the final outcome.

The variety of initial conditions may bear consequences which shape and constrain future decisions of different business organisations.[60] Initially insignificant circumstances may turn out to be amplified: small causal events in history can thus become important due to the success of a technology, a product or an organisation. Levinthal (1995, p. 26) has shown that even if all organisations face the same environment, they may be led, as a result of these different starting points, to adopt distinct organisational forms. Thus observed differences in organisational form may in large part reflect variation in their founding conditions. If path-dependent behaviour dominates, nothing can guarantee that the fusion of necessity and chance, typical of path-dependent evolution, will lead to the optimum outcome. The example of the QWERTY keyboard, analysed by Paul David, is famous: the interdependency and complementarity between users – for whom the incentive to adopt a given technical solution depends on the number of individuals who have already adopted it – and the switching cost of retraining personnel – following a change in the arrangement of the keys – means the QWERTY keyboard has continued to dominate the market, even though other keyboards which allowed faster typing

---

[60] Hodgson (1998b, pp. 36, 47); Dosi and Metcalfe (1991, p. 133).

were introduced in its wake (David, 1985, pp. 281ff.). In the presence of increasing returns to scale, path-dependence may generate 'an outcome not necessarily superior to alternatives . . . and not entirely predictable in advance'.[61] This may cause a 'lock-in effect' in a sub-optimal condition that involves a market failure. However, as pointed out by Paul David, path-dependence is neither a necessary nor a sufficient condition for market failure.[62]

Organisations may contribute to the persistence of non-optimal solutions inasmuch as they have interest in containing a self-sustaining pattern of actions despite their being socially sub-optimal.[63] As highlighted by Pagano (1991, p. 327):

If it is true that technology influences property rights, the opposite also is true: property rights influence technology. This implies that we have to face very complicated cumulative processes where property rights influence themselves via technology and technology influences itself via property rights.

In this context, simple efficiency stories may well lose their meaning. Each outcome is likely to be path dependent and inefficient interactions between property rights and technology are likely to characterise the history of economic systems.

---

[61] Arthur (1989, p. 128). Chandler provides ample evidence of the dramatic cost advantages of the economies of scale and scope of the new capital-intensive industries of the Second Industrial Revolution. He notices that the first movers and closer followers that made the tripartite investment 'in manufacturing, marketing, and management essential to exploit fully the economies of scale and scope quickly dominated their industries. Most continued to do so for decades' (Chandler, 1992, p. 82). 'This integrated learning', which makes it possible to introduce new products and 'to lower unit costs by benefiting from economies of scale and scope', tends to create powerful barriers to entry. The example of the evolution of the chemical and pharmaceutical industries is particularly striking in this respect. As Chandler shows, in these two industries the barriers, built on an integrated set of dynamic capabilities, were so high 'that after the 1920s of the 50 largest chemical companies and the 30 largest pharmaceutical companies, only 2 chemical companies and no pharmaceutical companies were able to enter their respective industries' (Chandler, 2003: chapter 1, pp. 7–11, *passim*).

[62] David (1997); see also Bonaccorsi and Giuri (2003, pp. 50–1). For a sceptical position on the QWERTY story and on the concept of path-dependency, see Margolis and Liebowitz (1998, pp. 21–2).

[63] A more extended analysis of these issues is in Pitelis (1991, p. 19); Hodgson (1993b, pp. 24–5); and Screpanti (1995, pp. 68ff.).

Selection does not necessarily favour optimal outcomes because path-dependence with increasing returns and cumulative interactions between property rights and technology may prevent the emergence of efficient property rights. It has been shown that when governance structures are complex entities made up of many independent elements, 'selective forces tend to lose their power to drive a population to optimality' (Dosi and Marengo, 2000, p. 86). Moreover, as regards self-sustaining organisational patterns, large organisations can afford the high cost of external influence activities that succeed in persuading public bodies, political parties, public opinion and consumers by manipulating and distorting information and through lobbying activity. This confirms that there is a two-way relationship between organisations and markets. On the one hand, markets tend to select organisations; but on the other, the existence of the markets themselves depends on the appropriate functioning of organisations that regulate markets.[64]

Path-dependent and localised knowledge do not impede transmutable, non-ergodic, processes because even if movement is easiest to adjacent states, 'there are typically many adjacent states' (Loasby, 2004a, p. 271). Furthermore, the lock-in effects may be attenuated by creative learning, which produces unexpected novelty, new waves of better technologies, new entrepreneurial vision, the dynamics of positive externalities and interaction between internal and external knowledge.[65] As a consequence, the development of capabilities will be the result of a *path-dependent* process, which is however not *path-determined*. At each step, the direction of process could be changed 'because of the influence of new events in selecting among the different attractors of the system'.[66] Under path-dependent processes, agents are still able to change the conditions in which they operate, inventing and creating their future.

To sum up, creative learning may imply the introduction of new technologies that can suddenly change the direction of the development path, demolishing lock-in effects and unmasking new economic opportunities.

[64] This point is put forward in Pagano (1991, pp. 327, 337) and Hodgson (1993a, pp. 92–3).
[65] Antonelli (2004, pp. 250ff.) For further discussion on network externalities and switching costs, see Shapiro and Varian (1999: chapters 1, 5, 6, 7).
[66] Antonelli (2004, p. 250). See also Niman (2004, pp. 283ff.), who argues that the creation of new capabilities and the start-up of new innovative business organisations may threaten the market power of large incumbent firms and nullify their cost advantage.

Increasing radical uncertainty

This final sub-section of this section on structural change addresses the increase in the level of uncertainty in economic processes that is rooted in the sweeping changes that have taken shape since the 1970s.

During the 1950s and 1960s the economic development of industrialised countries was based on a high degree of predictability and stability of demand, ready availability of unskilled labour and mass production of standardised goods. In this period, the reduction of average costs was mainly due to the possibility of expanding the volume of production of final consumer goods, so as to enjoy significant economies of scale and economies of growth. Furthermore, oligopolistic rivalry and the routinisation of innovation processes within large firms contributed to reducing the level of uncertainty.[67]

In the 1970s several conditions prevailing during the 1950s and 1960s were progressively transformed. As was mentioned in the discussion on the increasing need for knowledge (section 1.4), production organisation was influenced by a number of factors that generated radical uncertainty,[68] in particular:

• Instability of demand and volatility of prices, exchange rates and interest rates
• Saturation of numerous mass markets that increasingly became substitution markets generally characterised by slow growth
• Growing pressures to innovate
• Increased internalisation of competition and in particular the growing competitiveness of some developing countries.

Subsequently, in facing increasing competitiveness and unstable and slow-growing demand, firms sought to expand their market share by differentiating and personalising their production. In this context, developing production structures that are able to reduce average costs and respond to the growing differentiation of consumer models has proved to be more and more essential in seeking to build a competitive advantage.[69] In short, for many firms innovation has become an

---

[67] The influence of oligopolistic rivalry and the routinisation of innovative activity within large business organisations is discussed in Baumol (2002: chapter 3).
[68] For a more detailed analysis on these points see Morroni (1992: pp. 175ff.).
[69] On the concept of competitive advantage, see Porter (1985: p. 3).

increasingly important means to save on input requirements and to match market needs.

1.7 Institutional and market conditions

Business organisations' efficiency and efficacy are also related to institutional conditions. Undeniably, the level of transaction, organisation and transformation costs crucially depends on the institutions governing the process of exchange and organisational coordination. I adopt here North's (1990, pp. 3–7, 1994, p. 361) definitions of institution and organisation. *Institutions* are considered 'the rules of the game in society. . . that shape human interaction', while conversely, social *organisations* are 'the players'.

Organisations

Social organisations are groups of people coordinated to perform tasks in order to achieve individual and collective aims. There are many different kinds of social organisations, including:

- Firms and networks of firms (e.g. family firms, managerial corporations, public companies, regulated firms, partnerships and state-owned companies)
- State or public organisations (e.g. international organisations, central and local administrations, public offices, the judiciary, anti-trust and regulatory authorities)
- Elected political bodies (e.g. political parties, city councils, parliaments)
- Third-sector organisations (e.g. voluntary associations, non-governmental organisations (NGOs), non-profit enterprises, trade unions, professional and trade associations, trusts and foundations, clubs, various associations, consumers' and workers' cooperatives, social cooperatives and social enterprises)
- Social and religious bodies (e.g. families, churches, etc.).

In the introduction to the book a firm was defined as an autonomous legal entity that produces and sells goods or services. Naturally, not only firms but many other social organisations may also sell goods and services. However, for other social organisations this does not form part of their major aims and therefore can be regarded as a secondary or occasional activity, while what identifies a firm, in relation to other social organisations, is that its *main* activity is selling goods and services.

A person who is member of a firm may also belong to other social organisations. For instance, she may be a member of a family, a trade union, a professional association, a voluntary group, a club and a political party. Moreover, a social organisation may be constituted by a set of social organisations. Thus there are lower-level organisations that are connected through a higher-level organisation. For example, a firm may belong to a network of firms and to a trade association.

Institutions

Institutions are mechanisms created in order to regulate interpersonal relationships and facilitate coordination. They consist in rules such as explicit and implicit regulations, laws and jurisprudence, as well as accepted norms, customs and formal and informal codes of conduct. Institutions exist to reduce the costliness of exchanging, protecting rights and enforcing agreements. 'When it is costly to transact, institutions matter.'[70]

Firms' decision-making processes and organisational settings are affected by institutions such as the legal system, which determines the set of rules that govern property rights and corporate control establishing 'socially acknowledged and enforced rights'.[71]

As far as property rights are concerned, the adoption of new patterns of ownership has enormously influenced the growth potential of enterprises. For instance, the creation of limited liability companies, the expansion of the stock market and the related formation of public companies removed 'the most important limitation on the growth and ultimate size of the business firm when it destroyed the connection between the extent and nature of a firm's operations and the personal position of the owners' (Penrose, 1959, p. 6).

---

[70] North (1994, p. 360; cf 1990, pp. 3–7); Denzau and North (1994, p. 4). See also Loasby (1999, p. 46) and readings in Ménard (2004a, 2004f).
[71] Hodgson (2001, p. 312). On this point, see also Dosi and Marengo (2000, p. 82).

Within the legal system, laws particularly important in shaping firms' decision-making are those that regulate corporate control, enforcement and dispute resolution activities. These include laws designed to:

- Regulate capital markets, financial and banking systems
- Discipline accounting practices and set book-keeping standards
- Regulate independent auditing that verifies corporations' financial statements
- Set the civil law of contracts, labour legislation, industrial relations and union agreements
- Empower anti-trust authorities, establish mechanisms of contract enforcement
- Establish the rules concerning business organisation bankruptcies
- Punish fraud, account fiddling, corporate corruption and misconduct
- Devise protection systems to cope with social costs of economic transformations, 'creative destruction' and business organisation failures.

The 'symbiotic' interaction between institutions and organisations

The institutional setting is instrumental in the profitability of activities undertaken by firms. Accordingly, incremental change in institutional conditions comes from the perception that business organisations 'could do better by altering the existing institutional framework'. However, in the presence of incomplete information and consequent erroneous models, the institutional change resulting from the incentive structure provided by existing institutions and property rights is not necessarily efficient, in that information feedback is typically insufficient to correct these subjective models (North, 1990, pp. 7, *passim*). Moreover, some institutions are not created

to be socially efficient; rather they . . . are created to serve the interests of those with the bargaining power to devise new rules. If economies realize the gains from trade by creating relatively efficient institutions, it is because under certain circumstances the private objectives of those with the bargaining strength to alter institutions produce institutional solutions that turn out to be or evolve into socially efficient ones. (North, 1990, p. 16)

Well-designed institutions play a part in reducing the degree of uncertainty surrounding transactions by establishing a stable 'structure to human interaction' through common laws and code of behaviour.[72]

Enforcement, corruption and influence activities

There are certain institutions consisting in laws and rules specifically designed to mitigate adverse selection and moral hazard problems that may characterise both market and organisational relationships. The strength and the degree of compliance with these laws affect economic efficiency and the competitiveness of firms. *Low enforcement* and *high influence* and *corruption* entail significant transaction and organisation costs that may lead to market and organisational failures. Let us elaborate on these three important factors:

- *Enforcement* signifies the ability to oblige the parties either to respect the contract or to pay the injured party compensation. The inability of the legal system to ensure appropriate enforcement of contracts increases uncertainty and consequently transaction costs as well.
- *Influence activities* are attempts to influence a decision-maker undertaken by a person who possesses some critical information. Under conflict of interests, the informed party may misrepresent, distort or fail to report the information needed by the decision maker.[73] Influence activities may take place both outside and inside organisations.
  Within organisations, employees may divert efforts by trying to influence or lobby superiors in order to affect organisational decisions concerning the distribution of benefits or quasi-rents

---

[72] North (1990, p. 6, see also pp. 59–60, 69).

[73] The concept of influence activities was originally developed by Milgrom and Roberts (1986, pp. 18ff.) with reference to exchanges between interested parties in the market. Subsequently, they focused mainly on influence activities within organisations (Milgrom and Roberts, 1990a, pp. 89ff., 1992, pp. 167, 179, 192–6, 375, 600). An anticipation of these themes may be found in Knight's (1921a, pp. 252–4) considerations on moral hazard. Cf. Kreps (1990a, p. 768); Foss (1996c, p. 83); Baron and Kreps (1999, p. 85).

among members of the organisation.[74] Influence costs arise even if
the central authority does not make suboptimal decisions, is
incorruptible and is aware of the influence activity, because 'the
time, effort, and ingenuity devoted to attempts at influence are
unavailable for more productive activities' (Milgrom and Roberts,
1992, p. 196, cf. 1990a, pp. 80–2 *passim*). We cannot but agree
with Milgrom and Roberts that influence activities 'are one of the
important costs of centralized control'. However, it is difficult to
share their statement that 'these costs are largely eliminated when
there is no decision maker with authority to make decisions that
employees wish to influence' (1992, p. 196). A central point is that
influence activities arise not only in organisations, but even on
markets in the presence of asymmetric information, heterogeneous
knowledge and conflict of interests. In decentralised structures,
influence activities exhibit different features compared to those
observed in organisations, but are not absent. For instance, sellers
may spend economic recourses in order to hide defects of their
products or to convince buyers that their products are endowed
with advantages that do not actually correspond to reality. Business
organisations may influence, deceive or even bribe and corrupt
authorities that are supposed to control their functioning and
behaviour. Again, manipulation of information by firms may
encompass consumption styles, cultural aspects, ideologies and
even political issues.

- *Corruption* consists in dishonestly using decision-making power or
  privileged information to obtain an advantage. It involves a hidden
  exchange, between two parties, which violates the law or codes of
  behaviour. An illustrative example, using the agency relationship,
  may be illuminating. Put simply, the agency relationship refers to a
  situation in which one party (the 'agent') is required to act on behalf of
  another (the 'principal'). There is corruption when the agent – for
  instance, an elected official or a civil servant – acts against the interest
  of the principal, the state or the citizens, and in favour of a third

---

[74] For employees, quasi-rents are payments beyond those they could expect to
obtain by quitting and taking another job, while rents are payments beyond
those required to attract them to the job in the first place (Milgrom and Roberts,
1999, p. 47; cf. Milgrom and Roberts, 1992, p. 269).

party – the corrupter – from whom he receives a bribe. Therefore in the corrupt exchange there are three parties: principal, agent and corrupter.[75]

The foregoing distinction between the three parties involved in the corrupt deal can be applied also to the private sector. For instance, a chief executive (CEO) of a company may falsify balance sheets in order to influence the stock market in a way that damages stockholders but favours certain lender banks that then reward the CEO. In this example, the CEO is of course the agent, stockholders are the principal and the banks are the third party, the corrupter. To taken another example, one could cite a manager who sells secret information to a competing firm (della Porta and Vannucci, 1999, p. 17).

Bribes are transfers that may be profitable for the agent and the third party. If one considers only these two parties, the corrupt exchange does not *per se* represent an economic inefficiency. The costs of corruption arise on account of the damage to the principal, which corresponds to the amount by which the principal is cheated, and most of all on account of economic inefficiencies stemming from the presence of strong negative externalities. Such externalities arise 'because productive decisions are distorted, either from favoring those who pay bribes or from punishing those who refuse' (Milgrom and Roberts, 1990a, p. 80). This drives honest dealings out of the market. Furthermore, if trust – understood as confidence in the honesty of the opposing party – facilitates economic activity,

---

[75] Della Porta and Vannucci (1999, p. 17) point out that:

> The functionary of a democratic government can be . . . conceived as a system of principal–agent relationships between electorate, elected official, and bureaucrats. The 'contract' that public administrators stipulate with the state – and therefore with the citizens the state represents – imposes respect of certain rules restricting discretionary power of the agent . . .

In this respect, the principal is a collective entity whose interests are often not easily defined. As observed by Lambsdorff (2002b, pp. 97–8), in the standard principal-agent model the interests of the principal are clearly specified and it is commonly assumed that 'a benevolent principal has full control over the legal framework, over reward and penalties'. In presenting corruption as an agency relationship, I do not refer to these assumptions that are too restrictive and patently in contradiction with the characteristics of various environments where corruption permeates economic relations.

corruption may, by contrast, result in further significant costs.[76] Nor should it be overlooked that corruption needs camouflage, which entails a cost corresponding to the economic resources employed to keep the unlawful transactions secret, while a corrupt exchange itself requires the development of private mechanisms for enforcement that are, of course, expensive. Problems are also encountered in relation to threats of disclosure which lock-in the two parties (the agent and the corrupter) even after the corrupt deal has been accomplished. Last but not least, if we consider public services, inefficiency may be deliberately pursued in order to obtain bribes from citizens who seek to secure a better service as an exception from the normal ill-functioning bureaucratic procedure. This observation indicates that inefficient administration and bureaucracy may not be due to the lack of individual abilities or resources, as might at first sight seem, but instead hide corruption.[77]

Legality, individual freedoms and economic development

Public and private corruption is not unjust only because it obviously entails a loss for the principal and for other subjects who refuse to pay a bribe, and because it increases the costs of economic activities, as indicated above; what must also be stressed is that corruption also generates ' dynamic inefficiency' by preventing the development over time of individual abilities, the growth of efficient local firms and investment in the region by enterprises located in other areas.[78] Therefore, scant enforcement power on the part of the legal system and severe corruption negatively affect economic competitiveness.

Prahalad (2005: chapter 5), who has focused on the consequences of corruption for economic development, convincingly argues that, in poor countries, corruption represents a major impediment to poverty alleviation because it inhibits the creation of markets and hinders the development of entrepreneurial abilities and buying power. Thus

---

[76] *Ibid.* On this also Leibenstein (1982, pp. 274–5).

[77] Vannucci (1997, pp. 37, 46–9). For further discussion and bibliographical references on the relationship between corruption and inefficiency, see also della Porta and Vannucci (1999); Lambsdorff (2002a, 2002b); Vannucci and della Porta (2003); Burguet and Che (2004); Vannucci (2004: chapter 2).

[78] On dynamic inefficiency, see Vannucci (1997, p. 49).

institutional conditions limit or favour, as the case may be, individual abilities and opportunities. Amartya Sen has pointed out that appropriate institutional arrangements may enhance individual abilities ('capabilities' in his terminology). He has highlighted the important connection between abilities and freedom. On the one hand, a person's ability ('capability') is a kind of freedom: the freedom to achieve 'alternative functioning combinations (or, less formally put, the freedom to achieve various lifestyles)'. On the other hand, individual abilities ('capabilities') are fostered by ensuring substantive freedom of exchange and transaction, political liberties, education, social powers and access to health care. Accordingly, development can be regarded as an integrated process of expansion of substantive freedoms, which may explain why Sen argues that 'freedoms are not only the primary ends of development, they are among its principal means' (Sen, 1999, pp. 10, 75, 297, *passim*).

Economic policies and market conditions

Both economic policies and market conditions shape the performance of firms.

Fiscal and monetary policies are obviously particularly important in determining exchange rates and therefore the international competitiveness of firms. A crucial role is also played by industrial and anti-trust (or competition) policies, which greatly affect the way in which business organisations operate.

The structure of markets is linked to the number of sellers and buyers, entry and exit conditions (e.g. entry barriers, brand identity, absolute cost advantage, sunk costs, access to inputs), and the rivalry among existing competitors depending on the size and technology of incumbent firms, concentration, product differences, information complexity, or differences in cost structures.[79] As emerges from the extensive literature on market structure, possible collective outcomes resulting from individual firms' choices affect profitability.

---

[79] On these factors, see the study of 'competitive forces' in Porter (1985, pp. 4ff.), and the analysis on market structure and 'basic conditions' of supply and domand in Scherer (1980, pp. 4–5). On entry and exit conditions, see also Baumol (1982, pp. 1ff.).

Moreover, the market breadth and fast pace of growth enhance efficiency. As far as extension of the market is concerned, a publisher who operates, for instance, on the large and growing English-reading market features a completely different type of organisation and level of efficiency compared to a publishing company that sells books in a language used by no more than a few million people. On the other hand, the market enlargement derives from the decrease in communication and transport costs as well as from demographic growth that creates additional demand.

With regard to the evolution of consumption models, some interesting interconnected phenomena are emerging. First and foremost, a process of identification and creation of collective interests is taking place in consumption activities. This is a rather new phenomenon because traditionally – i.e. since the rise of trade unions– the process of identification has taken place within production activities. Moreover, consumers are increasingly reacting to advertising-driven manipulation and to the lack of information on the characteristics of commodities through the creation of consumers' associations and autonomous information networks. Thus as the options and possibilities of consumption choices widen and become more complex, consumers are increasingly engaged in a process of discovery and creation of new combinatory consumption possibilities, 'new and favourable options'. From this point of view, consumers are considered as 'active producers of their consumption set' (Bianchi, 1998a, p. 7). Finally, consumers are increasingly concerned with the firms' social responsibility regarding working conditions, human rights and environmental aspects, as some recent corporation cases show.[80]

Key concepts

abilities
authority
basic conditions
complementarities
corruption
data

[80] Commission of the European Communities (2001). On firms' social responsibility, see sections 4.1, 4.2.

economising
enforcement power
externalities
forecasting (complete, perfect, imperfect, incomplete
  forecasting)
flows
funds
heterochronia
indivisibility (of production element and processes; economic
  and technical indivisibility)
influence activities
information
innovation
institutions
knowledge
market
market failures
missing markets
norms
optimisation
organisation
path-dependence
power
practical knowledge
risk (objective and subjective risk)
selection
set-up process
stakeholders
sunk costs
tacit knowledge
team production
theoretical knowledge
trust
uncertainty (radical, substantive, procedural, weak uncertainty)
variety

2 | Decision-making

THIS chapter addresses organisational decision-making. Figure 2.1 lists the main elements that influence decision-making mechanisms within the firm, which include property structure, hierarchical relationships and in particular the allocation of control rights and responsibilities (who participates in decision-making), rules regulating collegial decisions, the aims of the firm, incentive structure and the motivations of stakeholders and the degree of rationality of the actors' behaviour. These elements are linked one to another by mutual and close interaction. They are strongly sensitive to basic conditions, listed in the bottom right-hand rectangular block in figure 2.1, and deeply influence organisational coordination of the development of capabilities, the governance of transactions and determination of the scale dimension of processes, represented in the triangular block of figure 2.1.

For the sake of brevity, the main links between the decision-making elements may be summarised by the following causal chain. The firm's property structure affects control rights. The allocation of responsibilities and control rights plays a role in establishing the aims of the firm that shape its incentive structure, while the latter then influences individual behaviour within the decision-making processes, along with the kind of rationality that is related to the level of abilities. Abilities are, in turn, linked, to the degree of uncertainty and other basic conditions. This extremely simplified chain is complicated, in reality, by the influence of various *basic conditions* outlined in chapter 1, by the numerous possible *feedbacks* which bring about a two-way relationship between the different decision-making elements and finally by the uneven and changing distribution of *contractual power* among the various stakeholders. Let us consider the various decision-making elements one by one.

Decision-making

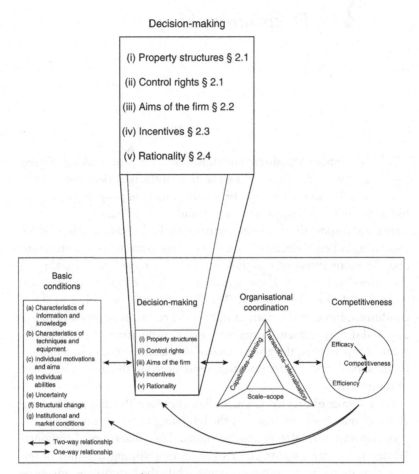

Figure 2.1. Decision-making.

2.1 Property structures, power and control

Firms, like all social organisations, involve both *power* and *control*. It is self-evident that the allocation of control rights and thus decision-making processes within the firm are affected by property structures. However, determinants of ownership structure and the relationship between property, organisational setting and control are in many circumstances rather complex and controversial.[1]

---

[1] For a broader discussion of related issues, see, for instance: Galbraith (1967: chapter 5); Demsetz (1983, 1995, 1997); Demsetz and Lehn (1985); Grossman

Residual rights of control and residual returns

According to the theory of property rights, pioneered by Grossman and Hart (1986, p. 252), ownership of an asset gives residual rights of control and residual return. Residual rights of control consist in an exclusive and alienable right to decide on the use of the asset 'in any way not inconsistent with a prior contract, custom, or law', while residual return is given by the net income that is left over after paying all costs. Under this perspective, profits are correctly regarded as a 'residual' obtained by the owner of physical assets.

Possessing the *residual* control and income rights eliminates the difficulty of writing contracts that assign these rights in all the different circumstances that may occur during the contract term. The allocation of responsibilities and decision rights may turn out to be efficient whenever the value of the assets strongly depends on the way in which they are used. In other words, one simple implication of the property rights theory is that, *ceteris paribus*, a party is more likely to own an asset if her use of the asset influences its productivity or value. For instance, 'it is usually thought efficient for someone to own the house they live in or the car they drive (as long as they can afford to . . .). Presumably, the reason is that the person with the most influence on the house's or car's value is the user' (Hart, 1995a, pp. 30, 49–50).

Residual control and income rights contribute to explaining the role of the firms' boundaries in offering incentives. However, actual residual rights of control over the firm's decisions depend on (i) the patterns assumed by ownership structures, (ii) the institutional context that can limit decision rights and (iii) specific contracts that can delegate control or assign the use of a specific asset, as in the following cases.

and Hart (1986); Hart and Moore (1990); Harris and Raviv (1991); Milgrom and Roberts (1992: chapters 9, 15); Hart (1995a, 1995b); Thompson and Wright (1995); Buzzacchi and Colombo (1996); Freeland (1996, 2001); Hansmann (1996); Shleifer and Vishny (1997); Cowling and Sugden (1998); Bianco and Casavola (1999); Schumann (1999); Helper, MacDuffie and Sabel (2000); Zingales (2000); Bianchi, Bianco and Enriques (2001); Hodgson (2001: chapter 19); Screpanti (2001: chapter 5); Tylecote and Visintin (2002); Roe (2003); Bianco (2004). Valuable collections of writings on the subject are in: Keasey, Thompson and Wright (1999a, 1999b, 1999c, 1999d); Barca and Becht (2001); Gugler (2001); McCahery *et al.* (2002); Calderini, Garrone and Sobrero (2003); Ménard (2004b: part III, 2004e: part II).

First, in modern economies there is a large variety of different property structures. These include: family firms,[2] managerial corporations, public companies, state companies, partnerships,[3] non-profit firms, cooperatives of consumers and workers' cooperatives. Accordingly, the owner of the firm's assets may be a single person, a group of shareholders, or a legal entity. In many of the above cases, *responsibilities and rights of control* are separate from *ownership*. Even within the same sector of activity, differences in property structures may be quite pronounced.

Secondly, the limits of residual rights of control are stated by law and therefore depend on environmental institutional conditions that greatly affect the definition of firms' property rights. For example, in the employment relationship, rules against discrimination or rules stating that employees may be fired only for a 'just cause' are examples of legal restrictions on control rights. It worth noting that, in some circumstances, the requirement that terminations can be enacted only for a 'just cause' does not necessarily represent a mere cost for the firm; rather, it may turn out to be advantageous for the firm to bear this cost in situations in which 'efficient production requires that workers invest in firm-specific skills', because this limitation on firing makes employees 'more likely to invest in acquiring those skills' (Milgrom and Roberts, 1992, p. 290).

Finally, residual rights of control may be limited by contracts that explicitly delegate decision rights or assign the use of the asset to another person. There are many circumstances in which ownership of physical assets does not necessarily imply control and power, and control and power do not derive exclusively from ownership. The separation of ownership and direction strongly limits the explanatory power of the property rights theory *as it stands*.[4] Incentives for efficiency may

---

[2] An enterprise can be called a 'family firm' if an entrepreneurial family that owns a share of the firm displays a deep and long-lasting commitment by being involved in its strategic decisions (Schumann, 1999, p. 225).

[3] Partnerships consist in an organisation of two or more persons to carry on a business, sharing gains and losses. Accounting firms, law practices, architectural firms, consulting firms, medical clinics are often organised as partnerships (Milgrom and Roberts, 1992, pp. 522–3).

[4] As Holmström points out, 'the problem is that there are really no firms in these models, just representative entrepreneurs' (1999, p. 100); on this see also Love (2005, pp. 392–3).

be found and implemented even if the direction is separated from ownership. In large business organisations decision rights, normally assigned to ownership, are frequently delegated to management or a board of directors, according to specific contracts and internal decision rules. In a corporation, the board of directors has the power to set dividends, to hire, fire and establish the compensation of executives, to decide the corporate strategy, reject merger offers or instead approve and submit them to shareholders and so on.[5]

It follows that the analysis of organisations cannot be based exclusively on property rights and incentive considerations.[6] Individual behaviour and the level of individual abilities may also shape the aims of the firm and the distribution of responsibilities. On the other hand, the aims of the firm and the distribution of responsibilities ultimately influence the firm's property structure. This means that the creation of individual abilities, the accumulation and social distribution of knowledge and the development of organisational learning 'cannot be reduced simply to either incentive or property rights allocation'. 'Stylised facts on the patterns of learning at the level of firms, industries and countries can hardly be interpreted as equilibrium responses to distributions of property rights.'[7]

Ownership forms

In various different economic systems there are certain predominant ownership forms. Divergent patterns of corporate governance have evolved in various industrialised countries according to the specific characteristics of the market of corporate control. In the Anglo-American framework, corporate governance is generally characterised by a highly diffuse ownership structure although there is a remarkable variability of ownership concentration across businesses. In US- or

---

[5] Milgrom and Roberts (1992, pp. 214, 498); Demsetz and Lehn (1985, pp. 1155ff.).

[6] By contrast, Foss and Foss (2000, p. 66) argue that 'many of the explanatory concepts and insights of the KBA [knowledge-based approach] can *themselves* be interpreted in term of OE [organisational economics] (using the language of property rights economics)'. On a critical analysis of this position see Dosi and Marengo (2000, pp. 83–4).

[7] In Dosi and Marengo's (2000, pp. 83–4) view, this is one of the basic tenets of competence and evolutionary perspectives.

UK-style public companies, the distinguishing feature of a public company is that it has a high number of small owners. An individual shareholder has no actual control power because the ownership of shares is dispersed across a vast number of small investors (Milgrom and Roberts, 1992, pp. 214, 498; Hart, 1995b, p. 680). 'With the dispersion of shareholding, the owners become rentiers who are de facto indistinguishable from the bondholders' (Screpanti, 2001, p. 288).

In Germany since the 1970s, a particular property and control form, labelled 'corporate capitalism', has assumed importance. This form is characterised by giant hierarchically organised manufacturing companies, one of whose major features is the presence of shareholding blocs led by banks. The banks involved each exert control over at least one of these blocs, with the result that small individual shareholders effectively have no residual control. But the crucial point is that for, each of these banks, the controlling shareholder is actually constituted by other big companies (mainly banks). Consequently, the bank managers 'can collectively control the entire system' (Screpanti, 2001, *ibid.*).

In Italy, corporate governance is characterised by a high degree of ownership concentration 'achieved mainly by using pyramidal groups', both for listed and unlisted companies. Governance structures appear to be built around (a) 'family capitalism', (b) very limited involvement by banks or other financial companies and (c) a considerable presence of state ownership that has been sharply declining in recent years (Bianco and Casavola, 1999, pp. 1057–8).

In Japan, a property and control form called *Keiretsu* has assumed importance. It consists of a company coalition held together by complex structures of cross-shareholding linkages and by personal ties among managers. For instance, given a group of, say, twelve top companies, constituting the core of a *Keiretsu*, if each of these companies succeeds in acquiring 5 per cent of shares in the other companies belonging to their group then they can jointly become completely autonomous from external shareholders. It follows that the managers can, if they act jointly, '*legally* control the entire group'.[8]

---

[8] Screpanti (2001, p. 288); on this see also Aoki (1988: chapter 4).

In American public companies, German corporate capitalism and the Japanese *Keiretsu*, the firm's control is in the hands of executives. Other organisational forms that imply a separation of ownership and control are, for instance, contracts which allocate decision rights and licensing agreements, or networks of firms that are based on outsourcing and contracting out. These specific organisational forms are based on mutual monitoring, common learning processes and long-term relations, and substitute for ownership in protecting specific assets by controlling opportunistic behaviours within networks of firms.[9]

Control rights over other firms may be allocated by specific governance contracts that assign the responsibilities and decision rights to a non-owner chief firm. In leasing contracts, responsibilities and some rights of control may be delegated to the leaseholder.

Contracts may establish, or various situations may imply, that the owners of the organisation's assets are not the exclusive recipients of the residual returns. In managerial corporations, executives' and top managers' earnings are linked to residual returns of the firm or are forms of profit-sharing. A further example is the existence of lenders as residual claimants, as is the case when a firm is unable to pay its debts. In such circumstances, 'increases in its earnings may have to be paid to the lenders'.[10]

Furthermore, residual income and residual control are not always bundled together on a one-to-one basis. For instance, it sometimes happens that two parties share control 50:50, but have a differential profit share. Another example is represented by a situation where employees receive a profit-based incentive. In this case, they are residual income claimants even if they have no voting rights.[11] In short, ownership, control and residual returns are not always tied together.

The financial patterns of firms vary among countries. Canada, the United Kingdom and the United States have traditionally been characterised by heavier reliance on equity financing than many other industrial countries. In the 1980s there was a rise of debt linked to

[9] Holmström and Roberts (1998, pp. 73, 80, 83–9) and Helper, MacDuffie and Sabel (2000, pp. 244ff.).

[10] Milgrom and Roberts (1992, p. 291); and Holmström and Roberts (1998, p. 85); cf. Demsetz (1995, pp. 110ff.).

[11] These examples are drawn from Hart (1995a, p. 64).

the wave of takeovers. Takeovers often involve refinancing firms using a large amount of debt and concentrating equity ownership in the hands of fewer large investors (Milgrom and Roberts, 1992, pp. 489, 528).

Third-sector organisations are neither state nor private commercial organisations.[12] They display a wide variety of legal, property and organisational forms. Some have owners who maintain control over the organisation (firm-like organisations such as social enterprises or non-profit cooperatives), whereas in others ownership is spread among their members and the actual control and liability is attributed to the representative board (as in associations or charitable organisations). Third-sector activities are usually financed by donors or public policies and often performed by volunteers. As stressed by Bacchiega and Borzaga (2003, pp. 37–8), when the redistributive component is substantial and a non-profit organisation needs extensive support to be derived from donations and sustained by volunteer labour, then control rights are usually assigned to volunteers or donors, or alternatively to trustees or local community representatives. But if no redistributive component is involved, 'either because there is a paying demand for the service or because the public authority fully subsidises the organisation,' control rights are likely to be allocated in such a manner as to deal with the market and organisational failures that may arise in the provision of personal and community care services. In these circumstances, control of the organisation can be efficiently assigned to consumers, or workers and managers.[13]

In conclusion, any consideration of the crucial aspects of property structures and financial patterns must take into account the level of concentration of ownership, the debt–equity ratio, the power of the board of directors and the amount of shares held by the management. These specific features assumed by corporate governance affect firms' decision-making and performance through the selection of executives and managers, and the generation of distinctive sets of incentives for the various parties involved. As shown by Tylecote and Visintin (2002, pp. 81ff.), examining data from six industrialised countries,

---

[12] Hayek (1979, pp. 49–51) described as the third sector 'the independent sector' distinct from state or public organisations, on the one hand, and commercial or private organisations, on the other. See also Whelan (1999, pp. 10, 80).

[13] Bacchiega and Borzaga (2003). See also Hansmann (1996: chapter 12).

the performance of firms is influenced by the 'fit' between their corporate governance system and the 'technological regime' (which reflects the specific characteristics of technical change, such as the degree of visibility, novelty, appropriability and organisational implications) of the sectors in which they are operating.

2.2 Aims of the firm

Aim-setting is a crucial aspect that distinguishes formal organisations from other social organisations (Greve, 2003, p. 148). A firm's aims and strategy reflect the incentives embedded in the property and institutional structures. They are also the result of a compromise between the conflicting interests of diverse stakeholders. Moreover, the degree of competition and market power are also important elements in shaping the firm's aims.

The stakeholders of a firm include: the executives, managers and employees; the entrepreneur–owner or shareholders; lenders and investors (e.g. unit trusts or mutual funds, insurance companies, pension funds, financial intermediaries); suppliers; customers; trade unions; local communities represented by NGOs and public authorities. Since different stakeholders generally have conflicting interests and very different contractual power, the firm's conduct and performance emerging as the outcome of their interactions may be dissimilar from the original intentions and aims of the individuals who were personally involved in the decision-making processes. In effect, the original aims of the firm may even be subverted. Moreover, some groups of stakeholders may pursue specific sub-goals which conflict with the firm's aims (Williamson, 2002, p. 428).

In a situation of perfect competition, firms cannot but maximise profit. However, under market structures that are not characterised by perfect competition, business organisations may have various possible aims with a different degree of importance. In addition to profits, one may cite an increase in revenue, the value of assets, market shares, power, prestige, or a focus on employment and public approval; naturally, growth and the accumulation of capital can form part of an organisation's aims, but so can production of socially useful goods and services, protection of the natural environment, or production of goods and services under non-profit distribution constraints.

Clearly, the specific strategy adopted by firms to achieve their various aims influences the organisational setting.

In general, private organisations are designed in a way that seeks to motivate the managers and employees to pursue the owners' aims, usually represented by profits, growth, power and prestige. The owner of the firm's assets is entitled to receive the net income that is produced by the firm. To be the residual claimant represents a strong incentive for the proprietor to increase efficiency and efficacy because these two variables directly affect residual returns. Therefore, the owner of the firm's assets has a keen interest in checking that the various members of the firm work according to its aims.

When the contractual strength of other stakeholders, such as consumers and local communities, is strong, public approval with regard to quality standards, workers' conditions, preservation of the natural environment or philanthropic actions may be very important. The latter goals, implying an increase in production costs and thus contrasting with the aim of short-run profit, may nevertheless give a positive image of the firm, which thereby heightens its sales, market share and long-run profit perspectives.

On the other hand, as explained by the managerial theories of the firm, the CEO or the top management may derive benefits from aims other than profit, such as the size of the firm and the rate of change in size. Early insights by Herbert Simon and Edith Penrose prefigured managerial theories of the firm.[14] For instance, Simon (1959, p. 296) observes that often 'under modern conditions the equity owners and the active managers of an enterprise are separate and distinct groups of people, so that the latter may not be motivated to maximise profits'.

---

[14] See Milgrom and Roberts (1992, pp. 39–40, 178). As far as managerial theories of the firm are concerned, see Baumol (1959); Marris (1964, 2002, p. 68). Interestingly, Galbraith (1967, pp. 124–5) observes that where Baumol and Marris accept 'the separation of ownership from control in mature corporation and its implication for profit maximisation, . . . they would go on, as here, to examine the modern corporation as an instrument of planning that transcends the market'. In this passage Galbraith echoes Coase (1937), who is, however, not mentioned, and anticipates a central point of transaction cost economics latterly developed by Williamson (1985). On this, see the interesting reappraisal of Galbraith's theory of the firm in Dunn (2001b, pp. 13–14, 28, 2001c, pp. 158, 173 n. 8).

Penrose (1959, pp. 27–8) maintains that 'salaried managers have little or nothing to gain by paying out more than is necessary to keep existing shareholders from complaining in force, to attract any additional capital that may be needed'. Certainly it is hardly open to doubt that the main motivations of executives and managers include not only income, fringe benefits, the desire for recognition, prestige and self-realisation, but also the craving to acquire control and accumulate power as a positional good.[15] All these aims are linked to the continuing growth of the firm. As remarked by Ernesto Screpanti, 'only those managers who correctly define their personal goals and efficiently pursue them are selected and rewarded. The correct personal goals are those coinciding with the growth of the firm.'[16]

In state firms, the level of efficacy, in relation to the needs of customers and users, is directly linked to the contractual and political power of citizens, consumers and users. A low contractual and political power of consumers, citizens and local communities may bring about low efficacy in relation to the needs of customers and users. This situation is further aggravated if state firms operate in a monopolistic position, as is often the case. Low efficacy derives from the fact that the state firm only partially pursues official aims, which consist in meeting customers' needs, while devoting itself instead to the pursuit of non-explicit or hidden goals that correspond to the interests of some other stakeholders with stronger contractual and political power.

In third-sector organisations, the aims and strategy depend not only on interaction between persons who have actual control rights and the other stakeholders, but also on the original organisational mission and the shared values of their members. Third-sector organisations have a plurality of aims and roles, such as production of goods and service under non-profit constraints, the provision of social services

[15] An interesting case study on the effects of the struggle for control on organisational changes can be found in Freeland (2001, pp. 33ff., 296ff.). Freeland argues that M-form at General Motors was initially created to re-establish and ensure owner control over the corporation, and the evolution over the time of this particular organisational form within General Motors has been the result of conflict and compromise between owners and managers.

[16] Screpanti (2001, pp. 165–7, 289). For a critical discussion and bibliographical references concerning empirical research on management compensation and the firm's performance, see Demsetz (1995, pp. 110–36).

and other goods with the goal of meeting the needs of disadvantaged persons, advocacy activities and the distribution of resources among individuals.[17]

In third-sector firms the members usually have an interest in pursuing the aims of the organisation they join. This mitigates, but does not nullify, a possible conflict of interests in defining aims and in pursuing a power position and other benefits within the organisation. Within the third sector, there are business organisations which operate under the non-profit constraint (non-profit organisations). The non-profit distribution constraint has been traditionally considered as a consumer protection device against opportunistic behaviour; however it has been widely recognised that without an appropriate control and incentive structure, this does not constitute a sufficient condition to prevent the onset of opportunistic behaviour and the exploitation of consumers (Bacchiega and Borzaga, 2003, p. 30).

Consumer-owned cooperatives and workers' cooperatives do not pursue profit maximisation. Customer-owned cooperatives aim to sell to their members at lower prices than profit maximisation would imply (Milgrom and Roberts, 1992, p. 41). Workers' cooperatives may be considered representative organisations whose strategy reflects the aims of all their members.[18] In these employee-owned cooperatives, aims and strategy are related to the employees' interests.

2.3 Incentives and motivations

Incentive structures are important determinants of the evolutionary dynamics of business organisations. Stakeholders of the firm respond to various types of incentives and sanctions that shape their actions. Four main kinds of incentives and sanctions can be discerned: (i) market incentives and sanctions; (ii) incentive or sanction contracts between independent contracting parties; (iii) incentives and sanctions

---

[17] Bacchiega and Borzaga (2003, pp. 27–9, 33). Advocacy activities consist in advocating for, protecting and advancing the legal, human and service rights of a particular group of citizens with a weak position (people with disabilities, disadvantaged groups and so on).

[18] On the distinction between representative and corporate organisation, see Screpanti (2001, pp. 26–7).

provided by organisations that regulate the functioning of the market; and (iv) organisational incentives and sanctions (see table 2.1). The first three types of incentives and sanctions operate within markets, while the fourth takes place within firms. All four are subject to efficacy and efficiency problems, involving both benefits and costs.

Market incentives

Markets provide high-powered incentives. Within markets, firms are directly exposed to the incentives and sanctions that consist mainly in profits and losses. In addition, within markets variations in prices and quantities foster compatible behaviour among agents provided that they possess all relevant information about qualities, prices and the behaviour of the opposing party.

However, in cases of pre-contractual and post-contractual informational asymmetries, markets may provide incentives not to transmit the relevant information through the market or may even go so far as to manipulate information. In these cases, market incentives may bring about prohibitively high transaction costs, market failures, or missing markets.[19]

Pre-contractual informational asymmetries may cause adverse selection. The used-car market, examined in detail in section 1.1, is just one example among the frequent cases of the conscious withholding of relevant private information by one of the bargainers. Examples of adverse selection abound in the literature. Take, for instance, an example referring to the labour market and product market: a job applicant is generally better informed about her abilities than is a potential employer; analogously, a producer may be better informed about the quality and reliability of his products than are possible consumers.

Post-contractual information asymmetries, which consist in lack of relevant information after the agreement, may give rise to moral hazard problems. This may imply that after the contract one party

---

[19] Models and applications on asymmetric information and heterogeneous knowledge initially came from the early 1970s analysis of second-hand cars, insurance, credit and labour markets, mainly as a result of contributions by George Akerlof, Michael Spence and Joseph Stiglitz, who were awarded the Nobel Prize in 2001. See, for instance, Akerlof (1970); Spence (1974); Rothschild and Stiglitz (1976); Stiglitz and Weiss (1981).

Table 2.1. *Incentives and sanctions*

Kind of incentives and sanctions (I&S)	Area	Examples
1. Market I&S	Within the market	Profits and losses
2. I&S contracts between independent contracting parties	Within the market	Explicit contractual incentives. Insurance contracts with deductible clause or experience rated. Posting a bond that is forfeited or setting penalties if the counterpart does not respect the terms spelled out in the contract
3. I&S provided by organisations that regulate market functioning	Within the market	Incentives and sanctions provided by courts, anti-trust bodies, central banks, Security and Exchange Commission (SEC), etc.
4. Organisational I&S	Within organisations	Explicit contractual incentives; for instance, piece-rate, higher wages paid to more senior workers, stock options, and so on Implicit and discretional (extra-contractual) incentives. For example, access to resources and equipment, possibilities of learning and career advancement, flexible timetables, shifts and holiday periods, location and type of workplace, status symbols, facilities, and so on

chooses actions that are not observable and enforceable by the other party. The other party's inadequate information makes it impossible or very costly to find out whether the terms of the contract have been respected. Moral hazard problems are frequently found in principal–agent relationships. This is because the agent's interests usually differ from the principal's and the principal has little possibility of evaluating whether the agent has performed satisfactorily (Milgrom and Roberts, 1992, p. 195).

Contractual incentives

Independent contracting parties often endeavour to overcome problems arising from informational asymmetries in the market by means of incentive contracts, monitoring, screening, or signalling policies. These are devices frequently adopted to give information, limit the possibility of pre-contractual or post-contractual opportunism and increase enforceability in relationships between independent parties. In this section we shall focus on incentives, while monitoring, screening, or signalling policies will be considered in detail later (section 5.1).

One very common example of incentive contracts between independent contracting parties is that of insurance contracts, such as:

- Contracts with a *deductible clause* (in theft and fire insurance), which encourage the policyholders to behave carefully in protecting their property from thieves and fire by obliging them to bear the initial part of any loss and therefore to share the risk.
- Contracts with *experience-rated payments* (in car insurance), which encourage safe driving habits among policyholders by imposing higher rates on those responsible for traffic accidents.

Incentive contracts may also involve posting a bond that is forfeited or setting penalties if the other party does not respect the terms spelled out in the contract. The amount of these penalties may be established in advance or may be linked to the losses the other party causes. For instance, penalties are frequently applied in contracts with suppliers where the commodity and services are provided after the agreed date or if the quality of goods and services fails to reach the agreed level. However, difficulties in enforcing the payment of penalties may arise, at times on account of the lack of power to compel payment of the penalty or due to the fact that the other party may lack sufficient capital to pay.

Incentives provided by organisations within the market

The third kind of incentives and sanctions that operate within markets are those provided by organisations expressly designed to control the functioning of markets. Well-known examples are courts, anti-trust bodies, central banks, the Security and Exchange Commission (SEC, a US body which examines prospectuses describing investments for which funds are sought from the public), auditing, quality standard control bodies and certification and accreditation organisations. Incentives and sanctions provided by these organisations crucially depend on the *institutional context*. Laws and various rules enacted by expressly designed organisations may provide appropriate incentives and sanctions that aim to overcome the problem of market failures or missing markets by reducing informational asymmetries and increasing enforceability.

Incentives within organisations

Business organisations are characterised by a division of labour. A division of labour requires coordination which, in turn, needs motivation. Within firms, market incentives and sanctions are filtered by the organisational set-up and depend on the ownership and financial structure. This can result in a rather complex reward system which may be far more complicated than suggested by many simplified models. In fact, there is no single set of incentive mechanisms, but several sets 'which act at different levels of the organisation, with different timings and with different intensity' (Cohendet, Llerena and Marengo, 2000, p. 103). The incentive structure is characterised by high variability in individual incentive intensity according to the different roles assumed and the contractual strength possessed by members of the organisation.

Unified governance through vertical integration within one business organisation offers the advantage of averting the market failures that can arise from conflicts of interest, informational asymmetries and knowledge heterogeneities between independent contracting parties. On the other hand, in business organisations, strong conflicts of interest may arise among its stakeholders – for instance, between owners and executives, between managers responsible for different areas, or between managers and the workforce, or among colleagues in work teams. Employees may shirk their responsibilities and have no interest in transmitting the relevant information to decision-makers within the organisation. Therefore, even within organisations various conflicts of interest and cognitive limitations may lead to moral hazard and to influence activities.

Organisational coordination consists in transforming the actors who pursue mutually conflicting aims into a 'cooperative system' with common aims, by mediating conflicting interests through the implementation of appropriate human resource policies (Nonaka and Takeuchi, 1995, p. 37). When ownership and control are separated, risk, return and control may not be aligned, and incentives are a tool designed as a remedy. Generally, the owner of the firm's assets has a keen interest in providing the managers and employees with incentives to reduce moral hazard problems and enhance productivity and ability to respond to the market requirements (Garud and Shapira, 1997, p. 253). The failure of a business organisation, or simply poor efficiency, and efficacy, are often attributable to lack of abilities or interest in finding an appropriate incentive structure capable of mediating between the different interests of stakeholders so as to devise a strategy that assures a competitive advantage.

As demonstrated by Bacchiega and Borzaga (2003, pp. 29–30), third-sector organisations are characterised by incentive structures that induce the groups of agents involved (donors, volunteers, but also workers and managers) to behave consistently with the organisational goals. The members of third-sector organisations are often not only producers but also customers of the services provided. Both aspects tend to reduce moral hazard problems because they limit possible conflicts of interest in setting aims. Common aims encourage altruistic behaviour and mutual satisfaction based on reciprocity and solidarity.

State organisations may be characterised by a low-powered incentive structure due to the absence of a residual claimant, or because they are able to sustain huge losses for a protracted period of time without going bankrupt, relying on the taxpayers to pay the excessively high production costs. In efficient state organisations this problem is usually overcome by controls on efficiency carried out by internal managers and by expressly designed external organisations. However, if the political pressure of citizens and taxpayers is not strong enough, interest in controlling efficiency declines, allowing the allocation of quasi-rents among the organisation's members. A low-powered organisational incentive structure is frequently a consequence of this scant interest in controlling efficiency. But if the contractual and political powers of consumers, citizens and local communities are strong enough, and if institutions are well designed, state organisations succeed in devising the appropriate incentive structures that ensure very high efficiency despite the absence of a residual claimant.

Organisations can fail for the same reason as markets do, because of adverse selection and moral hazard phenomena due to conflicting interests among different stakeholders under radical uncertainty. In spite of this analogy, it is important to note that organisations are created specifically to cope with conflicts of interest by enforcing market contracts and implementing powerful incentives to manage conflicting interests and limit opportunism. As maintained by Barzel (2001, p. 19), 'changing a market relationship into an employment relationship induces a radical change of incentives. This change seems to be the main force for getting the parties to act in conformity with each other's desires, and correspondingly affects the guarantees that others look for.'

Internal incentives have a marked influence on judgments by the firm's members concerning the cost/benefit ratio and personal motivation to action. Personal motivation is conditioned not only by the firm's incentive structure, but in some cases there are intrinsic motivations linked to a specific role and the satisfaction derived from doing a good job. In some workplaces, personal motivations are also influenced by the allocation of responsibilities and roles, the manner in which risk is shared and the definition and redefinition of the aims of the organisation. Most people act mainly according to their role, which consists in sets of obligations and rights. Specific roles, the sense of belonging to the organisation and reciprocity relations tend to limit self-interested behaviour, as do moral codes and shared aims and interests. Identity, understood as the 'person's self-image' linked to their social category and role, is an important supplement to monetary incentives, which as sole motivators can be both 'costly and ineffective'.[20]

Within organisations, there is a tension between identification with the organisation and its goals and the pursuit of self-interest based on the desire to reduce effort, improve one's own relative position or accumulate power, according to the different roles played by the organisation's members. If it is undeniable that within organisations individual aims and behaviour are, to a certain extent, affected by the mechanisms of identification, Simon (1992, p. 6) is absolutely right in maintaining that economic analysis cannot merely concern the self-interested behaviour of completely isolated individuals, nor the disinterested or altruistic behaviour of individuals who, with complete self-denial, give up their own interests and rights in the interests of the organisation. Individual economic behaviour is the result of the intertwining and continuous reshaping of original individual aims based on self-interest, and the aims of the various organisations to which the individuals belong.

Internalising activities within one organisation usually facilitates monitoring and the observation and reward of outcomes. Organisations have a very wide range of potential rewards and punishments. Some of these are explicitly spelled out in the employment contracts, such as pay policy, while others may be implicit, very subtle and discretionary. Well-designed performance-based compensation systems motivate the firm's members and indicate the aims that are to be achieved. Performance evaluation can be a powerful tool for communicating to employees what is valued, norms of behaviour and organisational culture.

Incentive pay policy includes such aspects as piece-rate compensation, sales commission, discretionary bonus, a higher wage paid to more senior workers, or promotions policy. It may also involve group incentives such as profit-sharing or gain-sharing plans, or it may take the form of efficiency wages, deferred compensation, menus of contracts, management by objectives (MBO) and, for executives, options and compensation contracts based on share-price performance.[21] For

---

[20] Akerlof and Kranton (2005, pp. 11–12). See this paper also for an in-depth analysis of non-pecuniary sources of worker motivation.

[21] I do not address the analyses that model how firms design compensation contracts to induce employees to act in the interest of their employers. On

example, the rising pattern of wages over a worker's career implicitly involves a bond that is forfeited if the worker is caught cheating. 'A worker caught cheating after several years of employment stands to lose the high wages paid to more senior workers' (Milgrom and Roberts, 1992, p. 195). Under gain-sharing plans, when a work team meets predetermined targets, all the members receive bonuses. A menu of contracts consists in offering employees the possibility of choosing, according to their needs, among a variety of different methods of determining pay. MBO is a practice under which the employees and their supervisors negotiate the criteria and standards against which an employee's performance will be evaluated. Another common example of incentives within firms is the provision of stock options for executives, giving them the right to buy the corporation's stock at a specified price in the future. The underlying concept is that the presence of stock options will motivate the executives to work so that the market price of the stock rises above the price specified in the options. This enables them to make money by buying the stock cheaply (Milgrom and Roberts, 1992, pp. 134, 401, 413–14).

There is a wide range of human resource (HR) policies, including extra-contractual and largely discretionary incentive tools, that frequently influence motivation even more than economic incentives. Among often-mentioned features, it is worth citing: access to resources and equipment, assignment of tasks, job design, possibilities of learning and career advancement and worker participation. Equally important are autonomy and flexibility, crèches, choice of close colleagues or team members, timetables, shifts and the possibility of choosing holiday periods, location of the workplace within the firm's premises (e.g. on the higher and panoramic floor or in the basement under the stairs), office furniture and other status symbols, parking and other facilities, etc. Furthermore, for executives non-monetary rewards may include access to special dining rooms, sports facilities, company jets and membership in clubs. Some of these compensation

motivations, incentives and agency theory see: Jensen and Meckling (1976, pp. 303ff.); Fama (1980, pp. 307ff.); Holmström (1982, pp. 408ff.); Holmström and Milgrom (1991, pp. 556ff.); Laffont and Tirole (1993); Lazear (2000, pp. 1346ff.). For excellent overviews on the subject, see Milgrom and Roberts (1992: chapters 6, 7, 11, 12, 13); MacLeod (1995, pp. 3ff.); Prendergast (1999, pp. 7ff.); Gibbons (1998, pp. 115ff.); and Baron and Kreps (1999: chapters 5, 10–12, appendix C); Meccheri (2005, pp. 55ff.).

devices have a symbolic value, others substantial economic implications; all are no less relevant in motivating the firm's members than contractual and monetary incentives.

Yet it should not be overlooked that, like market incentives and sanctions, even organisational incentives and sanctions involve efficacy and efficiency problems.

Due to contract-writing costs and difficulties in enforcing contracts, it may be impossible to enforce a contract that 'makes pay (or anything else) contingent on a worker's *total* contribution to firm value'. The employee's short-run performance can be 'a misleading forecast of long-run performance; as a result, the worker's total, long-run contribution to firm value typically cannot be measured precisely, especially if such measurement must be taken by a neutral outsider' (Gibbons, 2000, p. 10).

With team production, group incentives are often applied. Such incentives increase reciprocal control within the team. Under team production, total output depends on the organisational structure and is not simply the sum of separable outputs of each of its members. With team production the productivity of any one worker is not independent of other workers' productivity, so that not only are individual effort and behaviour impossible to measure, but individual output may itself be impossible to ascertain and individual marginal productivity impossible to measure.[22]

Multi-tasking refers to a situation in which an employee has several tasks and a variety of responsibilities. Consequently, the employee's contributions take place along numerous dimensions. But if the performance of each task cannot be measured independently, severe difficulties arise in establishing incentives that motivate an equal and efficient allocation of an employee's time and effort among different tasks, in that employees will inevitably devote more attention and time to the activity that proves to have the highest incentive rate. Furthermore, strengthening the tie between compensation and output

---

[22] On team production, see Alchian and Demsetz (1972, pp. 195–6); Holmström (1982, pp. 408ff.); Aoki (1984, pp. 28–9). Team production involves not only the immeasurability of individual marginal productivity, but also a 'blatant affront to the principle of methodological individualisms' (Winter, 1988, p. 165).

of a single task may kill intrinsic motivation in a job that requires several tasks to be performed.[23]

The fairness of incentive schemes is evaluated by employees in terms of the outcomes (distributive justice) and of the process by which their performance is assessed and compensated (procedural justice). However, under informational asymmetries, comparisons concerning how each employee has performed relative to her peers can result in mistaken evaluations that kindle incentive legitimacy problems.

Performance-related pay systems, by strengthening the tie between compensation and output, can place employees under an excessive burden of risk, insofar as the outcome of the employees' work is not fully under their control. This exposes employees to risks they are unlikely to accept (Baron and Kreps, 1999, pp. 277–9). When incentives are established on performance targets based on past performance in the same task, employees are exposed to the ratchet effect that consists in punishing yesterday's good performance by setting higher standards today. If workers are aware that future standards will depend on current performance, they may oppose this incentive system and reduce productivity (Milgrom and Roberts, 1992, pp. 232–4, 240–1, 391). A possible solution to the ratchet effect is to incentivate improvements over time instead of designing incentives based on absolute levels of productivity measured at a given moment in time.

If radical uncertainty and conflicts of interest are present, a paradox arises. Organisational incentives and sanctions are designed to counter the consequences of radical uncertainty and conflicts of interest by limiting internal moral hazard phenomena and aligning members' behaviour to the aims of the firm. However, radical uncertainty and conflicts of interests are the very elements that make it difficult, if not impossible, to design an optimal incentive structure within complex organisations. This makes it highly unlikely that the alignment of the members' behaviour to the aims of the firm can be maintained solely through rewards and punishments. 'Ceteris paribus, the further . . . conditions depart from perfect knowledge, the less capable are such mechanisms of motivating actors and ensuring initiative'. Under radical uncertainty, informational deficiencies leave

---

[23] On the effects of incentives on multi-task activities, see the classic paper by Holmström and Milgrom (1991, pp. 556ff.).

incentives and sanctions 'susceptible to distortion and manipulation' (Freeland, 1996, p. 488), making them inadequate tools for control of the organisation if they are not supported by policies that encourage strong relations of reciprocity and create commitment to outcomes, voluntary compliance, identification and consent. Such policies are obtained through a mediation activity that manages the inevitable conflicts of interest among the firm's members concerning the distribution of the resources and the organisational setting and practices. Mediation mainly consists in negotiation and information activities that indicate possible mutual advantages for conflicting parties.

Organisational decision-making thus emerges as the result of both conflict and cooperation among the organisation's members, whose behaviour is based on individual motivations, these being in turn linked to the incentive structures produced by the various organisational settings and decision-making mechanisms.

In conclusion, with intrinsically imperfect and costly incentives and sanctions, the *relative revealed performance* of a business organisation is a consequence of its ability to craft incentives and carry out a mediation activity that proves to be *less costly* and *more adequate* to foster efficiency and efficacy.

2.4 Ability-based rationality

Along with the incentive structure considered in section 2.3, the level and the type of rationality are elements of prime importance in shaping decision-making mechanisms within organisations. The level and type of rationality are ability-based in the sense that both depend on 'the gap between agent's abilities and the difficulty of the decision problem to be solved'.[24] The firm's stakeholders interact on the basis of their theoretical, practical knowledge and information-processing ability. In the last analysis the needs and aims that drive their behaviour are forged by the knowledge and abilities they are able to acquire from experience.

---

[24] Heiner (1983, p. 562) treats the analytical consequences for the agent's behaviour of this gap that he terms 'C–D gap'. Concepts analogous to ability-based rationality are discussed in Grandori (1995, p. 11) and Raffaelli (2003, p. 127).

It is worth emphasising that both cognitive limits and the abilities to search for alternatives are distributed across individuals to a variable degree. Moreover, the same person may show substantial differences in these limits and abilities according to the situation at hand. Since the kind of rationality is linked to the individual level of abilities, rational behaviour cannot be identified with a 'universal assumption' pertaining to a single type and level of rationality. A more plausible picture is that individuals (and organisations themselves) 'shift from one decision strategy to another according to the nature of the problems' (Grandori, 1995, pp. 11, 84). In this respect, we cannot but agree with Robin Marris who disputes 'the right of some economists to appropriate the (unqualified) word 'rational' for what is by implication only one type of process and a rather narrow type at that'. Rationality is a much broader concept than is assumed in standard microeconomic theory.[25]

In the following I consider different types and degrees of ability-based rationality according to whether or not there is a gap between the ability possessed and that required.

Perfect rationality

Individual behaviour is the result of a two-stage process: *making* a decision and putting the decision *into action*. Perfect-rational behaviour consists in a perfect-rational action as a consequence of perfect-rational decision-making. Perfect-rational decision-making requires a situation in which individuals can fully evaluate all the consequences of each action according to their preferences in order to maximise their utility.[26] In other words, it implies that individuals must be able to estimate all possible future pay-offs consequent upon their actions. This means that individuals possess complete theoretical knowledge

---

[25] Marris (1992, pp. 195–6). See also Williamson (1999a, p. 20) and Loasby (2003a, pp. 285–90).

[26] 'Among the vast literature on perfect rationality see, for instance, Walliser (1989, p. 9), according to whom strong (or perfect) rationality may be decomposed into two half-steps: 'the first one treats the available data to define the agent's expectations on his environment and himself (cognitive rationality), the second one relies on these expectations to find out a selected action (instrumental rationality).'

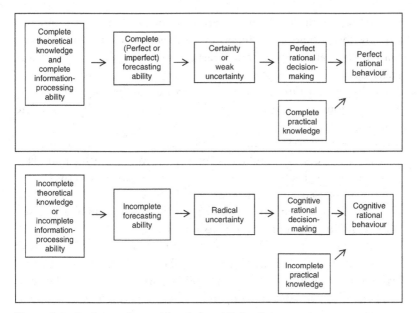

Figure 2.2. Perfect and cognitive rational behaviour.

and information-processing ability. Furthermore, perfect-rational action requires complete practical knowledge (figure 2.2).

Complete theoretical knowledge signifies that the decision-maker has full knowledge of the alternatives and consequences – i.e. a clear representation of the choice problem faced, which also involves the stationarity of the 'world' and a complete, consistent and stable preference ordering. If theoretical knowledge is initially not complete, perfect-rational decision-making requires that it must be, at least, exchangeable so that the necessary knowledge can be completed (at a known cost) through the market functioning.

Complete information-processing ability corresponds to the ability necessary to make whatever difficult calculations are needed to effect the optimal choice. It implies that individuals engage in logically correct reasoning.

Complete theoretical knowledge and information-processing ability make it possible to acquire complete forecasting ability. With complete forecasting ability individuals know the actual outcomes of all the possible events – or, at least, the probability distribution of all possible events. In the former case, they are in a situation of perfect forecasting, certainty or nil uncertainty. In the latter case, individuals are in a situation of imperfect forecasting or weak uncertainty. Both perfect and imperfect forecasting need the absence of radical uncertainty.[27]

Finally, perfect-rational behaviour depends on the ability to convert perfect-rational decisions into real actions. This requires complete practical knowledge.

It is important to stress that the completeness of all three individual abilities are necessary conditions for perfect-rational behaviour. This corresponds to a situation in which there is no gap between the abilities possessed and those required. Even an animal behaves in a perfectly rational way whenever the gap between abilities possessed and the abilities required is equal to zero. Consider the example of the laboratory rat faced with two buttons: the first gives it access to food and the second gives it a mild electric shock. If the buttons are not inverted in a random way, nobody will be surprised if the rat behaves in a perfectly rational manner by quickly learning just to press the food button and avoiding the button that gives the shock.

Under perfect rationality individuals optimise. Optimising behaviour consists in pursuing the best choice from the exhaustive list of all possible alternatives and in turning this decision into an appropriate action.[28] Optimisation is based on clarity, consistency and evaluation of consequences in terms of prior preferences. This implies the absence of errors – or, at least, systematic errors (see column (1) of table 2.2). Behaviour which is consistent with the above narrow definition of rationality is plausible whenever choices are simple, are

---

[27] As Tirole (1999, p. 756) points out, 'with [perfectly] rational agents contingencies are never unforeseen'. If parties are assumed 'to behave rationally', 'at the very least they know how payoffs relate to the final contract and investments'. Under some conditions, with perfectly 'rational actors the contingencies are not unforeseen even though they cannot be described ex ante' (Tirole, 1999, pp. 744, 746). What is required for perfect rationality is that agents can, at least, 'probabilistically forecast their possible future payoffs (even if other aspects of the state of nature cannot be forecast)' (Maskin and Tirole, 1999, p. 83).

[28] Optimisation problems involve the definition of an objective function which gives the mathematical specification of the relationship between the choice variables, whose optimal values have to be determined (e.g. the level of output), and some variables whose values have to be maximised or minimised (e.g. profit, market share, or cost).

Table 2.2. Ability-based rationality

	Ability-based rationality	
	Perfect rationality *(1)*	*Cognitive rationality* *(2)*
Abilities	Complete	Incomplete
Forecasting	Complete forecasting under certainty, objective or subjective probabilistic risk (weak uncertainty)	Incomplete forecasting under radical uncertainty
Situation at hand	Possible alternatives and outcomes fully specified. Immutable, ergodic, closed systems	Incomplete knowledge of alternatives and outcomes. Transmutable, non-ergodic, open systems. The future may be different from the past in an unexpected way
Decision-making processes aimed toward	'The best'	'The better'
Behaviour	*Optimisation* Anticipatory, calculated and consequential action	1. *Simplification* Action-based on routinised procedures, division of labour and knowledge, and sequential decisions 2. *Learning* Searching for alternatives
Possibility of errors	No systematic errors	Possible systematic errors
Alternatives	Given	Created
Choice	No real choice	Real choice
Result of the analysis	Determination of 'the one best way'	Determination of tendencies
Analysis of	States of equilibrium	Processes
Relevant analytical element	Constraints	Opportunities

made recurrently with substantial and rapid feedback and involve significant motivation.[29]

Cognitive rationality

At the opposite extreme of perfect rationality stands the case of 'absent rationality' (zero abilities), which is irrelevant to economic analysis. Between these two extremes there is an intermediate state of rationality characterising individuals who operate in conditions of radical uncertainty (substantive and/or procedural uncertainty) in which there is a gap between the ability possessed and that required. I term *cognitive rationality* this intermediate state between perfect rationality, which is linked to complete abilities, and absent rationality, which corresponds to randomness.[30] The concept of cognitive rationality used here implies the following related and partially conflicting aspects.

First cognitive rationality involves *reasoning* on the links between causes and effect regarding the achievement of benefits and the reduction of costs. Reasoned choices imply *per se* a cost, because ratiocination is a time- and energy-consuming activity. Therefore reasoning on causes and effects has an opportunity cost.[31]

The second aspect of cognitive rationality is given by *cognitive constraints* deriving from the individual's information-processing abilities and cognitive biases, together with the unpredictability of the future, which were discussed in chapter 1 (section 1.5).

Thirdly, cognitive rationality implies problem-solving procedures which are developed on the basis of individual abilities that 'pre-exist the acquisition of information from the environment'.[32] These problem-solving procedures imply the ability to search for information, to

---

[29] March (1997, pp. 10ff.); Denzau and North (1994, p. 10). On the relationship between optimisation and rationality, see Fedderke (1997, pp. 339ff.); Lawson (1997, pp. 186–7).

[30] The above definition of cognitive rationality has several analogies with the definition of the 'drastically weakened form' of 'cognitive rationality' provided by Walliser (1989, pp. 10–11, 13–14).

[31] Brain tissue is a high energy consumer. The brain accounts for about one-fifth of human energy (Loasby, 1999, p. 32).

[32] These characteristics of problem-solving procedures are discussed in Dosi and Egidi (1991, p. 167). The definition of cognitive rationality proposed in this book is consistent with the framework concerning decision-making processes provided by these two authors.

select different decision strategies (heuristics, routines, appropriateness), to look for alternative courses of action, to generate new languages and new behaviour and to deal with possible unforeseeable changes in environmental conditions by calling on creativity; in brief, the ability to construct new representations of problems. Individuals build their future by exploiting their ability to plan.[33] As noted by Loasby (1999, p. 6, 2001, p. 393), radical uncertainty makes room for imagination and mental processes that cannot fully rest on logical processes. Imagination and creativity are particularly important when 'the purpose of many decisions is not to respond to events but to introduce change'.[34] Effectively, then, the notion of cognitive rationality incorporates two important aspects: on the one hand, cost and cognitive constraints, on the other, learning and creative abilities.

The notion of cognitive rationality is closely akin to Simon's concept of bounded rationality.[35] However, I prefer the expression 'cognitive rationality' instead of the widely used bounded rationality for the following reasons.

- First, the adjective 'cognitive' suggests the search for alternatives that is an essential feature of the kind of rationality considered here.
- Secondly, as observed, 'the very term "bounded rationality" could be misleading insofar as it hints at some notional benchmarks of "full" rationality' (Dosi, 2002, p. 214). A similar idea is expressed by Loasby (2004a, p. 264) who argues that ' "bounded rationality"

---

[33] The concept of imagination was used by Joseph A. Schumpeter in his theory of the innovating entrepreneur and was more recently reintroduced by George Shackle and Ludwig Lachmann. For references to, and a discussion of, how imagination and intuitive processes explain entrepreneurial actions, see De Vecchi (1995, pp. 145–6); Harper (1996, pp. 88–92); Sabel and Zeitlin (1997, p. 11); Witt (1998, pp. 67ff.; 1999, pp. 390ff.); Loasby (1999, pp. 7, 31, 36ff.). On the human ability to construct new representations of problems, see Egidi and Rizzello (2003, p. 13).

[34] This two-fold nature of cognitive rationality is also captured in the expression 'bounded cognition' coined by Loasby (2002b, p. 1229).

[35] Simon's concept of bounded rationality 'is used to designate rational choice that takes into account the cognitive limitations of the decision maker' (Simon, 1987b, pp. 291, 293). 'Bounded rationality . . . assumes that the decision maker must search for alternatives, has egregiously incomplete and inaccurate knowledge about the consequences of actions and chooses actions that are expected to be satisfactory (attain targets while satisfying constraints)' (Simon 1997b, p. 17). This definition includes both incomplete information-processing abilities and incomplete theoretical knowledge of the full list of possible outcomes.

is not a good label for the view of human nature on which Simon sought to base his analysis, because it has been interpreted as an exception to the norm of unbounded rationality'.

• Thirdly, bounded rationality has progressively assumed numerous different and opposing meanings in the literature on the theory of the firm. On the one hand, bounded rationality has been interpreted as a 'universal assumption', rival and alternative to that of perfect rationality (Grandori, 1995, p. 11). On the other, bounded rationality has become an 'umbrella concept', which diverges considerably – as Simon himself has repeatedly stressed – from his own original idea.[36] This umbrella concept is large enough to include within bounded rationality optimisation under constraints, the optimal search-stopping rule, costly information and knowledge with farsightedness and perfect information-processing abilities.

• In order to avoid possible misunderstandings on the definition of bounded rationality, Radner (2000, pp. 633, 643ff.) proposes to distinguish between 'costly rationality', when there are costs of observation, communication and computation, and 'truly bounded rationality', closer to Simon's original meaning. This distinction is essential. Nevertheless, instead of using the expression 'truly bounded rationality', I prefer to use the shorter expression 'cognitive rationality', which emphases the *learning dimension* of this kind of rationality.

Ambiguities in decision-making

Decision-making under incomplete abilities and unanticipated disturbances involves ambiguity, inconsistency, ill-defined situations and opaqueness of the relationship between actions and environmental feedbacks (table 2.2). A forceful account of ambiguity and inconsistency in decision-making can be found in March (1988b, 1997), who distinguishes four kinds of ambiguity concerning: (i) preferences; (ii) relevance; (iii) history; and (iv) interpretation of

---

[36] For instance, see Simon's illuminating critique on the misuse of the definition of bounded rationality that is included in Rubinstein (1998, pp. 187ff.); see also Simon (1991, p. 26). Interesting comments on the misleading interpretation of bounded rationality as a hidden form of optimisation are in Gigerenzer and Selten (2001a, pp. 4–5); cf. Dunn (2001a, pp. 570–1).

decision processes. On the first point, March argues that where preferences are studied through the revelation of a series of choices, preference consistency has been difficult to find. Experimental findings show that human beings often act as if their different actions belong to different domains, with preferences that are conflicting and change over time.[37]

Rationality, optimisation and uncertainty

Under radical uncertainty one might assume that at least some kind of 'local optimisation' is still possible by making a choice among the subset of alternatives actually known to the chooser. In other words, the hypothesis of exogenously constrained knowledge might allow the theory to remain within the 'domains of optimisation'. However, in this context, the term 'optimisation' loses its meaning. In order to clarify this point, some examples of exogenous limits to rationality can be made by referring to the two types of radical uncertainty deriving from lack of information-processing abilities (procedural uncertainty) or from incomplete theoretical knowledge of all possible outcomes (substantive uncertainty).

Consider first the case of lack of information-processing abilities in relation to the complexity of the situation at the hand. This case may be illustrated by two famous examples: Rubic's cube and the chess game.

As argued by Ronald Heiner, Rubic's cube has

43 trillion possible initial positions from which to unscramble the cube. Minimizing the number of moves to solve the cube would require an extremely complex pattern of adjustment from one particular scrambled position to another . . . consequently cube experts have developed rigidly structured solving procedures that employ a small repertoire of solving patterns to unscramble the cube.

(Heiner, 1983, pp. 563–4)

---

[37] March (1988a, pp. 12–15, 1997, pp. 10–14); see also Dosi and Marengo (2000, p. 81). A seminal case study that has provided evidence on decision processes is contained in Cyert, Simon and Trow (1956). The data from this case study show that the criteria of choice are not the same from one choice to another: 'one choice may be made on the basis of relative costs and saving, while the next may be based entirely on non-monetary criteria. Further, few, if any, of the choices were based on a single criterion' (Cyert, Simon and Trow, 1956, p. 248).

A small repertoire of simplified procedures and rule-governed behaviour tend to be adopted each time they help to reach a target that is judged satisfactory in terms of saving of time and resources. They are adopted even if this leads away from optimisation. Under limited information-processing ability, non-optimal representation may be stable because 'discovering an optimal solution by trials (mutations) should be successful' but could be incredibly costly, 'in terms of computation and mental effort'.[38]

As far as the chess game is concerned, it is a game of perfect information: 'No probabilities of future events need enter the calculation.' The chess player's difficulty in behaving rationally is 'a matter of complexity' in relation to the information-processing ability of the players. Simon shows that no chess champion is able to follow an optimisation procedure because no one has sufficient computing ability to consider the whole tree of possible alternatives. For instance, expert chess players can look at as many as 100 possibilities in selecting a move or strategy; 100 even though a large number, is somewhat smaller than the 10^{120} that would perhaps constitute the total number of 'possible games of chess'. Each of the two players applies a rational strategy in order to beat the adversary even if neither can follow a perfectly rational strategy. Consequently, the winning chess player is not one who has employed the best strategy in relation to all possible strategies, but someone who implemented a strategy which is better than the opponent's. The winner has thus demonstrated greater abilities. Therefore, a winning strategy does not necessarily have to be the best strategy.[39] Playing better than the adversary cannot be confused with applying the optimal strategy. As in the chess game example, firms that are relatively more efficient will enjoy a competitive advantage.

However, unlike the case of the chess game and also Rubic's cube, firms do not always operate in a closed and deterministic situation of perfect information, but they make important choices and establish relational agreements that may even involve a significant lapse of time in a hard-to-predict world. Consider the example of substantive uncertainty deriving from the possibility of unforeseeable innovation. We

---

[38] Egidi (2002, p. 128); see also Egidi and Narduzzo (1997, pp. 678ff.).
[39] Simon (1972, pp. 412–17, 1976, pp. 440–1, *passim*, 1987a, p. 283); cf. Egidi (1992a, pp. 10–11).

have seen that technological change implies a high degree of uncertainty because of the difficulties in predicting the economic consequences of future improvements. Incomplete forecasting ability is due to ignorance of the rate and direction of innovative activity – in other words, to the fact that the future is partially unknown. This has relevant effects on consumption and investment activities. For instance, the choice of ordering a particular piece of equipment for delivery in six months' time could be considered a mistake on the part of the purchaser if, in the months following the order, an unpredictable technological improvement allows a new model of similar equipment with lower running costs and higher productivity to come onto the market.

If individuals do not know the actual future outcomes and are not aware of the incompleteness of their knowledge of possible outcomes, they may still believe that they can optimise, but they might ultimately make a choice that turns out to be the worst rather than the best. In the case of incomplete theoretical knowledge, therefore, the expression 'local choice' seems to be more appropriate than the expression 'local optimum'. In this second example, individuals likewise search for 'the better'. That is to say, it is the quest to improve one's own relative situation through simplification, which decreases the abilities required, and learning, which increases the abilities possessed. What is considered 'the better' depends on individual local knowledge-based on previous individual achievement or the performance of competitors or opponents. Individuals possessing local knowledge can make only a limited number of plans and, as a consequence, they select their choices from a limited number of alternative courses of action.[40]

It is now widely recognised that in conditions of radical uncertainty, 'decision-making systems remain incompletely specified' and this prevents genuine optimisation (Loasby, 1976, p. 137). Discussion on the

---

[40] Choosing 'the better' means choosing on the basis of a satisfying outcome that can be regarded as a 'reservation threshold' – i.e. the minimum level required to make the outcome of the choice satisfying. This minimum level has been called 'aspiration level'. Simon (1955, pp. 239ff., 1972, p. 415) introduced the word 'satisficing [= satisfying] to denote problem solving and decision-making that sets an 'aspiration level' and 'searches until an alternative is found that is satisfactory by the aspiration level criterion'. See also Molm (1997, pp. 13–14) and Screpanti (2001, pp. 54–62). The concept of 'level of aspiration' has

incompatibility between radical uncertainty and optimisation can be traced back as far as Frank Knight, Joseph A. Schumpeter and John Maynard Keynes. It is worth considering in detail their positions on the question.

Knight (1921a, p. 311) holds that profits 'arise out of the inherent, absolute unpredictability of things, out of the sheer brute fact that the results of human activity cannot be anticipated and then only in so far as even a probability calculation in regard to them is impossible and meaningless'. Schumpeter (1912, pp. 93–4) argues that the entrepreneur is motivated by: 'the desire for power accumulation', doing things for 'the sake . . . of success'; and moreover, by the 'distinctly anti-hedonistic' feeling of the 'joy of creating, of getting things done'. With remarkable analogies, Keynes (1936, p. 161) maintains that 'a large proportion of our positive activities' can be undertaken only as a result of a spontaneous and optimistic urge to action 'and not as the outcome of a weighted average of quantitative benefits multiplied by quantitative probabilities'. In the often-quoted passage on animal spirits, he refers to reasonable calculation as the basis of decision-making:

if the animal spirits are dimmed . . . , leaving us to depend on nothing but a mathematical expectation, enterprise will fade and die; . . . individual initiative will only be adequate when reasonable calculation is supplemented and supported by animal spirits, . . . human decision affecting the future . . . cannot depend on strict mathematical expectation since the basis for making such calculation does not exist.[41]

Individuals and entrepreneurs, as portrayed above by these three great economists, are not optimising subjects. This does not mean that they behave in an irrational way.[42] 'Reasonable calculation supplemented and supported by animal spirits' (Keynes, 1936, *ibid.*) can be seen as rational decision-making.

After the Second World War, an important article by Alchian (1950, p. 255) stressed the incompatibility between uncertainty and profit

attracted the interest of experimental psychologists since at least the 1930s; see, for instance, Frank (1935) and Lewin *et al.* (1944).
[41] Keynes (1936, pp. 162–3, *passim*); cf. Dequech (1999, pp. 419ff.).
[42] On the rationality of the Schumpeterian entrepreneur, see De Vecchi (1995, pp. 20, 25 n. 36). On non-optimising entrepreneurial decision-making, see Shane (2003, pp. 39–45).

maximisation. 'The only way to make "profit maximisation" a specifically meaningful action', he wrote, 'is to postulate a model containing certainty'. The theme of the incompatibility between profit maximisation and radical uncertainty has been discussed by many authors with different perspectives and analytical aims. For instance, Cyert and Pottinger assert that the 'profit maximisation assumption . . . fails under empirical scrutiny chiefly because decisions made under uncertainty will almost never lead to maximisation of profit.'[43] Dosi and Egidi (1991, pp. 173–4) observe that if individuals can find a new alternative, this logically implies that they are not optimising. In general, the emergence of a novelty prevents optimisation because it becomes impossible to identify all the alternatives. Whenever individuals have no 'information about the joint distribution of all the relevant random variables, then there is little reason to believe that . . . there will be a well-defined "optimal" investment or adoption strategy' (Rosenberg, 1996, p. 340).

Multiple rationalities within the theory of the firm

Given the incompatibility between optimisation and radical uncertainty, neoclassical economists exclude the possibility of unanticipated contingencies and save the assumption of perfect rational behaviour, which offers the undoubted analytical advantages of simple mathematical formalisation and precise predictions. Accordingly, they tend to limit the theory of the firm to certainty or weak forms of uncertainty characterised by fully pre-specified and closed systems that allow complete abilities, with free or costly information. As pointed out by Paul Davidson, mainstream contributions tend to assume certainty or probabilistic risk and end up considering probabilistic risk and uncertainty as synonymous, while they neglect true (or radical) uncertainty[44] because they believe, as Robert Lucas claims, that 'in case of uncertainty, economic reasoning will be of no value'.[45] However,

---

[43] Cyert and Pottinger (1978, p. 211) conclude that 'the way to go about searching for a better theory is to begin by trying to get hold of an empirically satisfactory account of how firms make decisions under uncertainty'.

[44] Davidson (1991a, p. 129); cf. Machina (1987, pp. 121ff.).

[45] Lucas (1981, p. 224) quoted in Loasby (1999, p. 1). The conventional neoclassical theory of the firm, agency and property right theories, and some transaction

positions in this regard are not unanimous. The importance of radical uncertainty in the economic processes is increasingly acknowledged by some authoritative mainstream economists. For instance, Hart (1995a, p. 81) maintains that 'in reality, a great deal of contractual incompleteness is undoubtedly linked to the inability of parties . . . to *think* very carefully about the utility consequences of their actions. It would therefore be highly desirable to relax the assumption that parties are unboundedly rational.' A similar and even stronger position is expressed by Radner (1996, p. 1372), who rightly holds that 'significant features of the organisation of firms . . . can only be explained by a satisfactory theory of truly bounded rationality' (or 'cognitive rationality with radical uncertainty' following the taxonomy presented in this book).[46]

The analytical advantages of the assumption of perfectly rational behaviour notwithstanding, a key point of this book is that radical uncertainty cannot be neglected. Discarding *a priori* the possibility of radical uncertainty prevents an understanding of the existence and growth of many firms. In fact, excluding from the analysis the possibility of radical uncertainty deprives the theory of the firm of a crucial element that is linked to the essence of the firm itself. *Firms can be seen as tools to cope with a hard-to-predict world.*[47]

The unknowable nature of future events and cognitive limits help to explain why individuals join and develop business organisations. Firms can reduce the cost of radical uncertainty, which originates from substantive uncertainty, because they constitute a reserve of resources and capabilities, develop new knowledge through learning processes and settle long-term relational agreements which give the employer

---

cost models assume *farsightedness* – i.e. that individuals are able to know the pay-offs associated with the all possible outcomes of their actions. This naturally excludes the possibility of radical uncertainty.

[46] See also Augier, Kreiner and March (2000, pp. 559ff.).

[47] In *The New Industrial State*, Galbraith regards firms as strategic planning units that are a response to the uncertain surrounding market processes. Anticipating subsequent literature, he outlines various possible ways utilised by firms for dealing with uncertainty: for instance, combining size with diversification, internalising external processes ('replacing markets'), controlling markets and using long-term contracts (Galbraith, 1967, pp. 25ff., 354); cf. Dunn (2001b, pp. 12ff., 2001c, pp. 164–7). On management's response to uncertainty, see Spender (1989, pp. 42–5, 186).

residual rights of control, thus allowing the work content to be modified if circumstances change. Moreover, whenever the complexity of routines required by a particular activity is beyond the ability of a single individual, team production, identification and codification of sub-problems and the division of labour and knowledge within a firm can create the necessary collective abilities.[48] The firm's coordination of different activities can overcome, or at least mitigate, the problem of procedural radical uncertainty stemming from the incompleteness of individual abilities.

If, then, firms are tools to cope with uncertainty, it is not only realistic to take into consideration the possibility of radical uncertainty within the theory of the firm, in the sense that it corresponds to what is observed in the real world, but it is also in accordance with the very object of the analysis.[49]

Nevertheless, recognition of the analytical importance of radical uncertainty by no means implies discarding optimisation techniques under certainty or probabilistic risk.[50] Perfect-rational behaviour can be postulated and optimisation techniques can be applied in all specific circumstances in which: (i) the problems at hand are well specified, (ii) the decision-makers' abilities are sufficient to cope with them and (iii) decision-makers perceive that it is worth bearing the cost of a consistent and calculated choice. Hence, I do not argue against the assumption of perfect-rational behaviour and optimisation techniques if they are applied in the specific circumstances where individuals have the relevant information and knowledge and sufficient computing ability to estimate all possible pay-offs.[51] I do criticise applications of assumptions 'outrunning applicability', i.e. applications in utterly

---

[48] This point has been highlighted, for instance, in Dosi and Egidi (1991, p. 184).

[49] Mariti (2003, p. 5). See the interesting considerations on realism in Mariti's (2003) discussion of Coase's methodological position. On the relationships between economics models and reality, see also the thorough analyses in Lawson (1997) and Mäki (2002a).

[50] As North (1990, p. 20) rightly notices: 'in those instances where something approximating the conditions described [by the neoclassical model] . . . exist, the neoclassical model has been a very effective model for analyzing economic phenomena.'

[51] Referring to Simon's chess game example, Kreps (1990a, pp. 772–3) concludes his textbook (*A Course in Microeconomic Theory*) by addressing the crux of this question:

implausible contexts.[52] I contend that in a comprehensive theory of the firm, *both* farsightedness and radical uncertainty must be considered according to the context. Therefore models based on perfect rationality and those based on cognitive rationality may be considered complementary if the different domains of application are clearly identified.[53] It hardly needs repeating that radical uncertainty has to be considered because firms establish relational agreements that involve 'long stretches of time' and unexpected events. Relational agreements within and between firms require the analysis of *processes*, in particular simplification (through routinised operating procedures, division of labour and performance feedback) and learning processes (table 2.2). The possibility of substantive (or fundamental) radical uncertainty is explicitly assumed within the Post Keynesian perspective, and the competence-evolutionary and cognitive perspectives,[54] while different degrees and kinds of uncertainty are presumed in most transaction cost studies.

> Played by the sort of individuals who populate the economies of this book, a chess match would be a boring affair; the players would come on stage, look at each other, and agree to whatever (forced) outcome the game happens to have. . . . But (of course) the implicit assertion is that economic situations are not in all respects so complex that equilibrium analysis is irrelevant . . . *The problem comes in applying the forms of analysis we have used* [in situations] . . . that involve *long stretches of time and much uncertainty* (emphasis added).

[52] Williamson (2002, pp. 426, 337 n. 8) warns against the overuse of maximisation techniques as a short-cut. 'Short-cut forms of analysis can be and are sometimes used uncritically. Overuse of maximisation, like overuse of natural selection, is a chronic hazard. Both work well in some circumstances but break down in others, whence there is a need to delimit the use of such methods to the "appropriate subset".' On the great damage caused by the misuse of powerful tools, see Loasby (2003a, pp. 289–90).

[53] Grandori (1995, pp. 10–11, 84–5). She correctly argues for the possible coexistence of different decision procedures according to the different situation to be faced ('actor with multiple rationalities') and claims that considering perfect rationality and bounded rationality as 'universalistic assumptions' (instead of 'behaviours to be explained' on the basis of the relationship between abilities possessed and abilities required) has had 'the result of sharpening the divide between economic and behavioural models of "economic man" and "administrative man"'.

[54] The competence–evolutionary perspective and the cognitive approach to economics largely overlap. Both analyse human problem-solving, decision-making and change, in order 'to explain the nature and evolution of organisations . . ., in a context characterised by structural uncertainty' (Egidi and Rizzello, 2003, p. 2).

Whenever, due to the presence of radical uncertainty, it is logically impossible to identify an optimum position that allows the objective function to be maximised (or minimised), there is no equilibrium solution and the analysis of processes and tendencies becomes unavoidable in the theory of the firm (table 2.2).[55] Accordingly, in this analytical context, the focus is not on equilibrium states, but rather on processes by which firms try to strengthen their competitiveness.

Known and unknown alternatives

There is a crucial difference, with non-negligible theoretical implications, between an analysis of the firm which takes into account *only* complete abilities and an analysis which considers *also* the possibility of incomplete abilities and radical uncertainty. Under complete abilities, all alternatives are known and economising means attaining 'the best'. When all alternatives are known, the decision-making process involves considering the cost of alternative courses of actions under specific constraints. In this case, binding constraints appear to constitute the relevant analytical element in determining the optimal choice. In contrast, under incomplete abilities, alternatives are not given and individuals endeavour to acquire new information. This learning process means that new opportunities can be discovered or created, and their consequences evaluated through lengthy and costly learning processes (Simon, 1987b, p. 292). In such conditions, economising consists in pursuing 'the better' and the decision-making process concerns the search for possible options in order to increase benefits and reduce costs. This entails real choice (table 2.2).[56]

In the case of incomplete abilities, constraints still play an important role, but the ability to look for and create opportunities then becomes the relevant analytical element. Moving towards consideration of the

---

[55] For a discussion on equilibrium versus multiple outcomes within modern organisational economics, see Augier, Kreiner and March (2000, pp. 559ff.). On tendencies and predictions, see Lawson (1997, pp. 32, 285–6).

[56] As highlighted by Harper (1996, p. 87), this is consistent with Karl Popper's characterisation of rational decision-making. 'What we need for understanding rational human behaviour . . . is something intermediate in character between perfect chance and perfect determinism' (Popper, 1972, p. 228). On real choice see the discussion in Shackle (1972); Loasby (1976); Dunn (2001a, p. 574).

economic impact of the search for new opportunities opens up the possibility of going beyond the narrow perspective that focuses exclusively on constraints: it widens the field of economic analysis to include the economic effects of creative learning, in the sense of active participation in the economic processes whereby individuals build their future through creation of genuinely new economic conditions.

Key concepts

adverse selection
agency relationship
corporate strategy
economising
maximisation
mediation activity
minimisation
moral hazard
opportunities
optimisation
property rights
profit
rationality (perfect and cognitive rationality)
residual returns of an asset
residual rights of control of an asset
separation of ownership and control
stakeholders
team production

3 | *Organisational coordination*

THE development of specific capabilities, the arrangement of transactions and the design of the operational scale of different processes are understood as the three main aspects of the firm's organisational coordination. The framework proposed in this book enables us to assess the effects of basic conditions and decision-making mechanisms on the possible interactions among these three aspects that are listed and emphasised in the large triangle in figure 3.1. Capability, transaction and scale–scope considerations interact in shaping the organisational performance and boundaries whenever *perfectly rational individuals* have to face costly transactional, organisational, technical and productive information and knowledge, and some specific characteristics of production elements, such as indivisibility and complementarities. The interplay and weight of these three single aspects of organisational coordination of the firm are strongly amplified if – in the presence of the above conditions concerning the characteristics of information, knowledge, production elements and processes – individuals have to cope with *substantial or procedural radical uncertainty* and consequently if individuals are cognitively rational instead of perfectly rational.

Sections 3.1–3.3 of this chapter are dedicated to the analysis of the capability, transaction and scale–scope aspects. This paves the way for section 3.4 that addresses the crucial point concerning the conditions under which these three aspects interact (for this reason section 3.4 is indicated in the core triangle in figure 3.1). However, before turning to this, I shall first of all examine the assets of the firm, assessing also how they relate to the three aspects of the firm's organisational coordination.

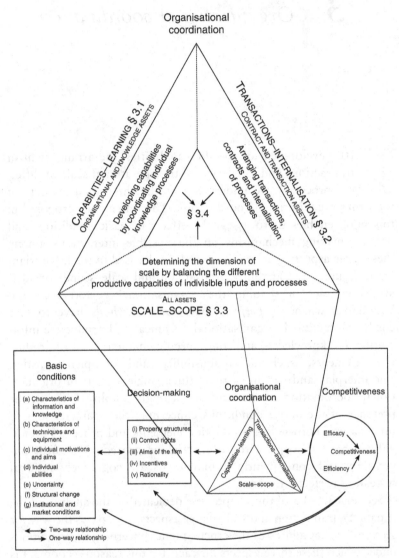

Figure 3.1. Organisational coordination.

The assets of the firm

For the sake of simplicity, we can distinguish five principal assets which constitute the resource endowments of a firm: knowledge, organisational, relational, physical and financial assets (figure 3.2).

Figure 3.2. The assets of the firm.

The characteristics of the specific resources available to firms and the manner in which these recourses are utilised strongly affect the organisation's revealed performance.[1]

Knowledge assets

The knowledge assets of a firm, which lie at the root of its capabilities, may be regarded as the 'learned knowledge' concerning organisational,

---

[1] On this point, see Wernerfelt (1984, pp. 59ff.); and Barney (1991, pp. 94ff.).

technical and relational aspects. The firm's knowledge is incorporated in the minds of its members, in a set of learned rules and routines, in the corporate culture and in a set of material artefacts such as machines, software, instruction books, products, etc. (Dosi, Faillo and Marengo, 2003, p. 12).

Knowledge of *organisational aspects* consists in knowledge of the social and technical interactions within the organisation and ultimately rests on knowledge about the 'match' between personnel and tasks and between employees working in teams (Prescott and Visscher, 1980, pp. 446ff.). Knowledge of organisational aspects is shaped by the development of informal interpersonal relations and interaction among learning processes. This knowledge of 'how to handle people' can be distinguished from knowledge of the techniques required to carry out service and manufacturing processes. *Technical knowledge* centres on activities such as administration, R&D innovation, legal services, marketing, finance, patent and production transformation activities. Lastly, *relational knowledge* is based on in the knowledge of agreements, contracts and transactions with suppliers and customers.

Organisational assets

Organisational assets consist in the organisation of knowledge, production processes, relational agreement and contracts. They involve a series of organisational relationships among the firm's members and routines consolidated over time. To address the organisation of knowledge, it is essential to ensure the organisation of existing skills according to the distribution of tasks within the organisation of work, and development of new skills through internal learning processes. Therefore the organisation of knowledge is linked to development of the firm's capabilities. The organisation of knowledge is based on the design of human resource (HR) policies (selection, pay and incentive systems, careers, etc.) that enhance motivation, coordination and integration. The organisation of processes, on the other hand, entails structuring the following activities: administration (strategy, direction, planning, allocation of resources, integration, control and coordination), R&D, innovation, marketing, legal and financial services and the coordination of all manufacturing operations (management of transformation activities, balancing of the productive capacities of equipments and intermediate processes). The organisation of contracts and relational agreements requires the management of relationships with suppliers, employees and customers.

The firm's organisation affects the efficiency and efficacy of individual resources because it affects the ways in which *resources* provide their *services* within the production process.[2] For instance, in team production the ways in which the members of the team provide their service depend, at least in part, on the team organisational setting. In other words, the members' skills are team-specific.

Relational assets

Relational assets are composed of relational contracts and agreements with the members of the firm (employees), upstream parties (suppliers) and downstream parties (customers). The value of relational assets depends on the reputation of the firm. Establishing relational agreements with employees or turning, instead, to external contracts with independent suppliers – in short, the alternative between make or buy – forms part of the arrangement of transactions that represents the second aspect of the organisational coordination of the firm.

The assets considered so far – namely, knowledge, organisational and relational assets – are intelligence-related and immaterial. In knowledge-based firms, the value of these intangible assets, as a whole, usually exceeds that of the physical assets. Consequently only a small proportion of their stock market value is attributable to ownership of physical assets; it depends, rather, on knowledge, organisational and transactional capital. While information and explicit knowledge (such as written information, data bases, patents and copyrights) are the property of the firm's owner, tacit organisational, technical and transactional knowledge embedded in its members is not possessed, in a strict sense, by the firm (Arrow, 1994a, p. 7). Hence, in knowledge-based firms, human resources play a predominant role.

---

[2] The origin of this distinction between productive resources and services comes from Edith Penrose's theory of the firm. Penrose (1959, p. 25) observes that 'it is never resources themselves that are the "inputs" in the production process, but only the services that the resources can render'. Penrose avoids the term 'factor of production' precisely because it makes no distinction between resources and services (cf. Best and Garnsey, 1999, pp. 188–9; Turvani, 2001b, p. 316). Georgescu-Roegen's (1970) production model develops (apparently independently from Penrose) a similar distinction in his definition of fund elements (see section 1.2). The idea of variable degrees of efficiency within the firm, according to different uses of resources, is discussed also in Leibenstein (1966, pp. 392ff.).

Physical and financial assets

Physical assets comprise fund elements such as land, equipment, buildings, raw materials, inventories and work-in-progress. The characteristics of physical assets, together with those of knowledge, organisational and relational assets, are related to the third aspect of organisational coordination, namely exploiting possible economies of scale and of scope by establishing the dimension of scale of different processes.

Finally, a business organisation is characterised by financial assets (shares and equities, bonds, net credits and liquidity). The subject of finance goes beyond the aims of the present book, although the present perspective could be expanded by including an analysis of the organisation of financial assets and capital structure. In particular, it would be a promising perspective for a future study to include an analysis of the implications of cash-flow management, decisions about dividends to be paid to shareholders and the choice between debt and equity. Inclusion of these issues would enrich the perspective presented in this book without changing its main propositions regarding the coordination of competencies, transactions and scale.

3.1 Capabilities

Production for the market implies that business organisations use individual abilities in order to acquire and develop capabilities to produce and sell particular goods and services that satisfy the potential demand, thereby enhancing their competitive advantage.[3] The development of capabilities involves the growth of the organisational, productive and transactional knowledge assets considered in the introduction to this chapter. There is now a large body of literature showing that the knowledge developed by business organisations plays an important part in explaining the differences in their revealed performance.[4] Following the conceptualisation proposed by Dosi,

---

[3] See, for instance, the following collections of writings on the topic: Hamel and Heene (1994); Lazonick and Mass (1995); Montgomery (1995); Foss and Knudsen (1996); Foss (1997b); Foss and Loasby (1998); Langlois, Yu and Robertson (2002: II, part I); Kay (2003: part I, II, III, IV).

[4] Among many contributions based on conceptual discussion, business history investigation, case studies or econometric estimates on the ways in which firms

Nelson and Winter (2000a, pp. 3ff.), we can distinguish between capabilities and competencies.[5]

The firm's *capabilities* are the abilities to produce specific goods and provide specific services for the market (for instance, to produce a type of software, computer or car).[6] The firm's capabilities are essentially the learning processes that are embodied in the knowledge capital of a business organisation. The firm's capabilities are clearly different from the mere sum of individual abilities and skills of its members. They are rather the result, accumulated over time, of the organisation and integration of the individual abilities of a collection of people.[7]

On the other hand, the firm's *competencies* can be defined as '"chunks" of organisational abilities identified in terms of performed tasks and knowledge-bases upon which they draw' (Dosi, Faillo and Marengo, 2003, p. 9). So one might talk of legal, medical, mechanical, chemical, accounting, administrative, managerial, organisational, marketing and sale competencies that contribute to forming the overall capabilities of the firm (*ibid.*).

Both capabilities and competencies are understood as potentialities that can be triggered in specific contexts.

use and develop capabilities and competencies, see Chandler (1990, 1992, 2003); Stalk, Evans and Shulman (1992); Bogner and Thomas (1994); Hall (1994); Klavans (1994); Zander and Kogut (1995); Pedeersen and Valentin (1996); Prencipe (1997); Mowery, Oxley and Silverman (1998); Delmas (1999); Appleyard, Hatch and Mowery (2000); Argote and Darr (2000); Flaherty (2000); Florida and Kenney (2000); Fujimoto (2000); Henderson and Cockburn (2000); Narduzzo, Rocco and Warglien (2000); Patel and Pavitt (2000); Pisano (2000); Szulanski (2000); Malerba *et al.* (2002); Giuri, Torrisi and Zinovyeva (2004); Mariani (2004). Klein and Hiscocks (1994) describe a number of structured techniques to address applied analysis of competencies.

[5] There is as yet no generally accepted vocabulary on capabilities; for a discussion on terminology used in the literature, see also Loasby (1998, pp. 163ff., 2002a, pp. 52–3); Dosi, Faillo and Marengo (2003, pp. 6ff.).

[6] According to Richardson (1972, pp. 139–40), who introduced the term 'capabilities', 'organisations will tend to specialise in activities for which their capabilities offer some comparative advantage'. Chandler (1990, p. 594) considers organisational capabilities 'the collective physical facilities and human skills' as they are 'organised within the enterprise'.

[7] Loasby (1998, p. 173). Lawson (1999, pp. 151ff., 2002, pp. 2ff.) applies the notion of competence not only at firm level but, interestingly, also at regional level.

The firm's specialisation and core capabilities

The firm's capabilities are not simply acquired but are created, and reflect its specialisation on the market. Competitive advantage and performance differences across firms are the result of the development of different capabilities from those possessed by others. The possession and control of rare, inimitable or difficult-to-substitute resources creates market power. Therefore, the more inimitable a firm's capabilities, the stronger its market position.[8] Accordingly, firms will tend to specialise in activities that are based on inimitable capabilities in order to maintain a competitive advantage over their competitors. 'Since the origin of all tangible resources lies outside the firm, it follows that competitive advantage is more likely to arise from the intangible firm-specific knowledge which enables it add value' to the inputs 'in a relatively unique manner' (Spender, 1996, p. 46).

Non-contestable capabilities are called *core capabilities*. Core capabilities are related to the set of specialised activities, routines, entrepreneurial, managerial and organisational skills that are embodied in a firm and which 'cannot be readily assembled through markets'.[9] This type of specific knowledge, which constitutes the basis of the firms' core capabilities, is built up according to the entrepreneur–manager's strategy and vision (Cohendet, Llerena and Marengo, 2000, pp. 96–8, 106).

The inimitability of core capabilities is linked to the existence of heterogeneous abilities which are based on asymmetric information and heterogeneous knowledge. The latter, in turn, is due to conflicts of interest among individuals as well as the specific characteristics of knowledge (tacitness, non-measurability, non-appropriability and non-exchangeability) and the possibility of an unpredictable response by some agent. In this context, existing knowledge must be acquired through experience and new knowledge must be built up. Specialisation allows saving on abilities and therefore favours the in-house

---

[8] On the relationship between market position, specialised knowledge and competencies, see: Richardson (1972, pp. 139–40); Demsetz (1988a, pp. 296–8, 1995, p. 11); Barney (1991, pp. 94ff.); Foss, Knudsen and Montgomery (1995, pp. 7ff.); Grant (1996, pp. 112ff.); Lawson (1999, pp. 153–4); and Hodgson (1998b, pp. 48–9); Turvani (2001b, pp. 314–15).

[9] Teece, Pisano and Shuen (1997, p. 205). See also Prahalad and Hamel (1990); Hamel (1994); Eriksen and Mikkelsen (1996).

learning processes which are essential for the innovative activity that increases efficiency and efficacy.[10]

The firm's specialisation requires a certain degree of social division of labour, which is encouraged by the opportunity to exchange goods and services and, as is well known, is linked to the extent of the market. Specialisation and social division of labour are among the most important determinants of the productivity growth that has characterised the years since 1800 in industrial countries.

Firms can take advantage of different forms of specialisation and division of labour according to two kinds of coordination mechanisms:

- Coordination by *management* within business organisations
- Coordination by *hybrid forms of organisation* (such as strategic alliances, franchising, collective trademarks, etc.).

Coordination and organisational competencies

Coordination and integration activities come into play above all when it is a question of managing relational agreements within and between firms. Relational agreements require organisational competencies which are a fundamental part of the management's knowledge and are represented by 'shared pieces of knowledge and routines concerning the governance of coordination and social interactions within the organisations and with outside entities (customers, suppliers, etc.)'.[11] Conceiving, creating, implementing and changing relational agreements that buttress the firm's organisation is one of the most important tasks of managerial activity.[12]

Coordination within business organisations involves deciding on the level of centralisation and the pattern of distribution of information – that is to say, which decisions are to be centralised and which are to be

[10] For a discussion of the relationship between the cognitive division of labour and innovative activity, see Pavitt (1998, pp. 433ff.).

[11] Dosi, Faillo and Marengo (2003, pp. 6ff). See also Dosi and Marengo (1994, p. 216); Teece, Pisano and Shuen (1997, p. 208).

[12] This point is stressed by Gibbons (2000, pp. 20, 37, *passim*) in his analysis of the firm's internal organisations. He argues that 'creating, maintaining and changing relational contracts seem to require real talent and inspirations' and that the informal managing of relational contracts is 'the key to superior organizational performance'. However he notices 'that current theory cannot even express (not to mention evaluate) much of what I am trying to say'.

left to different operational levels of the organisation or how to manage information and to communicate.[13] The information flows mainly in four directions: from outside to inside the organisation as well from inside to outside, upwards to support centralised decision-making and downwards to implement the management strategy.

Productive knowledge and the organisation of production processes are closely intertwined because the cognitive division of labour and the development of the firm's capabilities are dependent on the particular organisational setting. This becomes evident if one reflects on the adoption of different patterns of production. For instance, the adoption of Toyotism involved a major redefinition of the nature and distribution of productive and transactional knowledge.[14]

It is only in relatively recent times that the relationship between knowledge and organisation has begun to receive analytical attention. This scant attention has, however, some remarkable exceptions. For instance, Alfred Marshall stressed the link between organisation and knowledge. In a famous passage he argued that 'capital consists in a great part of knowledge and organisation . . . Knowledge is our most powerful engine of production; . . . Organisation aids knowledge; . . . it seems best sometimes to reckon Organisation apart as a distinct agent of production.'[15] As is known, this view that regards the firm as a way of organising knowledge has been completely neglected by the Marshallian *vulgata* that have influenced most microeconomic textbooks.[16]

---

[13] Milgrom and Roberts (1992, pp. 114–15). The role played by organisational coordination in developing specialised technical knowledge within firms was envisaged in Galbraith (1967, pp. 60ff.).

[14] Coriat and Dosi (1998, pp. 114ff.); Dosi, Faillo and Marengo (2003, p. 18). For a discussion on the different characteristics of Fordism and Toyotism, see Coriat and Dosi (1998, pp. 114–20).

[15] Marshall (1890, p. 115). Egidi and Rizzello (2003, p. 3) consider Marshall 'as the father of the cognitive approach to organisations'. On this, see also Arena (2003, pp. 221ff.); Loasby (2003b, pp. 202ff., 2004a, p. 263); Raffaelli (2003).

[16] This is due to the fact that the hypothesis of scarcity of knowledge is not compatible either with partial equilibrium price theory or the Arrow–Debreu model, where it is assumed that all commodities are scarce apart from knowledge, which is considered the only full and free commodity. In other words, the market develops its own informative and self-regulatory role only if we assume that individuals are able to acquire or are already in possession of all the relevant information. For interesting comments on this point, see: Hayek (1937, pp. 58–68); Arrow (1973, p. 142) (1994a, pp. 3ff.); Hahn (1981,

Dynamic capabilities and strategy

Building a 'business conception' about what 'business is to do' and designing the firm's strategy is the entrepreneurial activity *par excellence*.[17] Designing a strategy means identifying the basic long-term aims and objectives of a firm, and adopting the course of actions and the allocation of resources necessary to carry out these aims (Chandler, 1962, p. 13). Implementing a strategy means building the future in an incessantly changing world. This naturally involves the continuous emergence of trade-offs. Only by constant efforts to modify or adjust methods and introduce new ideas can trade-offs be appropriately managed and the intrinsic difficulties overcome. Strategy design, then, integrates with R&D, innovation and marketing activities. From this point of view, the entrepreneur is the 'agent of change' who discovers unexploited opportunities, 'prepares and shapes the cognitive process leading to novelty and builds 'new business conceptions'. In order to do this, the entrepreneur has to detect efficient and effective routines and to identify the appropriate incentive structure. In this respect, the role of the entrepreneur and that of the manager tend to overlap, because the coordination of resources cannot be separated from the process of creating resources.[18] As highlighted by Knight (1921a, pp. 211, 251), in operating as an interface between the internal organisation and the environment characterised by unanticipated turbulences, the managerial–entrepreneurial role involves judgement and conjectures that are mostly firm-specific and largely non-tradable.[19]

---

pp. 133–4); Stiglitz (1989, p. 23); Demsetz (1988a, pp. 281–3); Egidi (1992a, p. 9); Hodgson (1996, p. 261, 1998b, p. 37); Langlois (1998, p. 2); Loasby (1999, pp. 72, 84).

[17] On the business conception, see Witt (2000, p. 735). Cowling and Sugden (1998, pp. 61, 64) define a firm as a means of coordinating production from one centre of strategic decision-making. They argue that 'the power to make strategic decisions is the power to plan the overall direction of production in the firm'. In addition, see the discussion in Dunn (2000b, p. 429, 2002, pp. 66–73), who highlights that strategic decision-making and planning becomes essential 'in an uncertain (non-ergodic) environment'.

[18] Cohendet, Llerena and Marengo (2000, p. 109). On entrepreneurship, see the in-depth analyses contained in Shane (2003) and Kalantardis (2004), and the numerous essays collected in Livesay (1995); Westhead and Wright (2000); Foss and Klein (2002).

[19] On non-tradable entrepreneurial knowledge, see also Niman (2004, pp. 274–5).

Designing a strategy involves the formation of new capabilities in anticipation of the possible evolution of market conditions and new business creation. The formation of new capabilities is made possible by spotting possible future new markets and by developing or tracking down new abilities and skills. Building new capabilities, as Loasby (1998, p. 176) remarks, rests on 'a double conjecture, about the kind of future that it is reasonable to prepare for and about the appropriateness of particular capabilities to those kinds of future'. Often the rapid growth of a firm is determined by the strong success of a specific product, which is linked to the capacity to create a competitive advantage by exploiting technological opportunities in complementary commodities and matching potential demand.[20] Innovative firms invest in learning by creating new capabilities and new products that tend to change consumer tastes.[21]

In strengthening the firm's competitive advantage, the entrepreneurial or executive role in enhancing the firm's ability to learn is essential. This ability to learn is referred to as *dynamic capabilities*. Dynamic capabilities consist in the firm's ability to integrate, build and reconfigure internal and external knowledge to address rapidly changing environments.[22]

As far as dynamic capabilities are concerned, it is useful to consider Chandler's distinction between the technical capabilities that are required for the 'R' in R&D and the functional capabilities that are required for the 'D' in R&D, and for the production and distribution of new products. Technical capabilities are 'those learned by applying existing and new scientific and engineering knowledge to the creation of the new technologies and from which new products and processes can be commercialised' (Chandler, 2003: chapter 1, p. 5). In contrast, functional capabilities

---

[20] See Rosenberg (1969, pp. 111–12) and Marris (2002, pp. 68–9, 77) on the role of complementarities in technical change.
[21] Bianchi (1998a, pp. 9–11) and Gualerzi (1998, pp. 46ff.); cf. Rumelt (1994, p. xv) and Langlois (1997, p. 76).
[22] Teece, Pisano and Shuen (1997, p. 204); Fujimoto (2000, pp. 246ff.); Pisano (2000, pp. 129ff.); see also the related concept of combinative capabilities proposed by Kogut and Zander (1992, pp. 383ff.).

- 'are created by learning the product-related know-how'
- 'emerge from learning how to build and operate large-volume production facilities for the new product and how to recruit, train, and supervise the labor force essential to operating these facilities efficiently'
- 'are acquired in learning the nature of the product's customers and markets and building extensive, advertising, sales, and distribution systems to reach them'. (Chandler, 2003: chapter 1, p. 6.)

Dynamic capabilities come very close to the concept of core capabilities because the latter are an aspect of the firm's knowledge capital that is fundamental to the firm's competitive advantage. Differential success in research and innovation, together with different behaviour and strategies, are therefore determinants of firms' differential in revealed performances.[23]

Corporate culture

Corporate culture is constituted by a part of the firm's knowledge and organisational assets that is common to a substantial portion of the firm's members in spite of different cognitive maps and interests. However, corporate culture is more than shared knowledge: it is composed of a common set of rules, a shared way of thinking and ethical behavioural code, together with the beliefs, experiences, precedents and procedures that provide values and build up method and context as well as the language for the organisational activities.[24]

Managing corporate culture requires specific investment aimed at generating shared mental models which serve a dual function: for in addition to improving the *internal functioning* of the business organisation, they are also a factor in building its *external*

---

[23] Barney (1991, pp. 94ff.); Dosi, Nelson and Winter (2000a, p. 6); (Dosi and Winter, 1998, p. 339). The resources necessary for sustainable competitive advantage are termed 'strategic assets' (Foss, Knudsen and Montgomery, 1995, pp. 8–12).

[24] Hodgson (1996, p. 255). An early discussion on corporate culture is in Milgrom and Roberts (1992, pp. 132, 265, 597); Crémer (1990, pp. 255ff., 1993, pp. 351ff.); Kreps (1990b, pp. 168ff.). As stressed by Lazear (1995, p. 89) in his useful review on the issue, there is little consensus on the definition of corporate culture.

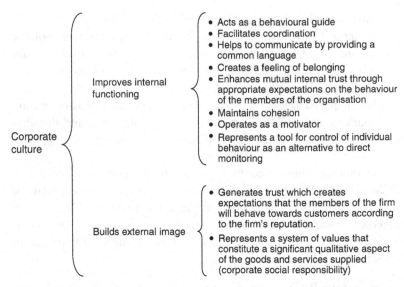

Figure 3.3. Corporate culture, internal functioning and external image.

image – i.e the way in which customers perceive its products and services (figure 3.3).

As far as internal implications are considered, corporate culture acts as a behavioural guide for the firm's members. The corporate spirit helps to communicate more efficiently by providing a common language; it facilitates coordination and creates a feeling of belonging by enhancing mutual internal trust and maintaining cohesion through appropriate expectations of the behaviour of the members of the organisation. In this respect, investing in corporate culture and reputation is an appropriate response to uncertainty.[25] Moreover, corporate culture operates as a motivator (together with economic compensations and other mechanisms) and may even represent a tool for control of individual behaviour as an alternative to direct monitoring (Lazear, 1995, pp. 89ff.).

With regard to the firm's external image, corporate culture can not only generate trust, which creates expectations that the members of the firm will behave towards customers according to the firm's reputation,

---

[25] See Kreps (1990b, pp. 168–9, 182–4, 191–4, 198–204) on the relationship between corporate culture, reputation and uncertainty.

but can also represent a system of values, capabilities and behaviour that constitute a significant qualitative aspect of the goods and services supplied by the business organisation. In many sectors of activity, these immaterial aspects of production are increasingly important in shaping the supply and demand conditions. In particular, it is interesting to note that, on the one hand, a rising number of firms is tending to base their advertising campaign on the positive aspects of their corporate culture while, on the other, customers are progressively more influenced in their choices by the behaviour and values of firms, as the growing concern about corporate social responsibility demonstrates.

3.2 Transactions

The second aspect of the organisational coordination of the firm is the arrangement of transactions and the internalisation of technologically separable processes. In this regard, it is useful to distinguish between transfers and transactions.

Definition of transfer and transaction

Transfer

A *transfer* takes place within a decomposable process when moving an intermediate output across two technologically separable processes within a firm. A production process is decomposable when it is technologically separable – that is, when it is possible to identify individual intermediate stages (or sub-processes) separable in time and space such that the product of one stage is a commodity utilised as an input in at least one other stage, and the various intermediate products that cross the 'frontier' from one stage to another may have an independent existence in the sense that they can be moved from one place to another while remaining 'unaltered for a certain time outside the production process'.[26]

A transfer may, or may not, involve internal prices. A transfer involves internal prices when firms adopt a division-by-division

---

[26] On the decomposability of processes, see Tani (1976, pp. 78–9) and Morroni (1992, pp. 70–1).

accounting system that takes into account exchanges of goods and services between various production units based on internal pricing.

Transaction

Transactions are regulated by contracts between independent agents who operate within markets and may involve either a transfer of a property right,[27] or renting a good (e.g. a tool, a car, or a house), or the provision of services through the market by an independent agent. A contract is a legally enforceable agreement, not necessarily written, between two or more parties. The essence of the contract is a commitment – that is to say, a contract is basically a form of promise.[28] A contract establishes the criteria to be used in deciding which course of action to undertake when unforeseen circumstances occur, who should have the power to decide and who has the power to resolve possible disputes if disagreements between the parties arise at a later moment of time. It gives guidance, attenuates misunderstandings through cultural alignment and may include the design of incentives. The existence of contracts does not need to depend on the possibility of opportunistic behaviour.

Transaction costs are the costs of exchange involved in framing and enforcing contracts: in other words, the costs of measuring 'what is being exchanged and of enforcing the consequent agreement'.[29] Accordingly, transaction costs are defined as the costs of using markets to satisfy economic requirements. They can be regarded as the costs to be borne in order to enjoy the advantages of division of labour. It is important to stress that in the analytical framework presented in these pages, transaction costs *always* involve an exchange between *independent agents*. This definition of transaction costs is akin to Ronald Coase's original meaning, the 'costs of using the price mechanism'.[30] Coase was the first to highlight the distinction between allocation of

---

[27] The definition of a transaction as 'transfer of ownership' goes back to Commons (1934, p. 58).

[28] See Love (2005, pp. 394–5); Masten (1999, pp. 25–6).

[29] North (1994, p. 360); see also North (1990, p. 27f.).

[30] Coase (1937, p. 38). See also Giovannetti (2003, pp. 1ff.); Hodgson and Knudsen (2003, p. 5); Mariti (2003, pp. 8, 14–16). Transaction costs literature now counts hundreds of contributions. Among the various collections of writings on the subject see, for instance: Pitelis (1993c); Medema (1995, 1998); Williamson and Masten (1995a, 1995b, 1999); Groenewegen (1996); Ménard (1997b, 2000, 2004b: part II, 2004c, 2004d, 2004g).

resources by 'entrepreneur-co-ordination' within the firm, which implies transfer by command, and allocation of resources 'by means of
the price mechanism', which involves a transaction through the
market.[31] In this context, the firm is seen as an autonomous administrative planning unit that supplants the price mechanism. Or, as Edith
Penrose put it, 'the larger this unit is, the smaller is the extent to which
the allocation of productive resources . . . is directly governed by
market forces and the greater is the scope for conscious planning of
economic activity'.[32] The Coasian distinction between allocation by
command within the firm and allocation by price mechanism within
the market implies a clear-cut dichotomy between the employment
contract and a market contract. The employment contract is based on
a relational agreement that is characterised by mutual obligations and
shared expectations about the behaviour of each party and by both
parties' interest in the relationship. It involves a general and broad
agreement on aims and on the parties' provisions. Some obligations
and expectations concerning the relational agreement are implicit,
others explicit and written in incomplete relational contracts or in
ethical and behavioural codes.[33] Other very common examples of
relational agreements are forms of collaboration among firms.

Composition of transfer and transaction costs

Transfer costs
Transfer costs of goods include all transport services. In certain cases,
transportation is a part of one single non-separable production process, such as the movement between two machines or loading and

[31] On resource allocation mechanisms, Coase argues that 'if a workman moves
from department Y to department X, he does not go because of a change in
relative prices, but because he is ordered to do so' (Coase, 1937, pp. 35–7, 1972,
p. 62). However, it should be noted that the workman may be ordered to move
from a department to another because the price of X has risen enough relative to
the price in Y to make the move worthwhile for the firm.

[32] Penrose (1959, p. 15). Similar considerations on the dichotomy between market
and hierarchy can be found in Galbraith (1967, pp. 25–7), who stressed that the
market can be replaced by organisational 'planning' and 'authoritative determination' in order to face 'unscheduled developments' due to market uncertainty. On this, see also Dunn (2001b, pp. 13–14, 28, 2001c, pp. 162ff.).

[33] The distinction between agreements and contracts is discussed in Barzel (2001,
pp. 2, 6, 10); see also Milgrom and Roberts (1992, pp. 131–2); Hodgson and
Knudsen (2003, p. 5).

unloading operations; in other cases transportation can be considered an intermediate process in itself that is part of a separable production process, such as the movement between two production units which carry out two intermediate processes. Transfer costs are 'really costs of production that are unavoidable in any economy with specialisation and a division of labor'. 'Many of the persons classified under Whole-sale and Retail Trade, for example, are really engaged in the physical movement of goods that would still have to take place even in a command economy with no market trading' (Hirshleifer and Glazer, 1992, pp. 378, 387).

The costs of the transfer of goods are given by the management costs of coordinating the transfer operations plus the physical movement costs. As indicated in table 3.1 (point 1), transfer management costs are the costs of: (1.1) coordinating the transport processes; (1.2) coordinating various intermediate warehouses; and (1.3) transfer accounting. Physical movement costs are the costs of: (1.4) auxiliary transformation and packaging processes; (1.5) transport and (1.6) warehousing.

Auxiliary transformation processes are needed where the semi-finished product requires a specific process to give it an independent existence outside the production process where it originated. Many examples could be given of products which require specific transformation where there is no continuity of operations – for instance, cellulose pulp to produce paper or glass paste, as both have to be dried and hardened to be transported outside the production unit. In fact, for molten glass to be utilised outside the production unit, additional hardening and packaging operations must be performed, while its re-use entails liquefying by heating. It is worth noting that continuity of operations is a technical condition, while vertical integration is a technical as well as a contractual condition. Continuity of operations may be assured even under very different contractual interfaces between successive intermediate stages. There may indeed be various ownership modes that can support continuity of operations (Williamson, 1997, p. 130).

The cost of warehousing depends on the quantity of semi-finished goods stored and the length of time they remain unused in the form of inventory. If these costs are to be taken into account, time must be included in analysis of the production process. Costs of auxiliary transformation processes and warehousing have considerable importance in many activities. Packaging, transport and warehousing between two production units are intermediate production processes in

Table 3.1. Components of transfer and transaction costs

Transfer Costs (production costs)

---

1. Transfer management costs and physical movement costs
    1.1 Costs of coordinating transport processes
    1.2 Costs of coordinating warehousing
    1.3 Accounting costs
    1.4 Costs of auxiliary transformation processes and packaging
    1.5 Transport costs
    1.6 Warehousing costs

Transaction Costs (exchange costs)

---

2. Contract and information–knowledge costs
    2.1 Taxes
    2.2 Government certificates and permits
    2.3 Middlemen payments
    2.4 Legal fees
    2.5 Contract-writing costs
    2.6 Costs of bargaining
    2.7 Information costs for the seller (signalling, advertising, marketing and information to potential buyers)
    2.8 Information and measurement costs for the buyer (screening, assessing qualities and recording prices)
    2.9 Costs arising from imperfectly specified contracts due to ignorance (radical uncertainty)
    2.10 Hold-up inefficiencies
    2.11 Costs of monitoring respect of the contract
    2.12 Enforcement costs

---

themselves. Even a technically integrated production unit has to move intermediate outputs within the establishment and, usually, to keep inventories between one sub-process and the next. The costs of energy and tools for moving goods and the costs of storing the intermediate products are considered part of the production process cost.

Transaction costs
Transaction costs encompass contract, information–knowledge and enforcement costs (see table 3.1, point 2). Thus their possible main

components are due to: (2.1) taxes; (2.2) government certificates and permits; (2.3) middlemen payments; (2.4) legal fees; (2.5) drawing up the contract; (2.6) bargaining; (2.7) information costs for the seller (signalling, advertising, marketing and information to potential buyers); (2.8) information and measurement costs for the buyer (search costs, costs of recording data, comparing the conditions of different suppliers, screening, assessing qualities, recording prices, selecting suppliers and deciding whether it is advantageous to exchange on the basis of transaction and bargaining benefits); (2.9) costs of imperfectly specified contracts due to ignorance of the other party's plans and possible outcomes (radical uncertainty); (2.10) hold-up inefficiencies; (2.11) costs of monitoring obedience to the contract; and, finally, (2.12) costs of enforcing the agreement.

Information–knowledge costs consist mainly in the costs of knowing the opposing party's behaviour and the possible outcomes of the interplay between agents, and of measuring the characteristics and the future performance of commodities. Information costs for the seller are due to the costs of signalling, advertising, marketing and informing potential buyers. Information costs for the buyer are mainly the costs incurred in searching and choosing among suppliers, screening, assessing qualities and recording prices.[34] Bargaining involves information and measurement costs because it consists essentially in acquiring information about the quality of the commodity traded, and the intentions and actual market power of the other party.

The cost of the monitoring aspect of the contract is mainly that of controlling the quality of outsourced semi-finished goods.

As indicated earlier (chapter 1, section 1.7), enforcement costs consist in the resources necessary to oblige the other party either to respect the contract or to pay the injured party compensation. Enforcement power reduces the degree of uncertainty about the behaviour of the other contractual party. Information–knowledge costs and enforcement power are interrelated because lack of enforcement power compromises the ability to forecast the other party's behaviour.

In considering the various components of transaction costs, a distinction can be made between *proportional* transaction costs that depend on the volume of goods and services exchanged and *lump-sum*

---

[34] On informational costs of the transaction, see Arrighetti (1998, p. 3) in which the author also carries out empirical tests on two samples of firms.

transaction costs that involve a fixed fee per transaction.[35] For instance, taxes and middlemen payments may represent proportional costs, while information–knowledge costs are largely independent of the volume exchanged. Lump-sum transaction costs cause economies of scale in buying inputs.

Transaction costs assume different relevance according to the characteristics of contracts, which are affected by the degree of knowledge of states of the world and the predictability of future events. Contracts may be perfect, imperfect, or incomplete. In the following three subsections we shall consider, respectively, the characteristics of these three different types of contracts.

Perfect contracts

Perfect contracts require *perfect knowledge and complete information processing ability* – that is to say, there must be no unexpected changes and the actual outcomes among all the possible events must be known and computed without cost. Individuals know the full list of all relevant contingencies and all consequences of possible actions. These assumptions, which we find in conventional microeconomic theory, entail nil uncertainty, perfect foresight, transmittable and marketable information and knowledge. In the presence of these conditions, parties can write agreemencts that consist in complete (spot or forward) contracts (point 1 in the left-hand block of figure 3.4).[36] Complete contracts involve complete:

- forecasting ability
- describability
- observability
- verifiability
- enforcement power.

Under *complete forecasting*, 'each party individually finds it optimal to abide by the contract's terms' and is unwilling to renegotiate the contract later on (Milgrom and Roberts, 1992, p. 127).

---

[35] For a discussion on this distinction see Hirshleifer and Glazer (1992, pp. 379ff.).
[36] A spot contract specifies delivery and payment at the instant of signing, while a forward contract, although signed today, indicates a specific future date for delivery and payment (Davidson and Davidson, 1984, p. 327).

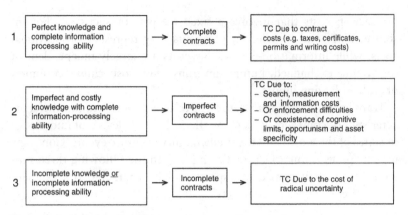

Figure 3.4. Individual abilities, contracts and transaction costs.

Note: TC = Transaction costs.

Complete describability consists in the ability to describe accurately and unambiguously in the contract what each party is to do in every possible contingency. Describability requires forecasting ability.

Complete observability implies that each party is able to know whether the contract's terms are being met.

Complete verifiability means that parties can write their mutual obligations and plans in such a way that, in the case of dispute, a neutral third party (say, a court) can establish the true significance of obligations and plans. Verifiability needs describability and observability.

Finally, *complete enforcement power* in turn requires verifiability. Describability matters whenever enforcement power is necessary, while it may be irrelevant if contracts are self-enforcing and, therefore, external enforcement is not necessary. A contract is self-enforcing when the benefits of respecting the contract exceed the cost.

With complete contracts, transaction costs are negligible and limited to contract costs such as taxes, certificates, permits, possible middlemen payments and writing costs. In these cases, spelling out in contracts the obligation binding on the parties can be a good alternative to ownership. Thus in the absence of any kind of uncertainty, transaction costs are not a problem: vertical disintegration and decentralisation are favoured.

Imperfect contracts

The label of 'imperfect contracts' is taken here as encompassing all contracts that imply knowledge costs such as measurement costs or contract-writing costs or the cost of 'bounded rationality with farsightedness' (see point 2 in the left-hand block of figure 3.4). All these costs may bring about significant transaction costs, but they do not prevent the contracting parties from computing the distribution of pay-offs, i.e. the benefits and costs deriving from their actions. Both contracting parties know the list of possible events and know or can estimate, at the very least, the probability distribution of all possible events (weak uncertainty and imperfect forecasting). This means that under imperfect contracts, parties must be endowed with the necessary information-processing ability, in order to establish an efficient course of action for each possible contingency. As a consequence, parties can optimise.

The literature based on these hypotheses has given rise to various models in which equilibrium positions spring from the interaction of perfectly rational contracting parties (as, for instance, in property rights, agency theories) or of boundedly rational – with farsightedness – contracting parties (as in transaction cost economics). In these approaches, contracts with costly information are usually defined as 'incomplete contracts'.[37] However, consistently with the distinction between imperfect and incomplete knowledge presented earlier in chapter 1 (table 1.2), I prefer to rename these contracts with costly information 'imperfect contracts', since they imply imperfect knowledge. I instead reserve the adjective 'incomplete' for those contracts designed under incomplete knowledge or incomplete information-processing ability and therefore under radical uncertainty (see table 3.2).

As far as imperfect contracts are concerned, for the purpose of our analysis it is sufficient to mention three kinds of transaction costs deriving, respectively, from: (i) search, measurement and information costs; (ii) contract-writing costs and enforcement difficulties; (iii) the

---

[37] On this, see the surveys by Hart and Holmström (1987, pp. 71ff.); Milgrom and Roberts (1992: chapters 6, 7); Hart (1995a, p. 23); Baker, Gibbons and Murphy (2002, pp. 39ff.); Gibbons (2003, pp. 755ff.). For an insightful comparative discussion of property right and agency theory, transaction cost economics and competence and evolutionary perspectives, see Dosi and Marengo (2000, pp. 80ff.).

Table 3.2. *Williamson's taxonomy on rationality and contracts: a comparison with some 'corresponding' definitions*

Williamson's taxonomy[a] (1)	Type of rationality and contract (2)	'Corresponding' definitions: type of rationality and contract		
		Radner's taxonomy[b] (3)	Hart's taxonomy[c] (4)	This book's taxonomy (5)
School of thought	Type of rationality and contract			
Orthodoxy – complete contracts	Hyperrationality – complete contracts	Perfect rationality	Perfect rationality – complete contracts	Perfect rationality with nil uncertainty – complete contracts
Transaction costs economics (and nearly-neoclassical theory of the firms)	Bounded rationality with farsightedness – incomplete contracts	Costly bounded rationality	Perfect rationality with lack of verifiability and enforcement difficulties – incomplete contracts	Perfect rationality with probabilistic risk (weak uncertainty) – imperfect contracts
Capabilities, behavioural and evolutionary approaches and organisation theory	Bounded rationality with myopia – incomplete contacts	Truly bounded rationality (Simon's bounded rationality)	Not considered	Cognitive rationality with radical uncertainty – incomplete contracts

Notes:
[a] Williamson (1999a, pp. 3, 24, table 1).
[b] Radner (1996, p. 1372, 2000, pp. 633, 643ff.).
[c] Hart (1995a, pp. 23, 81).

coexistence of 'bounded rationality with farsightedness', opportunism and asset specificity.

Costliness of measuring attributes of goods and services

First, measurement costs are the costs of obtaining information concerning the qualities and prices of products to be bought.[38] Measurement costs do not necessarily imply opportunism. Barzel's (2001, p. 37, n. 29) example is absolutely clear in this regard: 'Should people who spend (an "excessive" amount of) time picking and choosing among the apples in the apple bin be deemed "opportunists"? Aren't they simply taking care of their affairs?' Interestingly, in Coase's original conceptualisation of transaction costs the key element is constituted by search and information costs, while there is no reference to any notions of morally hazardous behaviour.[39] Moreover, transaction costs based on search and measurement costs do not require asset specificity. To sum up, whenever input measurement is particularly costly, vertical integration may be a response even if contracts do not imply any specific investment (Barzel, 2001, p. 46).

Lack of verifiability and enforcement difficulties

Secondly, imperfect contracts may derive from imperfect knowledge that makes agreements difficult to verify and enforce. Enforcement difficulties spring from the inability of a neutral outsider to verify the accomplishment of mutual obligations in the event of a contract dispute. This occurs because it may be hard to specify in advance, and unambiguously, all conditions regarding quantity, quality, price and possible external factors (Hart, 1995a, pp. 23–4, 81 *passim*). Differences in cognitive structures and languages among contracting parties may lead to misinterpretations and misunderstandings. Furthermore, when the number of potential events is very high, it may be extremely

---

[38] This expression has been introduced by Barzel (2001, pp. 31–2), who observes that: 'rather than focusing on "information", however, I focus on the more operational concept of "measurement". The switch is productive as measurement constitutes the quantification of information'.

[39] Links and differences between Coase's (1937) original theory and recent developments in the theory of the firm are discussed, for instance, in Williamson (1985, p. 78); Kay (1992, pp. 73ff.); Fransman (1994, pp. 719–23); Loasby (1994, p. 291, 1999, pp. 69ff., 81); Foss (1996c, p. 77); Slater and Spencer (2000, pp. 61ff.); Mariti (2003, pp. 1ff.); Love (2005, p. 389).

costly to spell out all conceivable circumstances in a contract, even if the contracting parties are able to estimate the pay-off distribution of possible actions. Statements describing complex situations are inevitably imprecise and ambiguous. It may therefore be prohibitively expensive to measure what each party agrees to yield to the other or to write a contract that describes all the circumstances according to all the possible changes in environmental conditions and decision-making, in such a way that a court can verify and enforce the contract. In these conditions, reneging is particularly problematic because 'what should be done in various circumstances is left unstated or ambiguous and thus open to differing interpretations' (Milgrom and Roberts, 1992, p. 133). When contracts leave out all the elements that are too costly to specify and to enforce, markets may fail to achieve the efficient allocation or may be missing, and transaction costs may arise even in the presence of perfect rationality and in the absence of opportunism and asset specificity.

As far as rationality is concerned, Hart (1995a, pp. 23, 81, *passim*) observes that, in 'transaction costs literature', contract-writing costs are usually regarded as a form of bounded rationality, in particular those costs that arise from difficulties in spelling out contracts so that parties will bind themselves to future courses of action and enter into a commitment that can be verified and enforced by a third party such as a court. However, Hart shows clearly that 'there is no contradiction' in assuming writing difficulties while on the other hand arguing that 'parties are unboundedly rational', in the sense that they 'can figure out the utility consequences of their inability to write an unambiguous contract'. Put differently, contract-writing costs and perfect rationality are not inconsistent concepts because the presence of contract-writing costs is not incompatible with the assumption that parties are able to estimate the distribution of pay-offs (Hart, 1995a, *ibid.*). In the same vein, Maskin and Tirole (1999, p. 83) show that if individuals are able to compute all the possible pay-offs of their actions, they are not boundedly rational but perfectly rational.[40]

In his theory of property rights, Hart (1995a, pp. 54–5) assumes contract-writing costs and indivisible and complementary production

---

[40] See also, Tirole (1999, pp. 741ff.) and Masten (1999, pp. 28–9) cf. Radner (1968, pp. 31ff.).

elements and processes. As a consequence, common ownership of highly complementary assets may resolve hold-up problems that stem from difficulties in writing plans down and in ensuring that they are verifiable and enforceable by an outside authority; furthermore, common ownership may lead to increasing returns, due to indivisibility and complementarities.

The coexistence of cognitive limits, opportunism and asset specificity
Thirdly, as in Williamson's (1985, pp. 13, 30–2) transaction cost economics, transaction costs may be associated with imperfect contracts that result from the *combined effects* of cognitive limits, opportunism and asset specificity. Cognitive limits and opportunism are two behavioural assumptions, while asset specificity is a transaction dimension.[41] Williamson (1985, p. 13, 1999b, p. 25) has greatly contributed to disseminating the idea, now generally accepted by economists, that the firm cannot be regarded as a mere production function (as in conventional neoclassical theory), but must rather be seen as a *governance structure*.

Bounded rationality with farsightedness. Williamson (1999a, p. 2, 1999b, p. 23) observes that 'orthodoxy ascribes hyperrationality'. By contrast, transaction cost economics assumes that 'human actors are intendedly rational but only limitedly so'.[42] These cognitive limits are not associated with myopia, as in the behavioural and capabilities approaches, but are instead present in conjunction with

---

[41] Williamson (1981, 1985, 1989, 1999a, 1999b) has played an essential role in developing transaction cost analysis in new directions and in particular in studying the various implications of opportunism and different transaction dimensions. On the very numerous empirical applications see, for instance, the following review studies: Walker and Weber (1984); Joskow (1988); Mahoney (1992); Shelanski and Klein (1995); Anderson (1996); Crocker and Masten (1996); Lyons (1996), Masten (1996); Coeurderoy and Quélin (1997); Rindfleisch and Heide (1997); Sobrero and Schrader (1998); Silverman (2002); Williamson (2002, p. 437); Carter (2003). In addition, see the papers in Williamson and Masten (1995b, 1999: part III); Ménard (2000: part VII).

[42] According to Williamson, bounded rationality 'is a condition of limited cognitive competence to receive, store, retrieve, and process information' (1996, p. 377). However, in the last few years, Williamson appears to have moved from a definition of bounded rationality as incomplete information computing ability toward a concept of bounded rationality as costly knowledge with farsightedness (see, for instance, 1999a, pp. 3, 24, table 1).

farsightedness. In this case, individuals are not precluded from assessing the negative consequences of another party's potential opportunism and evaluating the pay-offs associated with possible outcomes. This means that parties do not face unanticipated consequences. Bounded rationality with farsightedness may sound like a contradiction, yet if one defines bounded rationality as costly knowledge under weak uncertainty, the two concepts are compatible. In fact, under costly knowledge or weak uncertainty with complete information-processing ability, individuals are in a position to assess future pay-offs. This is the case of the example of second-hand cars, already mentioned, in which we have assumed that buyers know the distribution of bad- and good-quality cars and accordingly can maximise.

'Transaction cost economics', Williamson (1990a, p. 46) points outs, 'examines incomplete contracts in their entirety – hence the absence of surprise, victims and the like'. These particular cognitive limits correspond to a situation which implies that forward-looking individuals can correctly foresee the consequences of their own and the other party's ignorance. Using Williamson's words, 'limited but intended rationality is translated into incomplete but farsighted contracting'.[43] In this context, farsighted parties are able to spell out forward-looking contracts and identify the optimal governance structure. Columns of (1)–(2) table 3.2 (p. 152) summarise Williamson's taxonomy on rationality. In addition to Williamson's taxonomy, table 3.2 includes two columns ((3) and (4)) with some quasi-corresponding definitions provided by Radner (1996, 2000), Hart (1995a). Column (5) indicates the definition proposed in the present book. A table which compares different taxonomies may be useful

---

[43] Williamson (1996, p. 9, 1990a, p. 46, cf. 1999b, pp. 24–6). The assumption of farsightedness contrasts with the original interpretation of transaction costs provided by Coase (1937), who explicitly refers to 'difficulty of forecasting' and observes that 'it seems improbable that a firm would emerge without the existence of uncertainty'. Nonetheless, Coase does not draw the full consequences of such observations on uncertainty. One may observe that the main argument of Coase's critique of Knight's conception of the firm concerns not so much the concept of uncertainty which is central in Knight as, rather, the fact that Knight fails to make clear the existence of the cost of using the price mechanism and the advantages provided by the firm's coordination in superseding the price mechanism (Coase, 1937, pp. 40–1, 48–51). On this, see the comment in Slater and Spencer (2000, pp. 63–5).

because some disputes are mainly due to misunderstandings on definitions. Since corresponding definitions by different authors inevitably involve some slight semantic shifts, the correspondence suggested in table 3.2 is not strict and must be considered in a broad sense. With these necessary caveats, bounded rationality with farsightedness has some analogies with Radner's costly bounded rationality, and Hart's perfect rationality with lack of enforcement, or the perfect rationality with weak uncertainty proposed in this book. Indeed, many authors rightly consider bounded rationality with farsightedness as a form of perfect rationality under costly knowledge and weak uncertainty (imperfect knowledge). Brian Loasby has highlighted this point, arguing that there are two possible alternatives. If parties do not have the relevant information and knowledge, they contract in a situation of incomplete knowledge (radical uncertainty) and they cannot optimise. In contrast, if they are able to acquire (with a cost or without a cost) the relevant information and knowledge, at least in the form of the probability distribution of all possible outcomes, they operate in a situation of complete knowledge (perfect knowledge and certainty or imperfect knowledge and weak uncertainty) that allows perfect rationality and optimisation.[44]

Opportunism. Opportunism may be regarded as 'self-interest seeking with guile' and 'incomplete and distorted disclosure of information, especially . . . calculated efforts to mislead, distort, disguise, obfuscate, or otherwise confuse' (Williamson, 1985, p. 47). However, some authors tend to give a very broad notion of opportunism that encompasses 'honest disagreement' and which ends up identifying opportunism with mere self-interest.[45] As a consequence, opportunism appears to be ubiquitous.[46] But it is important to stress that opportunism lies

---

[44] Loasby (1999, p. 80); on imperfect knowledge, rationality and farsightedness I have already mentioned Hart (1995a, pp. 23, 81); see also the interesting discussion in Hodgson (1993a, pp. 85–6); Fransman (1994, pp. 732–4); Lindenberg (1996, pp. 130–2); Bianchi (1995, p. 187); Dosi and Marengo (2000, p. 87), Slater and Spencer (2000, pp. 68–73).

[45] See, for instance, Alchian and Woodward (1988, p. 66); and the comment by Love (2005, p. 383).

[46] On the very broad notion of opportunism used by some authors, the example given by Kreps (1990a, pp. 744–5, *passim*, n.a.) is enlightening:

Human beings are *boundedly rational and opportunistic* . . . Our use of the term 'opportunism' is stretched to mean that it is opportunistic to refuse to divulge

in the middle ground between self-interested reticent behaviour, whenever rules *do not imply the duty* to reveal the relevant information, and unlawful (or illegal) behaviour. In this middle ground, opportunism may range between *reticent or evasive behaviour*, whenever rules *do imply the duty* to reveal the relevant information (weak opportunism), and the *deliberate and active distortion* of relevant information, dissembling, purposeful cheating and breaching agreements *without committing a criminal offence* (strong opportunism).

Lack of interest in transmitting the relevant information and knowledge is not necessarily a form of opportunism. Merely self-interested reticent behaviour cannot be identified with opportunism when it is considered absolutely right, in order to acquire economic benefits, *not* to reveal a bit of privately possessed information. Suffice it to reflect on patents that are protected by law. Almost all economic processes are based on the competitive advantage springing from the existence of privately held information and knowledge, and therefore from different abilities among individuals. Consequently, we must distinguish between asymmetric information, as a basic source of competitive advantage, and purposeful cheating or withholding of information.[47]

Asset specificity. 'Asset specificity refers to durable investments that are undertaken in support of particular transactions, the opportunity cost of which investments is much lower in best alternative uses or by alternative users should the original transaction be prematurely

---

information that you hold and another lacks when the other person asks you to give up that information.

This stretches the notion of opportunism very far indeed, far beyond its most 'natural' usage. To amplify, suppose A owns a piece of land on which is buried some treasure. A doesn't know where the treasure is, and it is too expensive to dig up the entire plot to find it. B knows where the treasure is . . . According to this [very broad] definition of opportunism, it would be opportunistic of B to refuse to tell A where the treasure is, if A asks.

However, B is not bound to reveal the information to A. He can sell it to him. This notion of opportunism conflates opportunism and the absence of 'full cooperative' behaviour or altruistic behaviour. This explains the otherwise rather drastic assumption (made at the beginning of the quotation) that all individuals are always opportunistic. See also Williamson (1999b, pp. 39–40).

[47] This distinction is put forward by the resource-based and competencies perspectives; on this point see, for instance, Conner and Prahalad (1996, p. 477).

terminated' (Williamson, 1985, p. 55). Specific investment may concern both physical assets (such as dedicated equipment and site specificity) and intangible human assets (such as specific productive and transactional knowledge). Relation-specific investment, which may be difficult to redeploy, may cause hold-up inefficiency. If market conditions change and if it is impossible to draw up a complete contract, the party that invests in relation-specific assets exposes itself to a hazard, since the two parties have to negotiate over their future interactions.[48] Such bargaining may allow the opposite party to take advantage of the fact that the supplier's investment cannot be used elsewhere. Possible mistrust about the correctness or honesty of the other party may spring from the fact that in such conditions the individual is inclined to think that opportunistic or unlawful behaviour may be possible. In other words, mistrust is due to the fear of being cheated. The possibility of post-contractual opportunism triggers hold-up problems because it might prevent an efficient transaction from ever occurring when a party has to make a relation-specific investment. In these circumstances, the supplier may then be unwilling to make a specific investment, or may expend resources in contractual safeguards consisting in rewarding specific assets and in setting penalties in case the contract should be breached before its expiry. 'In either case, inefficiency results: either the market does not bring about optimal investment, or resources are expended on socially wasteful defensive measures' (Holmström and Roberts, 1998, p. 74). In the presence of co-specialised resources and hold-up problems, residual rights of control foster specific investments and unified property offers an alternative to contractual safeguards in protecting specific assets.[49] Asset specificity and the potential for opportunism are at the core of the hold-up problem. Undoubtedly, as emphasised by Williamson, in the presence of opportunism and asset specificity, transaction costs are higher and more relevant than in the above cases of measurement or writing costs.

---

[48] Shelanski and Klein (1995, p. 336); Holmström and Roberts (1998, p. 74). Klein, Crawford and Alchian (1978, pp. 105ff.) first highlighted the analytical implications of the hold-up problems.

[49] Milgrom and Roberts (1992, pp. 128, 137, 599, *passim*). Two resources are co-specialised if they are most productive when used together and lose much of their value if used separately to produce independent products and services (Milgrom and Roberts, 1992, p. 135).

To conclude this sub-section, in all three of the theories examined (measurement costs, difficulties of enforcement and the coexistence of 'bounded rationality', opportunism and asset specificity) transaction costs thus derive from imperfect contracts due to the presence of costly information and knowledge that do not prevent the parties from computing pay-offs associated with all possible events. In this case, it may be profitable to integrate vertically and carry out agreements within business organisations because unified ownership of physical assets (and other critical resources,[50] such as patents, brand names, software, etc.) confers the rights of control and enforcement in relational agreements whenever a situation not covered by contracts arises.

Incomplete contracts

Incomplete contracts are due to incomplete and heterogeneous knowledge of the possible outcomes (substantive radical uncertainty) or incomplete information-processing ability (procedural radical uncertainty) that generates incomplete forecasting about the other party's behaviour.[51] Point 3 in the left-hand block of figure 3.4 summarises the direct links between incomplete abilities, incomplete contracts and transaction costs.

If future contingencies are not even imagined, they cannot be planned for, and contractual commitments cannot be enforced. On the other hand, if individuals lack sufficient information-processing ability they may not be capable of framing correctly the problem they are confronted with or may not have the computing ability to assess the probability distribution of possible known outcomes. Both circumstances lead to incomplete contracts that have only a limited efficacy for achieving binding commitments.

In the case of *imperfect* contracts, examined in the previous subsection, transaction costs are the *costs of knowledge,* while in the case

---

[50] The theoretical implications of the concept of access to critical resources are discussed in Rajan and Zingales (1998, pp. 387ff.) and Kumar, Rajan and Zingales (1999, pp. 7ff.).

[51] On the relevance of cognitive aspects and, in particular, of uncertainty in determining transaction costs, see, for instance, Langlois (1984, pp. 28ff.); Dietrich (1994, p. 26); Conner and Prahalad (1996, pp. 477ff.).

of *incomplete* contracts, transaction costs are the *costs of sheer ignorance* due to radical uncertainty resulting from conflict of interests in a changing and complex world with fragmented and incomplete knowledge. In this latter case, individuals are characterised by cognitive rationality which may be considered close to the definition of truly bounded rationality or bounded rationality with myopia, as indicated in the comparison of the different taxonomies in table 3.2.

Radical uncertainty is a possible cause of transaction costs that does not necessarily require, or imply, opportunism. In fact, self-interested individuals with different aims and cognitive maps may react in an unexpected way to changes in environmental conditions that are not forecast and not spelled out by the contract. These reactions springing from the identification of new interests may conflict with the opposing party's interests and lead to a costly negotiation, generating deep disagreement and causing losses to one or both parties even if the two sides behave in a loyal, non-opportunistic, lawful and honest way.

On the basis of similar arguments Conner and Prahalad (1996, pp. 483–4) argue, from a resource-based or competence perspective, that transaction costs may be independent of opportunism and may derive from 'the irreducible knowledge differences between individuals'. Analysing the conditions under which transaction costs arise even in the absence of opportunism is certainly useful because it shows there are several sources of transaction costs, associated with cognitive problems, which are independent of possible opportunistic behaviour (such as measurement costs, contract-writing and enforcement costs, and cost of radical uncertainty). However, I would like to stress that, as evinced above, the knowledge-based considerations rather than the question of the existence or absence of opportunism are actually the key point.

In a world characterised by radical uncertainty, asset specificity is not a necessary condition for the existence of transaction costs. In many spot markets informational asymmetries and cognitive limitations are sufficient to trigger high transaction costs even in the absence of asset specificity. In claiming that radical uncertainty is a sufficient condition for the existence of transaction costs, I by no means wish to deny that opportunism and asset specificity are important factors contributing to the increase in transaction costs.

Asset specificity greatly aggravates transaction costs because it augments the cost of loss attendant on failure of agreement (Demsetz,

1988a, p. 289). It can hardly be doubted that asset specificity augments the loss should an unexpected contingency occur; consequently the need for contractual safeguards may be invoked, but these are difficult, costly and rather imperfect.

On the other hand, it is undeniable that both organisations and markets are subject to cheating, fraud, influence activities and lobbying. Therefore, Williamson (1999b, p. 39) is right in emphasising that the possibility of hazardous behaviour cannot be neglected, even if, as he himself recognises, 'most economic agents are engaged in business-as-usual, with little or no thought to opportunism, most of the time' (Williamson, 1993, p. 98). Firms, organisations of firms or organisations that control the market are essential tools to create trust and mitigate hazards. While a few market contracts are self-enforcing, most need the action of organisations that ensure enforcement and market functioning. These organisations, in turn, require expressly designed institutions. As discussed in chapter 1, section 1.7, the strength of institutions and the consequent degree of compliance with the laws affect the competitiveness of firms because weak enforcement, corruption, dishonesty and influence activities drive honest dealing out of the market and generate high transaction costs and economic inefficiency.[52] Organisations based on appropriate institutions can curb opportunism and create trust.

It is worth repeating that mitigating opportunism is not, however, the only source of gain. Organisations provide other no less important advantages: they involve reserves of physical and non-material human assets (tools, inventories and capabilities), and they also favour the development of learning processes and the exploitation of scale advantage.

We can conclude that under conflicting aims and in presence of at least one of two factors that cause cognitive limitations (incomplete theoretical knowledge of the possible outcomes and incomplete information-processing ability), agents are undeniably in a situation of radical uncertainty. In such a situation, transaction costs are essentially determined by cognitive limitations in the presence of conflicting

---

[52] Kumar, Rajan and Zingales (1999) and Beck, Demirgüç-Kunt and Maksimovic (2003) show through a cross-country analysis that better institutional development, measured by the efficiency of a country's judicial system, leads to larger average size of firms.

aims among individuals and are increased by the presence of opportunistic behaviour and asset specificity.

3.3 Scale and scope

The third aspect of organisational coordination consists in designing the operational scale of various processes in order to reach economies of scale and scope by balancing the different productive capacities of production elements and processes. If indivisibility and complementarity are considered as characteristics of processes and production elements, and some other relevant characteristics of production elements as well as information and knowledge are taken into account, then the balancing of different productive capacities of the various production processes becomes particularly relevant in shaping organisational boundaries and competitiveness.

Dimension of scale and increasing returns

The dimension of scale of a microeconomic unit, such as a firm, a production unit, a plant or a piece of equipment, is expressed by the maximum number of processes carried out per unit of time, which depends on the number of parallel processes and the duration of such processes. Therefore, the dimension of scale of a microeconomic unit is related to both size and speed.[53] The 'range of productive capacities' refers to the distance between the level of activation and that of the maximum productive capacity. The breadth of the range of productive capacities varies for different types of apparatus and their degree of adaptability.

For simplicity, I consider only three different ways in which an increase in the scale of production can take place:

• By substituting the old microeconomic unit with a new unit having greater productive capacity
• By multiplying the number of the same microeconomic units

---

[53] On the connection between size and speed see, for instance, Chandler (1990, p. 24) who offers ample historical evidence; see also Morroni (1992, 1999); Scazzieri (1993); Piacentini (1995). Heal (1999) provides a useful collection of essays on increasing returns and economies of scale.

- By juxtaposition, adding a new (different) microeconomic unit to the existing one.

An example may help elucidate the differences between these three ways of enlarging the scale of production. If we consider a microeconomic unit such as a computer, the scale can be increased either by replacing it with a more powerful and faster computer, or by multiplying the original computer (acquiring a certain number of identical computers), or by setting up a new, different, computer next to the old one. These three modes have dissimilar effects on the proportions in which various inputs are combined and in their qualitative characteristics; furthermore, these three modes apply not only to equipment, but also to plants, production units and firms, since economies of scale can be obtained by substituting, multiplying or juxtaposing machines within one plant, plants within one production unit, production units within one firm, or firms within one group.

In textbooks, returns to scale are generally defined as the relationship between an equiproportional increase in all inputs and the resultant increase in output. A change in the scale of production that leads to a variation of all inputs in the same proportion is conceivable. However, moving on to a larger scale of production usually involves a reorganisation of production that changes the relative requirements according to the relationships of complementarity between the different production elements. In short, an increase in the absolute quantities of the inputs involves a variation in proportions. When proportions between inputs change as scale dimension increases, the rate of change in the productivity of individual production elements increases differently. This can easily be clarified by an example. If the scale dimension of manufacturing a fabric increases, it may be supposed that the quantity of yarn increases in the same proportion to the output, with constant returns to scale. But the quantity of labour, space, stocks and energy will increase less than proportionately with respect to output, so that returns to scale may be high with regard to energy consumption, medium with regard to labour requirement and low with regard to stocks and space occupied.[54]

---

[54] The practice of separating the analysis of variations in proportions (partial or short-term adaptation) from variations in quantities (full or long-term adaptation) seems to be misleading, as there are good reasons for thinking that

The notion of returns to scale has an essentially technical nature because it refers to *physical quantities* and is therefore independent of prices of inputs and output. Economies of scale occur when a larger-scale dimension of a specific microeconomic unit leads to a lower total average cost of the product obtained. If prices are given, there is an inverse relationship between returns to scale and total average costs, so that the notions of increasing returns to scale and economies of scale can be taken as equivalent. If prices of inputs cannot be taken as given but may vary in relation to the quantities acquired, the concept of *economies of scale* should be used. This notion is more general because it includes both the possibility of returns to scale and reduction in the price of inputs when the quantities produced increase, as in the case of pecuniary economies.

Sources of economies of scale, learning-by-doing and growth

Figure 3.5 summarises the numerous sources of economies of scale, learning-by-doing and growth which derive, in the last instance, from some specific characteristics of information and knowledge, production elements and processes. Particular attention is drawn to replicability, indivisibility, complementarity, three-dimensionality of space, the set-up process and the statistical factors. These economies constitute a major factor in explaining the large size of many business organisations, even though they can only very rarely be considered absolutely determinant since knowledge and transaction aspects usually play an important role.[55] It is worth examining these various types of economies of scale and their sources one by one.

the proportions and quantities vary together. As pointed out long ago in Piero Sraffa's path-breaking article (Sraffa, 1925), increasing returns to scale derive from the possibility of augmenting the inputs in optimal proportions to the various dimensions of scale, while decreasing returns to scale occur when there is a restriction that prevents some elements of production from increasing in optimal proportions (Sraffa, 1925, pp. 7, 23–4; cf. Sraffa, 1926, pp. 44ff.; Morroni, 1998a, pp. 209ff., 1998b, p. 402).

[55] A detailed analysis of the different sources of economies of scale is found, for instance, in Pratten (1971, 1988, 1991, pp. 15ff.); Scherer (1980, pp. 81ff.); Morroni (1992: chapter 11); for a brief discussion on some common misinterpretations, see the appendix of chapter 11 of Morroni (1992). For a historical analysis of the impact of economies of scale and of scope on enterprises' strategy, structure and dynamics, see Chandler (1990, 1992).

(1) Economies of productive capacity balancing

An increase in the dimension of scale of the whole process may lead to a better balancing between the productive capacities of indivisible and complementary sub-processes and production elements that otherwise would be not fully utilised. Economies of productive capacity balancing are linked to the indivisibility and complementarity characteristics of many funds that are considered in chapter 1, section 1.2. These economies derive from the possibility that an increase in the whole process could bring about a more efficient utilisation of fund productive capacities. Where there are indivisible and complementary fund elements, bottlenecks in productive capacity may arise. These bottlenecks often lead to idle times and waste of the productive capacities of some devices or machines. In the presence of indivisible and complementary funds, a high volume of production is often necessary to render their different productive capacities compatible. In other words, the problem of the presence of idle time or underutilisation of the productive capacity of funds, due to economic or technical indivisibility, is solved by increasing the dimension of scale. Naturally, the greater the cost of funds used, the more desirable it is to reduce idle time.[56] However, indivisibility and complementarity of processes and goods are not the only source of economies of scale. There is interaction with other mutually reinforcing factors that are discussed below (see figure 3.5).

(2) Economies of threshold dimensions

Such economies arise from the presence of set-up processes. Set-up processes are independent of the scale of the overall production process. Economies of scale derive from the fact that as overall scale dimension increases, the cost of set-up processes remains constant for all possible scale dimensions. Average costs of the set-up process decrease because the cost is divided by an increasing number of units produced.

---

[56] The role played by unused productive services as an inducement to expansion of the firm was highlighted by Penrose (1959, pp. 66–70), while the effects of indivisibilities and complementarities on the idle times of funds were analysed by Georgescu-Roegen (1969, pp. 71ff., 1986, pp. 245ff.). See also Tani (1988, pp. 3ff.); Best and Garnsey (1999, pp. 188–9); Morroni (1992: part 1, 1999).

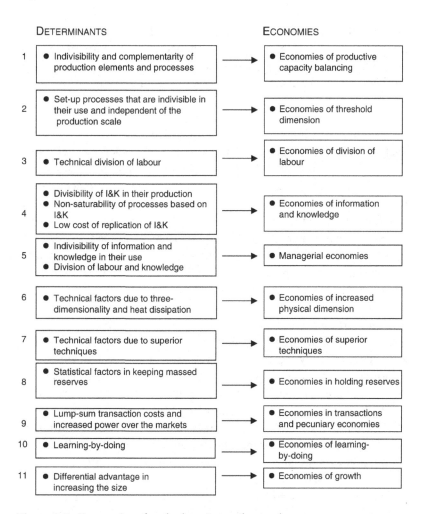

DETERMINANTS   ECONOMIES

1. • Indivisibility and complementarity of production elements and processes → • Economies of productive capacity balancing

2. • Set-up processes that are indivisible in their use and independent of the production scale → • Economies of threshold dimension

3. • Technical division of labour → • Economies of division of labour

4. • Divisibility of I&K in their production • Non-saturability of processes based on I&K • Low cost of replication of I&K → • Economies of information and knowledge

5. • Indivisibility of information and knowledge in their use • Division of labour and knowledge → • Managerial economies

6. • Technical factors due to three-dimensionality and heat dissipation → • Economies of increased physical dimension

7. • Technical factors due to superior techniques → • Economies of superior techniques

8. • Statistical factors in keeping massed reserves → • Economies in holding reserves

9. • Lump-sum transaction costs and increased power over the markets → • Economies in transactions and pecuniary economies

10. • Learning-by-doing → • Economies of learning-by-doing

11. • Differential advantage in increasing the size → • Economies of growth

Figure 3.5. **Economies of scale, learning and growth.**
Note: I&K = Information and Knowledge.

(3) Economies of division of labour

An increased dimension of scale may imply a reorganisation of production that allows a further operational and cognitive division of labour. Economies of division of labour arise because not only is greater dexterity favoured, thus augmenting the quality and speed of production, but specialisation is enhanced, which saves on learning processes. This enables firms to employ staff with special skills'or to use special-purpose machinery (Pratten, 1991, p. 17). Generally, an increased division of labour leads to changes in the quality of outputs and other production elements, such as equipment and types of workers. Therefore, increasing division of labour and technical change are closely linked.[57]

(4) Economies of information and knowledge

Such economies of scale are mainly due to three factors: divisibility of information and knowledge in their production processes; non-saturability of processes based on information and knowledge; and low cost of replication of information and knowledge. Divisibility of information and knowledge makes it possible to apply the division of labour that generates increasing returns, as argued in (3). For instance, technical division of labour among computer experts who are working on the production of new software may be extremely pronounced. Moreover, non-saturability, which depends on the fact that the same amount of information is required regardless of the quantity produced by the firm, involves a super-fixed cost. As a consequence, costs of processes that are based on information and knowledge are fully independent of the scale of processes in which this information and knowledge is used. In other words, it makes no difference whether 1 unit or 1 million units of the same commodity are to be produced; the same amount of information is required.[58] This generates the threshold economies considered in (2). For instance, checking proofs or designing and producing a prototype (for later production of a serial model) implies economies of scale since these activities represent super-fixed costs that are independent of the scale at which books are published or cars are produced. Finally, it is usually much cheaper to reproduce or replicate information and knowledge than to produce it in the first place.[59] Replication means

---

[57] For a detailed historical reconstruction of the different analytical treatments of the relationship between division of labour and scale, see Scazzieri (1993, pp. 36ff.). On the relationship between division of labour and technical change, see Evangelista (1999, pp. 48ff.).

[58] On the re-use of knowledge that makes it possible to apply the same knowledge to more and more units of output, see Langlois (1999, p. 248).

[59] Arrow (1994a, pp. 4–5); cf. Shapiro and Varian (1999: chapter 1); Salanié (2000, p. 110); Winter (2005, pp. 224, 231).

transferability across time and space, and entails absorptive abilities. Low cost of replication of information and knowledge leads to strong increasing returns because it implies high fixed costs and very low marginal cost, as in the case of software. When low cost of replication does not hamper appropriability and hence tradability, the return grows strictly in proportion to the size of the market and the potential gains are enormous.

(5) Managerial economies of scale

These concern the capacities of the entrepreneur or executive staff to coordinate the various operational levels and intermediate stages. Managerial economies derive from economies of information and knowledge considered in (4). They are mainly due to the fact that administrative and organisational tasks can be allocated to specialist staff and that administrative and organisational activities, which consist mainly of cognitive activities, are, largely, independent of the number of commodities sold.[60] Moreover, organised managerial action allows replication of best practices across time and space. Temporal and spatial replication of productive knowledge generally requires considerable planning and training efforts. Nevertheless, if successful, replication involves significant increasing returns.

(6) Economies of increased dimension

These economies derive from the three-dimensionality of space. Consider the case of containers (cisterns, tubes, ovens): their cost increases approximately in proportion to the surface area of the walls, while their productive capacity increases in proportion to the volume (for example a two-fold increase in the diameter of a boiler gives about a four-fold increase in productive capacity).[61] In some productions an increase in plant size reduces not only the investment cost per unit of product, but also the average costs of the operation, by virtue of the reduction in heat loss obtained by lowering the surface/volume ratio of the plants. In the literature on this subject, economies of increased

---

[60] Demsetz (1995, pp. 11, 31–2) argues that these 'economies of scale to specialised knowledge acquisition' play an essential role in explaining the existence of the firm.

[61] See Robinson (1931, pp. 22–3); Scherer (1980, pp. 82–3); Pratten (1991, pp. 16–17).

dimension are sometimes misinterpreted because of the confusion between indivisibility and the three-dimensionality of space. This confusion originates from the fact that three-dimensional production elements, once installed and operating, such as pipe-lines, ovens, etc., are always technically indivisible. However, economies of increased dimension do not depend on indivisibility but derive strictly from the three-dimensionality of space. In fact, indivisibility implies only economies of scale of productive capacity balancing, considered in (1), or (partial adaptation) increasing returns in the utilisation of a *single* plant due to its better utilisation as the quantity produced increases. This latter phenomenon has nothing to do with economies of scale which, by definition, are associated with the utilisation of a new larger plant.

(7) Economies of superior techniques

An increase in scale dimensions often means that techniques giving increases in productivity can be used. For instance, as scale is increased, automatic machinery may be used instead of manually operated machinery. New machinery often implies greater productive capacity.[62]

(8) Economies in holding reserves

Economies in holding reserves derive from the operation of the law of large numbers. An increase in the overall quantities involved in production leads to a less than proportional increase in any type of stock and reserve (for instance, guarantee capital, circulating capital, raw materials and machine spare parts). According to the theorem of the central limit (or the law of large numbers), the greater the number of resources involved, the smaller, in proportion, is the quantity of inventory necessary to provide for possible unforeseen circumstances.[63] For instance, an increase in the number of machines of the same type used in the same enterprise gives a saving in the number of spare parts that

---

[62] Pratten (1991, p. 18). On the 'scale-augmenting' nature of embodied technical change, see Evangelista (1999: chapter 4).

[63] These are the economies of scale which Robinson (1931, pp. 26–7) called 'economies of massed reserves or resources'. In Penrose (1959, p. 94) the firm is seen as a pool of resources that constitutes a reserve for the firm's operation. Cf. Hodgson (1998b, p. 40).

need to be stocked to repair possible faults. Similarly, an increase in the quantity produced and sold involves a less than proportional increase in the inventories. It is a well-known fact that an inventory should increase only in proportion to the square root of the quantity produced and sold. In other words, if sales of an item double, the inventory should not be doubled – it should be increased by much less than 100 per cent of its original amount (Baumol, 1968, p. 10). These economies are therefore due to statistical factors in holding massed reserves. It is interesting to note that the same statistical factors are also at the base of the money multiplier that characterises the functioning of the bank system. This is another striking common element between the firm and money.

(9) Economies in transactions

Economies in transactions can be explained by the fact that contracts imply fixed threshold costs, and therefore an increasing quantity exchanged implies decreasing information, marketing, advertising, contract and control costs per production unit (Nooteboom, 1993, p. 288, 2003, p. 5). A further source of economies achievable through market processes lies in the fact that an increase in dimension of scale of a firm or group of firms, in relation to the scale of the industry, leads to greater power over input and output markets, other things being equal. Thus, a firm that uses more resources can enjoy advantages arising from the purchase conditions of raw materials and intermediate goods. These advantages in buying inputs are customarily called pecuniary economies. Similarly a large firm can obtain substantial advantages in raising capital. Moreover, an increasing dimension and accordingly an expansion of the market share may augment discretion in fixing the price of the output, even though – it hardly need be added – output pricing does not merely depend on the relative size of the firm, but may depend on sunk costs and entry conditions, as the literature on contestable markets has emphasised.[64] Finally, the larger is the business organisation, the more easily it can lobby for its own interests.

---

[64] On contestable markets, see Baumol (1982) and Baumol, Panzar and Willig (1982).

(10) Economies of learning-by-doing

Learning-by-doing implies progressive incremental innovations and improvements in dexterity through *accumulation of experience*. This leads to a fall in average cost as the cumulative quantities of output increase over time.[65]

(11) Economies of growth

Economies of growth arise when a firm achieves a differential advantage (over competitors) by increasing its size. They are partially due to indivisibility of some unused resource or to some particular competence or market positions that create a differential advantage in expanding the size of the firm. Economies of growth are not economies of scale. Economies of growth are available only during expansion and therefore disappear when the expansion has been completed (Penrose, 1959, pp. 99–101).

Economies of scale at different operational levels

Economies of scale are often discussed with reference to the firm, which is implicitly identified with a single plant consisting of one or more homogeneous pieces of equipment. However, for a better understanding of the effect of increased firm dimension this simplifying assumption has to be abandoned: one should instead consider the possibility that the same firm could have several production units, several plants, or several indivisible elements of production with different productive capacities. Failure to take account of the operational level at which economies of scale come into effect may generate substantial problems of interpretation. This is because economies of scale may assume very different forms according to whether they concern a piece of equipment, a plant, a production unit, or even a network of firms linked by collaboration relations. Each of these microeconomic units corresponds to what I define as an 'operational

---

[65] For a discussion regarding empirical evidence on the importance of learning curves see Levin *et al.* (1988); Sutton (1998, pp. 173–4); Argote (1999); Scherer (2000, p. 222). Learning-by-doing is one of the only two sources of economies of scale mentioned in Sutton's (1998) book, *Technology and Market Structure: Theory and History* (the second is set-up costs that I have considered in (2), p. 166).

level'. Economies of scale have the particular characteristic of acting at different operational levels and affecting individual intermediate stages to different degrees, so that average costs in relation to the quantities produced at the various operational levels and intermediate stages are interdependent. For example, if we suppose that there are significant economies of scale in distribution, the firms will tend to increase their production, even without achieving economies of scale at this operational level, simply in order to reach the threshold that will allow them to enjoy the economies of scale in distribution.

In essence, increasing the dimension of scale at a particular operational level may trigger a series of changes in production organisation which may involve a reduction in input requirements at other operational levels or at some related intermediate stages. This may lead, as a consequence, to an enhanced balancing between the different productive capacities of various funds and intermediate processes, entailing a reduction in productive capacity waste and a more efficient utilisation of production elements. However, an increased-scale-based reorganisation of the time profile of funds' utilisation is of course contingent upon the institutional environment which is responsible for setting rules and defining property rights, legal rights on assets' utilisation, industrial relations and labour legislation governing work time and shifts.[66]

To conclude, it is not sufficient to evaluate economies of scale at the level of the single microeconomic unit; the relations between the dimensions of scale of the various related intermediate stages and operational levels must be analysed.

Economies of scope

The expansion of the boundaries of the firm is favoured not only by economies of scale and growth but also by economies of scope or joint costs. Economies of scope arise if it is less costly to combine the productions of two or more commodities than to produce them separately. In other words, the production of x_1 and x_2 involves economies of scope if $c(x_1, x_2) < c_1(x_1, 0) + c_2(0, x_2)$.[67] As previously discussed in

---

[66] North (1990, p. 65) explores the interplay between techniques, institutions, transformation costs and transaction costs.

[67] On economies of scope, see Panzar and Willig (1981, p. 268); Chandler (1990, pp. 17ff., 2003: chapter 1).

chapter 1 (section 1.2), economies of scope derive from the presence of complementarities among different productions (the reader will remember the example of the production of honey and flowering crops). Economies of scope may come into being at firm, production unit, plant and production line level. For instance, at firm operational level there are economies of scope when it is less costly to produce two or more commodities in one firm than to produce them in two or more firms.[68] This occurs whenever it is possible to economise on some shareable component, material, equipment, knowledge and labour service by saturating their production capacities.

Economies of scope associated with capabilities are particularly important in a dynamic environment where the firm's ability to introduce new processes and new products is essential. Carrying out different activities allows a company to differentiate between production activities and individual abilities. This diversification reduces the negative economic consequence of the failure of one activity and makes it possible to cope with uncertainty.

In producing specific goods, a firm may develop capabilities that turn out to be useful for designing, producing and marketing new products in complementary technology or related markets. Economies of learning-by-doing become economies of scope when learning advantages are applied across a differentiated production associated with an increased number of different production lines. In greatly differentiated enterprises, what is learned in producing a specific output can often be transferred to the production of another good manufactured by the same firm.

The relationship between economies of scale and economies of scope

The possibility of exploiting the same knowledge, by virtue of transferability, replicability and re-utilisation across time and space, implies

---

[68] Analogously, there are economies of scope: at *production unit* level, when it is less costly to produce two or more commodities in one production unit than to produce them in separate production units (within the same firm); at *plant* level, when it is less costly to produce two or more commodities by means of one plant than to produce them by means of two or more separate plants (within the same production unit); and at *production line* level, when it is less costly to produce two or more commodities on one production line than on more than one production line (within the same plant).

both economies of scale and economies of scope. In the former case, a body of knowledge is shared over an increasing number of identical units of output, while in the latter, a body of knowledge is shared over among several slightly different products. For instance, the re-utilisation of knowledge has significant effects in the increase of productivity of the software industry where pieces of software code can be re-used in different applications.[69]

At the firm level, some competencies related to certain specific activities, such as administration, marketing, organisation, etc., or the central information system consisting in software and hardware, can be utilised for the production of a variety of commodities manufactured by different production units that belong to the same firm. This allows significant economies of scope and scale by utilising shareable competencies and equipment. For instance, applied research on the pharmaceutical industry shows that large firms are at a significant advantage in the management of research through the ability to exploit economies of scope (Henderson and Cockburn, 2000, p. 156).

Moreover, economies of scale and scope may be reaped, at the same time, by producing a single component that can be used in the production of a wide range of differentiated commodities. For example, a firm may exploit economies of scale in making small electric motors by using these motors to make food processors, hair dryers, fans, vacuum cleaners and various other goods. Another firm may enjoy economies of scale in the manufacture of liquid crystal displays, using them to produce calculators, wristwatches, electronic address books, and other commodities.[70]

However in certain circumstances, a trade-off between economies of scope and economies of scale may arise. Diversification may involve a cost when it leads to a loss of economies of scale inherent in standardised production. Basically, differentiated production will be more costly than standardised production when the loss of economies of scale is greater than the economies of scope obtainable by carrying out the different processes within the same firm or production unit. One obvious way to overcome this trade-off is to increase the dimension of

---

[69] Cusumano (1991, pp. 435–7); Langlois (1999, p. 251); Winter (2005, p. 231).
[70] These examples are drawn from Milgrom and Roberts (1992, p. 107) and attributed to specific firms, namely General Electric and Casio.

scale to the point of allowing significant economies of scale in the single processes. But this solution may be prevented by the limited extension of the potential market. A second possible solution is to introduce organisational or technical flexibility associated with the level of adaptability of the production processes of the various individual goods. For instance, a wide product mix may be obtained by using sub-contractors specialised in certain particular productions that enjoy economies of scale, rather than producing all the commodities in-house. Sub-contracting allows organisational flexibility, reduces fixed costs and increases the process adaptability.

It is also possible to enjoy economies of scope and economies of scale at the same time through technical flexibility. For instance, cutting down on set-up times for switching machines from one process to another is a key element in reducing the cost of producing differentiated goods with the same equipment. Decreasing set-up times makes it possible to produce a wide range of products in small batches (i.e. short production runs), without keeping large inventories, thereby reducing flexibility costs. Greatest flexibility is obtained when the same degree of economies of scale, for the overall output range, can be enjoyed in producing single-unit lots (i.e. one-of-a-kind) as in producing a single homogeneous product.

Computer-based technology is one of the crucial elements that helps to reduce set-up times, make reconfiguration easy and therefore increase technical flexibility, allowing economies of scope and economies of scale to be exploited at the same time. Through information technology (IT), a high degree of flexibility can be obtained while still maintaining the typical advantages of industrial production: the economies of scale (on the overall range of output). Before the advent of computer-based technology, when economies of scope were opposed to those of scale,[71] differentiated production required two or more lines operating in parallel, or else very long set-up times, with large quantities of semi-finished goods in inventories. With the spread of computer-based technology, industrial production acquired some of the elements typical of traditional artisan production (high flexibility and trade specialisation).[72] This notwithstanding, as illustrated by the

[71] On the nature of the flexibility–scale trade-off, see Dosi (1988, pp. 96–8).
[72] This is illustrated effectively by the literature on flexible specialisation (Piore and Sabel, 1984, pp. 6–18, 124).

implementation of the flow–fund model, which focuses on the time profile of production processes, alongside these similarities some important differences between artisan production and flexible industrial production can also be observed.[73] Artisan production has three basic characteristics: high flexibility, long idle times for tools and long training times for workers (high specialisation). Tools remain idle when the craftsman moves from one operation to the other, using the tools one at a time. The more operations performed by one craftsman, the longer the tool idle times will be, although the craftsman's tools are generally simple, so that the incidence of idle times on total average costs is relatively low. The great advantage of artisan production is generally its flexibility, which allows very small batches (or, indeed, single units) to be produced. But in many circumstances, new technology now provides the opportunity to enjoy the advantages of artisan (or handicraft) production, in terms of flexibility, and at the same time the advantages of industrial production, in terms of shortening idle times of equipment and exploiting economies of scale.

3.4 Links between the three aspects of organisational coordination

In this chapter, each of the three aspects of the organisational coordination of the firm has been considered at length. We are now in the position to answer a question that is a crucial issue of this study: to what extent and under what circumstances do capability, transaction and scale–scope considerations become significant and interact?

For ease of presentation, among all numerous possible interactions linking these three aspects of the organisational coordination of the firm, I consider four simplified cases:

---

[73] Morroni (1992, pp. 44–67, 182–4, 1999, pp. 199ff). Among empirical implementations of Georgescu-Roegen's flow–fund model to case studies see, for instance: Polidori and Romagnoli (1987) on the agricultural industry; Morroni (1992, 1999) on the textile industry and on electronic devices for telecommunication networks; Marini and Pannone (1998) and Pannone (2002) on the telecommunications industry; Birolo (2001) on the shoe industry; Bertolini and Giovannetti (2003) on the agri-food sector; Mir and González (2003) on the tile industry. Moreover, a software program has been specifically designed for facilitating the application of the flow–fund model to empirical analysis (Moriggia and Morroni, 1993).

- No weight of these three aspects and therefore no interaction among them
- No interaction among the three aspects because only transaction costs have significant weight, while capability and scale considerations are insignificant
- Significant weight of all three and interaction among them
- Very significant weight of all three aspects and intense interaction among them.

No weight of the three aspects of organisational coordination and no interaction among them

Let us first examine the case which, as in traditional microeconomic theory, is characterised by full and free relevant information and knowledge, complete information-processing ability, complete contracts, nil uncertainty, perfect rationality and divisibility of production elements. The continuous development of the firm's capabilities in order to create and maintain a competitive advantage is not necessary when relevant technical and productive information and knowledge consist of recipes for production, such as a blueprint of techniques available cost-free 'on the shelf' and comprehensible to everybody. If the potential adopters have the necessary knowledge and expertise to understand, use and take advantage of all production techniques, then *every firm can produce a particular commodity or service as well as another.* 'Production costs are independent of the organisational framework – essentially because technologies are public goods.'[74]

Moreover, under full and free information and knowledge and complete information-processing ability, there are no unexpected changes and the actual outcomes among all the possible events can be ascertained and computed without cost. Individuals know the full list of all relevant contingencies and all consequences of possible actions (perfect forecasting). Under 'unrestricted cognitive competencies', 'contract execution problems . . . never arise'.[75] In this case,

---

[74] Loasby (1994, p. 298, 1999, p. 84, 2004a, p. 260). For a discussion on the analytical implications of the assumptions regarding productive knowledge available to all, see also Demsetz (1988a, p. 287); Rosenberg (1990, p. 171); Langlois and Robertson (1993, p. 638); Winter (2005, p. 239).

[75] Williamson (1985, pp. 30–1, 1999a, p. 2). See also Laffont and Martimort (1997, pp. 204–5) on complete contracts within the theory of the firm.

contracts are complete and the State is 'the efficient enforcer' and agreements tend to be carried out *within* the market (Barzel, 2001, pp. 2, 6, 10). According to the foregoing conditions, transaction costs are negligible and limited to contract costs such as taxes, certificates, permits and possible middlemen payments. If transaction costs are insignificant, spelling out in contracts the obligation binding on the parties can be a good alternative to ownership and decentralisation is favoured. With complete contracts there is little scope for managerial coordination. As argued by Ronald Coase, when it is costless to transact, the efficient competitive solution of neoclassical economics applies.[76]

On the other hand, in conditions where inputs and processes are perfectly divisible,[77] uncertainty is absent and the specific characteristics of information and knowledge play an insignificant role, economies of scale internal to the firm are non-existent and the analytical problem of balancing the different processes and identifying the productive sequences can be ignored. Low transaction costs and absent economies of scale encourage decentralisation and firm specialisation that makes it possible to take advantage of the *ex post* consequences of division of labour on efficiency. This favours the creation of increasing returns external to individual firms but internal to the industry in its aggregate that are compatible with perfect competition.[78]

Under the foregoing circumstances, the development of capabilities, transaction costs and internal economies of scale are utterly negligible aspects of the organisation of the firm (see column (1) of table 3.3). Therefore, the conventional and standard simplified view of the firm as a mere production function is perfectly consistent. Obviously, the above conditions are seldom met in the real-world firms we all know.

[76] Coase (1960), quoted in North (1990, p. 15).

[77] In the standard microeconomic analysis, the possibility of indivisibility is usually excluded because indivisibility may imply the absence of an equilibrium solution. If some kind of indivisibility is present, the assumption of convexity on the production possibility set is precluded. When the set of feasible production is not convex there may be no equilibrium solution that maximises profit at given prices. See, for example, Arrow and Hahn (1971: chapters 3, 7); Salanié (2000, pp. 109–13).

[78] The argument of external economies of scale is, for instance, adopted in the recent growth literature (see Romer, 1989, p. 108, 1991, p. 88). On external economies of scale, see also n. 20, p. 255.

Table 3.3. *Different degrees of interaction among transaction, capability and scale considerations*

		Zero interaction (1)	Zero interaction (2)	Intense interaction (3)	Very intense interaction (4)
WEIGHT OF SINGLE ASPECTS	(1) TRANSACTION	Insignificant	≠ Significant	= Significant	< Very significant
	(2) CAPABILITY	Insignificant	Insignificant	≠ Significant	< Very significant
	(3) SCALE–SCOPE	Insignificant	Insignificant	≠ Significant	< Very significant
CONDITIONS	TRANSACT. I&K[a]	Full and free	≠ Costly	= Costly	≠ Cognitive limitations
	TECHNICAL I&K	Full and free	= Full and free	≠ Costly	≠ Cognitive limitations
	ORGANIS. I&K	Full and free	= Full and free	≠ Costly	≠ Cognitive limitations
	I&K CHARACT.	Not considered	= Not considered	≠ Set-up processes and low cost of reproduction	= Set-up processes and low cost of reproduction
	IPA[b]	Complete	= Complete	= Complete	≠ Incomplete
	INPUT CHARACT.	Divisibility and substitutability	= Divisibility and substitutability	≠ Indivisibilities and complementarities	= Indivisibilities and complementarities
	CONTRACTS	Complete	≠ Imperfect	= Imperfect	≠ Incomplete
	UNCERTAINTY	Nil	≠ Weak	= Weak	≠ Radical
	RATIONALITY	Perfect	= Perfect (or bounded with farsightedness)	= Perfect	≠ Cognitive rationality

	Zero interaction (1)	Zero interaction (2)	Intense interaction (3)	Very intense interaction (4)
BOUNDARIES OF THE FIRM	Full decentralisation	≠ Tendency toward vertical integration through unified ownership or toward forms of collaborations among firms	≠ Tendency toward expansion of the boundaries of organ. coordination within and among firms	< Strong tendency toward expansion of the boundaries of organ. coordination within and among firms

Notes:

[a] I&K = Information and knowledge.
[b] IPA = Information processing ability.

However, Harold Demsetz claims that 'it is a mistake to confuse the firm of economic theory with its real-world namesake. The chief mission of neoclassical economics is to understand how the price system coordinates the use of resources, not to understand the inner workings of real firms'.[79]

No *interaction among the three aspects of organisational coordination and weight of transaction considerations alone*

Consider now the case in which transaction costs are significant but they are not related to capability and scale–scope aspects, which play no role. This is the case when transactional information and knowledge is costly, technical and productive information and knowledge is free and full, computing ability is complete, radical uncertainty is absent and production elements are divisible (see column (2) of table 3.3).

Under the above circumstances, individuals possess all the cognitive abilities needed to select the relevant information and assess all possible consequences of their decisions (perfect rationality or 'bounded rationality with farsightedness'). However, on account of costly transactional knowledge, contracts are imperfect and significant transaction costs may ensue. As a consequence, managerial coordination may overcome the problem of imperfect contracts. There will be the tendency toward vertical integration through unified ownership or toward forms of collaborations among firms. The above set of conditions is explicitly or implicitly assumed, albeit with some notable exceptions, in most contributions on property rights and transaction cost economics.[80]

Note that apart from the hypothesis of costly transactional information and knowledge, the other conditions are the same as the first set. Accordingly, even in this second case capability and scale considerations have no weight. For a quick comparison of different conditions, see columns (1) and (2) of table 3.3.

---

[79] Demsetz (1983, p. 347); see also the discussion in Williamson (2002, p. 433).

[80] For a survey on these models and applications, see Gibbons (2003, pp. 755ff.). It is necessary to stress that some models of this vast literature provide a richer and more complex picture than this rather simplified version would appear to suggest. On this, see n. 82, p. 185.

In this second set of conditions, 'although information is treated as being costly for transaction or management control purposes, it is implicitly presumed to be free for production purposes'. As a consequence, 'what one firm can produce, another can produce equally well'.[81] Hence, the problem of development of the firm's capabilities, the balancing of productive capacities and exploitation of the potential for economies of scale and scope does not arise due to the assumptions pertaining to free and full technical and productive information and knowledge and divisibility of production elements. In conclusion, transaction costs are significant but not related to the other two aspects of the organisational coordination of the firm because these two latter aspects have no noteworthy weight.

Significant weight of the three aspects of organisational coordination and intense interaction among them

In sharp contrast, interplay among capability, transaction and scale–scope considerations is observed whenever the situation involves transactional, organisational and productive knowledge that is dispersed, heterogeneous, tacit and costly, imperfect contracts (weak uncertainty), indivisibility and complementarity of some production elements and the existence of set-up processes in using information and knowledge as well as the low cost of replication of some information and knowledge. Analogously to the previous set of conditions, this third set is not incompatible with the presence of perfect rationality understood as the ability of individuals to estimate the probability distribution of all possible future pay-offs consequent upon their actions. Moreover, in this third case as well, contracts are imperfect because of the presence of costly transactional information and knowledge. The main difference in comparison to the previous set of conditions consists, on the one hand, in the fact that not only transactional knowledge, but also organisational, productive

---

[81] Demsetz (1988a, p. 287). Conner and Prahalad (1996, pp. 490, 497) criticise some transaction cost models which assume that the technology is constant across organisational modes and that, consequently, the same productive activity can be carried out either within a firm or by a collection of autonomous contractors, since it is assumed that all firms can produce goods or services equally well.

and technical knowledge may be costly; on the other, that specific characteristics of production elements (such as indivisibility and complementarity) are present. Compare columns (2) and (3) in table 3.3.

First, if technical, productive and transactional knowledge is not available without cost, and an absorptive ability to interpret, appraise and use this knowledge is required, then the development of capabilities makes it possible to acquire firm-specific knowledge and the necessary absorptive ability. This specialised knowledge, which is grounded in specific learning processes, constitutes an element of competitive strength.

Secondly, significant transaction costs are due to the presence of imperfect contracts which favour substitution of the firm's market relations by organisational coordination within and among firms. The development of knowledge and capabilities through organisational coordination appears to be an appropriate response to the existence of transaction costs that result from multiple interpretations and misunderstandings among contracting parties. In this context, the role of management in developing information and knowledge among parties is crucial (Hodgson, 2004a, pp. 411–14, *passim*). If technical, productive and transactional knowledge is not full, the development of capabilities makes it possible to acquire the necessary transactional knowledge to favour specialisation and mitigate transaction costs. It must be stressed that 'transaction costs themselves are not fully exogenous; their magnitude depends on the conscious actions undertaken by firms' aiming 'to shape the transactional environment to their advantage' (Jacobides and Winter, 2004, pp. 3, 9).

Thirdly, relevant economies of scale and scope originate from the characteristics of production elements and processes, such as complementarity, indivisibility, three-dimensionality of space and set-up processes, and from some characteristics of information and knowledge that involve super-fixed costs.

Under the above conditions, these three aspects of the organisational coordination of the firm have a significant weight and are so inextricably interwoven that they appear to be the different sides of the same organisational problem. This will be analysed in detail in chapter 6, section 6.3. It suffices here to preview just a few main links. For instance, if knowledge is not full and free, each given dimension of scale (aspect (3), see table 3.3) corresponds to a given degree of cognitive division of labour and a given stage of development of capabilities through shared experiential learning (aspect (1)). Analogously, the arrangement of transactions (aspect (2)) requires the development of internal and external capabilities regarding transactional and productive knowledge (aspect (1)). Whenever unified governance enhances learning (aspect (1)) and this is crucial to the acquisition of the firm's competitive advantage, the firm has a high incentive to integrate or join or create organisations of firms (aspect (2)). If there are indivisible and complementary funds and intermediate processes, the integration of technologically separable processes within a firm or coordination of such processes among firms (aspect (2)) leads to a reorganisation of production which could involve economies of scale in other processes at a different operational level (aspect (3)). Learning processes (aspect (1)) and transactional knowledge (aspect (2)) involve economies of scale and scope (aspect (3)). In effect, increasing returns represent a crucial ingredient to both learning processes and transactional activities. Moreover, the internalisation of external intermediate processes – which eliminates transaction costs (aspect (2)) – means that the internal division of labour and knowledge must be adjusted (aspect (1)) and a new balance of the production capacities of different production elements and processes reached (aspect (3)). The causal relationship among these three aspects *also* runs in the opposite direction: the balancing of processes and determination of the scale (aspect (3)) affects the governance of transactions (aspect (2)), which in turn affects the structure of specialisation (aspect (1)).

To sum up, as roughly sketched in figure 3.6, what mainly determines this interaction among the three aspects of the organisational coordination of the firm is: the presence of costly transactional and productive information and knowledge, indivisibility and complementarity of production elements, set-up processes in using information and knowledge and low cost of replication of information and knowledge.[82]

---

[82] Some recent developments in theories of the firm, which assume perfect rational behaviour or bounded rational behaviour with farsightedness, have begun to consider more than one aspect of organisational coordination on the basis of

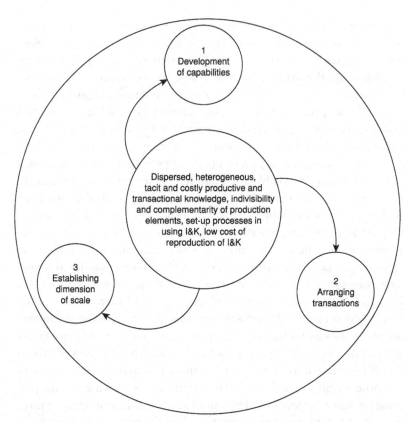

Figure 3.6. Interaction among the three aspects of organisational coordination.

Note: I&K = Information and Knowledge.

some conditions discussed in this sub-section. For instance, Hart (1995a, pp. 50–1), in his theory of the firm, assumes not only enforcement difficulties but also complementary assets. An implication of this theory is that with enforcement difficulties 'highly complementary assets should be under common ownership' which is characterised by increasing returns to scale. As a consequence, vertical integration is connected to economies of scale. On the other hand, some recent contributions belonging to transaction cost economics are increasingly paying attention to cognitive matters (see Williamson, 1999b, p. 38; and Ménard, 2004h, pp. 345–60; cf. the comment by Dosi and Marengo, 2000, p. 87). Finally, one can mention Demsetz's (1988a, pp. 295ff., 1995, pp. 11, 31–2) writings, in which he bridges cost-based considerations with an emerging knowledge-oriented perspective. Cf. the discussion in Love (2005, p. 386). See also section 6.3.

Very significant weight of the three aspects of organisational coordination and very intense interaction among them

The weight of the three aspects of organisational coordination and their interaction arising from the conditions discussed above (pp. 183–5) increases remarkably whenever cognitive limitations make it inevitable to operate under incomplete forecasting – i.e. under radical uncertainty that derives mainly from incomplete knowledge of possible outcomes (substantive uncertainty) or incomplete information-processing ability (procedural uncertainty). Both types of radical uncertainty reflect the actual conditions in which suppliers, members and customers of the firms have to operate in many significant circumstances.

Arguably, in such conditions developing new capabilities within the firm may be essential in order to mitigate the effects of both substantive and procedural radical uncertainty, and to strengthen the firm's competitive advantage. Furthermore, the incompleteness of contracts, which derives from radical uncertainty, favours substitution of the firm's market relations by managerial coordination, resulting in a strong tendency to expansion of the boundaries of organisational coordination within and between firms. A scenario of this kind in turn implies economies of scale that are attributable not only to the specific characteristics of information, knowledge and production elements (such as indivisibility, complementarity, the presence of set-up processes, low cost of replication of information and knowledge), but also to the decrease in the cost of keeping reserves, as well as the reduction in the negative economic consequences of the failure of one activity stemming from unforeseeable circumstances.

In conclusion, radical uncertainty strongly amplifies both the significance of capability, transaction and scale considerations and the interaction among such aspects, which emerges from the specific characteristics of information, knowledge and production elements (see column (4) in table 3.3). However, the converse is likewise conceivable: the specific characteristics of information, knowledge and production elements reinforce and magnify the effect of radical uncertainty on the interaction between learning processes, transactional relationships and the balancing of production capabilities. Focusing on the interaction among these three aspects of organisational coordination of the firm means concentrating the analysis on processes over time rather than on equilibrium states.

Key concepts

abilities
adaptability
asset specificity
capabilities
competencies
contract
corporate culture
corporate strategy
cost
decomposable production process
describability
dimension of scale
economies of scale
economies of scope
enforcement power
flexibility
hold-up problem
maximisation
observability
opportunism (weak and strong opportunism)
optimisation
organisational coordination
relational agreement
set-up process
skills
transaction
transaction costs
transfer
transfer costs
verifiability
vertical integration

4 | *Wrestling with uncertainty*

L IMITING uncertainty is indispensable in decision-making processes.[1] Uncertainty may be tempered in different contexts and by several means:

(i) *Within markets* between autonomous parties by means of special contracts which imply screening, signalling, monitoring, incentives and by means of organisations that ensure information, enforcement, regulation and dispute resolution activities.

(ii) *Between firms* by virtue of organisations of firms, such as hybrids or networks of firms, which provide a wide range of different combinations of market and organisational tools.

(iii) *Within firms* by keeping reserves and by long-term relational agreements. Long-term relational agreements, in turn, allow flexibility, the managing of conflicting interests among stakeholders, routinised operating procedures, division of labour, sequential aiming and learning (figure 4.1).

This chapter investigates points (i) and (ii) above – i.e. how uncertainty can be reduced and its negative economic effects mitigated within markets and organisations of firms, while chapter 5 is entirely dedicated to analysing in depth why firms represent a response to uncertainty (point (iii) above).

---

[1] The need to limit uncertainty in decision-making was stressed by Shackle (1958, pp. 106–7, 1959, pp. 22–5), who introduced the concept of bounded uncertainty; cf. Harper (1996, pp. 101–3, 117 n. 19). Loasby (2004a, pp. 267–8) notices that the emphasis on this point links the analyses put forward by George Shackle and Herbert Simon.

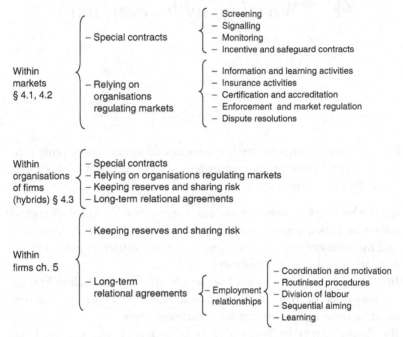

Figure 4.1. Wrestling with uncertainty.

4.1 Market contracts

Screening, signalling, monitoring, incentive and safeguard contracts are tools designed to reduce asymmetric information within markets and thus to limit the degree of uncertainty (table 4.1).

Under asymmetric information, *screening* is an activity undertaken by the uninformed party aiming to select the informed parties in order to attract only desirable buyers or sellers. This is generally achieved by providing a variety of options from which the informed parties select a particular one. The selection of a particular option reveals the relevant information and screens the informed party. In the literature, examples of screening are: a positively sloped experience–wage profile in order to reduce employee turnover and attract subjects who are less inclined to change job (where there are significant training costs); offering a wage based on measured performance in order to select the most productive job applicants; price differentiation – that is, setting prices of a line of related products (such as cars, computers, etc.) in order to

Table 4.1. Screening, signalling, monitoring and incentive contracts

Tool	Definition	Examples
Screening	Activity undertaken by the uninformed party aiming to select the informed parties in order to attract only desirable buyers or sellers	Positively sloped experience–wage profile, offering a wage based on measured performance and price differentiation
Signalling	Attempt by individuals who possess private information to communicate it	Product warranties, money-back guarantees, labelling and education
Monitoring	Control activities	Supervision, control of quality of good and services, sampling
Incentive and safeguard contracts	Contracts that establish a reward or a penalty for output performance	Contracts with deductible clause, experience-rated contracts or contracts that involve posting a bond

select different groups of customers and to maximise some objective function; or, finally, designing insurance contracts so that different policies are intended for different risk classes of buyers.[2]

Signalling is the attempt by individuals who possess private information to communicate it. In conditions of asymmetric information, agents may find it profitable to bear the costs of signalling activities. The more costly a signal or the more difficult to fake, the more credible it is. Product warranties, money-back guarantees or labelling are examples of signalling the good quality of products. Another kind

---

[2] The above examples are drawn from Milgrom and Roberts (1992, pp. 156–9), who extensively consider screening mechanisms and offer useful bibliographical references on the subject.

of signalling is education, whose level can generally be regarded as an indication of workers' productivity.[3]

Signals such as product warranties, money-back guarantees, or labelling are more credible if they are emitted by organisations associated with the expectation of duration and high sunk costs. For these organisations, the value of a good reputation is usually high because it is linked to the length of their life span which is presumed to be very long, even if top executives have a shorter time horizon and might be tempted to enjoy some short-run advantages and to lay some costs on the future directors' board.

Quality, social and eco-labels provide information, on a voluntary basis, to the firm's stakeholders concerning the quality of products, safety performance, occupational health and social and environmental records kept by business organisations. Recent decades have seen growing concern and expectations regarding the safety performance of products, as well as the social and environmental impact of business practices. Under mounting pressure from NGOs and consumer groups, companies have increasingly adopted labelling and voluntary codes of conduct covering working conditions, human rights and environmental aspects, in particular those of their sub-contractors and suppliers (Commission of the European Communities, 2001, p. 13). Signalling represents a transaction cost, while meeting established codes of conduct usually implies an increase in production costs. However, quality and social responsibility labels and voluntary codes of conduct reduce the risk of negative impact on a company's reputation that might arise from criticism of business practice, and positively enhance the firm's brands and image, thus resulting in higher profitability and growth. 'In recent years, socially responsible investing has experienced a strong surge in popularity among mainstream investors.' It contributes to minimising risks 'by anticipating and preventing crises that can affect reputation and cause dramatic drops in share prices'.[4] Given the voluntary nature of corporate social

---

[3] A broader discussion of signalling may be found in Frank (1988: chapter 5). On incentives to emit signals under asymmetric information, see also Arrow (1973, p. 143). The first systematic work on education as a signal is due to Spence (1974).

[4] Commission of the European Communities (2001, pp. 7, 20). In this *Green Paper*, it is noted that financial institutions are making increasing use of social

responsibility, the efficacy of labels and codes of conduct depends on their credibility, which must be based on proper implementation, compliance and verification by independent organisations.

Despite these positive effects of signalling, it should be stressed that signalling activities remain imperfect because in a complex world with private information they can distort reality and provide intentionally untrue information. Sometimes, individuals have difficulty in understanding whether certain signals launched on the market are credible or not.[5]

Monitoring consists in various control activities such as supervision, checking the quality of goods and service, etc. Monitoring, where possible, limits the information problem that lies at the basis of the moral hazard phenomenon.

Incentive and safeguard contracts between the principal and the agent (such as contracts with a deductible clause, experience-rated contracts or contracts that involve posting a bond) are another means available to limit the moral hazard problem. Incentive contracts, which have already been discussed in section 2.3, establish a reward or a penalty for output performance when inputs and effort cannot be ascertained. Most incentive contracts require organisations that guarantee the enforcement.

4.2 Organisations regulating markets

Let us now consider organisations expressly designed to reduce uncertainty and favour market functioning. Organisations which favour market functioning require an institutional environment that regulates exchange relationships within markets and relational

---

and environmental checklists to evaluate the risks of loans to, and investments in, companies. Being listed on an ethical stock market index can support a company's rating and therefore entails concrete financial advantages (Commission of the European Communities, 2001, *ibid.*).

[5] Baron and Kreps (1999, p. 581). Furthermore, subjects may 'disagree over the very meaning of the signal itself'. In the basic theory of market-signalling,

> there can be lots of possible market signaling equilibria in a given context because the question *What inferences are drawn from a signal that isn't part of the equilibrium?* can have many answers, all of them consistent with a signaling equilibrium. (Baron and Kreps, 1999, p. 584)

agreements within business organisations by setting laws and rules that govern property rights, commercial transactions, accounting practices, employment contracts and industrial relations. For example, incentive contracts are not sufficient to limit the effects of informational asymmetries if there are no institutions and organisations that compel enforcement of these contracts in case of dispute. It is worth stressing that in order to reduce uncertainty, organisations and institutions are both needed. For instance, the simple rule (an institution) that cars must stop to allow citizens to walk across a pedestrian crossing, established in the highway code, is of course not sufficient to reduce uncertainty without the action of police (an organisation) to enforce it.

The activities performed by organisations regulating markets are information, certification and accreditation services, enforcement and resolution of disputes (table 4.2).

Information and learning activities which favour market functioning and competition are provided by purpose-designed private and public organisations (such as consumer associations and cooperatives, specialised press, television shows dedicated to consumers, non-profit bodies, schools and universities, etc.). This type of organisation increases the welfare of all participants in exchange activities through the dissemination of information and the creation of knowledge that enhances individual abilities and fosters the development of trust and cooperation. However, as argued by Akerlof (1970, p. 488), these organisations, which have a positive effect on reduction of the extent of uncertainty, are not atomistic because they imply market power.

Insurance activities spread risk among policyholders and therefore reduce the costs of individual uncertainty in exchange activities (North, 1990, p. 126). They are normally carried out by insurance companies or public bodies that assess actuarial, ascertainable risk and pay compensation in certain eventualities to the policyholders who pay a premium.

Certification activities are aimed at increasing the credibility of corporate information on compliance with standards regarding product quality, balance sheets, safety performance, workplace conditions, occupational health and social and environmental records. Certification is performed by an independent organisation that verifies companies' conformity to the standard.

Table 4.2. *Organisations regulating markets*

Activities		Organisations
Information	Dissemination of information and the creation of knowledge that enhances individual abilities and fosters the development of trust and cooperation	Private and public organisations, such as consumer associations and cooperatives, specialised press, television shows dedicated to consumers, non-profit bodies, schools and universities, etc.
Insurance	Insurance activities spread risk among the policyholders and therefore reduce the costs of individual weak uncertainty in exchanging activities	Insurance companies and public bodies
Enforcement of market contracts	To oblige the parties either to respect the contract or to pay the injured party compensation	Public bodies with legally established powers of investigation and sanction (e.g. anti-trust bodies, courts, police, etc.)
Dispute resolution	Possible forms of dispute resolution among contracting parties: 1) take a binding decision 2) make a recommendation 3) indicate a solution by common consent.	Public or private organisations according to different national laws and traditions, e.g., trade associations, professional organisations, on-line cross-border dispute resolution services, etc.

Table 4.2. Organisations regulating markets (continued)

Activities		Organisations
Certification	Aimed at increasing credibility of corporate information on compliance with standards regarding accounts, financial statements, product quality, safety performance, workplace conditions, occupational health, social and environmental records	Certification organisations
Accreditation	A process similar to licensing wherein an accreditation body evaluates the capability of an applicant organisation to perform certification audits	Accreditation organisations

Accreditation is a process similar to licensing wherein an accreditation body evaluates the capability of an applicant organisation to perform certification audits. Accreditation organisations set standards, such as for product quality (e.g. ISO9000) or social accountability (e.g. SA8000),[6] and develop professional auditor training courses and guidance documents.

Certification and accreditation organisations are a response to the increasing demand for measuring, documenting and communicating these qualities. By providing credible signals, *certification and accreditation* organisations increase the transparency of business activities and the credibility of labels, and reduce the degree of uncertainty, and therefore the level of transaction costs, deriving from imperfect or incomplete knowledge. The European Union, along with international organisations such as the United Nations (UN), Organisation for Economic Cooperation and Development (OECD) and International Labor Organization (ILO), is promoting corporate social responsibility strategies as a response to a variety of social, environmental and economic pressures.[7] The negative effects on markets of scandals concerning the fiddling of accounts in some large American business organisations (e.g. the Enron case and others) have prompted the consideration of new laws and rules that ensure the genuine independence of auditors.

Enforcement and *dispute resolution* are performed by both public and private organisations. Control and enforcement are usually assured by public bodies with legally established powers of investigation and sanction (e.g. anti-trust bodies, courts, police, etc.), while

---

[6] 'Accountability' is understood as the capacity of an organisation to account for its actions towards interested parties through transparent procedures (see Grandori, 1995, pp. 206–7). For further details on accountability and certification activities, see Social Accountability International (2002, pp. 1–5).

[7] See the *Green Paper* presented by the Commission of the European Communities (2001, pp. 3ff.). The EU approach to corporate social reasonability is to integrate and promote the various international initiatives, such as UN and OECD guidelines and ILO labour standards based on the Declaration on Fundamental Principles and Rights at Work (freedom of association, abolition of forced labour, non-discrimination and elimination of child labour). These initiatives are not legally binding, but in the case of the OECD guidelines they benefit from the commitment of the adhering governments to promoting their actual observance by business (Commission of the European Communites, 2001, p. 6).

arbitration and dispute resolution are frequently carried out by public or private organisations according to different national laws and traditions (e.g. trade associations, professional organisations, on-line cross-border dispute resolution services, etc.). Various forms of alternative dispute resolution are also growing in importance.[8] In the *Green Paper* of the Commission of the European Communities (2002, p. 6), alternative methods of dispute resolution (also called mediation or conciliation) 'are defined as out-of-court dispute resolution processes conducted by a neutral third party'. There are three different kinds of alternative dispute resolution. The third party can:

- take a decision that is binding for one party
- make a recommendation to the parties who are free to follow it or not
- attempt to bring the parties together to persuade them to come to a solution by common consent, increasing the likelihood that, once the dispute is settled, the parties will be able to maintain their relations (Commission of the European Communities, 2002, pp. 7–9).

In short, most of the means that aim to reduce the uncertainty experienced by parties operating within markets imply the action of a variety of public and private organisations, which operate following laws and rules dictated by the institutional context. The market functioning requires the 'visible hand' of intentional organisations – such as state organisations, public bodies, courts, private third parties and arbitrators – that are based on appropriate institutions which ensure the enforcement of contracts and agreements.

---

[8] The promotion of alternative dispute resolutions is a priority declared by the EU institutions. On this see the Commission of the European Communities (2002, p. 5). Methods of alternative dispute resolution are increasingly applied in electronic commerce, employment relationships, commercial relations and family and civil mediations. For instance, alternative dispute resolutions in the field of e-commerce are 'the subject of recommendations issued by a number of international non-governmental organisations whose work is being closely followed by the Commission, such as the GBDe (Global Business Dialogue on e-commerce), the TABD (Transatlantic Business Dialogue) and the TACD (Transatlantic Consumer Dialogue)' (Commission of the European Communities, 2002, p. 12).

4.3 Hybrid forms

If specialisation in complementary different processes brings significant advantages, a successful response to uncertainty may be represented by hybrid forms intermediate between markets and hierarchies. For example, long-term supply relationships, strategic alliances, franchising, collective trademarks, symbiotic arrangements, equity cross-holdings, joint ventures (JVs), partnerships, consortia, supply chain systems, business associations and networks may guarantee an effective interface between parties.[9] In fact, when complementarities are highly specific, 'the interface between purchaser and supplier' has to be actively managed because the supplier needs to understand the purchaser's requirements in detail and the purchaser needs to understand and enhance the supplier's capabilities (Loasby, 1994, p. 299). Different firms have different firm-specific capabilities and ongoing interorganisational exchange facilitates the transfer and building of technical and productive knowledge. In this context, durable interfirm collaboration consisting in bilateral or multilateral structures may mitigate transaction costs and may be more effective than the pure price mechanism or single unified ownership. Lasting connections among firms enable them to benefit from the advantages of both integration and specialisation.[10]

As noted by Ménard (2004h, pp. 357–8), the literature on hybrids is unanimous about the role played by uncertainty in decisions regarding the level to which partners pool resources. Hybrids operate as a 'buffer'. Moreover, when radical uncertainty is due to a highly innovative environment and volatility of markets, there is an increasing need for complementary external capabilities that can be satisfied by collaboration among firms. As a consequence, 'radical uncertainty can favour disintegration, rather than integration'. This point has been

---

[9] Hybrid forms have increasingly attracted the attention of economists and business studies scholars. On the subject, see for instance: Mariti and Smiley (1983, pp. 437ff.; Williamson (1991); Milgrom and Roberts (1992, pp. 563–4, 575ff.); Grandori (1995, pp. 392–406); Grandori and Soda (1995); Gulati (1995); Masten (1996); Holmström and Roberts (1998); Mowery, Oxley and Silverman (1998); Ghosh and John (1999); de Jong and Nooteboom (2000); Helper, MacDuffie and Sabel (2000); Hodgson (2002a); Ménard (2003, 2004d, 2004h); and Nooteboom (2003).

[10] De Jong and Nooteboom (2000, p. 3); Brusoni, Prencipe and Pavitt (2001, p. 597).

underlined by Nooteboom (2003, pp. 14–15), who has provided ample empirical evidence.[11]

It is worth stressing that the advantage provided by hybrid forms in facing uncertainty is that they can use a very large variety of different possible *combinations of market and organisational tools* in order to mitigate uncertainty and transaction costs. First, hybrids can spell out market contracts to regulate relationships among the various firms belonging to the network. Secondly, they can resort to other organizations that regulate markets. Thirdly, they can take advantage of long-term relational agreements that allow flexibility, the managing of conflicts of interests, simplification (through routinised operating procedures, division of labour and sequential aiming) and learning processes (figure 4.1).

Hybrid organisations are neither markets nor hierarchies. Although these intermediate forms of organisational coordination are character-ised by a great diversity of agreements, 'the hybrid form of organiza-tion is not a loose amalgam of market and hierarchy but possesses its own disciplined rationale' (Williamson, 1991, p. 119). Hybrids are organisations composed of 'legally autonomous entities doing business together, mutually adjusting with little help from the price system, and sharing or exchanging technologies, capital, products, and services, but without a unified ownership'.[12]

Richardson (1972, p. 142) has emphasised that networks of firms exist because of the need to coordinate closely complementary but dissimilar activities. 'This co-ordination cannot be left entirely to direction within firms because the activities are dissimilar, and cannot be left to the market forces in that it requires . . . the matching, both qualitative and quantitative, of individual enterprise plans' (Richardson, 1972, *ibid.*). When such positive complementarities are present, economies of scale may be reaped by splitting production of

---

[11] On applied analyses see also Gulati (1995); Arrighetti, Bachmann and Deakin (1997); Nooteboom, Noorderhaven and Berger (1997); de Jong and Nooteboom (2000); Colombo and Delmastro (2001).

[12] Ménard (2004h, p. 348). In his insightful paper that analyses the attributes characterising hybrid organisations, Ménard (2004h, pp. 352–7) bridges some capabilities and transaction cost considerations. He takes into account both the possibility that contracts may be subject to unforeseeable revisions due to uncertainties and also the existence of asymmetries in resources and information as the main incentive to pool assets.

intermediate products into small, specialised firms. In effect, 'hybrid organisations exist because partners need to develop coordination, which requires interdependent investments'.[13]

Although a specific and detailed analysis of the complex theme of the various forms of collaboration among firms is beyond the aims of the present book, the analytical framework proposed here, which allows study of the relationships holding among basic conditions, decision-making mechanisms, organisational control and performance, could be applied not only in analysing the organisational coordination within firms but also within hybrid forms. Thanks to governance contracts, hybrids are able to enjoy the advantage provided by the three aspects of organisational coordination. In fact, interfirm cooperation: (i) favours learning processes; (ii) reduces uncertainty and transaction costs; and (iii) makes it possible to exploit economies of specialisation, scale and scope external to firms and internal to the group of firms. For instance, hybrids can enjoy economies of scale and scope in distribution channels, communication networks, network externalities, marketing, brand name and advertising (Nooteboom, 2003, p. 11).

Governance and licensing contracts or franchise arrangements allocate decision and control rights over a network of firms. These contracts serve some of the same purposes normally assigned to ownership (Holmström and Roberts, 1998, p. 84). Some contracts bind together firms in an interrelated managerial structure in such a way that the links among firms may be so strong that the networks can assume the form of 'quasi-firms'.

In hybrids, contracts – although incomplete (in the sense that this definition is used in this study) – play a significant role in coordinating partners. Ménard (2004h) indicates numerous crucial aspects usually regulated by contracts within hybrids: (i) the number of partners; (ii) duration and renewability; (iii) detailed specifications concerning quantities and quality standards; (iv) adaptation clauses; (v) rules for distributing the gains expected from joint actions; (vi) restrictions that delineate the domain of action of partners, limiting their autonomy; and (vi) complementary safeguards (e.g. financial hostages, mutual commitments guaranteed by specialised investment). Contractual

---

[13] Ménard (2004h, p. 357); cf. Spiller and Zelner (1997, p. 562f.).

safeguards in interfirm relationships are based on penalties to deter breach, on added information disclosure and specialised dispute settlement mechanisms (Williamson, 2002, p. 431).

However, as far as this last point is concerned, in many relationships among firms opportunistic behaviour is deterred and enforcement is achieved by extra-contractual tools and informal aspects such as reputation (based on continuity and recurrent transactions), mutual dependency, identification of shared goals among partners and social similarities.[14]

There are a multitude of hybrid organisational forms mid-way between the market and the firm that tend to reduce uncertainty by enhancing the transmission of information, as well as offering enforcement power and organisational safeguards for specific investment. Examples abound. Rupert Murdoch's media empire is based not on owning physical assets, but on crafting 'ingenious contracts that have given influence over an effective network of media players' (Holmström and Roberts, 1998, p. 85). The Japanese system of outsourcing rests on long-term, close relationships with a limited number of independent suppliers who often belong to one and the same association, as in the case of Toyota suppliers. A small number of suppliers permits comparative performance evaluation, keeps the cost of monitoring low and increases the frequency of transacting. Other examples are franchising contracts; mutual dependence as in the case of a single supplier; or inside contracting – i.e. utilising the labour services of employees of sub-contractors. Repeated interaction, interdependence, and organisational coordination allow information transmission to function fairly well even without unified ownership. Many hybrid organisations are characterised by 'highly frequent transactions with highly specific investments under conditions of great uncertainty but deliberately forgo the opportunity of vertical integration and often do not develop other classical safeguards against the

---

[14] Ménard (2004h, pp. 357–8, 362–6, *passim*); see also Loasby (1994, II, pp. 299–301); de Jong and Nooteboom (2000, p. 12). Sako (1992) provides theoretical and empirical analysis on the link between the type of buyer–supplier relations and corporate performance. She argues that the trust and interdependence present in many Japanese firms, obtained through obligational contractual relations, can be a powerful springboard from which to achieve corporate success.

hazards of opportunism'.[15] Moreover, forms of collaboration within networks of firms include practices that are generally considered highly vulnerable to opportunistic behaviour, such as broad open-ended contracts and heavy investment by suppliers in customer-specific assets, or joint product design efforts. In durable sub-contracting relationships, the interest in maintaining and renewing the joint activity leads to the creation of organisational mechanisms of reciprocity that guarantee loyalty so that concerns about 'hold-ups' do not prevent collaboration between individuals and organisations.[16] Firms can develop trust and collaboration over time by starting with small common projects scarcely vulnerable to opportunism, moving little by little to bigger subsequent projects that require specific investment. The example of the automobile industry is fairly clear: the success of Japanese firms in the United States and the adoption of many Japanese practices there 'makes it difficult to argue that vertical integration or detailed contracts' are the only way to support collaboration, learning and innovation (Helper, MacDuffie and Sabel, 2000, pp. 451, 471–4).

Among the key elements that lead to the increased pay-off of co-operation and the reduction of opportunism, a major role is played by the aim of achieving continuity of the relationship. Shared advances in knowledge prevent individuals and organisations from being tempted to exploit the ignorance of the other, as could occur in the case of mutually ignorant specialists. With the increasing need for knowledge in production activities, the knowledge relevant to the solving of problems tends to dwell in a variety of individuals who do not necessarily belong to the same firm. Therefore, under heterogeneous abilities, interorganisational exchange based on long-term relationships favours the development of firm-specific capabilities, fosters innovative activity and helps to cope with changing environments.

The presence of private governments (or 'authorities as distinct from hierarchies') is a core element in the architecture of hybrid organisations. 'One major characteristic of these devices is that they pair the autonomy of partners with the transfer of subclasses of

---

[15] De Jong and Nooteboom (2000, p. 12); cf. Holmström and Roberts (1998, p. 92).

[16] De Jong and Nooteboom (2000, p. 13); Helper, MacDuffie and Sabel (2000, p. 449); Loasby (2004a, pp. 270–1).

decisions to a distinct entity in charge of coordinating their action' (Ménard, 2004h, p. 366). For example, a group of millers who created a brand name for high-quality bread in France in the 1980s created an 'internal court' with three delegates operating as private judges for solving conflicts. In some circumstances, leadership emerges as a mode of coordination among partners. This usually comes about when a firm possesses specific capabilities or occupies a key position in the sequence of transactions required (Ménard, 2004h, pp. 30, 32).

It can thus be concluded that, in certain circumstances, radical uncertainty increases the need for external partners and long-term supply relationships.

Key concepts

hybrids
market
mediation activity
networks of firms
relational agreements
screening
signalling
uncertainty

5 | Uncertainty-decreasing strategies within firms

T HIS chapter tackles a key question that has been indicated, but not discussed in detail, in chapter 4: in what circumstances and in what ways are firms able to face radical uncertainty and mitigate its costs? This question is ignored in many theories of the firm because it makes formalisation difficult (or impossible).[1] Nonetheless, we cannot fail to address radical uncertainty because an answer to this question is absolutely crucial for a full understanding of organisational boundaries and behaviour. It is worth repeating that focus on hard-to-treat environmental conditions is motivated by the fact that radical uncertainty stands at the heart of the firms' functioning and growth, since *business organisations may be regarded precisely as a response to radical uncertainty*. Firms are useful instruments to prepare for an uncertain future, for two main reasons: (i) they are constituted by assets, such as equipment, warehouses and capabilities, that may represent useful reserves to face unpredicted contingencies; and (ii) they are based on long-term relational agreements that allow flexibility, the managing of conflicting interests among their stakeholders, simplification and learning. Section 5.1 of this chapter considers the role of reserves and relational agreements. In section 5.2 a particular type of relational agreement, the employment relationship, is analysed. Sections 5.3–5.6 investigate the properties of simplification and learning processes that are favoured by the employment

---

[1] See Walliser (1989, p. 9). In relation to this point, Gibbons (2000, pp. 40–1) argues:

> I am keenly aware that the economic approach [read: the theory of the firm based on agency, contract and game theory models] . . . is also quite narrow and even distorted. Examples abound . . . . Where I assume full rationality, reality may involve biases and heuristics . . . and attribution errors . . . Where I assume actions in a fixed context . . ., reality may involve not only shifts in context but feedback from actions to contexts . . . I hope to suggest that these issues are slowly moving onto some economists' radar screens and may be incorporated into models in organisational economics.

relationship. Simplification and learning are two mutually related ways adopted within firms to face radical uncertainty. Simplification and learning contribute to reducing substantive and procedural radical uncertainty because they decrease the gap between the abilities required and possessed. *Simplification* consists predominantly in: (i) adopting routinised operating procedures; (ii) sub-dividing problems and activities through division of labour and knowledge; and (iii) implementing adaptive behaviour by arranging goals in sequence and using performance feedback systems. Sections 5.3, 5.4 and 5.5 are dedicated to these three different ways of simplifying to reduce the capabilities required, while the final section 5.6 address learning processes intended to increase the abilities possessed.

5.1 Reserves and relational agreements

Reserves

Firms may increase flexibility by organising inventories that are buffers designed to deal with any unexpected and temporary imbalance. Reserves are characterised by increasing returns in the sense that the cost of keeping them decreases relatively as the organisation increases in size. Reserves are thus linked to the third aspect of organisational coordination of the firm discussed in chapter 3 (section 3.3, point (8)).

Multiperson business organisations can differentiate between activities, so that risk can be shared among the various activities. As Pratten (1988, p. 12) rightly observes, 'a large company's ability to spread risk may enable it to take greater risk. Large concerns have a greater opportunity for experimenting with new methods and introducing new products without jeopardising the future of the business if particular methods or products are unsuccessful.'

Moreover, a further way in which multiperson firms decrease the cost of radical uncertainty and increase flexibility is by embracing various individual abilities. The presence of different kinds of abilities provides 'a reserve when the list of future contingencies cannot be closed.'[2] This increases the flexibility of the firm in meeting the unforeseen.

---

[2] Loasby (1998, p. 176); see also Penrose (1959, p. 94); Arrow (1973, p. 147).

Finally, adjustments may be obtained by managing financial flows. The fact that such adjustment processes are possible is a particular characteristic of the functioning of business organisations.

Relational agreements

Relational agreements offer a second route to flexibility. The formation of relational agreements is mostly connected with the first and second aspect of organisational coordination of the firm–namely, the development of capabilities and the arrangement of transactions. When complete contracts are too costly or impossible, parties settle for relational agreements that frame their relationship over time. Usually only a few obligations and expectations concerning relational agreements are explicit and written in contracts or in ethical and behavioural codes, while most are implicit. The temporal dimension, associated with expected duration, is an essential element of the relational agreement and contracts, although the expected duration of a relational contract may vary. Some relational contracts are unlimited in time, such as tenures in the employment contract; others are automatically renewed unless one or other of the parties terminates the contract by giving notice, such as supply contracts, or rent contracts; still others have a temporary duration at the end of which a renewal is not guaranteed – e.g. research contracts, temporary employment contracts, etc.

Firms enter into different relational agreements according to their nature (e.g. partnership contracts among professionals, cooperation contracts among workers in a cooperative, employment contracts, etc.). By their very nature these relational agreements have a significantly informal nature. Among various relational agreements established by a firm, I shall discuss here the characteristics of the employment relationship, as it is of absolutely pre-eminent economic importance, not only in firms but also in many different types of organisations. Business organisations are generally characterised by the employment relationship, apart from family firms and workers' cooperatives that are composed only of their own members without employees.

5.2 The employment relationship

The employment contract is part of a broader relational agreement between the firm and the employee, which includes mutual obligation and expectations that are not spelled out in written form. For instance, corporate culture, concerning shared values and ways of thinking within the firm, is a major implicit and tacit component of the employment relationship. In the employment contract, whoever possesses legal control over the firm's assets has the authority to assign tasks and to allow employees access to critical resources that are crucial for developing the firm's competitiveness, to establish which assets should be used and how they should be used, and to decide the continuation of the employment relationship. With an employment contract, employees agree to obey the employer's directions according to the decision-making rights that are specified by the contract, by law and by union agreements, industrial relation rules and traditional and common practices. Generally, contracts establish the number of working hours and the occupational level. Legal rights concern such aspects as 'the right of employees to quit, to be free of intrusive surveillance' and 'not to be fired without a good cause and due process' (Baron and Kreps, 1999, p. 66). Of course, employment law covers a much larger range of matters – for instance, child labour, the length of the working week, minimum wage levels, health and safety, tax and social security payments, gender, race and religion discrimination, monitoring and surveillance activities, disabled individuals, union activities and collective bargaining, privacy rights, employment termination and so on.

Hierarchy, mutual dependency and contractual power

The employment contract involves authority and managerial coordination, but it implies mutual dependency according to the parties' contractual power. Managerial coordination gives executives and managers power over subordinates. This power has a two-fold nature: it is, understandably, desired as a means to achieve some personal or organisational aims, but it is not devoid of a negative side – i.e. it may often degenerate and become 'an end itself', seeking only to dominate and control other persons.[3]

Nonetheless, what is important to note is that authority is not always negatively perceived as an external imposition. To use Loasby's

---

[3] Russell (1938, pp. 10, 274–5). The distinction between hierarchy and authority is discussed in Ménard (1994, pp. 232ff.).

(1999, p. 101) words, 'people may be encouraged to join an organisation because they can accept the organisational definition of problems as their own and consequently know, without deliberation, what they should be thinking about'.[4] In short, the acceptance of authority simplifies decisions. It allows the members of an organisation to avoid, or at least to simplify, an energy- and time-consuming activity, i.e. choice.

For employers, one of the advantages offered by employment contracts is that long-term relationships allow recruitment and training costs to be amortised over a prolonged spell of time. Moreover, a permanent employment relationship not only ensures that firms continue to benefit from enhanced individual skills but also helps to create incentives that make it less attractive for the employee to abandon the firm and to take up a job with a rival company (Niman, 2004, p. 278). On the other hand, employees' contractual strength derives from the possibility of withdrawing the human capital attained and closely depends on the level of individual substitutability. Certain employees may have a network of connections with the firm's suppliers and customers, which would be jeopardised to the employer's detriment if the employee were to walk away.[5] Some knowledge developed by the employee may be easily transferable and used within other firms, while some firm-specific or relation-specific knowledge is an asset that the employee would lose as a result of changing job.

Contractual power between the employer and the employee depends mainly on the cost for both parties of terminating the employment relationship: the cost in terms of loss of value embodied in the employee's assets versus the cost of the employer's best alternative of finding and training a replacement. In general, the employee's contractual power is linked to legal rights, the value of the best alternative, the ability of the other side to threaten in return, control over resources, such as particular skills, or the exclusive possession of information.

---

[4] See also Simon (1992, p. 6). This surrendering of freedom on the part of the employee is an element of a more complex phenomenon termed 'labour alienation' by Marx (1867, pp. 799, 990). For a modern interpretation of this concept see, Screpanti (2001, pp. 18–19).

[5] Holmström and Roberts (1998, p. 85); Baron and Kreps (1999, pp. 65–6, 83).

The role of mutual dependence and alternatives in power relationships is lucidly expressed by Molm (1997, pp. 1, 29) in her book on power and social exchange:

One actor's dependence is the source of another's power. To the extent that dependence is mutual, actors in social relations have power over each other. And, to the extent that their dependencies are unequal, their relation will also be unequal, in terms of the benefits that each contributes and receives. More powerful, less dependent actors will enjoy greater benefits at lower costs.
Unequal dependencies give less dependent actors an advantage in the relation.

The employment relationship is generally characterised by an uneven, mutual dependence between employer and employees; 'it is generally felt that employees are more at risk . . . than are employers' (Baron and Kreps, 1999, p. 66).

Flexibility

We have seen that the specific difference between the employment contract and a spot contract with suppliers of goods and services is that the former implies the employer's authority and managed coordination. I wish to stress that authority and managerial coordination, which are an inherent part of the employment relationship itself, are essential in facing radical uncertainty. The central point is that an employment contract provides direction and discretionary power, understood as the employer's capacity to decide about the employee's activity during a long-term relationship – i.e. the authority to alter the work content, duties and responsibilities at a later date in response to circumstances that have been left unspecified in the contract. This makes it possible to achieve a remarkable degree of flexibility that reduces the cost of radical uncertainty by adapting decisions over time, according to the evolution of environmental conditions. In market contracting, on the other hand, flexibility is obtained through renegotiation of the contract. But, if radical uncertainty is present, the renegotiation process may be very costly due to transaction costs.[6]

---

[6] In modern economics, the analysis of the flexibility of the employment relationship was originally due to Coase (1937, pp. 35ff.) and further developed by

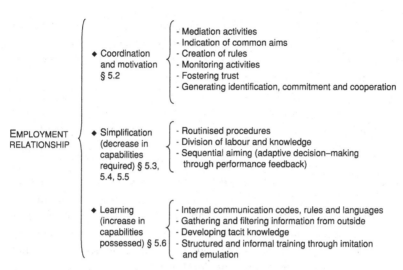

Figure 5.1. Uncertainty-decreasing strategies within the employment relationship.

From opportunism to opportunities: managing conflicts of interest

Coordination and motivation within the employment relation mitigate uncertainty. They are achieved through mediation activity in conflicts of interest, indication of common aims, creation of rules and monitoring activities, as well as the provision of incentives that boost loyalty

Simon's early work (1951, pp. 11ff.). In his seminal article, Simon stressed that 'the employment contract may be a functional (reasonable) way of dealing with certain kinds of uncertainty'. Simon showed that the employer acquires the right to postpone decisions about the employee's agenda, and in this way is able 'to postpone some of his decisions whose outcomes are contingent on future uncertain events' (Simon, 1978, p. 448). On the employment relationship, see also Pitelis (1993a, p. 9); Hart (1995a, p. 5); Langlois and Robertson (1995, p. 28); Conner and Prahalad (1996, pp. 487ff.); Foss (1996c, pp. 78, 84–6); Ménard (1997a, pp. 32–5); Holmström and Roberts (1998, pp. 74–9); Baron and Kreps (1999: chapters 4–9), Loasby (1999, p. 82). The book by Screpanti (2001, pp. 8–42, 183–95, 146–7, 157ff., 258–90) examines in depth the characteristics of the employment relationship within a Marxian perspective.

and reduce opportunism, foster trust and generate identification (figure 5.1). Identification and continuous association are powerful forces for reducing the inefficiencies that arise from moral hazard, as they create solidarity and stable expectations of members' behaviour and therefore trust (Simon, 1991, p. 41). Moreover, organisations provide a setting, through continuous association, which allows the accumulation of experiences that develop – or, one might add, in certain cases destroy – trust and therefore create stable expectations of the members' behaviour (Loasby, 1999, p. 105). The desire to maintain a good reputation and to continue the employment relation is another factor that enhances a climate of commitment, mutual loyalty and cooperation.[7] Trust is an essential and pervasive element within organisations because organisations cannot function effectively if all their members, from the low hierarchical levels to the chief executive officer (CEO), do not develop mutual confidence and are not 'willing to accept without question most of what they are told by people in other parts of the organisation' (Loasby, 1999, p. 101).

Long-term employment relationships allow more accurate access to information about employees' abilities and enable the firm to assess performance more accurately and along more dimensions (Baron and Kreps, 1999, p. 83). The specific characteristics of the employment contract together with the firm's contractual power provide the possibility of designing a vast range of pecuniary and non-pecuniary incentives and sanctions. An appropriate structure of incentives favours motivation, and the creation of shared goals and responsibility; it also fosters commitment, identification and cooperation, and facilitates the transmission of information and the development of a common language, principles and rules.

The opportunity to check reliability over time, effective control, promotion policies, incentive structures and management of conflicts of interest through mediation activity can eliminate – or at least substantially mitigate – the internal influence costs that spring from the attempt on the part of subordinates to influence the central authority by misrepresenting, manipulating and distorting information. In particular, participation in aims, identification, voluntary acceptance and consent on the part of the members of the organisation are

---

[7] Simon (1991, p. 41); a similar point of view is expressed in Hodgson (1993a, p. 90).

crucial in overcoming information failures, and help to surmount resistance to fiat and perfunctory compliance.[8] This is particularly true in the case of third-sector organisations, in which fiduciary relationships are favoured by the fact that workers and managers are interested in the service provided. 'The possibility of attracting motivated managers and workers tends to reduce agency problems and opportunistic behaviour, even if they do not disappear completely' (Bacchiega and Borzaga, 2003, pp. 43–4).

Overall, then, long-term relational agreements within firms, such as the employment contract, tend to limit uncertainty and its costs because they encourage trust, simplification and learning. Sections 5.3–5.5 are dedicated to the analysis of simplification procedures, while the final section 5.6 of the chapter addresses *learning* processes within the firm.

5.3 Routines

A possible and, indeed, a very common uncertainty-decreasing strategy consists in applying organisational routines, which are of great avail in coping with complexity because they reduce the quantity of necessary information and enhance coordination and predictability.

Organisational routines are recurrent interaction patterns learned by an organisation. They constitute the building blocks of the firm's competencies and capabilities (the first aspect of organisational coordination discussed in chapter 3).[9] Routines rest on skills that allow the members of the organisation to perform coordinated tasks in a highly relational and organisation-specific way. Under this perspective,

---

[8] On the complex relationship between informational deficiencies, control, participation in planning as sharing of power, consent and efficiency, see the discussion in Freeland (1996, pp. 486ff.).

[9] Attention to the role of routines in the theory of the firm was originally drawn by March and Simon (1958, pp. 160–1) and Cyert and March (1963, pp. 109–13). Nelson and Winter (1982, pp. 99–100, 160–1) take routines as the central unit of analysis of their evolutionary theory of the firm. See also Winter (1988, pp. 184, 189); Dosi, Nelson and Winter (2000a, pp. 4–5). In the recent fast-growing literature on these issues there is as yet no general consensus on what 'routines' are. On different definitions of routines, see Rura-Polley and Miner (2002, pp. 275–6). For a critical discussion on the economics and business literature dealing with routines and for vast bibliographical references on this theme, see Becker (2004, 2005).

skills are understood as 'quasi-modular components of routines' (Dosi, Nelson and Winter, 2000a, p. 4). Since organisational routines involve interaction, they are inherently collective phenomena. In contrast, recurrent patterns on the individual level, such as repetition of thought or action, are associated with the term 'habits'.[10] Habits are defined as 'a propensity to behave in a particular way in a particular class of situations' (Hodgson and Knudsen, 2004, p. 287).

Organisational routines are a key repository of both tacit, and explicit, production and organisation knowledge. As argued by Nelson and Winter (1982, p. 99), 'the routinisation of activity in an organisation constitutes the most important form of storage of the organisation's specific operational knowledge'. Organisational routines capture collectively held knowledge possessed by the organisation and can be inherited throughout the life of organisations as generations of members come and go.[11] They have a two-fold character: on the one hand, they can be regarded as a potential, which can subsist even unexpressed, i.e. a propensity to think and behave; on the other, they consist in an actual repetition of thought and action that is 'triggered by an appropriate stimulus or context.'[12] To designate the actual repeated performance within productive processes I use the expression *routinised operating procedures*.

Routines may refer to: (i) behavioural regularities, which are behavioural patterns and imply activity, and (ii) cognitive regularities, which are cognitive patterns, information-processing rules, heuristics, programmes, rules of thumb and decision-making rules (i.e. 'if . . . then' rules: 'If {condition *A*}, then {decide *B*}).[13]

As far as cognitive regularities are concerned, in complex and uncertain situations in which there is a high number of interrelated variables and acquiring the full relevant information is very costly or impossible, individuals and teams in business organisations tend to

---

[10] Becker (2004, p. 645); Hodgson and Knudsen (2004, pp. 286–7, 289).

[11] Baum and Singh (1994a, p. 7); Becker (2004, p. 660).

[12] Hodgson and Knudsen (2004, pp. 287, 290). On this point they quote the example of a firm with a Monday to Friday working week: 'During the week a number of routines can be energised. At other times the firm is inactive. But the routines do not all disappear at the weekend, to reappear mysteriously the next Monday morning. The routines-as-capacities remain. They can be triggered next week by appropriate stimuli.'

[13] Becker (2004, p. 645).

adopt constantly fixed parameters and certain formal or informal rules for the expected advantages in terms of saving on information-processing abilities, mental effort, learning times and resources. Adopting cognitive regularities implies a reduction in the capabilities required because it allows individuals to ignore some variables and follow sets of rules which lie in 'the long-term memory', thereby saving mental efforts.[14] In short, cognitive regularities make it possible to dispense with the highly energy-consuming activity of decision-making.

Behavioural regularities, which are simply fixed responses 'to defined stimuli' consisting in 'units or "chunks" of organised activity with a repetitive character', have a large component of embodied tacit knowledge. 'The interesting thing about routines is indeed that they are often found in contexts where nobody can explain what they are for except in the vague terms of "the way things are done around here".'[15] In organisations, routines are closely linked to roles. In fulfilling their role, the members of a firm are driven by 'a logic of appropriateness reflected in a structure of rules and definitions of identities'.[16]

Organisational routines enhance coordination and predictability for a number of reasons. Not only do they support a high level of simultaneity and make simultaneous activities mutually consistent, but they also give stability to the practices of a team and provide each of the members of the organisations with knowledge of the behaviour of the others on which to base her own decision.[17] Last but not least, they

---

[14] Egidi and Rizzello (2003, p. 11). Becker and Knudsen (2005, p. 756) show that empirical texts generally support the theoretical argument that routines help managers cope with radical uncertainty by freeing cognitive resources. For a detailed analysis of the existing empirical literature on effects of routines on organisations, see Becker (2004, p. 654).

[15] Dosi, Faillo and Marengo (2003, p. 6); Dosi, Nelson and Winter (2000a, pp. 4–5); cf. March and Simon (1958, p. 142).

[16] March (1988a, p. 17; 1997, p. 17); March, Schulz and Zhou (2000, p. 6); cf. Elster (1998, pp. 72–3; 1999, pp. 301–6).

[17] See Becker (2004, p. 654) for discussion and bibliographical references on this point. A key reference on predictable rule-based behaviour is Heiner (1983, pp. 370ff.) who argues that '*greater uncertainty will cause rule-governed behavior to exhibit inquiringly predictable regularities, so that uncertainty becomes the basic source of predictable behavior*'. On uncertainty-avoiding procedures in organisations, see Hofstede (1980, pp. 155–61).

establish a truce among the various members of the organisation (between team members and between managers and employees) who may have potentially conflicting interests.[18]

Organisational routines are characterised by stability and mutation, at the same time – stability, in terms of a 'stable sequence of inter-actions', and mutation represented by incremental adaptation to experience 'in response to feedback about outcomes' (Becker, 2004, pp. 649–53, *passim*). In fact, on the one hand, organisational routines 'take place when search has been eliminated, i.e. when the individual learning process stops' (Egidi and Rizzello, 2003, p. 11); on the other, organisational routines themselves are context-dependent and subject to transformations through learning processes because they evolve in an adaptive and creative manner whenever environmental conditions change. 'Routines are not inert', but typically change incrementally over time due to an internal dynamic deriving from the participants' response to the outcomes of previous iterations of a routine. This two-fold nature is only apparently contradictory. Indeed, there is a link between routinisation and change because stability and simplification constitute preconditions that facilitate learning and mutation by freeing up limited cognitive recourses. In other words, 'stability provides a baseline against which to assess changes'.[19] Arguably, technical change can be regarded as the generation of new organisational routines (Dosi and Egidi, 1991, pp. 183–5).

Just as habits replicate from individual to individual through imitation, routines replicate from organisation to organisation through a number of mechanisms such as the movement of employees from one organisation to another, consultants, codifiable information and instructions, knowledge embodied in equipment, the spread of rules emanating from state or public organisations or associations of employers, collaboration forms among firms and strategy imitation. However, not all organisational routines are easily replicable since some routines are repositories of knowledge that is not codified and are linked to idiosyncratic organisational settings. What is more, the copying or replication of routines is imperfect. This brings about variation in the evolution process. 'Variation is the evolutionary fuel,

---

[18] The importance of the role played by organisational routines in representing truces has been emphasised by Nelson and Winter (1982, pp. 107ff.).

[19] Becker (2004, pp. 649–51, 657–9, *passim*).

and the necessary basis for selection to work in any population, including a population of evolving firms.' Under this perspective, business organisations can be regarded as 'replicators' in that they constitute a 'cohesive whole' that interacts with their environment 'in a way that this interaction causes replication to be differential' (Hodgson and Knudsen, 2004, pp. 291–2, 295).

5.4 Division of labour

Technical division of labour among the members of the firm is a simplifying tool because it reduces the individual abilities required and makes saving on learning processes possible. Splitting activities into elementary operations decreases the complexity of tasks. Organisations solve complex problems by decomposing them recursively into sub-problems that can be solved more easily by different functional sub-systems of the firm. Problem-solving activity therefore leads to modifications in the internal division of labour and knowledge that enhance the potential for economising, as the latter term is defined in this study.[20]

Main effects of technical division of labour

Technical division of labour not only has the effect of simplifying and reducing learning time, but it also has many other important effects on the internal functioning of the firm. Division of labour:

- Facilitates repetition-based improvements that augment workers' dexterity
- Brings about a growth in productivity because it reduces idle times and thereby favours a more efficient utilisation and allocation of productive capacities
- Involves a reduction in production costs because, by dividing the work to be executed into different operations each requiring

---

[20] Egidi (1992a, pp. 8–12, 2002, p. 110); Egidi and Rizzello (2003, p. 8); Loasby (1998, p. 178); Ricottilli (2001, p. 4). Simplification and specialisation mechanisms related to learning processes are considered in Levinthal and March (1993, pp. 95ff.). On the relationship between the development of capabilities and division of labour, see Ramazzotti (2004, pp. 38ff.).

different degrees of skill, the firm can pay for the precise skill required for each operation[21]

- Leads to a change in the *quality* of production elements and outputs
- Last but not least, saves on the selection and internal transmission of information;[22] this saving appears to be of major importance today with the emergence of the new knowledge-based economy.

Specialisation and technical division of labour

Individual specialisation is based on technical division of labour within firms. It consists in the development of particular abilities by narrowing the range of activities through a process of technical division of labour and knowledge. Specialisation can be segmented into two dimensions: (a) the *number of operations* performed and (b) the *length of learning processes* per operation. In general, the narrower the range of operations performed and the longer it takes to acquire the necessary specific abilities to perform a single operation, the greater will be the specialisation.

To further clarify the meaning of these two dimensions of individual specialisation, consider the evolution of surgery in recent years. Specialisation in surgery has achieved a saving on knowledge, but it has also brought about, on the one hand, an increase in learning processes per operation and thereby in the ability to perform specific operations and, on the other, the introduction of innovative techniques. Knowledge per operation intensifies as individual specialisation grows. The saving on knowledge concerns the first dimension of specialisation, while the increase in learning time per operation and the consequent improvement in ability to perform specific operations concern the second dimension of specialisation.

Economies of individual specialisation may exist 'even if all individuals are *ex ante* identical'. In this case, 'the differences in productivity between various specialists are consequences rather than causes of the division of labour' (Yang and Ng, 1998, p. 4). There is a two-way

---

[21] As is well known, the improvement of dexterity was stressed by Smith (1776, I: pp. 17–21), while the concept of saving on different skills and reduction of idle times was put forward by Babbage (1832, pp. 172–3); cf. Tani (1986, p. 219, 1988, p. 10); Landesmann (1986, pp. 308–9); Morroni (1992, pp. 60–7).

[22] Arrow (1974b, p. 176); see also Screpanti (2001: chapter 5).

relationship between individual specialisation and heterogeneous and incomplete abilities. Heterogeneous and incomplete abilities among individuals favour specialisation, but at the same time the development of specialisation determines a distribution of learning processes that leads to individual heterogeneous and limited abilities.

Division of labour and specialisation not only favours better use of existing individual abilities, but it also promotes the creation of new abilities that influence the innovative activity. This second advantage of division of labour and specialisation is by far the most important.[23] As above, a two-way relationship can be discerned, in this case between division of labour and technical change. On the one hand, technical change ends up being shaped by the particular ways in which labour and knowledge are divided while, on the other, technical change affects division of labour.

Technical division of labour and individual specialisation should not be considered synonymous, unlike the interpretation adopted by most authors, as division of labour allows specialisation but may have opposite effects on the level of specialisation. If the division of labour reaches a point where the operations are very simple, it leads to deskilling phenomena and tends to nullify the need for learning and the content of the specialisation, with socially negative effects. Instead, if division of labour is kept within certain limits, it favours specialisation by enhancing learning processes and the development of job-specific skills. For instance, some new forms of division of labour linked to the application of new technologies (e.g. microelectronics and computers, new materials, new energy resources, medical technologies, biotechnology, aerospace techniques, etc.) tend to foster the development of new skills.

Division of labour and coordination

Technical division of labour and individual specialisation require intentional coordination of the individual abilities of the firm's members by the management, in order to ensure cooperation and distribution of

---

[23] Smith (1776, I: pp. 20–1). On the relationship between division of labour and innovation, see Rosenberg (1965, pp. 131–9); and Loasby (1999, pp. 131–2, 2003b, p. 15).

tasks. From this perspective, productive knowledge frequently resides in work groups or organisations rather than in individuals:

This is not simply a matter of the same knowledge being held by several individuals . . . Neither is it adequately captured by the image of complementary specialised skills being coordinated in the execution of a 'recipe' . . . It is crucially a matter of *distributed* knowledge, i.e. of complementary parts of the same functional unit of knowledge being held by several individuals and applied in a coordinated way, the coordination itself being a crucial aspect of the knowledge. (Winter, 2005, pp. 237–8)

The coordination of interdependent individual abilities establishes a social relationship among the members of the firm and favours the creation of specific capabilities.[24] Technical division of labour between the members of the firm transforms individual incomplete abilities into a firm's specific capabilities in producing goods and services. As division of labour and knowledge develop specialised roles, an increasing need for participation in decision-making and planning processes arises whenever 'directives impinge on an expert's sphere' of specific knowledge. Specialisation makes participation in decision-making processes and consent more rather than less important as a means of maintaining cooperation.[25]

Coordination is particularly important whenever division of labour fosters innovative activities that tend to break the stable patterns of routines. In fact, the generation of multifarious novelty is 'in some degree disruptive of the existing patterns of coordination' (Loasby, 2002a, p. 46) and creates asymmetric information and heterogeneous knowledge that requires organisational coordination and learning. The more the basic conditions undergo change, the less adequate such phenomena as centralisation, coercion and reliance on fiat appear to be. In a situation of complex interdependence and rapid unanticipated

---

[24] On the definition of the firm as a durable organisation coordinating indivisible and complementary inputs and the limited abilities of different individuals who cooperate to produce goods or services, see: Egidi (1992a, pp. 11–12); Foss (1997a, p. 310); Loasby (1998, p. 173); Hodgson (1998c, p. 38). The relationship between coordination, interdependency and specialisation is stressed by Simon (1991, p. 42); see also Egidi (1992b, p. 148).

[25] Freeland (2001, pp. 24, 29). For instance, Freeland (1996, p. 491) shows that 'within the M-form, failure to make use of divisional expertise will cause subordinates to view policies handed down from above as unjustified . . . with the risk of disrupting order within the firm'.

changes, the extensive reliance on monitoring and fiat may encourage perfunctory compliance rather than consummate performance. Consummate performance is a matter of taking the initiative to advance organisational objectives in a way that goes much beyond minimal effort based on self-interested calculation.[26] In such a context, there is then the need for coordination among specialised roles and active participation in decision-making processes on the part of the firm's members.

A firm's coordination activities are characterised by increasing returns because of managerial economies of scale in information acquisition and utilisation, as discussed in chapter 3. Thus, managerial capacities can be amplified as the company grows by adopting greater division of labour, hiring specialised employees and allocating many administrative and organisational tasks to specialist staff. With increased size and division of labour, a number of advantages are obtained: staff functions are designed to supply decision-making information to the CEO, communication is simplified and accelerated by technological innovations, techniques of cost accounting and budgetary control are brought to a high state of perfection and ways are devised to make large organisations manageable through decentralisation of operating authority and financial responsibility to product lines or territorial divisions.[27] Therefore, growth in the firm's size favours the division of labour into organisational and administrative sub-processes.

5.5 Sequential aiming and memory of the future

This section examines the third aspect of organisational simplification: sequential aiming. Sequential aiming consists in sequential attention to goals that allows adaptive decision-making on the basis of performance feedback (see figure 5.1, p. 211). It can in effect be regarded as a simplifying behaviour that identifies aims and adjusts intermediate goals to reality on the basis of information springing from the organisation itself and from the environment. The analysis of sequential aiming offered in this section can be seen as an outgrowth of Simon's

---

[26] Simon (1991, p. 32); Freeland (1996, p. 513, 2001, pp. 25, 312).
[27] Scherer (1980, p. 86); cf. Penrose (1959, pp. 92ff.); Demsetz (1995, pp. 31–2).

original idea,[28] in line with subsequent developments of the analysis of sequential decision-making and performance feedback under uncertainty.[29] Sequential aiming or similar dynamic mechanisms are often mentioned in analyses on the characteristics of knowledge, capabilities and transaction costs.[30] The increasing interest in the subject is testified by Greve's book (2003) which is entirely dedicated to a review of both theoretical and empirical literature on this issue. It also provides a theoretical framework and new extensive evidence concerning the effects of performance feedback on firms' behaviour.

Sequential aiming within business organisations simplifies individual decision-making because it helps their members to discern and pursue specific aims. It can be seen as a two-step process:

(i) Picking out aims and dividing them into intermediate goals or targets, thereby setting aspiration levels; breaking problems down into parts; establishing a particular operational and cognitive division of labour, looking for suitable information and choosing the appropriate means.

(ii) Determining a particular sequence of time horizons (or planning horizons) on the basis of an aspiration level and intermediate goals that have been identified, and implementing performance feedback systems.[31]

Let us look at step (i). First, sequential aiming consists in singling out specific aims so as to reduce the quantity of information and knowledge required. The simplification process may lead to the

---

[28] To my knowledge, Simon's first reference to sequential decision-making is in his article on the employment relationship (1951, p. 22). A more extensive discussion on this point is in the paper published four years later under the title 'A behavioral model of rational choice' (1955, pp. 250–3). See also Simon (1959, p. 297, 1972, p. 415). Cf. Lewin *et al.* (1944, pp. 333ff.).

[29] Analyses in a germane perspective appear in Cyert and March (1963, pp. 34ff., 118ff.); March and Olsen (1975, pp. 335); Kahneman and Tversky (1979, p. 32); Herriott, Levinthal and March (1985, p. 219); March (1988a, p. 11; 1997, p. 12).

[30] Brief references to some kind of adaptive sequential decision-making may be found, for instance, in: Arrow (1973, p. 138); Williamson (1985, pp. 56, 78–9, 1999b, p. 42); Dosi and Metcalfe (1991, pp. 141–2); Pitelis (1993b, p. 265); Levinthal and March (1993, p. 98); Denzau and North (1994, p. 12); Harper (1996, p. 21); Foss (1996c, p. 78); Shapira (1997a, p. 5); Dunn (1999, p. 211); Cohendet, Llerena and Marengo (2000, p. 106); Antonelli (2004, p. 156).

[31] Simon (1955, pp. 244, 248–52, 1959, p. 297). See also March (1988a, p. 3).

decomposition of single aims into different goals, specific targets, tasks and jobs, which in turn leads to the division of labour and knowledge within organisations. Selection of information and simplification in pursuing aims is essential whenever agents face a complex situation characterised by interaction among a high number of variables. Simon (1991, p. 37) rightly observes that 'one dimension of simplification is to focus on particular goals and one form of focus is to attend to the goals of an organisation'. Indeed, following the aims set out by organisations is generally believed to be a major determinant of success (Simon, 1991, *ibid.*).

In this first phase, various aspiration levels are identified in terms of goal-setting according to the decision-making mechanisms that characterise the firm, examined in chapter 2. An aspiration level is the level of future performance in relation to a particular organisational goal. Goals are judged appropriate if they meet the following criteria: (a) they are achievable on the basis of the abilities possessed; (b) they make it possible to economise (to increase benefits and decrease costs) in relation to the current situation or some reference level; and (c) they enable the firm to cope with competitive pressure.

The identification of goals and targets is characterised by the coexistence of two attitudes:

(a) *passive adjustment* based on assessment of past results or on the past performance of similar business organisations
(b) *active reaction* by identifying new aims that trigger a process of change.

As a consequence, firms' behaviour can be regarded as the result of both adapting to and transforming existing conditions. But the truly distinctive feature of adaptive behaviour within the firm is the tension between adjustment and innovation.[32] Innovative activity may constitute an attempt to overcome the existing trade-offs among conflicting aims. If abilities are heterogeneous, the propensity and ability to innovate varies among individuals. Even in the same environmental conditions, different levels of theoretical and practical knowledge

---

[32] On the coexistence of adaptive and innovative attitudes, see: Bianchi (1990, pp. 164–5); Sabel and Zeitlin (1997, pp. 5–6); Hodgson (1998a, p. 179); Runde (1998, p. 14 n. 19).

among individuals may lead one individual to behave in an adaptive way with very little innovation while inducing another to innovate.

Step (ii) of the sequential aiming process is the determination of a particular sequence of time horizons within which the process of increasing benefits and reducing costs takes place. This second step consists mainly in the implementation of performance feedback applied to each subsequent period of time (Greve, 2003, pp. 39ff.). Sequential aiming, through performance feedback, reduces the negative effects of radical uncertainty because it facilitates:

- learning processes
- flexibility in terms of adjustment, over time, of individual decisions to changing conditions
- reduction of the effects of evaluation and forecasting errors.

Let us consider the impact of these three aspects. First, the acquisition of information takes time because the capacity to collect information is limited at any single moment of time and also because the relevant information is often dated.[33] Aims and targets can be reshaped at each subsequent time horizon in order to take new information into account. Sequential aiming favours learning processes.

Secondly, sequential aiming means that existing plans can be revised according to changing conditions. It favours flexibility because, over time, plans can be modified and aims reshaped on the basis of past experience. Under conditions of uncertainty and irreversibility, the pursuit of aims that are set in sequence makes 'actions intertemporally flexible' in the sense that it keeps open a broad set of future options (Vercelli, 1995, p. 261).

Thirdly, sequential aiming makes it possible to reduce the effects of evaluation and forecasting errors. Shortening the time horizon reduces the degree of irreversibility of choices, i.e. the costs of switching. For example, hiring equipment for a limited period of time or hiring a worker on a short-term contract are two ways of reducing the degree of irreversibility that arises from asymmetric information on the actual qualitative nature of the equipment or worker hired.

Therefore, if environmental conditions are extremely volatile and uncertain, firms tend to arrange aims and targets in a sequence,

---

[33] On this point, see Arrow (1973, p. 138) and Stiglitz (1989, p. 7).

determining the time horizon of each aim and goal and thus deciding when an action should cease. The time horizon is in itself a goal in the sense that the decision on when an action should cease can be seen as establishing a limit to the investment of time allocated in pursuit of a particular aim.

The following example, based on a single aim, illustrates an extremely simplified sequential aiming procedure. Let us suppose that a firm wishes to reduce the average production cost with a given time horizon TH that is divided into different time periods (for instance, $T_1, T_2, \ldots T_n$). In the first period (T_1), the firm undertakes the goal of reducing average costs by a certain percentage. This goal is fixed according to: (a) the competitive pressure existing in the environment in which the firm operates; and (b) estimates of the possible cost reduction depending on abilities and skills available within the firm. In each subsequent period ($T_2, T_3, \ldots$) a new goal, consisting in a certain percentage of reduction of average cost, is established on the basis of the performance feedback concerning the previous experience and by evaluating the competitive pressure. In some periods, the results achieved may exceed the pre-set targets, while there may be other periods when the pre-set target fails to be met.

Naturally, in more complex situations a firm may have more than one aim and a single aim may be achieved by means of several goals. A high number of aims determines what can be called a multifocused strategy.

Sequential aiming consists in a feedback process of successive trials based on monitoring the success or failure associated with past adjustments. Firms thereby reshape their aims according to the degree of achievement. The goal at time T depends on the previous level of attainment at time T_{-1}. It follows that goals may change from point to point in this sequence of trials, with the difficulties experienced in reaching a goal depressing the level of the goal in the following period.[34] In a nutshell, sequential aiming allows a two-fold process: adapting performance to goal, and conversely, goal to performance. For example, Greve (2003, pp. 76ff., 111, 121, 136ff.) provides clear evidence from extensive applied investigations that search activities,

---

[34] Simon (1955, pp. 111–13, 1959, p. 297) and Herriott, Levinthal and March (1985, p. 219).

innovation and investment increase or decline when the firm's performance is above or below the aspiration level.

Goals change because preferences may, and usually do, change on the basis of personal experience and according to the evolution of environmental conditions. The present is linked to the future by the ability to plan and form mental images of possible future events on the basis of a creative re-elaboration of past experience. These actions, programmes or plans for the future, which are retained and recalled by the human mind, have been termed the 'memory of the future' (Ingvar, 1985, pp. 127–9). Planning, imagining and anticipating a 'world of the possible' is a specific human characteristic, linked to the firm's ability to innovate and create new opportunities.

Sequential aiming applies not only within firms but also within hybrids. Long-term forms of collaboration among firms frequently develop according to sequential aiming procedures because the result of their 'common project becomes the basis for deliberation over the shape of the next project' (Helper, MacDuffie and Sabel, 2000, pp. 445–6). In general, organised ongoing collaboration relations are founded on common interest in continuing the joint activity.

5.6 Learning

In the presence of environmental radical uncertainty, the development of capabilities through learning, which represents the first aspect of the organisational coordination of the firm, becomes a central issue in the theory of the firm and an important basis of competitive advantage. Learning processes, based on the building of a corporate culture and organisational capabilities and competencies, can limit radical uncertainty. This last section of the chapter is dedicated to the main properties of learning processes as an organisational response to radical uncertainty. It also analyses the close relationship between organisational learning and innovative activity. The development of an integrated set of dynamic capabilities, through learning, 'constitutes the foundation for continuing growth' (Chandler, 2003: chapter 1, pp. 7, 15). The evolutionary path through which techniques are developed and adopted is the result of the creation of capabilities. Accordingly, firms are here not only seen as collections of resources, 'repository of competencies' or 'loci of coordination', but also as loci of learning, in other words, as 'loci of creation, implementation, storage and diffusion of productive knowledge' (Dosi and Marengo, 2000, p. 81). Under this perspective, firms are regarded as *knowledge-creating organisations*.

Different forms of learning

Learning is understood as a means to increase the abilities possessed and involves a change in behaviour or knowledge on the basis of experience. There is a motivation to learn whenever there is a positive difference between the benefits of learning and its costs arising from the resources employed. The perceptions about institutional, organisational and market incentives, stemming from pay-offs associated with acquiring diverse types of knowledge, are the major driving forces of any learning process.[35] Nevertheless, it is conceivable that some learning benefits may not be strictly economic but instead rooted in motivations such as the need to make sense out of the diverse signals received by the senses, or the pursuit of personal self-esteem and self-realisation. Emotions linked to self-esteem and self-realisation play an essential role in favouring or discouraging learning.

Learning processes applied to information-processing ability consist in increasing the ability to take into account, classify and order different bits of information and compare benefits and costs. As far as practical knowledge is concerned, learning takes the form of an improvement in the ability to perform new operations. Since practical knowledge involves the adoption of automatic mechanisms of conduct, any improvement in practical knowledge is necessarily based on experience.

Learning may entail either adaptation or change. I term the first type of learning 'acquisitional learning', and the second type 'creative learning'.

Acquisitional learning can be described as a discovery of pre-existing information and an updating of theoretical knowledge in the light of incoming data that are given and available, as in long-run analysis in traditional static microeconomics. In these conditions, learning is manifested as the Bayesian revision of the probability distribution in the light of new information.

[35] Cohendet, Llerena and Marengo (2000, p. 102); cf. North (1990, pp. 75–8, 1994, p. 362).

Creative learning consists in the generation of knowledge and new opportunities. It involves a problem-formulation and problem-solving process that entails the development of the capacity to unlearn, and learn anew. Creative learning implies the capacity to change the representation of the environment, to interpret and re-elaborate relevant information, create new mental models and imagine alternatives (Loasby, 1999, p. 3; Hodgson, 2003a, p. 14).

These two types of learning mechanisms have opposite effects on uncertainty. Acquisitional learning, which increases information-processing ability, decreases procedural radical uncertainty. On the other hand, creative learning, which leads to innovative activity, thus bringing about the introduction of a novelty or the creation of unexpected opportunities, augments substantive radical uncertainty about possible outcomes.

When decision-makers are unaware of the state of radical uncertainty in which they are operating, learning activity prompts individuals to become conscious of their incomplete abilities, and thus destroys subjective certainty. Generally, however, agents are perfectly aware that they are facing an unpredictable future. In Hicks' (1977, p. vii) words, they 'do not know what is going to happen, and know that they do not know just what is going to happen'.

Organisational learning

Organisational learning is linked to the firm's ability to create new knowledge, spread it throughout the organisation and embody it in the output.[36] Development of the firm's capabilities can be obtained not only by coordination of internal learning processes, but also by hiring new members who have the necessary abilities, or by establishing collaboration forms among firms or through mergers with other organisations that have the required capabilities.[37] The benefits of organisational learning reside in the acquisition of a competitive advantage.

---

[36] Nonaka and Takeuchi (1995, p. 3). See the useful handbook on organisational learning edited by Dierkes *et al.* (2001). Argote's (1999) investigation on learning curves in organisations shows that organisations using similar processes and producing similar goods vary dramatically in the rate at which they learn.

[37] For further discussion on these issues see Teece *et al.* (1994, p. 198).

Organisational learning is driven by 'the search for a better performance' and inevitably modifies the environmental image of the members of the firm. In other words, organisational learning concerns 'the development of collectively-shared cognitive models and action repertoires' that form the necessary competencies to produce and sell commodities.[38] Organisational learning is never 'a purely cognitive process': it also implies social adaptation and 'modification of organisational rules' and routines (Dosi, Faillo and Marengo, 2003, pp. 15–16). In other words, 'learning becomes organisational when it is not only embedded in the minds of its members, but also when it is incorporated in the structures, files or routines of the organisation itself (Hodgson and Knudsen, 2003, p. 8). In this view, routines are conceived as learning units.[39]

Learning processes may be impeded by: (i) non-transmittability of knowledge due to tacitness; (ii) non-tradability of information and knowledge due to poor measurability or because it is in the interest of the holder not to exchange information and knowledge, in order to obtain a quasi-rent. Firms and organisations in general have both an *interest in* and the *ability to* organise internal learning even in the case of non-transmittable and non-tradable information and knowledge. On the one hand, they have an interest in advancing knowledge because they are aware that the ability to learn is the most enduring source of competitive advantage;[40] on the other, they are able to organise internal learning and enhance information handling because they:

(i) build up internal communication codes, rules and languages
(ii) gather and filter information and knowledge from outside
(iii) develop inside tacit knowledge
(iv) encourage internal training in a structured manner but also informally through imitation and emulation (figure 5.1, p. 211).

---

[38] Dosi and Marengo (1994, p. 221); Dosi, Marengo and Fagiolo (2005, p. 322); Dosi, Faillo and Marengo (2003, p. 13).

[39] See Schulz (2002, pp. 415, 418). On routine-based learning, see also Miner (1990, 1991) who focuses on organisational jobs as a special kind of routine. Formalised jobs consist in 'a range of possible enactments of a particular task . . . . For example, a receptionist's job entails tasks such as answering the phone, giving information, setting up appointments, and acting as a gatekeeper for the organisations. Each of these task may be done in a variety of ways.' (Rura-Polley and Miner, 2002, pp. 276–7).

[40] Levinthal (1995, p. 22); cf. Chandler (1992, p. 84, 2003: chapter 1, p. 5).

Business organisations create systems for internal communication and joint decision-making. Firms, by virtue of their very structure, allow the streamlining of communication. Indeed, firms and organisations in general can be seen as an intrinsic communication system. As Prescott and Visscher (1980, p. 460) put it, 'the firm is a structure within which agents have the incentive to acquire and reveal information in a manner that is less costly' than in possible alternative organisations. Three types of flow in the knowledge production process within the firm can be distinguished: top-down, bottom-up and horizontal flow (Screpanti, 2001, pp. 236–8). Communication is facilitated by the use of codes, which allow senders to transform their knowledge into a signal that is understood by the recipient. The adoption of common codes is a form of idiosyncratic co-specialisation that 'lowers knowledge transfer costs by increasing mutual understanding. Co-specialisation represents a specific, irreversible investment.'[41]

Division of knowledge reduces information flow within the organisation because members of the firm transfer only information and knowledge that are relevant for other members of the same firm. This selection of information to be used within the firm implies a form of power because it affects decision-making processes.

The identification of common aims within organisations, organisational control, common behavioural codes, incentives and continuing association tend to reduce conflicts of interest among members and help to deter possible influence activities and opportunistic behaviour that might hamper internal learning processes. Enhancing trust favours the transmission and acquisition of the information and knowledge that is essential to foster learning processes. Therefore, a fertile reciprocal breeding mechanism may be engendered: learning processes create a corporate culture that facilitates trust through appropriate expectations based on reputation mechanisms; trust, in turn, promotes internal learning processes.

Firms are learning organisations because they overcome the lack of interest in transmitting the relevant information between individuals, through the identification of common goals, and are able to offset the impossibility of transmitting tacit knowledge by means of the internal creation of non-explicit knowledge based on experience.

---

[41] Heiman and Nickerson (2002, p. 105). See Argote (1999, pp. 143ff.) on an empirical analysis on knowledge transfer within organisations.

Figure 5.2 illustrates a simplified example of this. The upper unshaded circle in figure 5.2 represents the market transmission of information and knowledge from agent *a* to agent *b*. Market transmission of information and knowledge between individuals or organisations derives from direct purchase of information and knowledge or from information incorporated in the goods or services exchanged, or is a by-product of the exchange activity.

In the market place, some bits of information and units of knowledge possessed by *a* may not be transmitted to *b* because of the lack of common interest or trust between the two individuals and the absence of a common language, or because knowledge is heterogeneous or tacit and therefore non-transmittable. In these cases market exchange does not occur (see table 1.1 in chapter 1, p. 28). In many relevant circumstances, information and knowledge that cannot be transmitted through the market can instead transferred internally within the organisations themselves. In figure 5.2, the central shaded flow of knowledge and information represents a flow of non-traded information and knowledge transmitted by organisational coordination. Furthermore, in-house transmission may allow replication that consists in the possibility of repeating a productive performance. Temporal and spatial replication involves substantial economies of scale and scope, but cannot happen 'without some organised managerial effort'.[42] Transmission and replication are made possible thanks to the identification of shared aims, the creation of a common code and the building of mutual trust.[43]

Though tacit knowledge cannot be transmitted either within the market or within organisations, it can be *created* within organisations through an interaction between their members in a 'generative relationship' that develops their knowledge, skills and performance (Hodgson and Knudsen, 2003, pp. 9–11). Firms enhance the creation of tacit knowledge by giving access to activities that enable individuals to acquire the necessary experience through learning-by-doing and learning-by-using. The tacit dimension of knowledge is present, more or less, in all production processes and in particular in innovative activities.

---

[42] Winter (2005, pp. 242, 244–5). On replication as knowledge transfer, see Winter and Szulanski (2001, pp. 730ff.).

[43] In this respect, Hahn (1989a, pp. 1–2) argues that 'traditional theory, by neglecting to give explicit attention to informational matters . . . has had very little to say' about organisations that are directly related 'to asymmetric or imperfect information'.

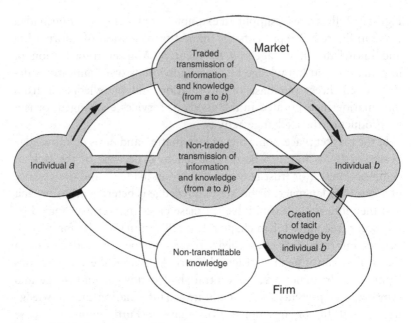

Figure 5.2. Information and knowledge transmission.

The creation of tacit knowledge by individual *b* within organisations is represented by the southeast shaded area of figure 5.2.

Discovering unexploited opportunities

Learning implies trial and error procedures. The errors tend to become eliminated as 'market experience reveals the infeasibility of some (hitherto sought-after) courses of action and the (hitherto unnoticed) profitability of other courses of action'.[44] Learning processes increase knowledge of possible services that may be obtained from available or new resources and thereby the possibility of discovering unexploited opportunities. If individuals possess complete abilities, 'all conceivably relevant available opportunities have been instantaneously grasped' (Kirzner, 1997, p. 9). Conversely, with incomplete and heterogeneous

---

[44] Kirzner (1997, p. 17); cf. Witt (2000, p. 735), where the 'business conception' is primarily understood as the identification of new opportunities for production and trade to be exploited. On the dynamics of mental models, see Denzau and North (1994, pp. 22–6).

abilities, which are the result of the accumulation of different individual experiences, what matters is the individual's 'image' of the environment. Under incomplete and heterogeneous abilities, there is the possibility that a single individual may be able to see, discover or invent opportunities that are not yet perceived by others. Thus whoever exploits new opportunities reaps the potential benefits. As emphasised by Kirzner (1997, p. 5), 'the discovery which reduces sheer ignorance is necessarily accompanied by the element of surprise'. Competitive advantage and instantaneous arbitrage are based on an ability differential among individuals. In most circumstances involving heterogeneous abilities and radical uncertainty, individuals not only try to identify existing opportunities that are not yet perceived by others, but they also attempt to broaden the set of available alternatives and to create new opportunities. In the latter case, learning brings about the exploration of unknown territory and the potential introduction of a genuine novelty. The discovery of new opportunities involves 'only differential access to existing information', while the creation of new opportunities implies the generation of new information and knowledge.[45]

Innovative activity and learning

A major objective of innovative business organisations is to facilitate the process of identification and discovery of unnoticed profit opportunities. Innovative activity can be regarded as a learning process. It is an intentional process of evolving capabilities and exploring new possibilities, in order to create, maintain and renew the competitive advantage. It involves a change in production techniques – i.e. in the

---

[45] Shane (2003, p. 20). The discovery process has been emphasised by NeoAustrian theorists; see, for instance, Harper's (1996, pp. 15–19, 89) critical exposition of Kirzner's (1989, pp. 20ff., 1997, pp. 3ff.) and Casson's (1982, pp. 146–8, 201) theories of entrepreneurship. The process of creation of new opportunities has been analysed by Penrose (1959, pp. 31–2, 52–6) and by some Post Keynesian and Schumpeterian economists. For the Post Keynesian position, see Davidson (1991a, 1994, 1996). On the Schumpeterian entrepreneur and connected theories on innovative activity, see Freeman (1994); Malerba and Orsenigo (1995); Balabkins (2003, pp. 209ff.); Ebner (2003, pp. 130ff.); and the critical discussion in De Vecchi (1995). As far as the process of creating alternatives is considered, see also Simon (1987b, p. 292).

method of production and/or in the quality of goods produced – but it may also be accompanied by a change in market conditions.

An advantage of basic research, stressed by Rosenberg (1990, p. 171), is that it allows a better understanding of how and where to conduct research of a more applied nature. The essential role of internal learning processes may help to shed light on why some private firms do basic research with their own money in spite of the existence of spillovers and non-appropriabilities. Even in cases in which 'there is no prospect of establishing proprietary control over the research findings', potential benefits may arise in terms of 'first-mover advantages' deriving from learning experiences that can represent a barrier to entry of new firms. What is relevant is not 'the size of spillovers, but whether the performing firm can capture enough of the benefits generated to yield a high rate of return on its investment' (Rosenberg, 1990, p. 167).

Quite often, the commercial success of an innovation is favoured by the possibility of making huge investments in R&D for product improvement.[46] On account of the high degree of unpredictability that surrounds the outcome of basic research in many important sectors of activities, 'large firms may be more willing to undertake basic research when they have a diverse range of products and strong marketing and distribution networks that increase their confidence that they will eventually be able to put the findings of basic research to some good commercial use' (Rosenberg, 1990, p. 168). Moreover, basic research is a long-term investment which usually requires stable commitments and long-term planning that may be better provided by large firms with a strong market position. Therefore, new business initiatives, grounded on basic research, learning processes and the development of capabilities, are generally carried out by large firms. This is, in fact, the case of most new business generated during the last decades of the twentieth century, which was created and built up by existing enterprises, 'and in large part by big or at least fair-sized ones'.[47] However, despite the acknowledgement of the essential function of corporate entrepreneurship, it should not be overlooked that, in some new

---

[46] Evangelista (1999: part two) provides an empirical analysis of the impact on innovative activity of knowledge-generating activities, such as R&D and design, and new technologies embodied in fixed capital.

[47] Drucker (2003, p. xi). The generation of new business by existing enterprises have been analysed in Sathe (2003).

technologies, start-up firms have a prominent role in the development of innovations, because creative and innovative activities can be favoured by the absence of rigid, authoritarian and hierarchical relationships, a circumstance that enhances diversity of options and tolerates variety.[48] 'In exploring unknown territory to the goal of better technologies', 'multiple sources of decision making' formed by numerous small business organisations are essential. This explains why innovations are often associated with multiple organisations or new entry to a field.[49]

In the United States this important role of new small firms and independent entrepreneurship has been powerfully conditioned by favourable environmental conditions, in particular, the government's anti-trust posture,[50] policies that lowered entry barriers, liberal licensing practices (as in the case of semiconductor patents), tolerance of a high degree of interfirm mobility on the part of highly skilled personnel, huge federal funding to research labs, in addition to the rise of the venture capital industry as one of the major innovations in the financial sector.[51] Last but not least, it is important to note the economic role of American universities in developing research projects which have led to useful industrial applications, and in providing qualified researchers who have created high-tech firms. Quite often, new innovative firms have been created by academic entrepreneurs supported by a financial commitment from venture capital firms.[52] In many hi-tech industries, this has resulted in a complex division of

---

[48] Rosenberg (1990, p. 168). On innovation and decreasing returns to hierarchy, see Screpanti (2001, pp. 239–41, 249–50).

[49] Rosenberg (2002, p. 36, *passim*). See also Loasby (1995, p. 472, 1999, p. 27).

[50] Rosenberg (2002, p. 8) mentions several anti-trust suits that have been of great significance 'in creating the necessary space for the activities of small firms.' He emphasises, however, that the impact of anti-trust policies on firms' behaviour derives not solely from the actual number of anti-trust cases that are brought into court, but also from the influence on business decision-making of the mere awareness of the possibility of intervention. For a description of competition laws in the United States and in the European Union, and for a general discussion on anti-trust policy, see Motta (2004: chapter 1).

[51] On changes in institutional environmental conditions, it is interesting to note that in the United States 'the contributions of the venture capital industry were vastly expanded around 1980 as the result of changes in the federal regulatory and tax changes that made huge new sources of capital available to high risk entrepreneurship in the new high tech sectors' (Rosenberg, 2002, p. 36).

[52] Rosenberg (2002, pp. 9, 36, 38–9, *passim*).

labour characterised by a large population of start-ups and few larger firms, 'investments by large firms in promising startup firms, joint ventures and licensing and, in some cases, the acquisition by large firms of small, promising startups'.[53]

Creating new opportunities is not just a matter of a once-and-for all decision. On the contrary, it is a process that takes time because it requires an effort on the part of individuals to refine their existing abilities, and on the part of firms to develop capabilities.[54] Innovative activity is sometimes a reaction to constraints, but it does not necessarily require a failure or a discrepancy between actual and expected outcomes or existing routines. It may rather be a response to competitive pressure or alternatively an attempt to reach a competitive advantage and to improve a situation already regarded as positive by increasing the firm's competitive strength.[55]

New capabilities are generated by an intensive outside–inside interaction and the ability to utilise outside knowledge (absorptive capacity). A firm relies on the capabilities of its members and of many formally independent organisations, and 'a firm may achieve distinctive advantages through the ways in which it combines these external capabilities with its own' (Loasby, 1998, p. 174). Carrying out basic research tends to increase the absorptive capacity to identify, assimilate and utilise new knowledge available from the environment. This is partly attributable to the fact that basic research requires in-house staff made up of scientists who can understand, interpret and evaluate the significance of new information and knowledge. 'The most effective way to remain effectively plugged in to the scientific network is to be a participant in the research process' (Rosenberg, 1990, p. 171).

The interaction among suppliers, customers and members of the firm involves redundancy in information and knowledge-sharing, resulting in a situation whereby overlapping information and knowledge is

---

[53] Rosenberg (2002, p. 33). See also Arora and Gambardella (1994, pp. 528–9).
[54] On the entrepreneurial characteristics (such as education, social position, motivation and the level of opportunity cost regarding alternative uses of resources and time) that favour the creation and exploitation of new opportunities, see Shane (2003: chapter 4).
[55] For the above reasons, Simon's (1972, p. 415) term 'satisficing', besides creating difficulties with proofreaders, may be misleading when referring to innovative activity. On the unsatisfactory nature of the 'satisficing' explanation, see Bianchi (1990, pp. 149ff.).

shared among members of an organisation and with individuals outside of the organisation. Redundancy of tacit and explicit knowledge encourages communication, and thus effectively facilitates learning.[56] As shown in Brusoni, Prencipe and Pavitt, who build their analysis on the case of the development of control systems for aircraft engines, multitechnology firms need to have knowledge in excess of that which is required for their internal production, as they must also address the task of coordinating 'networks of suppliers of equipment, components, and specialised knowledge', while at the same time maintaining a capability for systems integration. Accordingly, 'the division of labor' does not match 'the division of knowledge' (Brusoni, Prencipe and Pavitt, 2001, pp. 597–8, 608). 'By knowing more', multitechnology firms can cope with 'imbalances caused by uneven rates of development in the technologies on which they rely and with unpredictable product-level interdependencies' (Brusoni, Prencipe and Pavitt, 2001, *ibid.*).

External knowledge, which is available by means of transactions in the markets and technological interactions, is increasingly appreciated as 'an essential intermediary input in the production process of new knowledge.' Technological spillover and externalities undeniably also play a key role in the development of organisational capabilities. In particular, 'the amount of knowledge each firm can generate depends upon the amount of external knowledge available'. 'Knowledge networking consists in the . . . search for the sources of external technological knowledge . . . and in the intentional direction of internal research and learning towards complementary external knowledge' (Antonelli, 2004, pp. 61, 141, 173). The interaction among various learning processes from different sources, either internal or external to the firm, based on network externalities, is an element that explains the emergence of industrial districts or local production systems. Where complementarities between external and internal knowledge are important and pervasive, technological knowledge is viewed as

---

[56] Nonaka and Takeuchi (1995, pp. 11–14, 80–1) show that in many Japanese companies the concept of redundancy is brought to the point that 'a product development team is divided into competing subgroups that develop different approaches to the same project and then argue over the advantages and disadvantages of their proposals'.

a 'collective good' shared by interactive agents through intentional effort and participation (Antonelli, 2004, pp. 66–7).

Nonaka and Takeuchi have pointed out that creative learning processes within organisations consist in social interaction between tacit knowledge, which is rooted in experience, and explicit knowledge, which can be expressed in words and numbers. Organisational learning consists in a continuous and dynamic interaction between tacit and explicit knowledge:

> For tacit knowledge to be communicated and shared within the organisation, it has to be converted into words or numbers that anyone can understand. It is precisely during the time this conversion takes place – from tacit to explicit, and . . . back again into tacit, that organisational knowledge is created. Organisational knowledge creation is a spiral process in which the above interaction takes place repeatedly.
>
> (Nonaka and Takeuchi, 1995, pp. ix, 9–10, *passim*)

The conversion of tacit into explicit knowledge makes communication possible and allows non-transmittable and untradable knowledge to be turned into transmittable and tradable knowledge. This process involves different knowledge-creating entities, such as individuals, teams, firms and organisations of firms, and takes place at different levels because front-line employees, middle managers and top managers all play a part (Nonaka and Takeuchi, 1995, pp. 15, 56–7).

Learning as a firm-specific and path-dependent process

Learning is based on localised knowledge which is strongly selective in the sense that it does not so much imply a general body of knowledge as, rather, the effective capacity, largely rooted in practical knowledge, to execute a limited number of tasks in an efficient and efficacious manner.[57] Learning is likewise rooted in localised knowledge in that it is affected by the cognitive frames and actual capabilities of firms 'localised in historical time, in technical space, in the knowledge space' and 'in technological systems'.[58] Moreover, learning is firm-specific,

---

[57] The concept of localised technological change has been introduced by Atkinson and Stiglitz (1969, pp. 573ff.).

[58] Antonelli (2003, pp. 1ff., 2004, pp. 40ff., 247ff.), who offers an in-depth analysis of the characteristic of localised technological change. See also Dosi and Malerba (1996a, p. 4).

cumulative and path-dependent because is grounded in the specificity of the origins and accessibility of technological opportunities, and the ways the firm is able to store and augment its knowledge (Dosi and Winter, 2002, pp. 339–40). Every change in production techniques takes shape by means of adjustments that occur day by day and is the fruit of the history of the firm that adopts it, in the sense that it depends on the preceding sequence of choices as well as the specific model of accumulation of knowledge and experience. The acquisition and adaptation of new competencies and capabilities over time is a function of previously acquired knowledge. In other words, learning is a *firm-specific process* in which the different states represented by successively adopted techniques are not independent but are linked by causal relationships: learning is built on *what has already been learned.*[59]

Key concepts

authority
flexibility
habit
heuristics
hierarchy
innovation
learning (acquistional, creative and organisational learning)
opportunities
performance feedback
routines
selection
sequential aiming
skills
uncertainty

[59] Cohen and Levinthal (1990, pp. 499ff.); Malerba (1992, p. 606); Levinthal (1995, p. 31); Dosi and Malerba (1996a, p. 4); Loasby (1999, p. 58).

6 Conclusion: growth of the firm as the interplay between the three aspects of organisational coordination

T
HE central focus of this concluding chapter is on the growth process of the firm regarded as the result of the interplay between capability, transaction and scale–scope aspects. Management's ability to exploit the advantage provided by organisational coordination of the foregoing three aspects and to limit the negative effects of informational hazards and other counteracting forces are fundamental elements in understanding differences in the revealed performance of firms and their opportunity for growth. However, the firm's performance does not depend solely on managerial abilities, but also on the interplay among the various basic conditions and decision-making mechanisms.

This chapter is structured as follows. Section 6.1 deals with the various forms of the firm's growth: diversification, vertical and horizontal expansion. Section 6.2 focuses on diversification and flexible production. Section 6.3 outlines the cross-linked effects, in the growth process, between development of capabilities, arrangement of transactions and design of the operational scale. So tight-meshed are the links between these three aspects of the organisational coordination of the firm that they can be considered as three faces of the same analytical problem. We shall see that the analysis of the links between these three aspects offers a possible solution to the 'Cournot dilemma' on the incompatibility between increasing returns and competition. The final section 6.4 discusses the strengths and weaknesses that favour and hamper the expansion of the boundaries of business organisations.

6.1 The growth of the firm

Basically, the growth of the firm consists in an expansion of its boundaries, which are defined in terms of its managerial and administrative activities. This process leads to a widening of the organisational coordination of capabilities, transactions and processes.

The development of suitable capabilities is a necessary condition for the continuing growth of the firm. As highlighted by Penrose (1959, pp. 52–3, 66ff.), the process of expansion of the firm is related to the ability to adopt new forms of division of knowledge and to increase the quality of managerial services. The increase in knowledge not only sets in motion a productive opportunity for growth, 'but also contributes to the 'uniqueness' of the opportunity of each individual firm'.[1]

The growth of the firm is essentially a learning process accumulated in carrying out productive and transactional operations. The effects of such learning processes are, first, an expansion of the firm's opportunities and, second, 'the release of excess managerial resources that can be put to use in other, mostly related, business areas. Since the opportunity costs of unused, excess resources are zero', there will be a strong incentive for growth (Foss, 2002, p. 153).

The expansion of the firm may be achieved through two different routes: by acquiring another firm already in the business, or by expanding the original firm itself through investment in new productive capacity, hiring new staff, choosing new suppliers and looking for new distribution channels.

The merger and acquisition (M&A) solution implies advantages and costs. The main advantage is that the firm does not need to develop the capabilities and transaction relationships, as these are obtained along with the acquired firm. The costs are represented by difficulties in harmonising the different organisational and incentive structures. Many mergers have been designed 'to exploit complementarities, which often appear to be readily identifiable from outside, only to founder on the dissimilarities which may not be appreciated until people come face to face with incompatible know-how'. In some

---

[1] In the above passage Penrose highlights the connection between the development of knowledge and the growth of the firm. The origins of the knowledge-based growth theory of the firm may be traced back to Smith (1776) and Marshall (1890). On this, see Loasby (2002a, pp. 45–8). Penrose's methodology and analysis of the growth of the firm are admirably summarised in Best and Garnsey (1999, pp. 187ff.). For an appraisal of the 'Penrosian firm' in the light of recent advances in the economics of organisation, see also Garnsey (1998, pp. 523ff.); Clark (2000, pp. 219–26); Turvani (2001a, pp. 148ff.); Martino (2005, pp. 320ff.); and the various contributions in Pitelis (2002).

cases, the attempt to impose common codes and standards may hamper the creation and development of capabilities, potentially occasioning a decrease in the competitive advantage of the firm and the failure of the merger (Loasby, 1998, p. 174, 1999, p. 95). Costs in harmonising different organisational structures arise from 'conflicts of *corporate cultures*, political battles leading to *influence costs*, or misbehavior of the central office of the acquiring firm, which *reneges on promises* made to managers and employees of the formerly independent subsidiary' (Milgrom and Roberts, 1992, p. 574).

The firm's growth may assume three different forms: vertical integration, horizontal expansion and diversification. The integrated perspective adopted throughout this book can interpret all three of these forms of expansion of firm size.

Vertical integration can be described as expansion by internalising, under common ownership and management, the upward or downward production processes necessary for the production of a given good or service. Vertical integration is based on the development of capabilities used in activities that are connected in the chain of production and therefore need to be coordinated with one other (Foss, 2002, p. 153). Transaction cost considerations contribute to explaining vertical integration, but do not explain the other two important ways in which firms grow, namely, horizontal expansion and diversification.

Horizontal expansion is the result of increasing the size of a production process in order to produce a larger quantity of a given good or service. This involves a change in the dimension of scale that usually brings about a reorganisation of division of labour and knowledge and, as a consequence, a change in the quality of inputs and in individual abilities.

Diversification, which will be addressed in section 6.2, consists in an expansion of the size of the firm through the production of new goods or services.[2]

6.2 Diversification and flexible production

Diversification usually takes place in related business areas or towards areas in which the firm's capabilities or resources acquired in the past

---

[2] On diversification as essential elements of Edith Penrose's and Robin Marris' theories, see the comment by Marris himself (2002, p. 72). See also Dosi and Marengo (2000, p. 81).

imply a competitive advantage in carrying out these new activities. Firms usually expand their scope following the development of capabilities in similar activities that need analogous abilities or complementary components or equipment. Similar or complementary activities may best be performed under unified governance (Richardson 1972, pp. 139–40; Chandler, 1992, p. 83; Foss, 2002, p. 160). Alfred Chandler's historical analysis shows that the 'ability of large established firms . . . to enter *related product markets* helps to explain a significant change in the ways in which major new industries are coming to be created' (emphasis added).[3]

The instability of demand, the saturation of numerous markets and rising competitive pressures call for diversification that allows economies of scope or joint costs. The exploitation of economies of scope is favoured by the implementation of IT in production processes because it allows greater flexibility. Moreover, IT tends to link economies of scope to economies of scale. This leads to the spread of a new model of industrial organisation for firms and markets: large-scale flexible production. Thus, 'online' linkages between markets and producers, and flexible technology, allow 'custom-made' production in large establishments.[4]

However, there is no unequivocal relationship between the pursuit of greater flexibility and the size of production units or firms. In some cases, new technology allows a high degree of flexibility in large-scale production, while in other cases it encourages the economic potential of small firms or production units. This results in the presence of a variety of technical and organisational structures in different industries. Moreover, the 'locality of learning' and the 'opaqueness' of the environment imply the persistence of different organisational forms and size among firms, and the coexistence of diverse hybrid arrangements operating in the same sector of activity (Coriat and Dosi, 1998, p. 112; Ménard, 2004h, pp. 369–70).

---

[3] Chandler (1992, p. 96) noticed, by contrast, that unrelated diversification tended quite often to fail 'in maintaining long-term financial performance' because companies that move beyond the barriers created by their 'learned capabilities' could not capture 'economies of scale and scope to obtain lower unit costs'. They also encountered 'high barriers to entry erected by the first movers in the unrelated industries' (Chandler, 2003: chapter 1, pp. 10, 13–16, *passim*).

[4] Perez (1985, p. 461 n. 23). On flexibility, see Morroni (1991, 1992: chapter 12).

In spite of the significant economies of scale that characterise mass production, so highly prized is individual crafting that in many activities handicrafts have never been completely supplanted by cheaper industrial production, but have survived alongside it. Just as traditional artisan production was not ousted by the rise of mass production in the twentieth century, it seems likely that flexible industrial production (on a large or small scale) will not mean a complete decline in mass production. Depending on the sector of activity and the economic environment, large-scale flexible production may coexist not only with mass production, but also with other forms of production and market organisation, such as small-scale flexible industrial production, industrial production based on rigid technologies with flexible organisational systems and traditional artisan production.[5]

The presence of diverse types of firms within the same sector of activity may derive from heterogeneity in customer preferences that express a differentiated demand with regard to the output qualities, flexibility, learning processes and pre- and after-sales assistance.[6] The product of a large mass-production firm is very different, and meets quite different needs, compared to the analogous product supplied by a craftsman or by large-scale industrial flexible production. Distinct methods of production within specific organisation systems imply not only dissimilar final products, but also diverse auxiliary services, such as co-development of the characteristics of the goods and training in the use of the goods, etc. In a given sector the coexistence of several firms of contrasting sizes is not a necessary consequence of the absence of significant economies of scale. It may instead arise from the specific benefits inherent in the small scale of production, which allows a rather different relationship between manufacturers and customers in terms of contractual advantages, flexibility and learning opportunities.

The degree of diversification, the size distribution of firms and the possible predominance of one form of production over another in a geographical area or sector of activity depends on the interaction

---

[5] The macroeconomic effects of the predominance of one form of production over another on economic growth have generally been neglected in economic literature. One of the few noticeable exceptions is Nell's (1988: chapters 4, 5, 1996, pp. 394–5) analysis of the various types of adjustment mechanisms in prices and quantities corresponding to different forms of production.

[6] On the role of heterogeneity of demand and its effect on the industrial structure, see Bonoccorsi and Giuri (2003, pp. 59, 75ff.).

among the three aspects of the firm's organisational coordination, which in turn are affected by basic conditions, demand structure and the firms' decision-making mechanisms. Among these numerous elements, there is no one-way causal flow from basic conditions to firms' performances; on the contrary, all these elements are mutually interdependent.

6.3 Cross-linked effects in the growth of the firm

This section investigates the numerous links between the three aspects of organisational coordination, seeking to understand how they influence the growth of the firm. It develops further some arguments only sketched at the end of chapter 3 when we considered the basic conditions by virtue of which the three aspects of the organisational coordination of the firm assume a crucial and interactive role. We have seen that the interaction between the development of capabilities, arrangement of transactions and design of the operational scale is relevant in presence of radical uncertainty, indivisibility and complementarity of some production elements, limited transmittability or tradability of some bits of information or units of knowledge, low cost of replication of some bits of information and units of knowledge and the existence of super-fixed costs associated with the production of information and knowledge. We will now examine the main cross-linked effects that can arise between these three aspects of the organisational coordination of the firm whenever the above conditions prevail. In this context, let us consider, respectively, the following relationships: (a) capabilities–learning and scale–scope, (b) capabilities–learning and transactions–internalisation, and (c) transactions–internalisation and scale–scope.

Capabilities–learning and scale–scope

Productive knowledge is closely linked to the *dimension of scale* of production processes that results from a given organisational setting. Economies of scale imply the firm's capabilities and learned competencies necessary to exploit the properties of indivisible and complementary production elements and processes. These capabilities have 'resulted from solving problems of scaling up the processes of production'.[7] Put differently, for each given dimension of scale achieved and technique that can be chosen by the production unit, there are different stages of the development of abilities facilitating the use of specific machines and equipment.

Cognitive and operational division of labour is limited by the scale of the production process. Increasing scale implies further division of labour that entails a qualitative modification not only in some equipment, but also in the abilities and skills of some members of the firm, according to the new tasks linked to the changed organisational structure. In brief, increasing division of labour is a form of organisational innovation that involves different individual abilities and calls for new learning processes (see figure 6.1).[8] Moreover, a rise in dimension of scale allows an increase in the division of knowledge that brings about managerial economies of scale.

In producing specific goods, firms may develop capabilities that turn out to be useful for supplying new commodities in complementary technology. Re-utilisation of the same capabilities across time and space implies an opportunity to overcome the trade-off between economies of scale and economies of scope.

It thus becomes clear that there is a two-way relationship between scale–scope and capabilities considerations. On the one hand, the actual operational scale depends on technical and organisational knowledge that makes it possible to take advantage of the particular properties of production elements and processes. On the other, the increasing dimension of the scale of a firm's operations favours new organisational settings that involve a new division of knowledge and the development of new capabilities. These cross-linked effects show the strong relationship between organisation, knowledge and efficiency: different organisational modes associated with specific technical knowledge bring about dissimilar levels of efficiency.

---

[7] Chandler (1992, p. 84). In his economic and business history investigation, Chandler (1992, pp. 81, 99) describes the links between economies of scale and scope and the ways in which organisational learned competencies evolve in order to exploit the potential of such economies. On the relationship between specialised knowledge and economies of scale in direction and knowledge acquisition, see Demsetz (1995, pp. 11, 31–2).

[8] Turvani (2001a, p. 150). As noted by Robinson (1952, p. 54), a 'change in methods of production in a given state of knowledge is, strictly speaking, a contradiction in terms' (quoted in Lachmann, 1978, p. 221); see also Robinson

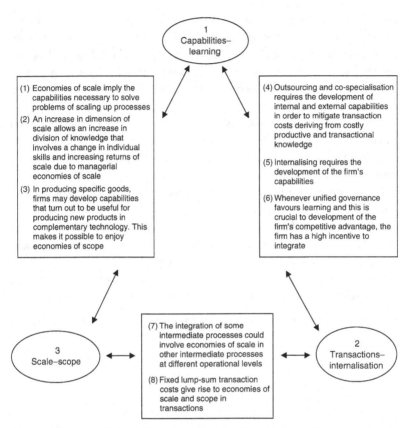

Figure 6.1. Cross-linked effects between the three aspects of organisational coordination.

Capabilities–learning and transactions–internalisation

Capability and transaction considerations turn out to be complementary if we recognise that *both* production *and* transaction processes involve an

(1980, pp. 220–1). In fact, 'the only techniques which may appropriately be considered 'perfectly known' to the firm are those that [it] is actually performing, and has been performing repetitively . . . [T]he firm gradually 'learns' a new method of production' (Winter, 1967, p. 11). On the link between the expansion of the firm, qualitative transformations of inputs and knowledge processes, see also Penrose (1959, p. 55, 1995, p. xiii); Georgescu-Roegen (1971, p. 244, 1986, p. 261); Harcourt and Kenyon (1976, pp. 111–12); Chandler (1992, pp. 81, 99); Morroni (1992, pp. 32–6, 44–7, 1999, pp. 195–6).

essential knowledge dimension.[9] A specific function of the entrepreneur–manager is to ascertain which distinctive abilities and competencies should be developed within the firm and which should instead be developed outside. This is linked to decisions about which activities to conduct internally and which to contract out. These decisions are then fundamentally HR decisions.[10]

Internalising technologically separable processes through vertical integration involves in-house learning processes aimed at developing the productive and technical knowledge necessary to perform the internalised processes.

In the presence of dispersed, heterogeneous and tacit knowledge, collaboration and co-specialisation among complementary producers entails costs that derive from expensive productive and transactional knowledge. On the other hand, collaboration needs the co-development of capabilities to reduce possible misunderstandings.

Outsourcing requires specific learning processes. In particular, outsourcing involves the development of:

(a) *internal capabilities*, in order to bargain, design suitable contracts, control quality and enforce contracts
(b) *external capabilities*, in order to educate suppliers, potential licencees and franchisees.[11]

---

[9] Williamson (1999b, p. 49) regards competencies-based and transaction-based approaches as both rival and complementary. Complementarities between the capabilities and transaction considerations are indicated, for example, in Dosi (1994, p. 231); Argyres (1996, pp. 129ff.); Spiller and Zelner (1997, pp. 561ff.); Dosi and Teece (1998, pp. 281ff.); Baron and Kreps (1999, p. 9); Langlois and Foss (1999, pp. 5, 14–17); Silverman (1999, p. 1123, 2002, p. 483); Dosi and Marengo (2000, p. 90); Brusoni, Prencipe and Pavitt (2001, pp. 597ff.); Heiman and Nickerson (2002, pp. 97ff.); Cohendet and Llerena (2002, pp. 2ff.); Madhok (2002); Dosi, Faillo and Marengo (2003, pp. 1ff.); Antonelli (2003, pp. 4ff.); Bonaccorsi and Giuri (2003, pp. 84–5); Hodgson and Knudsen (2003, pp. 1ff.); Nooteboom (2003, pp. 3 ff.); Hodgson (2004a, pp. 401ff.); Love and Roper (2005, pp. 33–4). Ménard (2004h, pp. 354); In a recent paper Jacobides and Winter (2004, pp. 3 ff.) persuasively argue that the co-evolution of transaction costs and capabilities is essential in shaping vertical scope over time.

[10] Chandler (1992, pp. 88–9) and Loasby (1994, p. 301) have highlighted the primary role of immaterial resources, such as human assets, in explaining the boundaries of the firm.

[11] Loasby (1994, p. 301); Foss and Eriksen (1995, pp. 44ff.); Baron and Kreps (1999, p. 9); and Foss (2002, pp. 160–1).

In multitechnology firms that rely on outsourcing, internal capabilities stretch beyond the boundaries of the firms' in-house production so that staff can relate to suppliers of equipment, knowledge and components (Brusoni, Prencipe and Pavitt, 2001, p. 598). Evidence from applied studies on franchise systems and durable interfirm collaboration among Japanese automakers, firms that produce aircraft engines and firms in electronics, food and biotechnology industries has shown the significant level of investments in specific human assets. Such investments are designed partly with the aim of enhancing the learning processes needed to master the different technologies adopted in specialised sub-units of the firms, but also for the purpose of training the staff members who have to arrange external relationships and have to command multiple technologies adopted by partners who produce various components or supply services.[12]

The consideration of cognitive matters offers an insight into the different reasons underlying vertical integration or safeguards in complementary relationships among partners. For instance, co-specialisation represents an idiosyncratic investment exposed to possible moral hazards, or more simply the transfer of knowledge possessed by some partners toward various competitors. In order to capture all the benefits that accrue from the development of productive knowledge and keep relevant information inside the firm, it may be in the firm's interest to hire individuals 'on a more permanent basis rather than secure the use of their services through a contract'.[13] Alternatively, in other circumstances, vertical integration and the abandonment of contracts mediated by the market may instead be motivated by the difficulty of developing suppliers' knowledge. For example, when Ford adopted the moving assembly line, in accordance with Tayloristic labour organisation, the main problem, according to a cognitive perspective, 'was . . . the difficulty of changing the suppliers' conception of their own business, and persuading them of the obsolescence of many of their existing capabilities' (Loasby, 1999, p. 97). The characteristics of capabilities possessed by firms operating in different

---

[12] Ménard (2004h, p. 356), for empirical evidence on this, see, for instance: Powell (1996); Prencipe (1997), Gambardella and Torrisi (1998), Mowrey, Oxley and Silverman (1998); Tunzelmann (1998), Lafontaine and Shaw (1999), Brusoni, Prencipe and Pavitt (2001, pp. 597–8), Takeishi (2001, pp. 403ff.).

[13] Niman (2004, p. 278). See also Heiman and Nickerson (2002, pp. 97ff.) on the contracting hazards involved in transfers of tacit and complex knowledge.

intermediate phases of the productive *filière* (or cluster) influence the effects of transaction costs on the level of integration. As argued by Grant (1996, pp. 119–20), 'if markets . . . transfer knowledge inefficiently. . ., vertically adjacent stages of production A and B will be integrated within the same firm if production at stage B requires access to the knowledge utilised in stage A'.[14] If capabilities are highly correlated along the productive *filière*, then a reduction of transaction costs will not lead to substantial dis-integration. In contrast, if capabilities are weakly correlated along the value chain, a reduction of transaction costs will lead to substantial dis-integration (Jacobides and Winter, 2004, pp. 29, 38).

On the other hand, transaction costs mould the trajectories of capability development (Jacobides and Winter, 2004, *ibid.*). Low transaction costs may favour external specialisation in single activities and social division of labour, while high transaction costs may induce the development of capabilities within the firm. But high transaction costs do not always imply a unified ownership. In some circumstances, organisational coordination of learning processes under forms of collaboration among firms may be more suitable than vertical integration. For instance, even in the presence of high transaction costs, the attempt to integrate complementary activities that are not truly similar, inasmuch as they are based on distinct technologies and may require 'different styles of management', 'is likely to produce lower quality or higher costs, or both' (Loasby, 1994, p. 299). In this case, a possible response to high transaction costs might be forms of collaboration among firms rather than unified ownership.

Organisational coordination not only makes it possible to avoid transaction costs and therefore 'avoid a negative', but it also provides the advantage over market relationships of enhancing the generation of new capabilities and can thus 'create a positive'. Whenever learning works better in a unified organisation than in two autonomous firms and whenever this is also essential for the development of capabilities on which the firm's competitive advantage is grounded, then a strong incentive for integration arises. Conversely, whenever learning works worse in a unified organisation than in two autonomous firms, there is an incentive toward keeping the firms autonomous. In other words, organisational coordination or dis-integration may prevail according to

[14] See also Demsetz (1988a, pp. 295ff.).

the governance structure that fosters learning and the creation of capabilities.

In conclusion, when asymmetric information and heterogeneous knowledge concerns not only transactions, but also production activities then, on the one hand, technology cannot be considered constant across organisational modes and, on the other, transaction costs and capability considerations can be seen as largely complementary.

Transactions–internalisation and scale–scope

Finally, consider the cross-linked effects between transactions and scale.[15] Transaction–internalisation and scale–scope considerations are related in many ways.

Firstly, when high transaction costs trigger the integration of technologically separable processes through unified ownership, they lead to a reorganisation of production that usually involves economies of scale and scope in other intermediate processes at different operational levels. For instance, an integration of manufacturing processes may lead to economies of scale and scope in managerial and administrative processes that are characterised by increasing returns due to the specific attributes of information and knowledge.

Secondly, transaction costs imply indivisibilities because they are linked to information problems and are therefore largely independent of the volume of goods and services exchanged. Fixed lump-sum transaction costs give rise to economies of scale and scope, and foster increasing dimension.

The relationship between size, total average cost and the quality of output

The boundaries of the firm depend on the relationship between size of the firm, total average costs and the quality of output. Total average costs are the sum of production and transaction costs, both of which are determined by organisation and technology. Firms pursue efficiency by reducing both production and transaction costs through

[15] Nooteboom (1993, pp. 283ff., 2003, p. 5); Hart (1995a, pp. 50–1); Lyons (1995, pp. 431ff.); Antonelli (2003, p. 6); Bonaccorsi and Giuri (2003, pp. 70–9, 84–7); Bertolini and Giovannetti (2003, pp. 1ff.); Lindbeck and Snower (2004) have jointly analysed transaction and scale–scope aspects.

modifications in the organisation of internal production and external relationships with suppliers. Production costs and transaction costs exert a reciprocal influence, and different organisational arrangements have contrasting effects on the various components of the total average cost and the properties that contribute to the final quality of the output. Therefore what matters is the final overall effect of different possible organisational arrangements among complementary activities on efficiency and efficacy.[16]

With asymmetric information and heterogeneous knowledge, different firms do not bear the same production costs for the same kind of activity. Moreover, under radical uncertainty, firms lack the necessary forecasting abilities to identify the optimum governance structure.[17] Nevertheless, they can identify and design, at each step, a *better* governance structure, in terms of total average costs and quality of the output, according to the changing environmental conditions.

Firms are likely to survive and grow when the net benefits, in terms of efficiency and efficacy, are greater than the net benefits of using the market (Hodgson and Knudsen, 2003, p. 11). Integration of processes within a firm is generally advantageous in the presence of high transaction costs, substantial managerial economies and low specialisation economies. However, sometimes high managerial economies and low specialisation economies may encourage organisational integration even in the presence of low transaction costs. On the other hand, high transaction costs and low specialisation economies may lead to substantial organisational integration even in the presence of scant managerial economies. When learning effects augment firm-specific capabilities, integration may be profitable even if market-based transaction costs are zero.[18] Finally, if specialisation brings about a sufficiently low cost

---

[16] Loasby (1998, p. 175); Jacobides and Winter (2004, p. 3). On the impossibility of assessing production and transaction costs separately, see also Milgrom and Roberts (1992, pp. 33–4); Langlois (1998, p. 10); Langlois and Foss (1999, pp. 6–10).

[17] On the insuperable difficulty of singling out an optimum governance structure under 'truly bounded rationality', see Hodgson (1993a, pp. 85–6) and Bianchi (1995, p. 187).

[18] This point has been exhaustively illustrated in Hodgson and Knudsen (2003, pp. 2–3), who show that, in some specific circumstances, dynamic learning effects may be sufficient to explain the existence of the firm. Their description provides a further reason in addition to the original explanation offered by transaction cost economics.

of production for specialised suppliers, the firm could outsource its inputs from an external supplier even if there were high transaction costs.

On the other hand, as previously noted, the need to coordinate the different productive capacities of the various fund elements does not necessarily involve an increase in size of the firm or production unit. If the production processes can be divided into different intermediate stages, a high volume of production may be obtained either by a larger firm or by an increased number of specialised firms belonging to an organisation of firms.[19] This demonstrates that the organisational outcome cannot be based solely on technical conditions, but involves entrepreneurial choices affected also by capability and transaction considerations according to the specific characteristics of basic conditions and internal decision-making mechanisms. As we shall see in greater detail in the next sub-section, the growth of the firm is not a necessary consequence of a single element.

Cournot's dilemma and the interaction among the three aspects of organisational coordination

In applied studies, lack of consideration of the joint effects of all three aspects of the organisational coordination of the firm (capabilities–learning, transactions–internalisation or scale–scope) may generate controversial results. Focusing exclusively on one of these three aspects may hamper a precise evaluation of the role of the aspect considered because its effects may be distorted by the hidden action of the other two interacting aspects excluded from the empirical analysis.

Empirical evidence from an interesting applied study on aircraft production (Bonaccorsi and Giuri, 2003) can clarify this point. This study shows that both engine suppliers and airframe manufacturers enjoy significant economies of scale in manufacturing, R&D and marketing activities originating from indivisibility and complementarity effects at the human capital and technical infrastructure level. Yet in spite of the fact that both sectors share the same conditions for

---

[19] On this alternative, see Becattini (1979, p. 131), who quotes Marshall's (1975a, pp. 195–7) statement that 'the advantages of production on a large scale can in general be as well attained by the aggregation of a large number of small masters into one district as by the erection of a few large works'.

economies of scale, they exhibit very different market structures. The production of commercial jet engines is characterised by 'intense competition, a low level of concentration and strong instability of market shares', while aircraft production has witnessed 'a tremendous process of concentration' (Bonaccorsi and Giuri, 2003, pp. 52, 74). Therefore, the effect of economies of scale on market structure appears to be unimportant in the jet engine sector, but significant in the airframe sector.

Why does the presence of internal economies of scale not lead to a strong concentration or a monopoly in jet engine production? On the mere basis of scale considerations, we cannot answer this question. In other words, by focusing exclusively on the phenomenon of economies of scale, we cannot understand what in this sector prevents the occurrence of a shake-out pattern in which a large incumbent would be in a position to exploit economies of scale and thus to dominate the industry. In order to explain this divergent pattern between engine suppliers and aircraft manufacturers, the analysis must be broadened by also considering aspects linked to the development of technological knowledge and to transactions that take place within vertical relations among producers. The low concentration level in the production of jet engines is explained in terms of the multiple-sourcing strategy adopted by large aircraft manufacturers, who have an interest in entering into transactional relations with many engine suppliers so as to exploit different technical capabilities. In this case, supplier heterogeneity enhances the learning processes that strengthen the competitive advantage of the aircraft manufacturer, because each customer relation is a source of specific learning. Aircraft manufacturers 'do not just demand products, but rather co-develop them' with suppliers, by looking for new solutions that integrate engine and airframe (Bonaccorsi and Giuri, 2003, pp. 79, 84).

The above example demonstrates that economies of scale considerations are important but not sufficient to explain the size of the firm and the market structure: knowledge and transaction cost considerations may also be essential. This indicates a possible solution to the long-standing conundrum, known as 'Cournot's dilemma', regarding the incompatibility between competition and internal economies of scale. Marshall observed that 'some, among whom Cournot himself is to be counted', have considered 'internal economies . . . apparently without noticing that their premises lead inevitably to the conclusion that, whatever firm first gets a good start will obtain a monopoly of the whole business of its trade'.[20] In other words, since internal economies of scale involve a reduction in average total cost as the size of *a single firm* increases, the growth of a firm implies a rise in its efficiency that may lead this firm to dominate the entire market, driving all others out of a given sector. Therefore, the tendency toward monopoly conditions seems inevitable. Nevertheless, empirical evidence shows that in numerous sectors of activity there is competition among firms of different sizes in spite of the presence of significant internal economies of scale.[21] At the end of the 1970s, Arrow (1979, p. 156) observed that 'this dilemma has been thoroughly discussed; it has not been thoroughly resolved'.

A perspective that considers not only economies of scale *per se*, but also the knowledge–development and transaction–arrangement dimensions may provide a solution to the contradiction between empirical evidence and Cournot's dilemma regarding the incompatibility between internal economies of scale and competition.[22] This integrated perspective offers an explanation which reconciles internal economies of scale with competition, clarifying why internal economies do not necessarily lead to a natural monopoly in many sectors of activity (as in the example of jet engine production). In fact, in many instances, transactional relationships and the development of technical

---

[20] Marshall (1890, pp. 378, 380 n. 1); cf. Cournot (1838, pp. 96ff.). Marshall attempted to reconcile the problem of the incompatibility between competition and increasing returns by abandoning the static analysis in favour of a dynamic analysis of the life cycle of the representative firm in which knowledge, skill and entrepreneural inventiveness play an important role. Pigou (1913, pp. 21–2) tried to circumvent such a dilemma by referring to the role of external economies that represent the only possible cause of increasing returns which is compatible with the static analysis of competitive equilibrium. In the 1920s, Marshall's analysis and subsequent developments of microeconomic theory by Pigou and others became the object of strong criticism and an intense debate known as the 'cost controversy' (see, for instance, the discussion and references in Prendergast, 1992, pp. 447ff.; Hart, 1996, pp. 353ff.; Marchionatti, 2001, pp. 43ff., 2003, pp. 49ff.; Raffaelli, 2003, pp. 113–14). As far as this controversy is considered, interesting analytical similarities between the contributions of Knight (1921b, 1924, 1925) and Sraffa (1925, 1926) to this debate have been highlighted in Marchionatti (2003, pp. 65ff.).

[21] On this see Pratten (1988) and Martin (2003), who provide very useful surveys on empirical findings concerning economies of scale in various industries.

[22] Knowledge-based considerations have been recently highlighted by Niman (2004, pp. 282–3) as a possible solution of Cournot's dilemma.

knowledge may offer advantages which offset those provided by a large dimension of scale even if the benefits in terms of economies of scale could be substantial. In this respect, the analysis of the connections between the three aspects of organisational coordination seems to offer a rich agenda and fruitful perspectives for future theoretical and empirical research.

6.4 Strengths and weaknesses

This concluding section of the book addresses some important factors that mould the growth and size of the firm. *Potential advantages* deriving from the cross-linked effects between development of capabilities, arrangement of transactions and design of the operational scale may be cancelled out by several external and internal *counteracting forces* and *weaknesses* which limit the firm's growth – or, in more extreme cases, lead to its bankruptcy. These counteracting forces include:

(i) institutional and market constraints
(ii) limited market dimension or downward-sloping demand curve, fixed supply of inputs and difficulties in raising capital that affect in particular small and new firms
(iii) errors of strategy due to cognitive inertia and myopia
(iv) rising organisational costs.

Institutional and market conditions have been discussed at length in chapter 1. Therefore, it suffices here perhaps to recall the three main environmental constraints on growth: inefficient institutional context, credit rationing policies and corruption.

As far as point (ii) is concerned, a downward-sloping demand curve, fixed supply of inputs, or difficulties in raising capital may limit or impede the expansion of the firm. However, the problem of a downward-sloping demand curve for existing products may be overcome by diversifying production. As Penrose (1995, pp. xiii, xvii) reminds us, there is no reason why the 'firm should see its prospect of growth, its productive opportunities, in terms of its existing products only'. A firm may expand through continuous diversification. In other words, a firm can use its knowledge and experience in developing new markets and in producing new commodities. In facing unfavourable demand conditions for their products, some firms can expand the total output by differentiating, while others may not be able to make the necessary changes in the range of products. In the latter case, 'failure to grow is often incorrectly attributed to demand conditions rather than to the limited nature of entrepreneurial resources' (Penrose, 1995, *ibid*.).

Analogously, difficulty in raising capital 'may often be just as well attributed to a lack of appropriate entrepreneurial services, in the sense that a different entrepreneur in the same circumstances might well achieve different results' (Penrose, 1959, p. 37).

If the firm is not confined to a particular location by the supply of resources or by local demand, limits to the local supply of inputs may be overcome by establishing new production units in other locations characterised by the abundance of required inputs (Penrose, 1959, p. 44).

In setting the firm's strategy, firms are subject to misperception, errors in identifying aims and imprecision in performance measuring that may lead to unnecessary changes or prevent timely response to problems.[23] The management may make erroneous decisions because of various forms of cognitive inertia and myopia. Ignoring some variables and applying routinised operating procedures greatly simplifies decision-making, but implies the possibility that the routines adopted could turn out to be inefficient because they may prove to have overstepped their domain of validity. Erroneous decisions may be due to the tendency to adopt routinised operating procedures that have proved efficacious in the past, extending them 'beyond their original domain' in which they had been tested.[24]

As far as cognitive myopia is concerned, Levinthal and March (1993, p. 95ff.) distinguish among temporal, spatial and failure myopia, as follows.

(a) *Temporal myopia* is the tendency of an organisation to privilege the short run and to disregard the distant future (e.g. the tendency to exploit old competencies instead of investing in development of new knowledge).

---

[23] Greve (2003, pp. 65–6, 152). On misperception, see Langlois (1997, pp. 76ff.) who brings evidence from the history of the computer industry.

[24] Egidi (2002, pp. 109–10). The experimental results offered by Egidi and Narduzzo (1997, pp. 678ff.) support this view.

(b) *Spatial myopia* consists in focusing on the close neighbourhood and ignoring changes in environmental conditions. 'Learning gives advantage to results in the spatial neighbourhood of current action' (Levinthal and March, 1993, p. 103). When environmental conditions change, as inevitably they do, the matches between organisations well adapted to their previous environments and the new environments are at risk.

(c) *Failure myopia* may spring from neglecting the possibility of failure and overestimating the possibility of success. 'Individuals are more likely to attribute their success to ability and their failure to luck' (Levinthal and March, 1993, p. 105). As a result, successful people have confidence in their ability and tend to underestimate difficulties. Since organisations select successful people to managerial positions, top management may risk overlooking the possibility of failure. Overconfidence may lead to disaster (Levinthal and March, 1993, p. 109).

These different forms of cognitive inertia and myopia may bring about difficulties in finding the right balance between exploitation of available knowledge, abilities and skills (i.e. the pursuit of higher efficiency), and exploration of new possibilities and alternatives. Sometimes firms persist in the adoption of procedures that have been successful in the past and are unable to innovate according to the evolution of technologies and markets. This kind of cognitive inertia has been called the 'success trap'.[25]

Rising organisational costs may have different causes: (i) difficulty in allocating rights and responsibilities; (ii) difficulty in vertical communication within organisations; (iii) difficulty in enlisting organisational loyalty, establishing rewards and focusing incentives that attenuate

---

[25] March (1991, pp. 71ff.) and Levinthal and March (1993, p. 106). On different forms of inertia and myopia, see also Dosi and Marengo (1994, pp. 226, 231); Rumelt (1995, pp. 106ff.); Egidi (2002, p. 109). Fransman (1994, pp. 751ff.) analyses the IBM case as an example of myopia deriving from loosely coupled information and knowledge. Fransman shows that during the 1980s in IBM there was a growing disjuncture between the information possessed by the company concerning the increasing performance of microprocessors and substitutability of smaller computers and mainframes, and the company's knowledge–belief regarding the ability of the mainframe to sustain its profitability and growth.

internal opportunism and conflicts of interest; and (iv) difficulty in accepting the modifications of the organisational set-up that are associated with the firm's growth process. These difficulties are made even worse in organisational contexts in which preferences are inconsistent and ill defined, technology is unclear (i.e. the organisation processes are not understood by its members) and the participation of decision-makers is fluid in the sense that it 'changes capriciously', as in the 'garbage can model of organizational choice' by Cohen, March and Olsen (1972, pp. 1ff.).

First, unclear allocation of rights and responsibilities makes decision-making mechanisms inefficient. Secondly, the firm's growth can imply that top management may lose touch with events affecting the decisions. This causes problems in vertical communication within organisations, leading to decreased efficiency and efficacy, and resulting at times in *quid pro quos* between managers and subordinates. Thirdly, difficulty in establishing rewards and focusing incentives may involve the possibility of shirking, high cost of coordination, monitoring and control, influence activities, collusion, subverted inspections, parochial interests and unimplemented decisions. If increasing coordination and control difficulties are encountered due to mounting organisational complexity, then it may prove necessary for a rising share of the labour force to be dedicated to administration, engendering growing burdens of bureaucracy as a firm grows larger.[26] Finally, the firm's growth process is generally characterised by changes that aim to strengthen its competitive position. These changes usually involve transformations in division of labour and knowledge, in the organisational set-up and in the power structure, which may meet with resistance on the part of some members of the firm who are unwilling to accept or strongly oppose any modification in the existing equilibria. For instance, the owner of the physical assets or the top managers may have no interest in the growth of the firm if this implies the development of capabilities that they are unable to control and hence an alteration of power relationships.

---

[26] Useful introductions to the large and important body of literature dedicated to these typical inefficiencies inside organisations are: Hart (1989, pp. 131ff.); Holmström and Tirole (1989, pp. 63ff.); Putterman and Kroszner (1996a, pp. 1ff.); Gibbons (2000, pp. 1ff., 2003, pp. 753ff.); Baker, Gibbons and Murphy (2002, pp. 39ff.).

All these cases, which lead to rising organisational costs, derive from some sort of management incapability or internal weaknesses. In standard neoclassical long-run analysis, limited organisational capacity is traditionally seen as a cause of decreasing returns and therefore as the element that determines the optimum size of the firm. However, there are neither solid theoretical reasons nor empirical evidence to assume limited organisational capacity or the inevitable weakening of appropriate incentives that make organisational costs slope upward. From a theoretical point of view, a firm can, in fact, hire and employ new resources to expand to any ultimate size and can increase its organisational capacity by adopting the Smithian division of labour, allocating many managerial and administrative tasks to specialist employees. With increasing size, its managerial and administrative functions can undergo reorganisation in order to maintain – or, indeed, increase – efficiency and efficacy. Moreover, firms may craft appropriate (monetary and non-monetary) incentives to motivate internal communication, learning processes and loyalty.

There is ample evidence of the numerous ways adopted by firms to counter the rising organisational costs that impede their growth. The presence of giant firms, which operate in many crucial industries (such as the automotive industry, aviation, banking, IT, large retailers, department stores, mail order houses, insurance, pharmaceuticals, clothing, etc.) with a number of employees which, in certain cases, is of the order of hundreds of thousands of people, constitutes irrefutable evidence of this ability to counteract rising organisational costs. Recent concentration processes in many sectors of activity confirm, beyond any doubt, the observations by Penrose (1959, p. 261) and Chandler (1992, pp. 80–3, 90–8), in whose opinion there is no proof that diseconomies of scale will inevitably arise at some point of the firm's growth and that large or giant firms will eventually become inefficient.[27] Concentration processes and the very rapid growth of business organisations in the IT sector since the 1980s demonstrate that the advantages provided by organisational coordination may contribute to overcoming various possible counteracting forces.

---

[27] The links between Penrosian analysis and Chandler's historical investigation and conceptualisation are indeed numerous. Suffice it to mention Penrose (1959) and Chandler (1961). Cf. Fransman (1994, pp. 742, 748); Best and Garnsey (1999, p. 200).

An essential point is that difficulty in adapting organisational capacity may affect the magnitude of the firm's growth rate at any moment, but does not entail a limit on the expansion of its size beyond a certain point. Such a constraint on the rate of growth is due to the necessity of 'bedding down' and training new managers who have to carry out the various activities required for growth.[28] Accordingly, 'so-called managerial diseconomies *must* eventually come into play if it is assumed that there is no change in knowledge and hence no change in the quality and type of managerial service'.[29] It follows that the internal countervailing forces to the firm's growth operate only if organisational knowledge is insufficiently developed by the management. It is evident here that the potential for learning processes to take place within the firm leads to the logical impossibility of determining the *optimum size* of the firm and therefore 'destroys the notion of the firm's optimum size'.[30]

In the last analysis, the crucial internal factor that can limit the firm's growth is thus the management's inability to avoid errors of strategy, together with the failure to create the necessary knowledge for exploiting advantages provided by the cross-linked effects of development of capabilities, arrangements of transactions and design of operational scale. Otherwise stated, the long-term competitive strengths and weaknesses of firms reflect their 'learned capabilities as well as those of their competitors from abroad and related industries' (Chandler, 1992, p. 99).

[28] Penrose (1995, p. xii) has put the issues very well:

Managerial resources with experience within the firm are necessary for the efficient absorption of managers from outside the firm. Thus, the availability of 'inherited managers' with such experience limits the amount of expansion that can be planned and undertaken in any period of time . . .

Once a substantial increment of growth is completed, however, the managerial services devoted to it become available for further expansion. There was no obvious and inevitable limit to this process and therefore the limit to its rate of growth would not necessarily limit the ultimate size of the firm . . .

Even growth by acquisition and merger does not escape the constraints imposed by the necessity of using inputs from existing managerial resources to maintain the coherence of the organization.

[29] Penrose (1959, p. 55). This quotation shows that learning on the part of the management team is at the heart of Penrose's theory of the growth of the firm.

[30] Foss (2002, p. 153). On this logical impossibility, see also Marris (2002, pp. 65, 71–2, 75); and Georgescu-Roegen (1964, p. 296); Morroni (1992, pp. 141–2); Penrose (1995, p. xii).

This conclusion introduces an unavoidable subjective element concerning the way in which the firm's management is able to grasp opportunities and contrast counteracting forces. Subjective and discretionary choices by management are influenced by the specific manner in which the different stakeholders' interests are weighed in decisions and by the various basic conditions. Moreover, it shows that the boundaries of the firm cannot be attributed solely to one single cause, but are instead the result of the interplay between negative factors, which are represented by the counteracting forces listed above, and opportunities for growth that derive from the three aspects of the firm's organisational coordination.

The informal nature of the managing of relational agreements and the subjective and discretionary properties of decision-making processes greatly affect the firm's revealed performance, its growth and therefore its boundaries. The members of a business organisation are linked by a network of information exchanges and socio-economic relationships, and interact according to rules that they can often influence. Continued growth is obtained 'through the utilisation and expansion of organizational learning'. The quality of managerial resources and, more generally, of the firm's specific capabilities, are essential in understanding the firm's strategy and changing boundaries.[31] This subjective element of managerial choice moulds the specificity of each firm and yields a large variety of outcomes. The fundamental implication of these considerations is that the firm's efficiency and efficacy, and thus its revealed performance, size and boundaries, have to be regarded as 'time- and path-dependent' phenomena subject to the constantly evolving influence of the multifaceted basic conditions and the different internal decision-making mechanisms.

Key concepts

cognitive myopia (temporal, spatial and failure myopia)
diseconomies of scale
diversification
economies of scope

---

[31] Chandler (1992, pp. 88–9, 92). On firm-specific entrepreneurial knowledge and judgement, see Knight (1921a, pp. 311–12); Penrose (1959: p. 63); Ricketts (1987, pp. 232ff.).

entrepreneurship
flexibility
growth of the firm
horizontal expansion
opportunity cost
vertical integration

Glossary

Italics denote cross-references. Bibliographic references to related literature can be found in the sections of the book indicated in the marginal **Section** column.

Abilities individual abilities consist in *information-process-* **Section 1.4**
ing ability and *theoretical* and *practical knowledge.*
See also *capabilities, competencies, skills.*

Absorptive capacity the faculty to identify, understand, **Section 1.1**
interpret, appraise, assimilate, retain, process and
utilise *information* and *knowledge* from the environment. See also *appropriability.*

Accountability the capacity of an organisation to account **Section 4.2**
for its actions towards interested parties through
transparent procedures.

Acquisitional learning see *learning.*

Adaptability the production of a single commodity is more **Section 3.3**
adaptable the less its average cost varies with the
quantity produced. See also *flexibility.*

Adverse selection may arise when informational asymmet- **Sections 1.1,**
ries and pre-contractual opportunism lead to a **2.3**
selection that is adverse to one party's interest. In
presence of adverse selection markets may be
missing. See also *moral hazard, missing market.*

Advocacy activities consist in advocating, protecting and **Section 2.2**
advancing the legal, human and service rights of a
particular group of citizens with a weak position
(people with disabilities, disadvantaged groups and
so on).

Agency relationship where one party (the 'agent') is required to act on behalf of another (the 'principal'). — Section 1.7

Appropriability of information and knowledge *information* and *knowledge* are appropriable if the holder can capture and protect the economic advantages that derive from possessing them. See also *absorptive capacity*. — Section 1.1

Asset specificity refers to relation-specific durable investments that are undertaken in support of particular *transactions*; the *opportunity cost* of such investments is much lower in best alternative uses. See also *hold-up problem, investment*. — Section 3.2

Asymmetry effect when subjects show risk aversion for gains, risk preference for losses, and weigh losses more heavily. See also *information-processing ability*. — Table 1.4

Authority *power* over individuals or organisations, which is legitimated by *rules*, originating from accepted social relations, or based on influence over opinions. — Sections 1.3, 1.7, 2.1, 5.2

Basic conditions result from the interplay between the environmental conditions that business organisations face and the internal conditions created by business organisations themselves according to external constraints and opportunities. They are mainly constituted by the following interacting and mutually reinforcing factors: (a) characteristics of *information* and *knowledge*, (b) characteristics of techniques and equipment, (c) individual motivations and aims, (d) individual *abilities*, (e) degree of *uncertainty*, (f) structural change and (g) institutional and market conditions. — Section I.3, Chapter 1

Business organisation see *firm*.

Business unit see *production unit*.

Capabilities the firm's abilities to produce and sell specific goods or services that satisfy the potential demand, according to the firm's specialisation and knowledge — Section 3.1

capital. The firm's capabilities are the result of
coordination and accumulation of the individual
abilities possessed by the members of the business
organisation. Capabilities are understood as potentialities that can be triggered in specific contexts. See
also *abilities, competencies, routines, skills.*

Cash flow net income (after payment of fixed interest) plus   Introduction to
depreciation provisions, i.e. the flow of money that   Chapter 3
is available for payment of taxes, dividends or
investment.

Chief executive officer (CEO) the highest-ranking officer of   Section 2.2
a corporation.

Cognitive myopia It is possible to distinguish among three   Section 6.4
types of cognitive myopia:
Failure myopia overconfidence that may lead to neglecting the possibility of failure and to overestimating
the possibility of success.
Spatial myopia focusing on the close neighbourhood of
current action and ignoring changes in environmental conditions.
Temporal myopia the tendency to privilege the short run
and to disregard the distant future.

Cognitive rationality see *rationality.*

Competencies the firm's competencies are organised cap-   Section 3.1
acities of a business organisation to perform
individual activities (for instance, mechanical, chemical, legal or organisational competencies). Competencies are understood as potentialities that can be
triggered in specific contexts. See also *abilities,
capabilities, routines, skills.*

Complementarities interdependencies among *funds*, inter-   Sections 1.2, 1.6
mediate phases of a single production process, dif-
ferent production processes or activities, innovations
or consumption goods. For instance, complementarities among indivisible *funds* determine fixed-
coefficient type of production, complementarities
among different processes lead to *economies of*

scope, while complementarities among various intermediate stages of a given production process give rise to the need to balance the different productive capacities of the various intermediate stages. See also *indivisibility*.

Complete contract see *contract*.

Complex system a complex system is constituted by structural linkages and the interactions of ensembles of different elements exhibiting a collective behaviour that is very different from what might have been expected from simply scaling up the behaviour of the individual units.   Section 1.4

Component a physically distinct portion of the final product that performs a well-defined function and is linked to other components through a set of interfaces defined by the product architecture.   Section 1.2

Conglomerate firm a firm that controls a group of subsidiary companies engaged in a variety of dissimilar and unrelated activities.   Introduction, Section 1.2

Consortia collaboration forms among firms regulating the joint realisation of projects whereby sub-processes are carried out by different firms, usually entitled to a separate gain share. See also *hybrids*.   Section 4.3

Context effect when history and presentation of the decision task influence perception and motivation in decision-making. See also *information-processing ability*.   Table 1.4

Contract a legally enforceable agreement, not necessarily written, between two or more parties.   Section 3.2
  Complete contract an agreement that can be fully verified and legally enforced by a third party (such as a court). See *enforcement power, verifiability*.
  Forward contract although signed today, it indicates a specific future date for delivery and payment.
  Imperfect contract a contract in a situation of costly information and knowledge (weak *uncertainty*).

Incomplete contract a contract in a situation in which it is impossible to specify in the contract all the circumstances that may occur.

Self-enforcing contract a contract is self-enforcing when the benefits exceed the costs of respecting the contract.

Spot contract involves delivery and payment at the instant of signing.

Corporate culture that part of knowledge capital which is common to a substantial portion of the members of the firm in spite of different cognitive maps and interests. It is a set of values, principles, experiences, precedents, expectations and procedures about how things should be done. — Section 3.1

Corporate strategy identifying the basic long-term aims and objectives of a firm, and adopting the course of actions and the allocation of resources necessary to carry out these aims. — Sections 2.1, 2.2, 2.3, 3.1

Corporation a firm that acts as a legal entity separate from its owners who have limited liability for the corporation's debts. — Section 2.1

Corruption dishonestly using decisional *power* or privileged *information* to obtain advantages. It involves a hidden exchange, between two parties, which violates the law or codes of behaviour. — Section 1.7

Co-specialisation resources are co-specialised when specialisation makes them complementary. Co-specialised resources are most productive when used together and lose much of their value if used separately to produce independent products and services. — Sections 3.2, 6.3

Cost the value of the resources needed for an economic operation. See also *opportunity cost, sunk costs*. — Sections 3.2, 3.3

Creative learning see *learning*.

Data derive from the senses, either directly or as reported by others, and consist in various signals that reach the brain from the outside world. See also *information*. — Section 1.1

Decomposable production process a production process is
  decomposable when it is possible to identify
  individual intermediate stages (or sub-processes)
  separable in time and space, and when the product
  of one stage is a commodity utilised as an input in at
  least one other stage.   Section 3.2

Describability the ability to describe accurately and unambiguously in the contract what each party is to do in
  every possible contingency. It requires *forecasting*
  ability. See also *observability, verifiability*.   Section 3.2

Dimension of scale the dimension of scale is expressed by
  the maximum number of processes carried out per
  unit of time by a given *microeconomic unit*. It
  depends on the number of parallel processes and the
  duration of such processes. Therefore, the dimension
  of scale is related both to size and speed. See also
  diseconomies of scale, economies of scale.   Section 3.3

Diseconomies of scale occur when a larger *dimension of*
  scale of a specific *microeconomic unit* leads to a
  higher total average cost of the product obtained.
  See also *economies of scale*.   Section 6.4

Diversification the firm's diversification consists in producing several different goods or services. It usually
  takes place in related business areas or towards areas
  in which the firm's *capabilities* or resources acquired
  in the past imply a competitive advantage in carrying
  out these new activities. See also *growth of the firm,*
  horizontal expansion, vertical integration.   Section 6.2

Economies of scale occur when a larger *dimension of scale*
  of a specific *microeconomic unit* leads to a lower
  total average cost of the product obtained. See also
  diseconomies of scale.   Section 3.3

Economies of scope (or joint costs) there are economies of
  scope if it is less costly to combine the productions of
  two or more commodities than to produce them
  separately. This occurs whenever it is possible to   Sections 3.3, 6.2

use the same component, material, equipment, knowledge and labour service for more than one product line.

Economising increasing benefits and reducing costs. It may take different forms according to the kind and level of *rationality*. See also *optimisation, sequential aiming*. Sections 1.3, 2.4

Enforcement power the ability to oblige the parties either to respect the *contract* or to pay the injured party compensation. See also *self-enforcing contract* under *contract*. Sections 1.2, 1.7, 3.2, 3.4

Enterprise see *firm*.

Entrepreneurship an activity that entails the discovery, or creation, and exploitation of new *opportunities*. See also *innovation, learning*. Sections 3.1, 5.6

Environmental conditions see *basic conditions*.

Equity securities issued by a firm that represent *property rights* (such as stocks or warrants convertible into stocks). Introduction to Chapter 3

Ethical behavioural code a set of *rules* governing an organisation, which are not enforced by legally binding sanctions. Section 1.1

Externalities actions of one party that affect the revenue, the *cost* or the utility of another and that are not mediated through the *market*. Sections 1.1, 1.6, 1.7, 4.3, 5.6

Firm (or business organisation or enterprise) a social *organisation* and a legal entity that produces and sells goods or services by means of a set of human, physical and financial resources coordinated, combined and monitored under an administrative structure. See also *conglomerate firm, corporation*. Introduction, Section I.2

Flexibility in production systems, flexibility is the capacity to change the mix of products according to market evolution (operational flexibility) or to the qualities Sections 3.3, 5.1, 5.2, 5.5, 6.2

of output mix (strategic flexibility). See also *adapt-ability*.

Forecasting   Section 1.5,
    Complete forecasting requires: (i) complete theoretical Table 1.2
knowledge of all possible events; and (ii) complete
information-processing ability to classify, order and
compare all possible events and actual outcomes.
Complete forecasting ability can be divided into
perfect and imperfect forecasting:

    Imperfect forecasting corresponds to weak *uncertainty*
and implies *objective risk* when individuals know the
objective probability distribution of all possible
contingencies or *subjective risk* when they can only
estimate the subjective probability distribution.

    Incomplete forecasting arises when individuals do not
have complete knowledge of the list of all possible
events or lack sufficient information-processing
ability in assessing, classifying and comparing states
or events. Incomplete forecasting implies radical
uncertainty.

    Perfect forecasting implies knowledge of the actual
outcomes among all possible events and thus is
characterised by nil *uncertainty*.

Forward contract see *contract*.

Flows *production elements* that either enter as inputs into Section 1.2
only one production process (e.g. raw materials or
energy) or emerge as outputs from one production
process (e.g. the finished product and waste). See
also *funds, limitational flows*.

Framing effect when choices are dependent on the descrip- Section 1.5,
tion of the decision problem, i.e. on the way Table 1.4
information is provided. See also *information-processing ability*.

Franchising collaboration form regulating the relation- Section 4.3
ship between one firm (the franchisor) and other
firms (the franchisees). The franchisee owns and
runs her firm using the franchisor's brand name and
often buying commodities for resale from the

franchisor. The franchisor collects royalties and fees from franchisee for use of the brand and usually also provides technical assistance, training, advertising, supervision and other services. See also *hybrids*.

Funds production elements that participate in many processes, entering and leaving the process (e.g. a piece of agricultural land, a loom, a computer, a worker). The services provided by funds are measured by time. See also *flows, input, production elements*.   Section 1.2

Growth of the firm an expansion of its boundaries, which are defined in terms of its managerial and administrative activities. The firm's growth may assume three different forms: *diversification, horizontal expansion* and *vertical integration*.   Section 6.1

Habit recurrent pattern on an individual level.   Section 5.3

Heterochronia heterogeneity of time horizons among individuals.   Section 1.3

Heuristics methods of looking for information and solutions relevant to the problem at hand.   Section 5.3

H-form (holding form) type of divisional structure in which a holding financially controls other firms. See also *M-form, U-form*.   Introduction

Hierarchy formalised chain of authority relations.   Section 5.2

Holdings see *H-form*.

Hold-up problem a hold-up problem arises when a party that has to make a relation-specific *investment* is vulnerable to the other party's post-contractual *opportunism*. A hold-up problem might prevent an efficient *transaction* from ever occurring. See also *asset specificity*.   Sections 3.2, 4.3

Horizontal expansion the firm's horizontal expansion consists in an increase in the size of the production process   Section 6.1

of a given good of service. See also *diversification, growth of the firm, vertical integration.*

Hybrids *organisations* composed of legally autonomous entities doing business together and sharing or exchanging technologies, capital, products, and services thanks to long-term contractual relations that do not imply a unified ownership (for instance, *consortia, networks, franchising,* collective trade marks, *joint ventures,* etc.).   Section 4.3

Ideologies shared frameworks of *mental models,* which groups of individuals possess on the basis of their interests.   Section 1.4

Imperfect contract see *contract.*

Incomplete contract see *contract.*

Indivisibility   Section 1.2
Economic indivisibility the impossibility of exchanging and paying for a good in exact correspondence with the quantity used (i.e. economic indivisibility in relation to quantities) and with the time strictly necessary for its use (i.e. economic indivisibility in relation to time).
Indivisibility of production elements a production element is defined as indivisible when it is impossible to divide it for exchange, production or consumption purposes.
Indivisibility of production processes a process is indivisible if it is characterised by a particular size above and below which it cannot take place: in other words, if it is impossible to activate processes that have the same proportions of inputs and outputs, but on a smaller or larger scale.
Technical indivisibility the impossibility of dividing a particular good, once it is exchanged, into amounts usable for production or consumption.

Industrial district (or local production system) cluster of firms taking advantage of proximity to one another in a defined area, using common infrastructures,   Section 1.1

enjoying external economies and sharing similar interdependent *competencies*.

Influence activities the attempt to influence others' deci- Section 1.7
sions. Under conflict of interests, the party holding information may misrepresent, distort, or fail to report the information needed by the decision-maker. Influence activities may take place both inside organisations and beyond them in market and political decision processes (advertising, lobbying, etc.) See also *corruption*.

Information is an organised set of *data*. A bit of information Section 1.1
is an indivisible set of *data*. See also *knowledge*.

Information-processing ability the ability to assess prob- Section 1.4
abilities, receive, store, classify, order, retrieve, enumerate and compare bits of information. See also *asymmetry effect, context effect, framing effect, practical knowledge, reference point effect, status quo effect, theoretical knowledge*.

Inheritance the process of transmission of characteristics Section 5.3
through imitation and learning that ensures the duplication or propagation of selected *routines*. See also *selection* and *variety*.

Innovation recombining resources into a new form. It may Sections 1.4,
involve the introduction of new goods or services, 1.6, 3.1, 5.6
organisational settings, production processes, *markets*, consumption models and raw materials. Innovations give rise to surprise and inconsistency of expectations. See also *entrepreneurship, learning, opportunities, uncertainty*.

Input *production element* that enters into one production Section 1.2
process as a *flow* (e.g. raw materials or energy) or that participates in many processes as a *fund* (e.g. a piece of agricultural land, a loom, a computer, a worker).

Institutions current laws and jurisprudence, as well as Sections 1.7, 4.2
accepted customs, formal and informal *rules, norms*, codes of conduct. Institutions regulate interpersonal

relationships and facilitate coordination. Institutions exist to reduce the costliness of exchanging, protecting rights and enforcing agreements.

Investment is an expenditure of money or utilisation of resources that generates a potential flow of future benefits. See also *asset specificity, hold-up problem*. Section 3.2

Job a formalised job is a set of tasks. For instance, a receptionist's job entails tasks such as answering the phone, giving information, setting up appointments, and acting as a gatekeeper for the organisations. Section 5.6

Joint venture jointly owned and managed *firm* constituted by two or more "mother" firms. See also *hybrids*. Section 4.3

Knowledge beliefs, skills and emotional attitudes. Knowledge derives from the ability to search, select, memorise, structure, compute, embody and use bits of relevant *information* within a cognitive system. A unit of knowledge is a piece of knowledge that cannot be further divided. See also *abilities, information processing ability, practical knowledge, tacit knowledge, theoretical knowledge*. Section 1.1

Learning a change in knowledge or behaviour on the basis of experience. Section 5.6
    Acquisitional learning can be regarded as the discovery of pre-existing information and an updating of theoretical knowledge in the light of incoming data that are given and available.
    Creative learning consists in the generation of new knowledge and opportunities. It involves a problem-formulation and problem-solving process that entails the development of the capacity to unlearn, or learn anew. Creative learning implies the capacity to change the representation of the environment, to interpret and re-elaborate relevant information, create new mental models and imagine alternatives.
    Organisational learning the cumulative process of acquisition of new capabilities developed by the firm and embodied in the output. Organisational learning is driven by the search for a better performance that

will make it possible to increase the competitive advantage.

Limitational flows *flows* that are transformed in strict proportions during the production process (for instance, the yarn in the weaving process).
Section 1.2

Management by objectives (MBO) incentive system under which the employees and their supervisors negotiate the criteria and standard against which an employee's performance will be evaluated.
Section 2.3

Market a social structure in which autonomous parties engage in exchange.
Section I.3, 4.1

Market failures situations in which *markets* fail to achieve efficient allocation. Market failures are due to asymmetric *information* and heterogeneous *knowledge*, *externalities* and *economies of scale*.
Sections I.3, 1.1

Maximisation to find a maximum of the objective function (e.g. the maximum profit or market share) with respect to the choice variable whose values have to be optimised (e.g. the optimum level of output). Maximisation and *optimisation* are so closely connected that in the literature they are often taken as synonymous. See also *minimisation, rationality*.
Section 2.4

Mediation activity the management of conflict of interests between opposing parties by means of information and negotiation activities aiming to arrange agreements that are mutually advantageous.
Sections 2.3, 4.2, 5.2

Mental models representations that individual cognitive systems build to perceive, define and codify the information through which individuals make sense out of the environment, design their problem-solving activity and construct their strategy. See also *theoretical knowledge*.
Section 1.4

M-form (multidivisional form) multidivisional structure within an enterprise coordinated by strategic planning and incentives. See also *H-form, U-form*.
Introduction

Microeconomic unit a firm, a *production unit*, a plant or a Section 3.3
piece of equipment.

Minimisation to find a minimum of the objective function Section 2.4
(e.g. the minimum cost) with respect to the choice
variable whose values have to be optimised (e.g. the
optimum level of output). See also *optimisation,
maximisation, rationality*.

Missing markets markets for certain commodities are Section I.3, 1.1,
missing when these markets do not exist and 1.5, 2.3, 3.2
therefore trade does not take place even if some
agents would be willing to buy or to sell these
commodities. Sources include informational asymmetries, knowledge heterogeneities and *adverse
selection*.

Moral hazard when potential opportunistic actions chosen Section 2.3, 5.2
by one party after the *contract* are not observable and
enforceable by the other party. Moral hazard is a form
of post-contractual opportunism. See also *adverse
selection enforcement, observability*.

Networks of firms forms of collaboration among firms in Section 4.3
which the interdependence and coordination is not
pre-defined, but selected in relation to changing
circumstances. See also *hybrids*.

Norms social models of behaviour. Section 1.7

Observability implies that each party is able to know Section 3.2
whether the *contract*'s terms are being met. See also
describability, verifiability.

Opportunism may be regarded as self-interest, seeking with Section 3.2
guile and incomplete and distorted disclosure of
information, especially calculated efforts to mislead,
disguise, obfuscate, or otherwise confuse without
committing a criminal offence.
  Strong opportunism deliberate and active distortion of
  relevant information, dissembling behaviour and
  breaching agreements.

Weak opportunism reticent and evasive behaviour, whenever rules imply the duty of revealing the relevant information.

Opportunities occasions which make it possible to econo- | Sections I.4, mise – that is, to increase benefits or reduce costs. | 2.4, 5.6 With incomplete and heterogeneous *abilities*, unexpected and unexploited opportunities can be sought or created by means of *learning*. See also *economising, entrepreneurship*.

Opportunity cost the opportunity cost of an activity is the | Introduction, value of the next-best alternative that has to be | Section 3.2, 6.1 forgone in order to undertake the activity in question. See also *asset specificity, cost*.

Optimisation attaining the "best" choice from the exhaust- | Sections 2.4, ive list of all possible alternatives. Optimisation | 3.2 problems involve the definition of an objective function which gives the mathematical specification of the relationship between the choice variables, whose optimal values have to be determined (e.g. the level of output), and some variables whose values have to be maximised or minimised (e.g. profit, market share, or cost). Optimisation and *maximisation* are so closely connected that in the literature they are often taken as synonymous. See also *economising, minimisation, rationality*.

Organisation a social organisation is a set of people | Section 1.7 coordinated to perform tasks in order to achieve individual and collective aims.

Organisational coordination consists mainly in: (i) de- | Section I.3, veloping specific *capabilities* by coordinating and | Chapter 3 motivating learning processes; (ii) arranging *transactions* with suppliers and customers, and establishing the degree of internalisation of processes; (iii) designing the *dimension of scale* by balancing the different productive capacities of indivisible and complementary inputs and processes.

Organisational learning see *learning*.

Output *production element* that exits from one production process as a *flow* (such as the finished product and waste).   Section 1.2

Partnership an *organisation* of two or more persons to carry on a business, sharing gains and losses. Accounting firms and law practices, architectural firms, consulting firms and medical clinics are often organised as partnerships. See also *firm*.   Section 2.1

Path-dependence a process is path-dependent where initial conditions and the subsequent sequence of steps exert strong effects on its development and on the final outcome.   Section 1.6

Perfect rationality see *rationality*.

Performance feedback see *sequential aiming*.

Piece-rate compensation incentive system by which em-ployees are paid a sum according to each piece produced.   Section 2.3

Power ability to do something. In relationships between individuals or organisations, the ability to control, affect or decide the behaviour of an individual or an *organisation.* This kind of power derives from a number of factors: endowments possessed (such as wealth, particular *abilities*, exclusive possession of inputs or *information*), force defined as the ability to exert physical coercion, legal right and *authority*.   Sections 1.3, 4.3

Procedural uncertainty see *uncertainty*.

Practical knowledge knowing how to do something. It consists in applying the appropriate course of action on the basis of a solution of a problem-solving procedure. See also *abilities, information-processing ability, theoretical knowledge*.   Section 1.4

Production elements *flows* or *funds*.   Section 1.2

Production unit (or a business unit) a unit consisting of one   Section 1.2
    or more plants situated in one or more departments,
    within a single establishment or in neighbouring
    establishments. The production unit is responsible
    for organising the production of a single commodity
    (or a range of commodities) and the corresponding
    production methods.

Property rights confer on the owner of an asset *residual*   Section 2.1
    rights of control and *residual returns* of the asset.

Profit a *residual return* obtained by owners of a firm after   Section 2.1
    all costs have been paid.

Public company a *corporation* whose ownership is dis-   Section 2.1
    persed across a vast number of small investors who
    have no actual control power.

Quasi-rent a return beyond the minimum needed to keep a   Section 1.7
    resource in this current use, in other words beyond
    the return that could be expected from employing
    this resource in an alternative use.

Ratchet effect when future incentives will depend on   Section 2.3
    current performance, employees may oppose this
    incentive system by reducing today's productivity.

Radical uncertainty see *uncertainty*.

Rationality   Section 2.4
    Cognitive rationality incorporates a wide range of
        possible degrees of rationality under constraints on
        information-processing *abilities* and cognitive
        biases. It corresponds to the capacity to search for
        information, select different decision strategies
        (appropriateness, *heuristics*, *routines*), look for
        alternative courses of actions, generate new behav-
        iour and cope with unforeseeable changes in environ-
        mental conditions. See also *knowledge, forecasting,*
        uncertainty.
    Perfect rationality implies complete *knowledge* of all
        possible courses of actions and of the full list of

possible outcomes, and complete information-processing *abilities*. Under perfect rationality individuals are able to estimate all possible future pay-offs consequent upon their actions.

Reference point effect when choices are evaluated by individuals in relation to the way their current situation differs from some reference level rather than to the absolute level of their current situation. See also *information-processing ability*.   Table 1.4

Relational agreement a relational agreement is characterised by mutual (implicit or explicit) obligations and shared expectations about the behaviour of each party and by both parties' interest in maintaining the relationship over time. It involves a general and broad agreement on aims and on the parties' provisions. See also *contract*.   Sections 3.2, 5.1

Residual returns of an asset the net income that is left over after all costs have been paid.   Section 2.1

Residual rights of control of an asset the exclusive and alienable right to decide on the use of the asset in any way not inconsistent with a prior contract, custom, or law.   Section 2.1

Risk   Section 1.5
    Objective risk when individuals know the objective probability distribution of all possible contingencies.
    Subjective risk when individuals know the subjective probability distribution of all possible contingencies. See also *forecasting ability, uncertainty*.

Routines organisational routines are coordinated units of activity with a repetitive character. They constitute the building blocks of the firm's *competencies* and *capabilities*. See also *skills*.   Section 5.3

Rules formal or informal regulations that constrain the behaviour of individuals and *organisations,* and the interaction among them. See also *institutions*.   Section 1.7

Screening an activity undertaken by the uninformed party   Section 4.1
   aiming to select the informed parties in order to attract
   only desirable buyers or sellers. This is generally
   achieved by providing a variety of options from which
   the informed parties select a particular option. The
   selection of a particular option reveals the relevant
   information and screens the informed party.

Selection constitutes the mechanism for preservation of   Sections 1.6,
   routines that are successful in meeting competition.   5.3
   Markets and business organisations provide a setting
   for the selection of new ideas. See also *inheritance*,
   variety.

Self-enforcing contract see *contract*.

Separation of ownership and control a situation in which   Section 2.1
   the *residual rights of control* and the *residual returns*
   of an asset belong to diverse parties.

Sequential aiming identifying and pursuing specific aims   Section 5.5
   that are set in a sequence. Sequential aiming is
   adaptive decision-making on the basis of performance feedback, according to change in conditions
   over time and to the possibility of learning from
   experience.

Set-up process a process that is independent of the scale of   Sections 1.2,
   the production process in which it is used; for   3.3
   instance, machine set-up operations, checking proofs
   or designing a product. It implies super-fixed costs
   that lead to a sharp reduction in average cost as the
   total volume of production increases.

Signalling the attempt by individuals who possess private   Section 4.1
   information to communicate it (for instance, prod-
   uct warranties, money-back guarantees or labelling,
   education, quality labels, and social and eco-labels).
   The more costly the signal or the more difficult to
   fake, the more credible it is.

Skills individual skills consist in knowing how to perform   Sections 3.1,
   specific tasks in the production of goods or services.   5.3

They are relational and organisation-specific abilities that constitute building blocks of organisational *routines*.

Spot contract see *contract*.

Stakeholders persons who derive advantages and bear costs resulting from the action of the firm, including the following: executives, managers and employees; the entrepreneur–owner or shareholders; lenders and investors (i.e. unit trusts or mutual funds, insurance companies, pension funds, financial intermediaries); suppliers; customers; trade unions; local communities represented by NGOs; public authorities. **Sections 1.3, 2.2**

Status quo effect in decision-making when the current status is favoured compared to alternatives not experienced. See also *information-processing ability*. **Table 1.4**

Stock options the right to buy the corporation's stock at a specified price in the future. If the market price of the stock rises above the price specified in the options, it is possible to make money by buying the stock at the (cheaper) specified price. **Section 2.3**

Strategy see *corporate strategy*.

Structural change a mutation of the economic system and of the industrial organisation due to changes in production techniques, market conditions and the composition of demand. **Section 1.6**

Substantive uncertainty see *uncertainty*.

Sunk costs are those costs that can never be recouped. See also *cost*. **Sections 1.2, 1.7, 3.3, 4.1**

Tacit knowledge *knowledge* that cannot be expressed directly in words, numbers, formulae and designs, like knowing how to walk or ride a bicycle. All knowledge concerning a particular *skill* or technique has a tacit dimension that can never be made completely explicit. **Section 1.1**

Team group of individuals who are interdependent in their   Sections 1.2,
tasks, who see themselves and are seen by others as a   2.3
social entity embedded in a larger social system. See
team production.

Team production production in which the contribution of   Sections 1.2,
each member of the *team* is dependent on other   2.3
members' productivity. As a consequence, individual
marginal productivity is impossible to measure.

Theoretical knowledge bits of information embodied in a   Section 1.4
cognitive system. It is formed of a complex set of
elements: ability to put stimuli in the right interpretative box, knowledge of actual states of the world
and outcomes, awareness of *rules*, capacity to
construct *mental models, ideologies*, ability to
identify aims, discover *opportunities* and recognise
pay-offs. See also *abilities, information-processing
ability, practical knowledge.*

Third-sector organisations are neither state nor private-   Section 2.1
commercial organisations. Third-sector activities are
usually financed by donors or public policies and
often performed by volunteers. They display a wide
variety of legal, property and organisational forms.
Some have owners who maintain control over the
organisation (firm-like organisations such as social
enterprises, non-profit cooperatives), while in others
the ownership is spread among their members and
the actual control and liability is attributed to the
representative board (as in associations or charitable
organisations).

Transaction an act of exchange within markets, which may   Section 3.2
involve either a transfer of a *property right*, or
renting a good (e.g. a tool, a car, or a house), or the
provision of services by an independent agent. See
also *transaction costs, transfer, transfer cost.*

Transaction costs costs of exchange, i.e. the costs of using   Section 3.2
markets to satisfy economic requirements. Transac-
tion costs encompass contract, information, knowledge and enforcement costs. Their possible main

components are due to: (i) taxes; (ii) government
certificates and permits; (iii) middlemen payments;
(iv) legal fees; (v) contract-writing costs; (vi) bargaining costs; (vii) information costs for the seller;
(viii) information and measurement costs for the
buyer; (ix) costs of imperfectly specified *contracts*
due to ignorance of the other party's plans and
possible outcomes; (x) *hold-up* inefficiencies; (xi)
costs of monitoring respect of the contract; and,
finally, (xii) costs of enforcing the agreement. See
also *transaction, transfer, transfer cost.*

Transfer a logistic operation across a technologically   Section 3.2
separable interface within a *firm*. A transfer takes
place within a *decomposable production process* and
does not involve a contract-based relationship. See
also *transaction, transaction costs, transfer cost.*

Transfer costs are given by the management costs of   Section 3.2
coordinating the transfer operations plus the phys-
ical movement costs. They include: (i) coordinating
the transport processes; (ii) coordinating various
intermediate warehouses; (iii) transfer accounting.
Physical movement costs are the costs of: (iv)
auxiliary transformation and packaging processes;
(v) transport and (vi) warehousing. Transfer costs
are a component of production costs. See also
transaction, transaction costs, transfer.

Trust confidence in the correctness and honesty of the   Section 1.1
opposite party. Trust is characterised by two
components. The first is calculative. This is generated as a result of experience: (a) it is a consequence
of a credible commitment on the basis of knowledge
of the opposite party's interest; or (b) it derives from
membership in the family, community, culture, or
religion (characteristic-based trust), or in organisations that ensure respect for rules, ethics or professional standards (institution-based trust). The
second component of trust is non-calculative in the
sense that it is based on the *a priori* belief that the
opposite party will behave in a correct and honest

way. Correctness and loyalty may imply a behaviour
that is against one's own interest.

U-form (unitary form) firm structure in which control   Introduction
rights are unified in one centralised unit. See also
H-form, *M-form*.

Uncertainty   Section 1.5
  Radical uncertainty when individuals do not know the
  future pay-offs. It includes as a sufficient condition
  one of the two following types of uncertainty:
  Procedural uncertainty this derives from cognitive limits
  in classifying, ordering, computing and comparing
  all possible outcomes.
  Substantive uncertainty this stems from incomplete
  knowledge of all possible outcomes.
  Weak uncertainty (probabilistic risk) when individuals
  know the objective or subjective probability distribution of all possible contingencies (*objective and
  subjective risk*). See also *forecasting ability*.

Variety springs from the existence of different *abilities*   Section 1.6
among individuals and from the fact that individuals
are placed in different contexts. Different individual
abilities imply potentially dissimilar patterns of
connections between available bits of information.
See also *inheritance, selection*.

Verifiability means that two parties can write their mutual   Section 3.2
obligations and plans in such a way that, in case of
dispute, a third party (e.g. a court) can determine the
true significance of obligations and plans. Verifiability needs *describability* and *observability*. See also
contract.

Vertical integration unified governance, under common   Sections 3.2,
ownership and management, of two or more   3.4, 6.1
successive stages. Vertical integration is a technical
as well as a contractual condition. See also *diversification, growth of the firm, horizontal expansion*.

Weak uncertainty see *uncertainty*.

References

Note: Pages quoted in the text always refer to the original edition unless the reprint or the translation date is indicated in these references between square brackets.

Agliardi, Elettra (1998), *Positive Feedback Economies*, Macmillan, London

Akerlof, George A. (1970), 'The market for "lemons": quality uncertainty and the market mechanism', *Quarterly Journal of Economics*, n. 84, pp. 488–500; repr. in slightly adapted form in Barney and Ouchi (1986, pp. 27–39)

Akerlof, George A. and Kranton, Rachel E. (2005), 'Identity and the economics of organizations', *Journal of Economic Perspectives*, 19(1), Winter, pp. 9–32

Alchian, Armen A. (1950), 'Uncertainty, evolution and economic theory', *Journal of Political Economy*, 58, pp. 211–21; repr. in slightly adapted form in Barney and Ouchi (1986, pp. 305–19); repr. in Williamson (1990b, pp. 23–33); repr. in Hodgson [1998d, vol. II, pp. 253–63]

Alchian, Armen A. and Demsetz, Harold (1972), 'Production, information costs, and economic organization', *American Economic Review*, 62, pp. 777–95; repr. in slightly adapted form in Barney and Ouchi (1986, pp. 129–55); repr. in Demsetz (1988b, pp. 119–43); repr. in Medema (1995, vol. I, pp. 25–43); repr. in Williamson and Masten (1995a, pp. 47–66); repr. in Buckley and Michie (1996, pp. 75–102); repr. in Casson (1996, pp. 92–110); repr. with minor abridgements in Putterman and Kroszner [1996b, pp. 193–216]; repr. in Keasey, Thompson and Wright (1999c, pp. 327–45); repr. in Williamson and Masten (1999, pp. 35–53); repr. in Foss (2000, vol. I, pp. 223–47); repr. in Langlois, Yu and Robertson (2002, vol. I, pp. 196–214); repr. in Kay (2003, pp. 353–72); repr. in Ménard (2004a, pp. 148–66)

Alchian, Armen A. and Woodward, Susan (1988), 'The firm is dead: long live the firm. A review of Oliver E. Williamson's *The Economic Institutions of Capitalism*, *Journal of Economic Literature*, 36(1), March, pp. 65–79; repr. in Ménard (2004g, pp. 98–112)

Allais, Maurice (1953), 'Le comportement de l'homme rational devant le risque: critique des postulats et axiomes de l'école américaine', *Econometrica*, 21, October, pp. 503–56

Allsopp, Vicky (2002), 'Trust, time and uncertainty', in Dow and Hillard (2002, pp. 81–96)

Alt, James E. and Shepsle, Kenneth A. (eds.) (1990), *Perspectives on Positive Political Economy*, Cambridge University Press, Cambridge, repr. [1995]

Anderson, Erin (1985), 'The salesperson as outside agent or employee: a transaction cost analysis', *Marketing Science*, no. 4, pp. 234–54

——— (1996), 'Transaction cost analysis and marketing', in Groenewegen (1996, pp. 65–83)

Anderson, Erin and Schmittlein, David C. (1984), 'Integration of the sales force: an empirical application', *Rand Journal of Economics*, 15 (3), Autumn, pp. 385–95

Andersson, Åke E., Batten, David F. and Karlsson, Charlie (eds.) (1989), *Knowledge and Industrial Organization*, Springer-Verlag, Berlin-Heidelberg

Anheier, Helmut K. and Ben-Ner, Avner (eds.) (2003), *The Study of Nonprofit Enterprise: Theories and Approaches*, Kluwer Academic/ Plenum Publishers, New York

Antonelli, Cristiano (1999), *The Microdynamics of Technical Change*, Routledge, London

——— (2003), 'The economics of governance: the role of localized knowledge in the interdependence among transaction, coordination and production', Laboratorio di Economia dell'Innovazione Franco Momigliano, Università di Torino, preliminary version, in Green, Miozzo and Dewick (2005)

——— (2004), *The System Dynamics of Localized Technical Change: Ingredients, Governance and Processes*, Laboratorio di Economia dell'Innovazione Franco Momigliano, Università di Torino, preliminary draft, May

Aoki, Masahiko (1984), *The Co-operative Game Theory of the Firm*, Blackwell, Oxford

——— (1988), *Information, Incentives, and Bargaining in the Japanese Economy*, Cambridge University Press, Cambridge; repr. [1992]

Aoki, Masahiko, Gustafsson, Bo and Williamson, Oliver E. (eds.) (1990), *The Firm as a Nexus of Treaties*, Sage, London

Appleyard, Melissa M., Hatch, Nile W. and Mowrey, David C. (2000), 'Managing the development and transfer of process technologies in semiconductor manufacturing industry', in Dosi, Nelson and Winter (2000b, pp. 183–207)

Archibugi, Daniele and Lundvall, Bengt-Åke (eds.) (2001), *The Globalizing Learning Economy*, Oxford University Press, Oxford

Arena, Richard (2003), 'Organization and knowledge in Alfred Marshall's economics', in Arena and Quéré (2003, pp. 221–39)

Arena, Richard and Longhi, Christian (1998a), 'Introduction', in Arena and Longhi (1998b, pp. 1–19)

(eds.) (1998b), *Markets and Organization*, Springer, Berlin

Arena, Richard and Quéré, Michel (eds.) (2003), *The Economics of Alfred Marshall: Revisiting Marshall's Legacy*, Palgrave Macmillan, Basingstoke and New York

Argote, Linda (1999), *Organizational Learning: Creating, Retaining and Transferring Knowledge*, Kluwer Academic Publishers, Boston

Argote, Linda and Darr, Eric (2000), 'Repositories of knowledge in franchise organizations: individual, structural and technological', in Dosi, Nelson and Winter (2000b, pp. 51–68)

Argyres, Nicholas S. (1996), 'Evidence on the role of capabilities in vertical integration decisions', *Strategic Management Journal*, 17(2), pp. 129–50

Arora, Ashish and Gambardella, Alfonso (1994), 'The changing technology of technological change: general and abstract knowledge and the division of innovative labour', *Research Policy*, 23, pp. 523–32

Arora, Ashish, Fosfuri, Andrea and Gambardella, Alfonso (2001), 'Markets for technology and their implications for corporate strategy', *Industrial and Corporate Change*, 10(2), pp. 419–51

Arrighetti, Alessandro (1998), 'Exchange operational costs and long-term relationships between firms', WP 7/1998, Istituto di Scienze Economiche, Università degli Studi di Parma, Parma

Arrighetti, Alessandro, Bachmann, Reinhard and Deakin, Simon (1997), 'Contract law, social norms and inter-firm cooperation', *Cambridge Journal of Economics*, 21, pp. 171–95

Arrow, Kenneth J. (1962), 'Economic welfare and the allocation of resources for invention', in Nelson (1962, pp. 609–25); repr. in Needham (1970, pp. 415–31); repr. in Stephan and Audretsch (2000, vol. I, pp. 61–77)

(1973), 'Information and economic behavior', Lecture presented to the Federation of Swedish Industries, in Arrow [1984], *The Economics of Information: Collected Papers of Kenneth J. Arrow*, Volume 4, Blackwell, Oxford, pp. 136–52

(1974a), *The Limits of Organization*, W.W. Norton, New York

(1974b), 'On the agenda of organizations', in Marris (1974, pp. 214–34); repr. in Arrow (1984, vol. IV: pp. 167–84)

(1979), 'The division of labor in the economy, the polity, and society', in O'Driscoll (1979, pp. 153–64)

(1984), *The Economics of Information: Collected Papers of Kenneth J. Arrow*, Volume 4, Blackwell, Oxford

(1994a), 'Information and the organization of industry', *Rivista Internazionale di Scienze Sociali, Lectio Magistralis*, Catholic University of Milan, Occasional Paper, April–June, pp. 3–15

(1994b), 'Methodological individualism and social knowledge', *American Economic Review, Papers and Proceedings*, 84(2), May, pp. 1–9

Arrow, Kenneth J., Colombatto, Enrico and Perlman, Mark (eds.) (1996), *The Rational Foundations of Economic Behavior*, Macmillan, London

Arrow, Kenneth J. and Hahn, Frank H. (1971), *General Competitive Analysis*, Holden–Day, San Francisco

Arrow, Kenneth, J., Ng, Yew-Kwang and Yang, Xiaokai (eds.) (1998), *Increasing Returns and Economic Analysis*, Macmillan, London

Arthur, W. Brian (1989), 'Competing technologies, increasing returns, and lock-in by historical events', *Economic Journal*, 99, March, pp. 116–31; repr. in Boettke and Prychitko (1998, pp. 244–59); repr. in Heal (1999, pp. 350–65)

Atkinson, Anthony B. and Stiglitz, Joseph E. (1969), 'A new view of technological change', *Economic Journal*, September, pp. 573–8

Augier, Mie, Kreiner, Kristian and March, James G. (2000), 'Introduction: some roots and branches of organisational economics', *Industrial and Corporate Change*, 9(4), pp. 555–65

Augier, Mie and March, James G. (eds.) (2002), *The Economics of Choice, Change and Organization: Essays in Memory of Richard M. Cyert*, Edward Elgar, Cheltenham

(eds.) (2004), *Models of a Man: Essays in Memory of Herbert A. Simon*, MIT Press, Cambridge, MA

Babbage, Charles (1832), *On the Economy of Machinery and Manufactures*, 2nd edn. enlarged, Knight, London; 4th edn. Frank Cass, London (1932)

Bacchiega, Alberto and Borzaga, Carlo (2003), 'The economics of the third sector: toward a more comprehensive approach', in Anheier and Ben-Ner (2003, pp. 27–48)

Backhaus, Jürgen (ed.) (2003), *Joseph Alois Schumpeter: Entrepreneurship, Style and Vision*, Kluwer Academic Publishers, Dordrecht

Baets, Walter R.J. (1998), *Organizational Learning and Knowledge Technologies in a Dynamic Environment*, Kluwer Academic Publishers, Dordrecht

Baily, Martin Neil and Winston, Clifford (eds.) (1988), *Brookings Papers on Economic Activity: 3 – 1987, Special Issue on Microeconomics*, The Brookings Institution, Washington, DC

Baker, George, Gibbons, Robert and Murphy, Kevin J. (2002), 'Relational contracts and the theory of the firm', *Quarterly Journal of Economics*, 117(1), February, pp. 39–84; repr. in Ménard (2004d, pp. 114–59)

Balabkins, Nicholas W. (2003), 'Adaptation without attribution? The genesis of Schumpeter's innovator', in Backhaus (2003, pp. 203–20)

Balakrishnan, Srinivasan and Wernerfelt, Birger (1986), 'Technical change, competition and vertical integration', *Strategic Management Journal*, no. 7, pp. 347–59

Baranzini, Mauro and Scazzieri Roberto (eds.) (1986), *Foundations of Economics*, Blackwell, Oxford

Barca, Fabrizio and Becht, Marco (eds.) (2001), *The Control of Corporate Europe*, Oxford University Press, Oxford

Barnett, William A., Cornet, Bernard, D'Aspremont, Claude, Gabszewicz, Jean and Mas-Colell, Andreu (eds.) (1991), *Equilibrium Theory and Applications: Proceedings of the Sixth International Symposium on Economic Theory and Econometrics*, Cambridge University Press, Cambridge

Barney, Jay B. (1991), 'Firm resources and sustained competitive advantage', *Journal of Management*, 17(1), pp. 99–120; repr. in Langlois, Yu and Robertson [2002, vol. II, pp. 94–115]

Barney, Jay B. and Ouchi, William C. (eds.) (1986), *Organizational Economics: Toward a New Paradigm for Understanding and Studying Organizations*, Jossey-Bass, San Francisco

Baron, James N. and Kreps, David M. (1999), *Strategic Human Resources: Frameworks for General Managers*, J. Wiley & Sons, New York

Barro, Robert J. (ed.) (1989), *Modern Business Cycle Theory*, Blackwell, Oxford and Harvard University Press, Cambridge, MA

Barzel, Yoram (2001), 'A theory of organizations to supersede the theory of the firm', September, preliminary version, http://www.econ.washington.edu

Baum, Joel A.C. (ed.) (2002), *Companion to Organizations*, Blackwell, Oxford and Malden, MA

Baum, Joel A.C. and Singh, Jitendra V. (1994a), 'Organizational hierarchies and evolutionary processes: some reflections on a theory of organizational evolution', in Baum and Singh (1994b, pp. 3–20)

(eds.) (1994b), *Evolutionary Dynamics of Organizations*, Oxford University Press, Oxford

Baumol, William J. (1959), *Business Behavior, Value and Growth*, Macmillan, New York

(1968), *Economic and Operations Analysis*, Prentice Hall, Englewood Cliffs, NJ, 4th edn., [1977]

(1982), 'Contestable markets: an uprising on the theory of Industry structure', *American Economic Review*, 72(1), pp. 1–15

(2002), *The Free-Market Innovation Machine: Analyzing the Growth Miracle of Capitalism*, Princeton University Press, Princeton

Baumol, William J., Panzar, John Clifford and Willig, Robert D. (1982), *Contestable Markets and the Theory of Industry Structure*, with contributions by Elizabeth E. Bailey, D. Fisher, H.C. Quirmbach, Harcourt Brace Jovanovich, San Diego, rev. edn. [1988]

Becattini, Giacomo (1979), 'Dal "settore industriale" al "distretto industriale". Alcune considerazioni sull'unità d'indagine dell'economia industriale', *Rivista di Economia e Politica Industriale*, January, English trans. from Italian of a new version 'Sectors and/or districts: some remarks on the conceptual foundations of industrial economics', in Goodman and Bamford, with Saynor [1989, pp. 123–35]

(ed.) (1987), *Mercato e forze locali: il distretto industriale*, Il Mulino, Bologna

Becattini, Giacomo, Bellandi, Marco, Dei Ottati, Gabi and Sforzi, Fabio (eds.) (2003), *From Industrial Districts to Local Development: An Itinerary of Research*, Edward Elgar, Cheltenham

Beck, Thorsten, Demirgüç-Kunt, Asli and Maksimovic, Vojislav (2003), 'Financial and legal institutions and firm size', World Bank Policy Research Working Paper 2997, March

Becker, Gary S. (1962), 'Irrational behavior and economic theory', *Journal of Political Economy*, 70, pp. 1–13

Becker, Markus C. (2004), 'Organizational routines: a review of the literature', *Industrial and Corporate Change*, 13(4), pp. 643–78

(2005), 'The concept of routines: some clarifications', *Cambridge Journal of Economics*, 29, pp. 249–62

Becker, Markus C. and Knudsen, Thorbjørn (2005), 'The role of routines in reducing pervasive uncertainty', *Journal of Business Research*, 58, pp. 746–57

Bell, Daniel and Kristol, Irving (eds.) (1981), *The Crisis in Economic Theory*, Basic Books, New York

Belussi, Fiorenza and Gottardi, Giorgio (eds.) (2000), *Evolutionary Patterns of Local Industrial Systems*, Ashgate, Aldershot

Belussi, Fiorenza, Gottardi, Giorgio and Rullani, Enzo (eds.) (2003), *The Technological Evolution of Industrial Districts*, Kluwer Academic Publishers, Dordrecht

Benson, George C.S. (1989), 'Codes of ethics', *Journal of Business Ethics*, 8 (5), pp. 305–19

Bertolini, Paola and Giovannetti, Enrico (2003), 'The internationalisation of an agri-food district', preliminary version, Dipartimento di Economia Politica, Università degli Studi di Modena e Reggio Emilia, Modena

Best, Michael H. (1990), *The New Competition: Institutions of Industrial Restructuring*, Polity Press, Cambridge, repr. [1996]

Best, Michael H. and Garnsey, Elizabeth (1999), 'Edith Penrose, 1914–1996', *Economic Journal*, 109(453), February, pp. 187–201

Bewley, Trueman (ed.) (1987), *Advances in Economic Theory: Fifth World Congress*, Cambridge University Press, Cambridge

Bianchi, Marcello, Bianco, Magda and Enriques, Luca (2001), 'Pyramidal groups and the separation between ownership and control in Italy', in Barca and Becht (2001, pp. 154–87)

Bianchi, Marina (1990), 'The unsatisfactoriness of satisficing: from bounded rationality to innovative rationality', *Review of Political Economy*, no. 2, pp. 149–67

(1995), 'Markets and firms: transaction costs versus strategic innovation', *Journal of Economic Behavior and Organization*, 28(2), pp. 183–202

(1998a), 'Introduction', in Bianchi (1998b, pp. 1–18)

(ed.) (1998b), *The Active Consumer: Novelty and Surprise in Consumer Choice*, Routledge, London

Bianco, Magda (2004), 'Analisi d'opera: Roe M., *Political Determinants of Corporate Governance: Political Context, Corporate Impact*, Oxford University Press, Oxford, 2003', *Rivista di Politica Economica*, March–April, pp. 357–73

Bianco, Magda and Casavola, Paola (1999), 'Italian corporate governance: effects on financial structure and firm performance', *European Economic Review*, 43, pp. 1057–8

Birolo, Adriano (2001), 'Un'applicazione del modello "fondi-flussi" a uno studio di caso aziendale nel distretto calzaturiero della Riviera del Brenta', in Tattara (2001, pp. 193–215)

Boettke, Peter J. (ed.) (1994), *The Elgar Companion to Austrian Economics*, Edward Elgar, Cheltenham

Boettke, Peter J. and Prychitko, David L. (eds.) (1998), *Market Process Theories, Volume I: Classical and Neoclassical*, An Elgar Reference Collection, The International Library of Critical Writings in Economics, Edward Elgar, Cheltenham

Bogner, William C. and Thomas, Howard (1994) 'Core competence and competitive advantage: a model and illustrative evidence from the pharmaceutical industry', in Hamel and Heene (1994, pp. 111–47)

Boisot, Max and Canals, Agustí (2004), 'Data, information and knowledge: have we got it right?', *Journal of Evolutionary Economics*, 14, pp. 43–67

Bolle, Friedel (1999), 'Trust', in Earl and Kemp (1999, pp. 575–81)

Bonaccorsi, Andrea and Giuri, Paola (2003), 'Increasing returns and network structure in the evolutionary dynamics of industries', in Saviotti (2003, pp. 50–93)

Bonini, Nicolao and Egidi, Massimo (1999), 'Cognitive traps in individual and organizational behavior: some empirical evidence', *Revue d'Economie Industrielle*, no. 88, pp. 153–86

Bouckaert, Boudewijn and De Geest, Gerrit (eds.) (1999), *Encyclopedia of Law and Economics*, Edward Elgar, Aldershot, 5 vols.

Bowles, Samuel, Franzini, Maurizio and Pagano Ugo (eds.) (1999), *The Politics and Economics of Power*, Routledge, London

Brusco, Sebastiano (1982), 'The Emilian model: productive decentralisation and social integration', *Cambridge Journal of Economics*, 6(2), June, pp. 167–84; repr. in Lazonick and Mass [1995, pp. 223–40]

Brusoni, Stefano, Prencipe, Andrea and Pavitt, Keith (2001), 'Knowledge specialization, organizational coupling, and the boundaries of the firm: why do firms know more than they make?', *Administrative Science Quarterly*, 46, pp. 597–621

Buchanan, James M. and Thirlby, G.F. (eds.) (1973), *LSE Essays on Cost*, London School of Economics and Political Science, Weidenfeld & Nicolson, London

Buckley, Peter J. and Michie, Jonathan (eds.) (1996), *Firms, Organisations and Contracts: A Reader in Industrial Organization*, Oxford University Press, Oxford

Buigues, Pierre, Jacquemin, Alexis and Marchipont, Jean-François (eds.) (2000), *Competitiveness and the Value of Intangible Assets*, with a Preface by Romano Prodi, Edward Elgar, Cheltenham

Burchell, Brendan and Wilkinson, Frank (1997), 'Trust, business relationships and the contractual environment', *Cambridge Journal of Economics*, 21, pp. 217–37

Burguet, Roberto and Che, Yeon-Koo (2004), 'Competitive procurement with corruption', *Rand Journal of Economics*, 35(1), Spring, pp. 50–68

Burton-Jones, Alan (1999), *Knowledge Capitalism: Business, Work, and Learning in the New Economy*, Oxford University Press, Oxford, repr. [2001]

Buzzacchi, Luigi and Colombo, Massimo G. (1996), 'Business groups and the determinants of corporate ownership', *Cambridge Journal of Economics*, 20, pp. 31–51

Calderini, Mario, Garrone, Paola and Sobrero, Maurizio (eds.) (2003), *Corporate Governance, Market Structure and Innovation*, Edward Elgar, Cheltenham

Carabelli, Anna (1995), 'Uncertainty and measurement in Keynes: probability and organicness', in Dow and Hillard (1995, pp. 137–60)

Carmignani, Marcello and Vercelli, Alessandro (eds.) (1978), *Il mondo contemporaneo: economia e storia*, La Nuova Italia, Florence, 2 vols.

Carter, Richard (2003), 'Empirical tests of transaction cost economics: a critical review', paper presented at the Fifth International Workshop on Institutional Economics, *Explaining the Firm: Transaction Costs or Capabilities?*, June, University of Hertfordshire, Hatfield

Casson, Mark C. (1982), *The Entrepreneur: An Economic Theory*, Angus Robertson, Oxford

(1995a), *Entrepreneurship and Business Culture: Studies in the Economics of Trust*, vol. 1, Edward Elgar Aldershot

(1995b), *The Organization of the International Business: Studies in the Economics of Trust*, vol. 2, Edward Elgar, Aldershot

(ed.) (1996), *The Theory of the Firm*, An Elgar Reference Collection, The International Library of Critical Writings in Economics, Edward Elgar, Cheltenham

(1997), *Information and Organization: A New Perspective on the Theory of the Firm*, Clarendon Press, Oxford

Center for Business Ethics (1986), 'Are corporations institutionalizing ethics?', *Journal of Business Ethics*, 5(2), pp. 85–91

Chandler, Alfred D. Jr. (1962), *Strategy and Structure: Chapters in the History of the Industrial Enterprise*, 3rd printing, MIT Press, [1966], Cambridge, MA

(1977), *The Visible Hand: The Managerial Revolution in American Business*, Belknap/Harvard University Press, Cambridge, MA

(1990), *Scale and Scope: The Dynamics of Industrial Capitalism*, Belknap/Harvard University Press, Cambridge, MA

(1992), 'Organizational capabilities and the economic history of the industrial enterprise', *Journal of Economic Perspectives*, 6(3), pp. 79–100; repr. in Foss (2000, vol. IV, pp. 274–95); repr. in Langlois, Yu and Robertson (2002, vol. III, pp. 415–36); repr. in Kay (2003, pp. 161–82)

(2003), *Shaping the Industrial Century: The Remarkable Story of the Evolution of the Modern Chemical and Pharmaceutical Industries*, 2nd volume of a two-volume series entitled *Paths of Learning Evolution of High Technology Industries Worldwide*, draft, April, forthcoming Harvard University Press, Cambridge, MA

Chandler, Alfred D. Jr., Hagström, Peter and Sölvell, Örjan (eds.) (1998), *The Dynamic Firm: The Role of Technology, Strategy, Organization, and Regions*, Oxford University Press, Oxford, repr. [1999]

Clark, Peter (2000), *Organisations in Action: Competition between Contexts*, Routledge, London

Coase, Ronald H. (1937), 'The nature of the firm', *Economica*, November, pp. 386–405; repr. in Stigler and Boulding (1953, pp. 331–51); repr. in slightly adapted form in Barney and Ouchi (1986, pp. 80–98); repr. in Coase [1988, pp. 33–55]; repr. in Williamson (1990b, pp. 3–22);

repr. in Medema (1995, vol. I, pp. 5–24); repr. in Buckley and Michie (1996, pp. 40–58); repr. in Casson (1996, pp. 36–55); repr. in Putterman and Kroszner (1996b, pp. 89–104); repr. in Keasey, Thompson and Wright (1999c, pp. 307–26); repr. in Williamson and Masten (1999, pp. 3–22); repr. in Foss (2000, vol. II, 239–55); repr. in Langlois, Yu and Robertson (2002, vol. I, pp. 85–104); repr. in Ménard (2004a, pp. 51–70)

(1960), 'The problem of social cost', *Journal of Law and Economics*, 3, October, pp. 1–44; repr. in Coase (1988, pp. 95–156); repr. in Ménard (2004b, pp. 341–84)

(1972), 'Industrial organization: a proposal for research', in Fuchs (1972, pp. 59–73); repr. in Coase [1988, pp. 57–74]; repr. in Williamson and Masten (1995a, pp. 3–17); repr. in Williamson and Masten (1999, pp. 54–68)

(1988), *The Firm, the Market and the Law*, University of Chicago Press, Chicago, repr. [1990]

(1991), 'The institutional structure of production', Nobel Lecture, 9 December, *American Economic Review*, September 1992; repr. in Coase (1994, pp. 3–14); repr. in Williamson and Masten (1995a, pp. 643–53); repr. in Persson [1997, pp. 11–20]; repr. in Ménard (2004d, pp. 3–9)

(1994), *Essays on Economics and Economists*, The University of Chicago Press, Chicago

Coeurderoy, Régis and Quélin, Bertrand (1997), 'L'économie des coûts de transaction: Un bilan des études empiriques sur l'intégration verticale', *Revue d'Economie Politique*, 107(2), March–April, pp. 145–81

Cohen, Michael D., March, James G. and Olsen Johan P. (1972), 'A garbage can model of organizational choice', *Administrative Science Quarterly*, 17(1), March, pp. 1–25

Cohen, Wesley M. and Levinthal, Daniel A. (1989), 'Innovation and learning: the two faces of R&D', *Economic Journal*, 99, September, pp. 569–96; repr. in Mansfield and Mansfield [1993, pp. 458–85]

(1990), 'Absorptive capacity: a new perspective on learning and innovation', *Administrative Science Quarterly*, 35, pp. 128–52; repr. in Martin and Nightingale [2000, pp. 499–523]; repr. in Langlois, Yu and Robertson (2002, vol. II, pp. 69–93)

Cohendet, Patrick and Llerena, Patrick (2002), 'Dual theory of the firm between transactions and competences', draft, forthcoming, *Revue d'Economie Industrielle*, no. 110, 2005, pp. 175–98

Cohendet, Patrick, Llerena, Patrick and Marengo, Luigi (2000), 'Is there a pilot in the evolutionary firm?', in Foss and Mahnke (2000, pp. 95–115)

Colombo, Massimo G. and Delmastro, Marco (2001), 'The choice of the form of strategic alliances: transaction cost economics and beyond', in Plunket, Voisin and Bellon (2001, pp. 17–34)

Commission of the European Communities (2001), *Promoting a European Framework for Corporate Social Responsibility*, Green Paper, Brussels, http://www.europe.eu.int/eur-lex

(2002), *Alternative Dispute Resolution in Civil and Commercial Law*, Green Paper, Brussels, http://www.europe.eu.int/eur-lex

Commons, John R. (1934), *Institutional Economics: Its Place in Political Economy*, Macmillan, New York, repr. with a new Introduction by Malcolm Rutherford, 2 vols., Transaction Publishers, New Brunswick, NJ [1990]

Conner, Kathleen R. and Prahalad, C.K. (1996), 'A resource-based theory of the firm: knowledge versus opportunism', *Organization Science*, 7 (5), pp. 477–501; repr. in Foss (2000, vol. IV, pp. 123–67)

Coriat, Benjamin and Dosi, Giovanni (1998), 'Learning how to govern and learning how to solve problems: on the co-evolution of competences, conflicts and organizational routines', in Chandler, Hagström and Sölvel (1998, pp. 103–33); repr. in Dosi (2000, pp. 294–324); repr. in Hodgson (2002b, pp. 95–123); repr. in Lazaric and Lorenz (2003b, pp. 221–51)

Cosmides, Leda and Tooby, John (1996), 'Are humans good intuitive statisticians after all? Rethinking some conclusions from literature on judgment under uncertainty', *Cognition*, 58, pp. 1–73

Cournot, Augustin (1838), *Recherches sur les Principes Mathématiques de la Théorie des Richesses*, Hachette, Paris; new edn. with appendix by Léon Walras, Joseph Bertrand and Vilfredo Pareto, Introduction and notes by Georges Lutfalla, Librairie des Sciences Politiques et Sociales Marcel Rivière, Paris [1938]; English trans. by N.T. Bacon, 1897, *Researches into the Mathematical Principles of the Theory of Wealth*, Macmillan, New York, 1927, repr. A.M. Kelley, New York, 1971

Cowling, Keith and Sugden, Roger (1998), 'The essence of the modern corporation: markets, strategic decision-making and the theory of the firm', *The Manchester School*, 66(1), January, pp. 59–86

Cozzi, Terenzio and Marchionatti, Roberto (eds.) (2001), *Piero Sraffa's Political Economy: A Centenary Estimate*, Routledge, London

Crémer, Jacques (1990), 'Common knowledge and the co-ordination of economic activities', in Aoki, Gustafsson and Williamson (1990, pp. 53–76), repr. in Foss [2000, vol. III, pp. 255–93]

(1993), 'Corporate culture and shared knowledge', *Industrial and Corporate Change*, 2(3), pp. 351–86

Crocker, Keith J. and Masten, Scott E. (1996), 'Regulation and administered contracts revised: lessons from transaction-cost economics for public utility regulation', *Journal of Regulatory Economics*, 9(1), pp. 5–39

Currie, Martin and Steedman, Ian (1990), *Wrestling with Time*, Manchester University Press, Manchester

Cusumano, Michael A. (1991), *Japan's Software Factories: A Challenge to US Management*, Oxford University Press, New York and Oxford

Cyert, Richard M. (1988), *The Economic Theory of Organization and the Firm*, Harvester Wheatsheaf, New York

Cyert, Richard M. and March, James G. (1963), *A Behavioral Theory of the Firm*, Prentice Hall, Englewood Cliffs, NJ; repr. Blackwell, Cambridge, MA, 1992

Cyert, Richard M. and Pottinger, Garrel (1978), 'Toward a better micro-economic theory', *Philosophy of Science*, 46(2), pp. 204–22; repr. in Cyert [1988, pp. 201–19]

Cyert, Richard M., Simon, Herbert A. and Trow, Donald B. (1956), 'Observation of a business decision', *The Journal of Business*, 29(4), October, pp. 237–48

Dasgupta, Partha (1988), 'Trust as a commodity', in Gambetta (1988, pp. 49–72)

David, Paul (1985), 'Clio and the economics of QWERTY', *Economic History*, 75(2), pp. 332–37; repr. in Mansfield and Mansfield (1993, pp. 319–24); repr. in Heal (1999, pp. 319–24); repr. in Martin and Nightingale [2000, pp. 281–6]; repr. in Kay (2003, pp. 607–12)

    (1997), 'Path dependence and the quest for historical economics: one more chorus on the ballade of QWERTY', Discussion Papers in Economics and Social History, no. 20, University of Oxford, Oxford

Davidson, Paul (1991a), 'Is probability theory relevant for uncertainty? A Post Keynesian perspective', *Journal of Economic Perspectives*, 5(1), pp. 129–43

    (1991b), *Money and Employment: The Collected Writings of Paul Davidson*, vol. 1, Macmillan, London

    (1991c), *Controversies in Post Keynesian Economics*, Edward Elgar, Aldershot

    (1994), *Post Keynesian Macroeconomic Theory: A Foundation for Successful Economic Policies for the Twenty-First Century*, Edward Elgar, Aldershot

    (1996), 'Reality and economic theory', *Journal of Post Keynesian Economics*, 18(4), Summer, pp. 479–508

Davidson, Paul and Davidson, Greg S. (1984), 'Financial markets and Williamson's theory of governance: efficiency versus concentration versus power', *Quarterly Review of Economics and Business*, 24, Winter; repr. in Davidson [1991b, pp. 324–38]

Day, Richard H. (2002), 'Adapting, learning, economizing and economic evolution', in Augier and March (2002, pp. 219–36)

de Jong, Gjalt and Nooteboom, Bart (2000), *The Causal Structure of Long-Term Supply Relationships: An Empirical Test of a Generalized Transaction Cost Theory*, Kluwer Academic Publishers, London

della Porta, Donatella and Vannucci, Alberto (1999), *Corrupt Exchanges. Actors, Resources, and Mechanisms of Political Corruptions*, Aldine De Gruyter, New York

Delmas, Magali A. (1999), 'Exposing strategic assets to create new competences: the case of technological acquisitions in the waste management industry in Europe and in the United States', *Industrial and Corporate Change*, 8(4), pp. 635–71

Demsetz, Harold (1983), 'The structure of ownership and the theory of the firm', *Journal of Law and Economics*, 26(2), pp. 375–90; repr. in Demsetz (1988b, pp. 187–201); part. repr. in Putterman and Kroszner [1996b, pp. 345–53]

(1988a), 'The theory of the firm revisited', *Journal of Law, Economics, and Organization*, pp. 141–61; repr. in Demsetz (1988b, 144–65); part. repr. in Williamson and Winter (1991, pp. 159–78); repr. in Langlois, Yu and Robertson [2002, vol. I, pp. 280–300]; repr. in Ménard (2004g, pp. 77–97)

(1988b), *Ownership, Control and the Firm: The Organization of Economic Activity, Volume I*, Blackwell, Oxford; repr. (1990)

(1995), *The Economics of the Business Firm: Seven Critical Comments*, Cambridge University Press, Cambridge, repr. [1997]

(1997), 'The firm in economic theory: a quiet revolution', *American Economic Review, Papers and Proceedings*, 87(2), May, pp. 426–29

Demsetz, Harold and Lehn, Kenneth (1985), 'The structure of corporate ownership: causes and consequences', *Journal of Political Economy*, 93 (6), pp. 1155–77; repr. in Demsetz (1988b, pp. 202–22); repr. in Keasey, Thompson and Wright (1999b, pp. 105–27)

Dennett, Daniel C. (1995), *Darwin's Dangerous Idea: Evolution and the Meanings of Life*, Allen Lane, London, repr. Penguin London, 1996

Denzau, Arthur T. and North, Douglass C. (1994), 'Shared mental models: ideologies and institutions', *Kyklos*, 47(1), pp. 3–31; repr. in Hodgson (2003b, pp. 214–41); repr. in Ménard (2004g, pp. 36–64)

Dequech, David (1999), 'Expectations and confidence under uncertainty', *Journal of Post Keynesian Economics*, 21(3), Spring, pp. 415–30

De Vecchi, Nicolò (1995), *Entrepreneurs, Institutions and Economic Change: The Economic Thought of J.A. Schumpeter (1905–1925)*, Edward Elgar, Aldershot

Dierkes, Meinolf, Berthoin Antal, Ariane, Child, John and Nonaka, Ikujiro (eds.) (2001), *Handbook of Organizational Learning and Knowledge*, Oxford University Press, Oxford

Dietrich, Michael (1994), *Transaction Cost Economics and Beyond: Towards a New Economics of the Firm*, Routledge, London

Dopfer, Kurt (1993), 'The generation of novelty in the economic process: an evolutionary concept', in Dragan, Steifert and Demetrescu (1993, pp. 130–53)

    (ed.) (2005), *The Evolutionary Foundations of Economics*, Cambridge University Press, Cambridge

Dosi, Giovanni (1984), *Technical Change and Industrial Transformation*, Macmillan, London

    (1988), 'Sources, procedures, and microeconomic effects of innovation', *Journal of Economic Literature*, 26(3), September; pp. 1120–71, repr. in Dosi [2000, pp. 63–114]

    (1994), 'Boundaries of the firm', in Hodgson, Samuels and Tool (1988, pp. 229–36)

    (2000), *Innovation, Organization and Economic Dynamics: Selected Essays*, Edward Elgar, Cheltenham

    (2004) 'A very reasonable objective still beyond our reach: economics as an empirically disciplined social science', in Augier and March (2004, pp. 211–26)

Dosi, Giovanni and Egidi, Massimo (1991), 'Substantive and procedural uncertainty: an exploration of economic behaviours in changing environments', *Journal of Evolutionary Economics*, 1(2), April, pp. 145–68; repr. in Dosi [2000, pp. 165–88]

Dosi, Giovanni, Faillo, Marco and Marengo, Luigi (2003), 'Organizational capabilities, patterns of knowledge accumulation and governance structures in business firms: an Introduction', 25 February, Pisa, paper presented at the Fifth International Workshop on Institutional Economics, *Explaining the Firm: Transaction Costs or Capabilities?*, June, University of Hertfordshire, Hatfield; LEM Working Paper Series, no. 11, Laboratory of Economics and Management, Sant'Anna School of Advanced Studies, Pisa

Dosi, Giovanni, Freeman, Chris, Nelson, Richard, Soete, Luc and Silverberg, Gerard (eds.) (1988), *Technical Change and Economic Theory*, Frances Pinter, London

Dosi, Giovanni and Malerba, Franco (1996a), 'Organizational learning and institutional embeddedness: an introduction to the diverse evolutionary paths of modern corporations', in Dosi and Malerba (1996b, pp. 1–24)

    (eds.) (1996b), *Organization and Strategy in the Evolution of the Enterprise*, Macmillan, London

Dosi, Giovanni and Marengo, Luigi (1994), 'Some elements of an evolutionary theory of organizational competences', in England (1994, pp. 157–78); repr. in Dosi [2000, pp. 211–35]; repr. in Foss (2000, vol. IV, pp. 50–73); repr. in Langlois, Yu and Robertson (2002, vol. III, pp. 646–70)

(2000), 'On the tangled discourse between transaction cost economics and competence-based views of the firm' in Foss and Mahnke (2000, pp. 80–92)

Dosi, Giovanni, Marengo, Luigi and Fagiolo, Giorgio (2005), 'Learning in evolutionary environments', in Dopfer (2005, pp. 255–338)

Dosi, Giovanni and Metcalfe, J. Stanley (1991), 'On some notions of irreversibility in economics', in Saviotti and Metcalfe (1991, pp. 133–59)

Dosi, Giovanni, Nelson, Richard R. and Winter, Sidney G. (2000a), 'Introduction: the nature and dynamics of organizational capabilities', in Dosi, Nelson and Winter (2000b, pp. 1–22)

(eds.) (2000b), *The Nature and Dynamics of Organizational Capabilities*, Oxford University Press, Oxford

Dosi, Giovanni and Orsenigo, Luigi (1988), 'Coordination and transformation: an overview of structures, behaviours and change in evolutionary environments', in Dosi *et al*, (1988, pp. 13–37); repr. in Langlois, Yu and Robertson [2002, vol. II, pp. 463–87]

Dosi, Giovanni and Teece, David J. (1998), 'Organizational competences and the boundaries of the firm', in Arena and Longhi (1998b, pp. 282–302)

Dosi, Giovanni, Teece, David J. and Chytry, Josef (eds.) (1998), *Technology Organization and Competitiveness: Perspectives on Industrial and Corporate Change*, Oxford University Press, Oxford

Dosi, Giovanni and Winter, Sidney (2002), 'Interpreting economic change: evolution, structures and games', in Augier and March (2002, pp. 337–53)

Dow, Sheila C. and Earl, Peter E. (eds.) (1999a), *Economic Organization and Economic Knowledge: Essays in Honour of Brian J. Loasby*, vol. I, Edward Elgar, Cheltenham

(eds.) (1999b), *Contingency, Complexity and the Theory of the Firm: Essays in Honour of Brian J. Loasby*, vol. II, Edward Elgar, Cheltenham

Dow, Sheila C. and Hillard, John (eds.) (1995), *Keynes, Knowledge and Uncertainty*, Edward Elgar, Aldershot

(eds.) (2002), *Post Keynesian Econometrics, Microeconomics and the Theory of the Firm: Beyond Keynes, Volume One*, 'Preface' by Geoffrey C. Harcourt, Edward Elgar, Aldershot

Dragan, Joseph C., Steifert, Eberhard K. and Demetrescu, Mihai C. (eds.) (1993), *Entropy and Bioeconomics: First International conference of the EABS Proceedings*, Rome, 28–30 November 1991, Nagard, Milan

Drucker, Peter F. (1993a), 'From capitalism to knowledge society', in Drucker (1993b, pp. 17–42); repr. in Neef [1998, pp. 15–34]

(1993b), *Post-Capitalist Society*, Butterworth–Heinemann, Oxford, repr. 1995

(2003), 'Foreword', in Sathe (2003, pp. xi–xii)

Dunn, Stephen P. (1999), 'Bounded rationality, "fundamental" uncertainty and the firm in the long run', in Dow and Earl (1999b, pp. 199–217)

(2000a), 'Whither Post Keynesianism?', *Journal of Post Keynesian Economics*, 22(3), Spring, pp. 343–64

(2000b), 'Fundamental uncertainty and the firm in the long run', *Review of Political Economy*, 12(4), pp. 419–33

(2001a), 'Bounded rationality is not fundamental uncertainty: a Post Keynesian perspective', *Journal of Post Keynesian Economics*, 23(4), pp. 567–87

(2001b), 'Toward a Post Keynesian theory of the multinational corporation: some Galbraithian insights', draft, Division of Economics at Staffordshire Business School

(2001c), 'Galbraith, uncertainty and the modern corporation', in Keaney (2001, pp. 157–82)

(2002), 'A Post Keynesian approach to the theory of the firm', in Dow and Hillard (2002, pp. 60–80)

(2004), 'Keynes, uncertainty and the competitive process', *Research in the History of Economic Thought and Methodology*, 22, pp. 65–91

Dupré, John (ed.) (1987), *Latest on the Best: Essays on Evolution and Optimality*, A Bradford Book, MIT Press, Cambridge, MA

Earl, Peter E. (ed.) (1988), *Behavioural Economics*, 2 vols., Edward Elgar, Aldershot

(2002), *Information, Opportunism and Economic Coordination*, Edward Elgar, Cheltenham

Earl, Peter E. and Kay, Neil M. (1985), 'How economists can accept Shackle's critique of economic doctrines without arguing themselves out of their jobs', *Journal of Economic Studies*, 12, pp. 34–48, repr. in Kay [1999]

Earl, Peter E. and Kemp, Simon (eds.) (1999), *The Elgar Companion to Consumer Research and Economic Psychology*, Edward Elgar, Cheltenham

Eatwell, John, Milgate, Murry and Newman, Peter (1987) (eds.), *The New Palgrave: A Dictionary of Economics*, 4 vols., Macmillan, London

Ebner, Alexander (2003), 'The institutional analysis of entrepreneurship: historist aspects of Schumpeter's development theory', in Backhaus (2003, pp. 117–39)

Egidi, Massimo (1986), 'The generation and diffusion of new routines', Conference on *Innovation Diffusion*, Venice, 17–21 March

(1992a), 'Colloquium with H.A. Simon, Introduction', in Egidi and Marris (1992, pp. 8–12)

(1992b), 'Organizational learning, problem solving and the division of labour', in Egidi and Marris (1992, pp. 148–73)

(1996), 'Routines, hierarchies of problems, procedural behaviour: some evidence from experiments', in Arrow, Colombatto and Perlman (1996, pp. 303–33)

(2002), 'Biases in organizational behavior', in Augier and March (2002, pp. 109–46)

(2004), 'From bounded rationality to behavioral economics', University of Trento, draft, November

Egidi, Massimo and Marris, Robin (eds.) (1992), *Economics, Bounded Rationality and the Cognitive Revolution*, Edward Elgar, Aldershot

Egidi, Massimo and Narduzzo, Alessandro (1997), 'The emergence of path-dependent behaviors in cooperative contexts', *International Journal of Industrial Organization*, 15(6), October, pp. 677–709

Egidi, Massimo and Rizzello, Salvatore (2003), 'Cognitive economics: foundations and historical evolution', Working Papers, 4, Department of Economics 'S. Cognetti de Martiis', Centro Studi sulla Storia e i Metodi dell'Economia Politica 'Claudio Napoleoni' (CESMEP), University of Turin

Einstein, Stanley and Amir, Menachem (eds.) (2003), *Police Corruption: Paradigms, Models and Concepts – Challenges for Developing Countries*, Office of International Criminal Justice (OICJ), Huntsville, AL

Elster, Jon (1998), 'Emotions and economic theory', *Journal of Economic Literature*, 36, March, pp. 47–74

(1999), *Alchemies of the Mind: Rationality and the Emotions*, Cambridge University Press, Cambridge

England, Richard W. (ed.) (1994), *Evolutionary Concepts in Contemporary Economics*, University of Michigan Press, Ann Arbor

Eriksen, Bo and Mikkelsen, Jesper (1996), 'Competitive advantage and the concept of core competence', in Foss and Knudsen (1996, pp. 54–74)

Evangelista, Rinaldo (1999), *Knowledge and Investment: The Sources of Innovation in Industry*, Edward Elgar, Cheltenham

Faber, Malte and Proops, John L.R. (1990), *Evolution, Time, Production and the Environment*, Springer-Verlag, Berlin

Fama, Eugene (1980), 'Agency problems and the theory of the firm', *Journal of Political Economy*, 88, pp. 288–307; part. repr. in Putterman and Kroszner (1996b, pp. 302–14); repr. in Keasey, Thompson and Wright (1999c, pp. 3–21); repr. in Foss [2000, vol. I, pp. 307–24]; repr. in Langlois, Yu and Robertson (2002, vol. I, pp. 69–93)

Fedderke, Johannes W. (1997), 'The source of optimality in action', *Cambridge Journal of Economics*, 21, pp. 339–63

Filippi, Francesco (2003), 'Daniel Kahneman e la psicologia delle decisioni', *Il Ponte*, 59(12), December, pp. 75–91

Fitzroy, Felix R., Acs, Zoltan J. and Gerlowski, Daniel A. (1998), *Management and Economics of Organization*, Prentice Hall Europe, London

Flaherty, M. Thérèse (2000), 'Limited inquiry and intelligent adaptation in semiconductor manufacturing', in Dosi, Nelson and Winter (2000b, pp. 99–123)

Florida, Richard and Kenney, Martin (2000), 'Transfer and replication of organizational capabilities: Japanese transplant organizations in the United States', in Dosi, Nelson and Winter (2000b, pp. 281–307)

Fontana, Giuseppe (2000), 'Post Keynesians and Circuitists on money and uncertainty: an attempt at generality', *Journal of Post Keynesian Economics*, 23(1), Fall, pp. 27–48

Fontana, Giuseppe and Gerrard, Bill (2004), 'A Post Keynesian theory of decision making under uncertainty', *Journal of Economic Psychology*, 25(5), pp. 619–37

Foss, Nicolai J. (1996a), 'Knowledge-based approaches to the theory of the firm: some critical comments', *Organization Science*, 7(5), pp. 470–76

(1996b), 'More critical comments on knowledge-based theories of the firm', *Organization Science*, 7(5), pp. 519–23

(1996c), 'The "alternative" theories of Knight and Coase, and the modern theory of the firm', *Journal of the History of Economic Thought*, 18, Spring, pp. 76–95

(1997a), 'The classical theory of production and the capabilities view of the firm', *Journal of Economic Studies*, 24(5), pp. 307–23

(ed.) (1997b), *Resources, Firms and Strategies: A Reader in the Resources-Based Perspective*, Oxford University Press, Oxford

(ed.) (2000), *The Theory of the Firm: Critical Perspectives on Business and Management*, 4 vols., Routledge, London

(2002), 'Edith Penrose: economics and strategic management', in Pitelis (2002, pp. 147–64)

(2005), *Strategy, Economic Organization, and the Knowledge Economy: The Coordination of Firms and Resources*, Oxford University Press, Oxford

Foss, Nicolai J. and Eriksen, Bo (1995), 'Competitive advantage and industry capabilities', in Montgomery (1995, pp. 43–69)

Foss, Nicolai J. and Foss, Kirsten (2000), 'The knowledge-based approach and organisational economics: how much do they really differ? And how does it matter?', in Foss and Mahnke (eds.) (2000, pp. 55–79)

Foss, Nicolai J. and Klein, Peter G. (eds.) (2002), *Entrepreneurship and the Firm: Austrian Perspectives on Economic Organization*, Edward Elgar, Cheltenham

Foss, Nicolai J. and Knudsen, Christian (eds.) (1996), *Towards a Competence Theory of the Firm*, Routledge, London, repr. [1999]

Foss, Nicolai J., Knudsen, Christian and Montgomery, Cynthia A. (1995), 'An exploration of common ground: integrating evolutionary and strategic theories of the firm', in Montgomery (1995, pp. 1–17)

Foss, Nicolai J. and Loasby, Brian J. (eds.) (1998), *Economic Organisation, Capabilities and Co-ordination: Essays in Honour of G.B. Richardson*, Routledge, London

Foss, Nicolai J. and Mahnke, Volker (eds.) (2000), *Competence, Governance, and Entrepreneurship: Advances in Economic Strategy Research*, Oxford University Press, Oxford

Foster, John and Metcalfe, J. Stanley (eds.) (2001), *Frontiers of Evolutionary Economics: Competition, Self-Organization and Innovation Policy*, Edward Elgar, Cheltenham

(eds.) (2004), *Evolution and Economic Complexity*, Edward Elgar, Cheltenham

Fox, Craig R. and Tversky, Amos (1998), 'A belief-based account of decision under uncertainty', *Management Science*, 44(7), July; repr. in Kahneman and Tversky (2000, pp. 118–42)

Frank, Jerome D. (1935), 'Individual differences in certain aspects of the level of aspiration', *American Journal of Psychology*, 47, pp. 119–28

Frank, Robert H. (1988), *Passions within Reason: The Strategic Role of the Emotions*, W.W. Norton, New York

Fransman, Martin (1994), 'Information, knowledge, vision and theories of the firm', *Industrial and Corporate Change*, 3(3), pp. 713–57; repr. in Dosi, Teece and Chytry (1998, pp. 147–91)

Freeland, Robert F. (1996), 'The Myth of the M-Form? Governance, Consent, and Organizational Change', *American Journal of Sociology*, 102(2), September, pp. 483–526

(2001), *The Struggle for Control of the Modern Corporation: Organizational Change at General Motors, 1924–1970*, Cambridge University Press, Cambridge

Freeman, Chris (1974), *The Economics of Industrial Innovation*, Penguin Books, 2nd edn. Frances Pinter, London, [1982]

(1994), 'The economics of technical change', *Cambridge Journal of Economics*, 18, pp. 463–514

Friedman, Milton (1953a), 'The methodology of positive economics', in Friedman (1953b, pp. 3–43)

(1953b), *Essays in Positive Economics*, University Press of Chicago, Chicago; 5th impression 1966, 1st Phoenix edn. [1966]

Fuchs, Victor R. (ed.) (1972), *Policy Issues and Research Opportunities in Industrial Organisation*, vol. 3 of *Economic Research: Retrospective and Prospect*, National Bureau of Economic Research, Cambridge, MA

Fudenberg, Drew and Tirole, Jean (1991), *Game Theory*, MIT Press, Cambridge, MA

Fujimoto, Takahiro (2000), 'Evolution of manufacturing systems and *ex post* dynamic capabilities: a case of Toyota's final assembly operations', in Dosi, Nelson and Winter (2000b, pp. 244–79)

Galbraith, John Kenneth (1967), *The New Industrial State*, Houghton Mifflin, Boston

Gambardella, Alfonso and Torrisi, Salvatore (1998), 'Does technological convergence imply convergence in markets? Evidence from the electronics industry', *Research Policy*, 27, pp. 445–63

Gambetta, Diego (ed.) (1988), *Trust: Making and Breaking Cooperative Relations*, Blackwell, Oxford

Garnsey, Elizabeth (1998), 'A theory of the early growth of the firm', *Industrial and Corporate Change*, no. 3, pp. 523–56; repr. in Storey (2000, vol. II, pp. 344–75)

Garrouste, Pierre and Ioannides, Stavros (eds.) (2001), *Evolution and Path Dependence in Economic Ideas*, Edward Elgar, Cheltenham

Garud, Raghu, Nayyar, Praveen Rattan and Shapira, Zur Baruch (1997a), 'Technological choices and the inevitability of errors', in Garud, Nayyar and Shapira (1997b, pp. 20–39)

(eds.) (1997b), *Technological Innovation: Oversights and Foresights*, Cambridge University Press, New York

Garud, Raghu and Shapira, Zur Baruch (1997), 'Aligning the residuals: risk, return, responsibility and authority', in Garud, Nayyar and Shapira (1997b, pp. 238–56)

Gatignon, Hubert and Anderson, Erin (1988), 'The multinational corporation's degree of control over foreign subsidiaries: an empirical test of a transaction cost explanation', *Journal of Law, Economics and Organization*, no. 4, pp. 305–36

Georgescu-Roegen, Nicholas (1964), 'Measure, quality and optimum scale', in Rao (1964, pp. 231–56); repr. in Georgescu-Roegen [1976, pp. 271–96]

(1969), 'Process in farming versus process in manufacturing: a problem of balanced development', in Papi and Nunn (1969, pp. 497–528); repr. in Georgescu-Roegen [1976, pp. 71–102]

(1970), 'The economics of production', *American Economic Review*, 60 (2), May, pp. 1–9 (The 1969 Richard T. Ely Lecture), repr. in Georgescu-Roegen [1976, pp. 61–9]

(1971), *The Entropy Law and the Economic Process*, Harvard University Press, Cambridge, MA, 4th printing, [1981]

(1976), *Energy and Economic Myths: Institutional and Analytical Economic Essays*, Pergamon Press, New York

(1979), 'Energy Analysis and Economic Valuation', *The Southern Economic Journal*, 45(4), pp. 1023–58

(1986), 'Man and production', in Baranzini and Scazzieri (1986, pp. 245–80)

Ghosh, Mrinal and John, George (1999), 'Governance value analysis and marketing strategy', *Journal of Marketing*, 63, Special Issue, pp. 131–45

Gibbons, Robert (1992), *A Primer in Game Theory*, Harvester Wheatsheaf, New York

(1998), 'Incentives in organizations', *Journal of Economic Perspectives*, 12(4), pp. 115–32

(2000), 'Why organizations are such a mess (and what an economist might do about it)', draft of a chapter of Gibbons (forthcoming)

(2003), 'Team theory, garbage cans and real organizations: some history and prospects of economic research on decision-making in organizations', *Industrial and Corporate Change*, 12(4), pp. 753–87

(2004), 'Four formal(izable) theories of the firm?', draft of two chapters of Gibbons (forthcoming)

(forthcoming), *Organizational Economics*, Princeton University Press, Princeton, in progress draft in http://www.mit.edu/rgibbons

Gigerenzer, Gerd (2002), *Reckoning with Risk: Learning to Live with Uncertainty*, Penguin Books, London

Gigerenzer, Gerd and Selten, Reinhard (2001a), 'Rethinking rationality', in Gigerenzer and Selten (eds.) (2001b, pp. 1–12)

(2001b) *Bounded Rationality: The Adaptive Toolbox*, MIT Press, Cambridge, MA, paperback edn. [2002]

Giovannetti, Enrico (2003), 'La divisione del lavoro è limitata dalla divisione del lavoro', preliminary version, Dipartimento di Economia Politica, Università di Modena e Reggio Emilia, Modena

Giuri, Paola, Torrisi, Salvatore and Zinovyeva, Natalia (2004), 'ICT, skills and organisational change: evidence from a panel of Italian manufacturing firms', preliminary version

Goodman, Edward and Bamford, Julia, with Saynor, Peter (eds.) (1989), *Small Firms and Industrial Districts in Italy*, Routledge, London

Grandori, Anna (1995), *L'organizzazione delle attività economiche*, Il Mulino, Bologna; 2nd edn., *Organizzazione e comportamento economico*, Il Mulino, Bologna, 1999; English rev. version, *Organization and Economic Behavior*, Routledge, London and New York [2001]

Grandori, Anna and Soda, Giuseppe (1995), 'Inter-firm networks: antecedents, mechanisms and forms', *Organization Studies*, 16(2), pp. 183–214

Grant, Robert M. (1996), 'Toward a knowledge-based theory of the firm', *Strategic Management Journal*, 17, Winter Special Issue, pp. 109–122

Green, Ken, Miozzo, Marcela and Dewick, Paul (eds.) (2005), *Technology, Knowledge and the Firm: Implications for Strategy and Industrial Change*, Edward Elgar, Cheltenham

Greenaway, David, Bleaney, Michael and Stewart, Ian (eds.) (1991), *Companion to Contemporary Economic Thought*, Routledge, London

Greve, Henrich R. (2003), *Organizational Learning from Performance Feedback: A Behavioral Perspective on Innovation and Change*, Cambridge University Press, Cambridge

Groenewegen, John, Pitelis, Christos and Sjöstrand Sven-Erik (eds.) (1995), *On Economic Institutions*, Edward Elgar, Aldershot

Groenewegen, John (ed.) (1996), *Transaction Cost Economics and Beyond*, Kluwer Academic Publishers, Dordrecht

Grossman, Sanford J. and Hart, Oliver D. (1986), 'The costs and benefits of ownership: a theory of vertical and lateral integration', *Journal of Political Economy*, 94(4), pp. 691–719; repr. in Williamson (1990b, pp. 252–80); repr. in Medema (1995, vol. I, pp. 219–47); repr. in Williamson and Masten (1995a, pp. 287–315); repr. in Casson (1996, pp. 423–51); repr. in Williamson and Masten (1999, pp. 151–79); repr. in Foss [2000, vol. III, pp. 63–89]; repr. in Langlois, Yu and Robertson (2002, vol. I, pp. 479–507); repr. in Kay (2003, pp. 401–29); repr. in Ménard (2004g, pp. 183–211)

Grossman, Sanford J. and Stiglitz, Joseph E. (1980), 'On the impossibility of informationally efficient markets', *American Economic Review*, 70(3), June, pp. 393–408

Gualerzi, Davide (1998), 'Economic change, choice and innovation in consumption', in Bianchi (1998b, pp. 46–63)

Gugler, Klaus (ed.) (2001), *Corporate Governance and Economic Performance*, Oxford University Press, Oxford

Guidi, Marco E.L. and Parisi, Daniela (eds.) (2005), *The Changing Firm: Contributions from the History of Economic Thought*, F. Angeli, Milan

Gulati, Ranjay (1995), 'Does familiarity breed trust? The implication of repeated ties for contractual choice in alliances', *Academy of Management Journal*, 38(1), pp. 85–112

Hagedoorn, John (1996), 'Innovation and entrepreneurship: Schumpeter revisited', *Industrial and Corporate Change*, 5(3), pp. 883–96

Hahn, Frank H. (1981), 'General equilibrium theory', in Bell and Kristol (1981, pp. 123–38); repr. in Hahn (1984, pp. 72–87)

(1984), *Equilibrium and Macroeconomics*, Blackwell, Oxford

(1989a), 'Introduction', in Hahn (1989b, pp. 1–4)

(ed.) (1989b), *The Economics of Missing Markets, Information, and Games*, Clarendon Press, Oxford

Hall, Richard (1994), 'A framework for identifying the intangible sources of sustainable competitive advantage', in Hamel and Heene (1994, pp. 148–69)

Hamel, Gary (1994), 'The concept of core competence', in Hamel and Heene (1994, pp. 11–33)

Hamel, Gary and Heene, Aimé (eds.) (1994), *Competence-Based Competition*, John Wiley & Sons, Chichester

Hansmann, Henry (1996), *The Ownership of Enterprise*, The Belknap Press of Harvard University Press, Cambridge, MA, repr. [2000]

Harcourt, Geoffrey C. (1982), *The Social Science Imperialists*, ed. Prue Kerr, Routledge & Kegan Paul, London

Harcourt, Geoffrey C. and Kenyon, Peter (1976), 'Pricing and the investment decision', *Kyklos*, 29(3), pp. 449–77, repr. in Harcourt [1982, pp. 104–26]

Hargreaves Heap, Shaun, Hollis, Martin, Lyons, Bruce, Sugden, Robert and Weale, Albert (1992), *The Theory of Choice: A Critical Guide*, Blackwell, Cambridge, MA, repr. [1998]

Harper, David A. (1996), *Entrepreneurship and the Market Process: An Enquiry into the Growth of Knowledge*, Routledge, London

Harris, Milton and Raviv, Artur (1991), 'The theory of capital structure', *Journal of Finance*, 46(1), March, pp. 297–355

Hart, Neil (1996), 'Marshall's theory of value: the role of external economies', *Cambridge Journal of Economics*, 20, pp. 353–69

Hart, Oliver (1989), 'An economist's perspective on the theory of the firm', *Columbia Law Review*, 89, pp. 1757–74; repr. in Buckley and Michie (1996, pp. 199–220); part. repr. in Putterman and Kroszner (1996b, pp. 354–60); repr. in Foss [2000, vol. I, pp. 130–47]

(1995a), *Firms, Contracts, and Financial Structure*, Clarendon Press, Oxford, repr. [1997]

(1995b), 'Corporate governance: some theory and implications', *Economic Journal*, 105, May, pp. 678–89; repr. in Keasey, Thompson and Wright (1999a, pp. 238–49)

Hart, Oliver and Holmström, Bengt R. (1987), 'The theory of contracts', in Bewley (1987, pp. 71–155); repr. in Foss (2000, vol. II, pp. 3–80)

Hart, Oliver and Moore, John (1990), 'Property rights and the nature of the firm', *Journal of Political Economy*, 98(6), December, pp. 1119–58; repr. in Williamson and Masten (1995a, pp. 316–55)); repr. in Foss (2000, vol. III, pp. 90–127); repr. in Ménard (2004b, pp. 504–43)

Hayek, Friedrich A. von (1937), 'Economics and knowledge', *Economica*, February, pp. 33–54; repr. in Buchanan and Thirlby [1973, pp. 43–68]

——— (1945), 'The use of knowledge in society', *American Economic Review*, 35(4), September, pp. 519–28; repr. in Hayek (1949, pp. 77–91); repr. in Townsend (1971, pp. 29–43); part. repr. in Putterman and Kroszner (1996b, pp. 66–71)

——— (1949), *Individualism and Economic Order*, Routledge & Kegan Paul, London

——— (1979), *Law, Legislation and Liberty: A New Statement of the Liberal Principles of Justice and Political Economy, Volume 3: The Political Order of A Free People*, University of Chicago Press, Chicago and Routledge & Kegan Paul, London, repr. [1981]

Heal, Geoffrey (ed.) (1999), *The Economics of Increasing Returns*, An Elgar Reference Collection, The International Library of Critical Writings in Economics, Edward Elgar, Cheltenham

Heiman, Bruce and Nickerson, Jack A. (2002), 'Towards reconciling transactions cost economics and the knowledge-based view of the firm: the context of interfirm collaboration', *International Journal of the Economics of Business*, 9(1), pp. 97–116

Heiner, Ronald A. (1983), 'The origin of predictable behavior', *American Economic Review*, 73(4), September, pp. 560–95; repr. in Ménard (2004b, pp. 74–109)

Helper, Susan, MacDuffie, John Paul and Sabel, Charles (2000), 'Pragmatic collaborations: advancing knowledge while controlling opportunism', *Industrial and Corporate Change*, 9(3), pp. 443–87

Henderson, Rebecca M. and Clark, Kim B. (1990), 'Architectural innovation: the reconfiguration of existing product technologies and the failure of established firms', *Administrative Science Quarterly*, 35, pp. 9–30

Henderson, Rebecca M. and Cockburn, Iain (2000), 'Measuring competence? Exploring firm effects in drug discovery', in Dosi, Nelson and Winter (2000b, pp. 155–82)

Herriott, Scott R., Levinthal, Daniel A. and March, James G. (1985), 'Learning from experience in organizations', *American Economic Review*, 75, pp. 298–302; repr. in March [1988b, pp. 219–27]

Hey, John D. (1991), 'Uncertainty in economics', in Greenaway, Bleaney and Stewart (1991, pp. 252–73)

(ed.) (1997a), *The Economics of Uncertainty, Vol. I: Risk*, An Elgar Reference Collection, The International Library of Critical Writings in Economics, Edward Elgar, Cheltenham

(ed.) (1997b), *The Economics of Uncertainty, Vol. II: Uncertainty and Dynamics*, An Elgar Reference Collection, The International Library of Critical Writings in Economics, Edward Elgar, Cheltenham

Hicks, John R. (1976), 'Some questions of time in economics', in Tang, Westfield and Worley (1976, pp. 135–51); repr. with the title 'Time in economics', in Hicks [1982, pp. 281–300]

(1977), *Economic Perspectives: Further Essays on Money and Growth*, Clarendon Press, Oxford

(1982), *Money, Interest and Wages, Collected Essays in Economic Theory, Volume II*, Blackwell, Oxford

Hirshleifer, Jack (1987), 'On the emotions as guarantors of threats and promises', in Dupré (1987, pp. 307–26)

Hirshleifer, Jack and Glazer, Amihai (1992), *Price Theory and Applications*, 5th edn., Prentice Hall, Englewood Cliffs, NJ

Hodgson, Geoffrey M. (1993a), 'Transaction costs and the evolution of the firm', in Pitelis (1993c, pp. 77–100)

(1993b), *Economics and Evolution: Bringing Life Back into Economics*, Polity Press, Cambridge

(1996), 'Corporate culture and the nature of the firm', in Groenewegen (1996, pp. 249–69)

(1997), 'The ubiquity of habits and rules', *Cambridge Journal of Economics*, 21, pp. 663–84, repr. in Hodgson (2003b, pp. 379–400)

(1998a), 'The approach of institutional economics', *Journal of Economic Literature*, 36, March, pp. 166–92, repr. in Hodgson (2003b, pp. 145–71)

(1998b), 'Evolutionary and competence-based theories of the firm', *Journal of Economic Studies*, 25(1), pp. 25–56

(1998c), 'The Coasean tangle: the nature of the firm and the problem of historical specificity', in Medema (1998, pp. 23–49)

(ed.) (1998d), *The Foundations of Evolutionary Economics: 1890–1973*, 2 vols., An Elgar Reference Collection, Edward Elgar, Cheltenham

(2001), *How Economics Forgot History: The Problem of Historical Specificity in Social Science*, Routledge, London

(2002a), 'The legal nature of the firm and the myth of the firm–market hybrid', *International Journal of the Economics of Business*, 9(1), pp. 37–60

(ed.) (2002b), *A Modern Reader in Institutional and Evolutionary Economics: Key Concepts*, Edward Elgar, Cheltenham

(2003a), 'On the limits of rational choice theory', Working Paper Series, 27, University of Hertfordshire, Business School, Hatfield

(ed.) (2003b), *Recent Developments in Institutional Economics*, An Elgar Reference Collection, Critical Studies in Economic Institutions, Edward Elgar, Cheltenham

(2004a), 'Opportunism is not the only reason why firms exist: why an explanatory emphasis on opportunism may mislead management strategy', *Industrial and Corporate Change*, 13(2), April, pp. 401–18

(2004b), 'Darwinism, causality and the social sciences', *Journal of Economic Methodology*, 11(2), June, pp. 175–94

Hodgson, Geoffrey M. and Knudsen, Thorbjørn (2003), 'Firm-specific learning and the nature of the firm: why transaction cost theory may provide an incomplete explanation', paper presented at the Fifth International Workshop on Institutional Economics, *Explaining the Firm: Transaction Costs or Capabilities?*, June, University of Hertfordshire, Hatfield

(2004), 'The firm as an interactor: firms as vehicles for habits and routines', *Journal of Evolutionary Economics*, 14, pp. 281–307

Hodgson, Geoffrey M., Samuels, Warren and Tool, Marc (eds.) (1994), *The Elgar Companion to Institutional and Evolutionary Economics*, 2 vols., Edward Elgar, Aldershot

Hodgson, Geoffrey M. and Screpanti, Ernesto (eds.) (1991), *Rethinking Economics: Markets, Technology and Economic Evolution*, Edward Elgar, Aldershot

Hofstede, Geert (1980), *Culture's Consequences: International Differences in Work-Related Values*, Sage, Beverly Hills and London

Holmström, Bengt R. (1982), 'Moral hazard in teams', *Bell Journal of Economics*, 13(2), pp. 324–40; repr. in Williamson (1990b, pp. 162–78); repr. in Foss (2000, vol. II, pp. 110–32); repr. in Langlois, Yu and Robertson [2002, vol. I, pp. 408–24]

(1999), 'The firm as a subeconomy', *Journal of Law, Economics and Organization*, 15, pp. 74–102, repr. in Ménard (2004d, pp. 59–87)

Holmström, Bengt R. and Milgrom, Paul (1991), 'Multitask principal-agent analyses: incentive contracts, asset ownership, and job design', *Journal of Law, Economics, and Organization*, 7, pp. 24–52; repr. in Williamson and Masten (1995a, pp. 553–81); part. repr. in Putterman and Kroszner (1996b, pp. 254–66); repr. in Williamson and Masten

(1999, pp. 214–42); repr. in Langlois, Yu and Robertson [2002, vol. I, pp. 556–4]; repr. in Ménard (2004e, pp. 385–510)

Holmström, Bengt R. and Roberts, John (1998), 'The boundaries of the firm revisited', *Journal of Economic Perspectives*, 12(4), Fall, pp. 73–94; repr. in Ménard (2004d, pp. 509–30)

Holmström, Bengt R. and Tirole, Jean (1989), 'The theory of the firm', in Schmalensee and Willig (1989, pp. 63–133); repr. in Foss (2000, vol. I, pp. 148–219)

Hunt, Joseph McVicker (ed.) (1944), *Personality and the Behavior Disorders: A Handbook Based on Experimental and Clinic Research*, 2 vols. The Ronald Press, New York [1945]

Ingvar, D.H. (1985), '"Memory of the future": an essay on temporal organization of conscious awareness', *Human Neurobiology*, 4, pp. 127–36

Jacobides, Michael G. and Winter, Sidney G. (2004), 'The co-evolution of capabilities and transaction costs: explaining the institutional structure of production', draft, forthcoming, *Strategic Management Journal*, 26 (5), pp. 395–413

Jensen, Michael and Meckling, William (1976), 'Theory of the firm: managerial behavior, agency costs and ownership structure', *Journal of Financial Economics*, 3, pp. 305–60; repr. in slightly adapted form in Barney and Ouchi (1986, pp. 214–75); repr. in Medema (1995, vol. I, pp. 44–99); repr. in Buckley and Michie (1996, pp. 103–167); part. repr. in Putterman and Kroszner (1996b, pp. 315–35); repr. in Keasey, Thompson and Wright (1999b, pp. 155–210); repr. in Foss (2000, vol. I, pp. 248–306); repr. in Langlois, Yu and Robertson [2002, vol. I, pp. 303–58]

Johnson, Eric J., Hershey, John, Meszaros, Jacqueline and Kunreuther, Howard (1993), 'Framing, probability distortions, and insurance decisions', *Journal of Risk and Uncertainty*, 7, pp. 35–51; repr. in Kahneman and Tversky [2000, pp. 224–40]

Joskow, Paul L. (1988), 'Asset specificity and the structure of vertical relationships: empirical evidence', *Journal of Law, Economics, and Organization*, 4(1), pp. 95–117; repr. in Williamson and Winter [1991, pp. 117–37]; repr. in Ménard (2004d, pp. 319–41)

Jussawalla, Meheroo and Ebenfield, Helene (eds.) (1984), *Communication and Information Economics.: New Perspectives*, with a Foreword by K. Boulding, North-Holland, Amsterdam

Kahneman, Daniel (2003), 'Maps of bounded rationality: psychology for behavioral economics', *American Economic Review* 93(5), December, pp. 1449–75

Kahneman, Daniel, Slovic, Paul and Tversky, Amos (eds.) (1982), *Judgment under Uncertainty: Heuristics and Biases*, Cambridge University Press, Cambridge

Kahneman, Daniel and Tversky, Amos (1979), 'Prospect theory: an analysis of decision under risk', *Econometrica* 47(2), pp. 263–91; repr. in Earl (1988, vol.1, pp. 253–81); repr. in Hey (1997a, pp. 1–29); repr. in Kahneman and Tversky [2000, pp. 17–43]

—— (1996), 'On the reality of cognitive illusions', *Psychological Review* 103 (3), pp. 582–91

—— (eds.) (2000), *Choices, Values, and Frames*, Russell Sage Foundation, Cambridge University Press, Cambridge

Kalantardis, Christos (2004), *Understanding the Entrepreneur: An Institutionalist Perspective*, Ashgate, Aldershot

Kay, John (ed.) (2003), *The Economics of Business Strategy*, An Elgar Reference Collection, The International Library of Critical Writings in Economics, Edward Elgar, Cheltenham

Kay, Neil M. (1979), *The Innovating Firm: A Behavioural Theory of Corporate R&D*, 'Foreword' by C. Freeman, Macmillan, London

—— (1992), 'Markets, false hierarchies and the role of asset specificity', *Journal of Economic Behaviour and Organisation*, 17, pp. 315–33; repr. in Pitelis (1993c, pp. 242–61); repr. in Kay [1999, pp. 73–92]

—— (1996), 'The economics of trust: a review of *Studies in the Economics of Trust* by Mark Casson', *International Journal of the Economics of Business* 3(2), pp. 249–60; repr. in Kay [1999, pp. 93–109]

—— (ed.) (1999), *The Boundaries of the Firm: Critiques, Strategies and Policies*, Macmillan, London

Keaney, Michael (ed.) (2001), *Economist with a Public Purpose: Essays in Honour of John Kenneth Galbraith*, Routledge, London and New York

Keasey, Kevin, Thompson, Steve and Wright, Mike (eds.) (1999a), *Corporate Governance, Volume I: Aspects of Corporate Governance*, An Elgar Reference Collection, The International Library of Critical Writings in Economics, Edward Elgar, Cheltenham

—— (eds.) (1999b), *Corporate Governance, Volume II: Governance Mechanisms. Part I*, An Elgar Reference Collection, The International Library of Critical Writings in Economics, Edward Elgar, Cheltenham

—— (eds.) (1999c), *Corporate Governance, Volume III: Governance Mechanisms. Part II*, An Elgar Reference Collection, The International Library of Critical Writings in Economics, Edward Elgar, Cheltenham

—— (eds.) (1999d), *Corporate Governance, Volume IV: Responses to Governance Issues*, An Elgar Reference Collection, The International Library of Critical Writings in Economics, Edward Elgar, Cheltenham

Keynes, John Maynard (1936), *The General Theory of Employment, Interest and Money*, Macmillan, London, repr. in *The Collected Writings of John Maynard Keynes, Volume VII*, ed. D. Moggridge, Macmillan, London [1971]

(1937), 'The general theory of employment', *Quarterly Journal of Economics*, February, repr. in *The Collected Writings of John Maynard Keynes, Volume XIV*, ed. D. Moggridge, Macmillan, London, [1971, pp. 109–23]

Khalil, Elias L. (ed.) (2003), *Trust*, An Elgar Reference Collection, Critical Studies in Economic Institutions, Edward Elgar, Cheltenham

Kirzner, Israel M. (1973), *Competition and Entrepreneurship*, Chicago University Press, Chicago

(1989), *Discovery, Capitalism, and Distributive Justice*, Blackwell, Oxford

(1997), 'Entrepreneurial discovery and competitive market process: an Austrian approach', *Journal of Economic Literature*, 15(1), March, pp. 60–85; repr. in Kirzner [2000, pp. 3–40]

(2000), *The Driving Force of the Market: Essays in Austrian Economics*, Routledge, London

Klavans, Richard (1994), 'The measurement of a competitor's core competence', in Hamel and Heene (1994, pp. 171–82)

Klein, Benjamin, Crawford, Robert and Alchian, Armen (1978), 'Vertical integration, appropriable rents, and the competitive contracting process', *Journal of Law and Economics*, 21, pp. 297–326; repr. in slightly adapted form in Barney and Ouchi (1986, pp. 39–71); repr. in Medema (1995, vol. I, pp. 100–29); repr. in Williamson and Masten (1995a, pp. 66–95); part. repr. in Putterman and Kroszner [1996b, pp. 105–24]; repr. in Keasey, Thompson and Wright (1999c, pp. 359–88); repr. in Williamson and Masten (1999, pp. 71–100); repr. in Foss (2000, vol. III, pp. 18–47); repr. in Langlois, Yu and Robertson (2002, vol. I, pp. 215–44); repr. in Ménard (2004d, pp. 175–204)

Klein, Jeremy A. and Hiscocks, Peter G. (1994), 'Competence-based competition: a practical toolkit', in Hamel and Heene (1994, pp. 183–212)

Klein, Saul, Frazier, Gary L. and Roth, Victor J. (1990), 'A transaction cost analysis model of channel integration in international markets', *Journal of Marketing Research*, 27(2), May, pp. 196–208

Knight, Frank H. (1921a), *Risk, Uncertainty, and Profit*, Houghton Mifflin, New York; repr. with a new 'Preface' by the author, The London School of Economics and Political Science, no. 16, London [1933]

(1921b), 'Cost of production and price over long and short periods', *Journal of Political Economy*, 29(4), April, pp. 304–35

(1924), 'Some fallacies in the interpretation of social cost', *Quarterly Journal of Economics*, 38(4), August, pp. 582–606

(1925), 'On decreasing cost and comparative cost: a rejoinder', *Quarterly Journal of Economics*, 39(2), February, pp. 331–33

Kogut, Bruce and Zander, Udo (1992), 'Knowledge of the firm, combinative capabilities, and the replication of technology', *Organization Science*, 3, pp. 383–97; repr. in Foss (1997b, pp. 306–26)

Koppl, Roger (ed.)(2004), *Evolutionary Psychology and Economic Theory*, Elsevier, Oxford

Krafft, Jackie and Ravix, Jacques-Laurent (1998), 'Theories of the Firm', in Arena and Longhi (1998b, pp. 237–61)

Kregel, Jan A. (1980), 'Markets and institutions as features of a capitalist production system', *Journal of Post Keynesian Economics*, III(1), Fall, pp. 32–48

Kreps, David M. (1990a), *A Course in Microeconomic Theory*, Harvester Wheatsheaf, New York

(1990b), 'Corporate culture and economic theory', in Alt and Shepsle (1990, pp. 90–143); repr. in Williamson and Masten (1995a, pp. 497–552); repr. in Buckley and Michie (1996, pp. 221–75); repr. in Foss [2000, vol. III, pp. 168–218]; repr. in Ménard (2004e, pp. 414–70)

Kumar, Krishna B., Rajan, Raghuram G. and Zingales, Luigi (1999), 'What determines firm size?', NBER Working Papers, w7208, July, http://gsbwww.uchicago.edu/fac/luigi.zingales/research/Pspapres/size.pdf

Kurz, Heinz D. and Salvadori, Neri (eds.) (1998), *Elgar Companion to Classical Economics*, 2 vols., Edward Elgar, Cheltenham

(eds.) (2003), *The Legacy of Piero Sraffa*, 2 vols., An Elgar Reference Collection, Intellectual Legacies in Modern Economics, Edward Elgar, Cheltenham

Lachmann, Ludwig (1978), 'Vicissitudes of subjectivism and the dilemma of the theory of the choice', in Lachmann [1994, pp. 218–29]

(1994), *Expectations and the Meaning of Institutions: Essay in Economics by Ludwig Lachmann*, ed. D. Lavoie, Routledge, London

Laffont, Jean-Jacques and Martimort, David (1997), 'The firm as a multicontract organization', *Journal of Economics and Management Strategy*, 6(2), Summer, pp. 201–34

Laffont, Jean-Jacques and Tirole, Jean (1993), *A Theory of Incentives in Procurement and Regulations*, MIT Press, Cambridge, MA

Lafontaine, Francine and Shaw, Kathryn L. (1999), 'The dynamics of franchise contracting: evidence from panel data', *Journal of Political Economy*, 107(5), October, pp. 1041–80; repr. in Ménard (2004d, pp. 469–508)

Lambsdorff, Johann G. (2002a), 'Making corrupt deals: contracting in the shadow of the law', *Journal of Economic Behaviour and Organization*, 48, pp. 221–41

(2002b), 'Corruption and rent-seeking', *Public Choice*, 113, pp. 97–125

Landau, Ralph, Taylor, Timothy and Wright, Gavin (eds.) (1996), *The Mosaic of Economic Growth*, Stanford University Press, Stanford, CA

Landesmann, Michael A. (1986), 'Conceptions of technology and the production process', in Baranzini and Scazzieri (1986, pp. 281–310)

Landesmann, Michael A. and Scazzieri, Roberto (1996a), 'Introduction', in Landesmann and Scazzieri (1996b, pp. 1–30)

(1996b), *Production and Economic Dynamics*, Cambridge University Press, Cambridge

Langlois, Catherine C. and Schlegelmilch, Bobo B. (1990), 'Do corporate codes of ethics reflect national character? Evidence from Europe and the United States', *Journal of International Business Studies*, 21, pp. 519–39

Langlois, Richard N. (1984), 'Internal organization in a dynamic context: some theoretical considerations', in Jussawalla and Ebenfield (1984. pp. 23–49)

(ed.) (1986), *Economics as a process: Essays in the New Institutional Economics*, Cambridge University Press, Cambridge

(1994), 'Risk and uncertainty' in Boettke (1994, pp. 118–22)

(1997), 'Cognition and capabilities: opportunities seized and missed in the history of the computer industry', in Garud, Nayyar and Shapira (1997b, pp. 71–94)

(1998), 'Transaction cost, production costs, and the passage of time', in Medema (1998, pp. 1–21)

(1999), 'Scale, scope and the reuse of knowledge', in Dow and Earl (1999a, p. 239– 53)

Langlois, Richard N. and Foss, Nicolai J. (1999), 'Capabilities and governance: the rebirth of production in the theory of economic organization', *Kyklos*, 53(2), pp. 201–18; repr. in Langlois, Yu and Robertson [2002, vol. I, pp. 4–19]

Langlois, Richard N. and Robertson, Paul L. (1993), 'Business organization as a coordination problem: Toward a dynamic theory of the boundaries of the firm', *Business and Economic History*, 22(1), pp. 31–41; repr. in Langlois, Yu and Robertson [2002, vol. III, pp. 635–45]

(1995), *Firms, Markets and Economic Change*, Routledge, London

Langlois, Richard N., Yu, Tony Fu-Lai and Robertson, Paul (eds.) (2002), *Alternative Theories of the Firm*, 3 vols., An Elgar Reference Collection, The International Library of Critical Writings in Economics, Edward Elgar, Cheltenham

Latsis, Spiro J. (ed.) (1976), *Method and Appraisal in Economics*, Cambridge University Press, Cambridge

Lawson, Clive (1999), 'Towards a competence theory of the region', *Cambridge Journal of Economics*, 23, pp. 151–66

(2002), 'Competence theories', preliminary version, Cambridge

Lawson, Tony (1997), *Economics and Reality*, Routledge, London

Lazaric, Nathalie and Lorenz, Edward (eds.) (1998), *Trust and Economic Learning*, Edward Elgar, Cheltenham

(2003a), *Knowledge, Learning and Routines, Vol. I: Knowledge and Learning*, An Elgar Reference Collection, Critical Studies in Economic Institutions, Edward Elgar, Cheltenham

(eds.) (2003b), *Knowledge, Learning and Routines, Vol. II: Routines*, An Elgar Reference Collection, Critical Studies in Economic Institutions, Edward Elgar, Cheltenham

Lazear, Edward P. (1995), 'Corporate culture and the diffusion of values', in Siebert (1995, pp. 89–133)

(2000), 'Performance pay and productivity', *American Economic Review*, 90(5), December, pp. 1346–61

Lazonick, William and Mass, William (1995), *Organizational Capability and Competitive Advantage: Debates, Dynamics and Policy*, An Elgar Reference Collection, The International Library of Critical Writings in Business History, Edward Elgar, Aldershot

Leibenstein, Harvey (1966), 'Allocative efficiency and X-efficiency', *American Economic Review*, 56, pp. 392–415, part. repr. in Putterman (1986 pp. 165–9)

(1982), 'The prisoners' dilemma in the invisible hand: an analysis of intrafirm productivity', *American Economic Review. Papers and Proceedings*, 72, pp. 92–7; repr. in Putterman and Kroszner [1996b, pp. 267–75]

Leijonhufvud, Axel (1986), 'Capitalism and the factory system', in Langlois (1986, pp. 203–23); repr. in Langlois, Yu and Robertson (2002, vol. III, pp. 149–69)

Levin, Richard C., Klevorick, Alvin, Nelson, Richard and Winter, Sidney (1988), 'Appropriating the returns from industrial research and development', in Baily and Winston (1988, pp. 783–820); repr. in Mansfield and Mansfield (1993, pp. 242–90)

Levinthal, Daniel A. (1995), 'Strategic management and the exploration of diversity', in Montgomery (1995, pp. 19–42)

Levinthal, Daniel A. and March, James (1993), 'The myopia of learning', *Strategic Management Journal*, 14, pp. 95–112; repr. in Lazaric and Lorenz (2003a, pp. 530–47)

Levy, David M. (2001), 'How the dismal science got its name: debating racial quackery', *Journal of the History of Economic Thought*, 23(1), pp. 5–35

Lewin, Kurt, Dembo, Tamara, Festinger, Leon and Snedden Sears, Pauline (1944), 'Level of aspiration', in Hunt (1944, vol.1, pp. 333–78)

Lindbeck, Assar and Snower, Dennis (2004), 'The firm as a pool of factor complementarities', Discussion Paper Series, 4242, Center for Economic Policy Research, in www.cepr.org/pubs/dps/DP4242.asp

Lindenberg, Siegwart (1996), 'Short-term prevalence, social approval, and the governance of employment relations', in Groenewegen (1996, pp. 129–47)

Livesay, Harold C. (ed.) (1995), *Entrepreneurship and the Growth of Firms*, 2 vols., An Elgar Reference Collection, The International Library of Critical Writings in Business History, Edward Elgar, Aldershot

Loasby, Brian J. (1967), 'Management economics and the theory of the firm', *Journal of Industrial Economics*, 15, July, pp. 165–76; repr. in Earl (1988, vol. I, pp. 461–72)

(1976), *Choice, Complexity and Ignorance: An Enquiry into Economic Theory and the Practice of Decision-Making*, Cambridge University Press, Cambridge

(1994), 'Organisational capabilities and interfirm relations', *Metroeconomica*, 45, pp. 248–65, repr. in Foss [2000, vol. II, pp. 288–303]

(1995), 'Running a business: an appraisal of economics, organization and management by Paul Milgrom and John Roberts', *Industrial and Corporate Change*, 4(2), pp. 471–89

(1998), 'The concept of capabilities', in Foss and Loasby (1998, pp. 163–82)

(1999), *Knowledge, Institutions and Evolution in Economics*, The Graz Schumpeter Lectures, 2, Routledge, London

(2001), 'Time, knowledge and evolutionary dynamics: why connections matter', *Journal of Evolutionary Economics*, no. 11, pp. 393–412

(2002a), 'The significance of Penrose's theory for the development of economics', in Pitelis (2002, pp. 45–59)

(2002b), 'The evolution of knowledge: beyond the biological model', *Research Policy*, 31 (8–9), 1227–39

(2003a), 'Closed models and open systems', *Journal of Economic Methodology*, 10(3), September, pp. 285–306

(2003b), 'Efficiency and time', in Arena and Quéré (2003, pp. 202–20)

(2004a), 'Economics after Simon', in Augier and March (2004, pp. 259–78)

(2004b), 'Hayek's theory of the mind', in Koppl (2004, pp. 101–34)

Lombardi, Mauro (2003a), 'The evolution of local production systems: the emergence of the "invisible mind" and the evolutionary pressures towards more visible "minds"', *Research Policy*, 32, pp. 1443–62

(2003b), 'Cognitive models, efficiency, and discontinuities in the evolution of industrial districts and local production systems', in Belussi, Gottardi and Rullani (2003, pp. 109–37)

Love, James H. (2005), 'On the opportunism–independent theory of the firm', *Cambridge Journal of Economics*, 29, pp. 381–97

Love, James H. and Roper, Stephen (2005), 'Economists' perceptions versus managers' decisions: an experiment in transaction-cost analysis', *Cambridge Journal of Economics*, 29, pp. 19–36

Lucas, Robert E. Jr. (1981), *Studies in Business Cycle Theory*, MIT Press, Cambridge, MA

Luini, Luigi (ed.) (1999), *Uncertain Decisions: Bridging Theory and Experiments*, Kluwer Academic Publishers, Boston

Luzzati, Tommaso (1999), 'A piece of evidence regarding the full rationality of economic agents', *Journal of Institutional and Theoretical Economics*, 155(3), pp. 567–72

(2003), 'Trivial choices and rationality', Studi e Ricerche del Dipartimento di Scienze Economiche, no. 94, University of Pisa, Pisa, pp. 1–18

Lyons, Bruce R. (1995), 'Specific investment, economies of scale, and make-or-buy decision: A test of transaction cost theory', *Journal of Economic Behavior and Organization*, 26, pp. 431–43

(1996), 'Empirical relevance of efficient contract theory: inter-firm contracts', *Oxford Review of Economic Policy*, 12(4), pp. 27–52

Macdonald, Stuart and Nightingale, John (eds.) (1999), *Information and Organization: A Tribute to the Work of Don Lamberton*, Elsevier, Amsterdam

Machina, Mark J. (1987), 'Choice under uncertainty: problems solved and unsolved', *Journal of Economic Perspectives*, 1(1), pp. 121–54; repr. in Hey (1997a, pp. 283–316)

MacLeod, W. Bentley (1995), 'Incentives in organizations: an overview of some of the evidence and theory', in Siebert (1995, pp. 3–42)

Madhok, Anoop (2002), 'Reassessing the fundamentals and beyond: Ronald Coase, the transaction cost and resource-based theories of the firm and the institutional structure of production', *Strategic Management Journal*, 23, pp. 535–50

Mahoney, Joseph T. (1992), 'The choice of organizational form: vertical financial ownership versus other methods of vertical integration', *Strategic Management Journal*, 13, pp. 559–84

Mäki, Uskali (2002a), 'The dismal queen of the social sciences', in Mäki (2002b, pp. 3–31)

(ed.) (2002b), *Fact and Fiction in Economics: Models, Realism, and Social Construction*, Cambridge University Press, Cambridge

Malerba, Franco (1992), 'Learning by firms and incremental technical change', *Economic Journal*, 102(413), pp. 845–59; repr. in Martin and Nightingale [2000, pp. 604–18]

Malerba, Franco, Nelson, Richard, Orsenigo, Luigi and Winter, Sidney G. (2002), 'A behavioral and evolutionary model of the dynamics of the computer industry', in Augier and March (2002, pp. 354–83)

Malerba, Franco and Orsenigo, Luigi (1995), 'Schumpeterian patterns of innovation', *Cambridge Journal of Economics*, 19, pp. 47–65

Malinvaud, Edmond (ed.) (1979), *Economic Growth and Resources*, Macmillan, London

Mansfield, Edwin and Mansfield, Elizabeth (eds.) (1993), *The Economics of Technical Change*, An Elgar Reference Collection, The International Library of Critical Writings in Economics, Edward Elgar, Aldershot

March, James G. (1988a), 'Introduction: a chronicle of speculations about decision-making in organizations', in March (1988b, pp. 1–21)

(1988b), *Decisions and Organizations*, Blackwell, Oxford

(1991), 'Exploration and exploitation in organizational learning', *Organizational Science*, no. 2, pp. 71–87, repr. in Langlois, Yu and Robertson (2002, vol. II, pp. 621–37)

(1997), 'Understanding how decisions happen in organizations', in Shapira (1997b, pp. 9–32)

March, James G. and Olsen, Johan P. (1975), 'The uncertainty of the past: organizational learning under ambiguity', *European Journal of Political Research*, 3, pp. 147–71; repr. in March [1988b, pp. 335–58]

March, James G. Schulz, Martin and Zhou, Xueguang (2000), *The Dynamics of Rules: Change in Written Organizational Codes*, Stanford University Press, Stanford, CA

March, James G. and Simon, Herbert A. (1958), *Organizations*, John Wiley, New York; 2nd edn. with the collaboration of Harold Guetzkow, Blackwell, Malden, MA and Oxford, 1993; repr. [1995]

Marchionatti, Roberto (2001), 'Sraffa and the criticism of Marshall in the 1920s', in Cozzi and Marchionatti (2001, pp. 43–80)

(2003), 'On the methodological foundations of modern microeconomics: Frank Knight and the "cost controversy" in the 1920s', *History of Political Economy*, 35(1), pp. 49–75

Margolis, Stephen E. and Liebowitz, Stanley J. (1998), 'Path dependence', in Newman (1998, vol. III, pp. 17–22)

Mariani, Myriam (2004), 'What determines technological hits? Geography versus firm competencies', *Research Policy*, 33, pp. 1565–82

Marini, Giovanni and Pannone, Andrea (1998), 'Network production, efficiency and technological options: toward a new dynamic theory of telecommunications', *Economics of Innovation and New Technology*, 7(3), pp. 177–201

322

References

Mariti, Paolo (2003), 'The BC and AC economics of the firm', Collana di
E-papers del Dipartimento di Scienze Economiche, Discussion Paper, 4,
Università di Pisa, Pisa, http://ssrn.com/author=17159
Mariti, Paolo and Smiley, Robert H. (1983), 'Co-operative agreements and
the organization of industry', *Journal of Industrial Economics*, 31(4),
June, pp. 437–51; repr. in Buckley and Michie (1996, pp. 276–92)
Marris, Robin (1964), *The Economic Theory of Managerial Capitalism*,
Macmillan, London, abridged and edited version with a new title,
Managerial Capitalism in Retrospect, St Martin's Press, New York,
[1998]
(ed.) (1974), *The Corporate Society*, John Wiley, New York
(1992), 'Implications for economics', in Egidi and Marris (1992, pp.
194–224)
(2002), 'Edith Penrose and economics', in Pitelis (2002, pp. 61–79)
Marshall, Alfred (1890), *Principles of Economics*, Macmillan, London, 8th
edn. 1920, repr. [1990]
(1975a), 'The theory of foreign trade and other portions of economic
science bearing on the principle of laissez faire', in Marshall (1975b,
vol. II, pp. 3–236)
(1975b), *The Early Economic Writings of Alfred Marshall, 1867–1890*, 2
vols., ed. J.K. Whitaker, Macmillan, London
Martin, Ben R. and Nightingale, Paul (eds.) (2000), *The Political Economy
of Science, Technology and Innovation*, An Elgar Reference Collection,
The International Library of Critical Writings in Economics, Edward
Elgar, Cheltenham
Martin, Stephen (2003), 'Globalization and the natural limits of competition', preliminary version, Department of Economics, Krannert School
of Management, Purdue University, Purdue, Indiana, March
Martino, Gaetano (2005), 'Change in the internal division of labour in
Edith T. Penrose's theory of the growth of the firm', in Guidi and Parisi
(2005, pp. 320–39)
Marx, Karl (1867), *Capital: A Critique to Political Economy*, vol. 1, trans.
from German by B. Frokes, introd. by E. Mandel, Penguin Books in
association with *New Left Review*, London, 1976, repr. [1990]
Maskin, Eric and Tirole, Jean (1999), 'Unforeseen contingencies and
incomplete contracts', *Review of Economic Studies*, 66, pp. 83–114
Masten, Scott E. (1984), 'The organization of production: evidence from
the aerospace industry', *Journal of Law and Economics*, 27, October,
pp. 403–17; repr. in Ménard (2004d, pp. 213–27)
(1996), 'Empirical research in transaction cost economics: challenges,
progress, directions', in Groenewegen (1996, pp. 44–64)
(1999), 'Contractual choice', in Bouckaert and De Geest (1999, pp. 25–45)

Masten, Scott E., Meehan, James W. Jr and Snyder, Edward A. (1991), 'The cost of organization', *Journal of Law, Economics and Organization*, 7(1), pp. 1–25

Mayumi, Kozo and Gowdy, John M. (eds.) (1999), *Bioeconomics and Sustainability: Essays in Honor of Nicholas Georgescu-Roegen*, Edward Elgar, Cheltenham

McCahery, Joseph A., Moerland, Piet, Raaijmakers, Theo and Renneboog Luc (eds.) (2002), *Corporate Governance Regimes: Convergence and Diversity*, Oxford University Press, Oxford

McFadden, Daniel (1999), 'Rationality for economists?', *Journal of Risk and Uncertainty*, 19(1), pp. 73–105

McGuire, C.B. and Radner, Roy (eds.) (1972), *Decision and Organization: A Volume in Honor of Jacob Marschak*, North-Holland, Amsterdam, 2nd edn., University of Minnesota Press, Minneapolis [1986]

Meccheri, Nicola (2005), 'Employment with alternative incentive schemes when effort is not verifiable', *Labour*, 19(1), pp. 55–80

Medema, Steven G. (ed.) (1995), *The Legacy of Ronald Coase in Economic Analysis*, 2 vols., An Elgar Reference Collection, Intellectual Legacies in Modern Economics, Edward Elgar, Aldershot

(ed.) (1998), *Coasean Economics: Law and Economics and the New Institutional Economics*, Kluwer Academic Publishers, Boston

Ménard, Claude (1994), 'Organizations as coordinating devices', *Metroeconomica*, 45(3), October, pp. 224–47; repr. in Ménard (2004e, pp. 316–39)

(1997a), 'Internal characteristics of formal organizations', in Ménard (1997b, pp. 30–58)

(ed.) (1997b), *Transaction Costs Economics: Recent Developments*, Edward Elgar, Cheltenham

(ed.) (2000), *Institutions, Contracts and Organizations: Perspectives from New Institutional Economics*, Edward Elgar, Cheltenham

(ed.) (2004a), *The Foundations of the Institutional Economics*, An Elgar Reference Collection, The International Library of the New Institutional Economics, vol. 1, Edward Elgar, Cheltenham

(ed.) (2004b), *Transaction Costs and Property Rights*, An Elgar Reference Collection, The International Library of the New Institutional Economics, vol. 2, Edward Elgar, Cheltenham

(ed.) (2004c), *Contracts in the New Institutional Economics*, An Elgar Reference Collection, The International Library of the New Institutional Economics, vol. 3, Edward Elgar, Cheltenham

(ed.) (2004d), *Modes of Organization in the New Institutional Economics*, An Elgar Reference Collection, The International Library of the New Institutional Economics, vol. 4, Edward Elgar, Cheltenham

(ed.) (2004e), *Institutional Dimensions of Modern Corporation*, An Elgar Reference Collection, The International Library of the New Institutional Economics, vol. 5, Edward Elgar, Cheltenham

(ed.) (2004f), *The Political Economy of Institutions*, An Elgar Reference Collection, The International Library of the New Institutional Economics, vol. 6, Edward Elgar, Cheltenham

(ed.) (2004g), *Controversies and Challenges in the New Institutional Economics*, An Elgar Reference Collection, The International Library of the New Institutional Economics, vol. 7, Edward Elgar, Cheltenham

(2004h), 'The economics of hybrid organizations', *Journal of Institutional and Theoretical Economics*, 160(3), September, pp. 345–76

Metcalfe, Stanley (1995), 'Technology systems and technology policy in an evolutionary framework', *Cambridge Journal of Economics*, 19, pp. 25–46

Milgrom, Paul and Roberts, John (1986), 'Relying on the information of interested parties', *Rand Journal of Economics*, 17(1), pp. 18–32

(1988), 'Economic theories of the firm: past, present, and future', *Canadian Journal of Economics*, 21, pp. 444–58; repr. in Buckley and Michie (1996, pp. 459–75); repr. in Foss (2000, vol. I, pp. 115–29)

(1990a), 'Bargaining costs, influence costs, and the organization of economic activity', in Alt and Shepsle (1990, pp. 57–89); repr. in Williamson and Masten [1995a, pp. 457–96]; part. repr. in Putterman and Kroszner (1996b, pp.162–74); repr. in Ménard (2004g, pp. 271–312)

(1990b), 'The economics of modern manufacturing: technology, strategy and organization', *American Economic Review*, 53(3), pp. 511–28

(1992), *Economics, Organization, and Management*, Prentice Hall, Englewood Cliffs, NJ

(1995), 'Complementarities and fit: strategy, structure, and organizational change in manufacturing', *Journal of Accounting and Economics*, 19, pp. 179–208

(1999), 'The internal politics of the firm', in Bowles, Franzini and Pagano (1999, pp. 46–62)

Miner, Anne S. (1990), 'Structural evolution through idiosyncratic jobs: the potential for unplanned learning', *Organizational Science*, 1, pp. 195–210

(1991), 'Organizational evolution and the social ecology of jobs', *American Sociological Review*, 56, pp. 772–85

Minsky, Hyman P. (1996), 'Uncertainty and the institutional structure of capitalist economies: remarks upon receiving the Veblen–Commons Award', *Journal of Economic Issues*, 30(3), June, pp. 357–68

Mir, Pere and González, Josep (2003), *Fondos, flujos y tiempo: un análisis microeconómico de los procesos productivos*, Ariel, Barcelona

Mises, Ludwig von (1949), *Human Action*, Yale University Press, New Haven

Molm, Linda D. (1997), *Coercive Power in Social Exchange*, Cambridge University Press, Cambridge and New York

Montgomery, Cynthia A. (ed.) (1995), *Resource-Based and Evolutionary Theories of the Firm: Towards a Synthesis*, Kluwer Academic Publishers, Boston

Moriggia, Vittorio and Morroni, Mario (1993), *KRONOS Production Analyser*, version 2.2, software for the flow–fund analysis of production processes in English, Italian, Spanish and Catalan, Edizioni ETS, Pisa

Morroni, Mario (1991), 'Production flexibility', in Hodgson and Screpanti (1991, pp. 68–80)

(1992), *Production Process and Technical Change*, Cambridge University Press, Cambridge

(1998a), 'Decreasing returns', in Kurz and Salvadori (1998, vol. I, pp. 209–12)

(1998b), 'Increasing returns', in Kurz and Salvadori (1998, vol. I, pp. 399–405)

(1999), 'Production and time: a flow–fund analysis', in Mayumi and Gowdy (1999, pp. 194–228)

Motta, Massimo (2004), *Competition Policy. Theory and Practice*, Cambridge University Press, Cambridge

Mowery, David C., Oxley, Joanne E. and Silverman, Brian S. (1998), 'Technological overlap and interfirm cooperation: implications for the resource-based view of the firm', *Research Policy*, 27(5), pp. 507–23

Narduzzo, Alessandro, Rocco, Elena and Warglien, Massimo (2000), 'Talking about routines in the field: the emergence of organizational capabilities in a new cellular phone network company', in Dosi, Nelson and Winter (2000b, pp. 27–50); repr. in Lazaric and Lorenz (2003b, pp. 333–56)

Needham, Douglas (ed.) (1970), *Readings in the Economics of Industrial Organization*, Holt, Rinehart & Winston, New York

Neef, Dale (ed.) (1998), *The Knowledge Economy*, Butterworth-Heinemann, Woburn, MA

Nell, Edward J. (1988), *Prosperity and Public Spending*, Unwin Hyman, Boston

(1996), 'Transformational growth and the long-period method', *Review of Political Economy*, 8(4), pp. 379–401

Nelson, Richard R. (ed.) (1962), *The Rate and Direction of Inventive Activity: Economic and Social Factors*, Princeton University Press, Princeton

Nelson, Richard, R. and Winter, Sidney G. (1982), *An Evolutionary Theory of Economic Change*, Harvard University Press, Cambridge, MA

Newbery, David M. (1989), 'Missing markets: consequences and remedies', in Hahn (1989b, pp. 211–42)

Newman, Peter (ed.) (1998), *The New Palgrave Dictionary of Economics and the Law*, 3 vols., Macmillan, London

Niman, Neil B. (2004), 'The evolutionary firm and Cournot's Dilemma', *Cambridge Journal of Economics*, 28(2), pp. 273–89

Nonaka, Ikujiro and Takeuchi, Hirotaka (1995), *The Knowledge-Creating Company: How Japanese Companies Create the Dynamics of Innovation*, Oxford University Press, Oxford

Nooteboom, Bart (1993) 'Firm size effects on transaction costs', *Small Business Economics*, 5(4), pp. 283–95

   (2002), *Trust: Forms, Foundations, Functions, Failures and Figures*, Edward Elgar, Cheltenham

   (2003), 'Governance and competence: how can they be combined?', Rotterdam School of Management, Erasmus University Rotterdam, Netherlands, paper presented at the Fifth International Workshop on Institutional Economics, *Explaining the Firm: Transaction Costs or Capabilities?*, June, University of Hertfordshire, Hatfield

Nooteboom, Bart, Noorderhaven, Niels G. and Berger, Hans (1997), 'Effects of trust and governance on relational risk', *Academy of Management Journal*, 40(2), pp. 308–38

Nooteboom, Bart and Six, Frédérique (eds.) (2003), *Trust Process in Organizations: Empirical Studies of the Determinants and the Process of Trust Development*, Edward Elgar, Cheltenham

North, Douglass C. (1990), *Institutions, Institutional Change and Economic Performance*, Cambridge University Press, Cambridge, repr. [1995]

   (1994), 'Economic performance through time', *American Economic Review*, 84(3), June, pp. 359–68

O'Driscoll, Gerald P. Jr (ed.) (1979), *Adam Smith and Modern Political Economy: Bicentennial Essays on the Wealth of Nations*, Iowa State University Press, Ames, IA

O'Driscoll, Gerald P. and Rizzo, Mario J. (1985), *The Economics of Time and Ignorance*, Blackwell, Oxford

Olson, Mancur and Kähkönen, Satu (2000), *A Not-So-Dismal Science: A Broader View of Economies and Societies*, Oxford University Press, Oxford

Ouchi, William G. (1980), 'Markets, bureaucracies and clans', *Administrative Sciences Quarterly*, 25(1), March, pp. 129–41; repr. in Ménard (2004d, pp. 345–57)

Pagano, Ugo (1991), 'Property rights, asset specificity, and the division of labour under alternative capitalist relations', *Cambridge Journal of Economics*, 15, pp. 315–42

Palay, Thomas M. (1985), 'Avoiding regulatory constraints: contracting safeguards and the role of informal agreements', *Journal of Law, Economics, and Organization*, 1(1), Spring, pp. 155–75

Palermo, Giulio (2003), 'The ontology of economic power in a critical realist perspective', Discussion Paper, 308, Università di Brescia, Brescia

Pannone, Andrea (2002), 'Accounting and pricing for the telecommunications industry: an operational approach', *Industrial and Corporate Change*, 10(2), pp. 453–79

Panzar, John Clifford and Willig, Robert D. (1981), 'Economies of scope', *American Economic Review*, 71(2), pp. 668–72

Papi, Ugo and Nunn, Charles (eds.) (1969), *Economic Problems of Agriculture in Industrial Societies*, Proceedings of a Conference of the International Economic Association, Rome, September 1965, Macmillan, London, and St Martin's Press, New York

Pasinetti, Luigi L. (1981), *Structural Change and Economic Growth*, Cambridge University Press, Cambridge

(1993), *Structural Economic Dynamics: A Theory of the Consequences of Human Learning*, Cambridge University Press, Cambridge

(ed.) (1998), *Italian Economic Papers, Volume III*, Società Italiana degli Economisti, Oxford University Press and Il Mulino, Bologna

Patel, Pari and Pavitt, Keith (2000), 'How technological competencies help define the core (not the boundaries) of the firm', in Dosi, Nelson and Winter (2000b, pp. 313–33)

Pavitt, Keith (1998), 'Technologies, products and organisation in the innovating firm: what Adam Smith tells us and Joseph Schumpeter doesn't', *Industrial and Corporate Change*, 7, pp. 433–52

Pedeersen, Torben and Valentin, Finn (1996), 'The impact of foreign acquisition on the evolution of Danish firms', in Foss and Knudsen (1996 pp. 150–74)

Penrose, Edith (1959), *The Theory of the Growth of the Firm*, 3rd edn., Blackwell, Oxford, Oxford University Press, Oxford, repr. [1997]

(1995), 'Foreword to the third edition' of Penrose (1959), pp. ix–xxiii; repr. in Langlois, Yu and Robertson (2002, vol. I, pp. 143–55)

Perez, Carlota (1985), 'Microelectronics, long waves and world structural change: new perspectives of developing countries', *World Development*, 3, March, pp. 442–63

Persky, Joseph (1990), 'A dismal romantic', *Journal of Economic Perspectives*, 4(4), Fall, pp. 165–72

Persson, Torsten (ed.) (1997), *Nobel Lectures: Economic Sciences 1991–1995*, World Scientific Publication, Singapore

Piacentini, Paolo (1995), 'A time-explicit theory of production: analytical and operational suggestions following a 'fund–flow' approach', *Structural Change and Economic Dynamics*, 6, pp. 461–83

Pigou, Arthur Cecil (1913), 'The interdependence of different sources of demand and supply in a market', *Economic Journal*, 23(89), March, pp. 19–24

Piore, Michael J. and Sabel, Charles F. (1984), *The Second Industrial Divide: Possibilities for Prosperity*, Basic Books, New York

Pisano, Gary (2000), 'In search of dynamic capabilities: the origins of R&D competence in biopharmaceuticals', in Dosi, Nelson and Winter (2000b, pp. 129–54)

Pitelis, Christos (1991), *Market and Non-Market Hierarchies*, Blackwell, Oxford

(1993a), 'Transaction costs, markets and hierarchies: the issues', in Pitelis (1993c pp. 7–19)

(1993b), 'On transaction (costs) and markets and (as) hierarchies', in Pitelis (1993c, pp. 262–76)

(ed.) (1993c), *Transaction Costs, Markets and Hierarchies*, Oxford University Press, Oxford, repr 1994

(ed.) (2002), *The Growth of the Firm: The Legacy of Edith Penrose*, Blackwell, Oxford

Plunket, Anne, Voisin, Colette and Bellon, Bertrand (eds.) (2001), *The Dynamics of Industrial Collaboration: The Diversity of Theories and Empirical Approaches*, Edward Elgar, Cheltenham

Polanyi, Michael (1966), *The Tacit Dimension*, Doubleday & Company, New York and Routledge and Kegan Paul, London; repr. Anchor Books, New York, [1967]

Polidori, Roberto and Romagnoli, Alessandro (1987), 'Tecniche e processo produttivo: analisi a "fondi e flussi" della produzione nel settore agricolo', *Rivista di Economia Agraria*, 42(3), pp. 335–72

Popper, Karl R. (1972), *Objective Knowledge: An Evolutionary Approach*, Oxford University Press, Oxford

Porter, Michael E. (1985), *Competitive Advantage: Creating and Sustaining Superior Performance*, Free Press, New York

Powell, Walter W. (1996), 'Inter-organizational collaboration in the biotechnology industry', *Journal of Institutional and Theoretical Economics*, 152(1), pp. 197–215

Prahalad, C.K. (2005), *The Fortune at the Bottom of the Pyramid*, Wharton School Publishing, Upper Saddle River, NJ

Prahalad, C.K. and Hamel, Gary (1990), 'The core competence of the corporation', *Harvard Business Review*, 68, May–June, pp. 79–91; repr. in Foss (1997b, pp. 235–56); repr. in Langlois, Yu and Robertson (2002, vol. II, pp. 327–39); repr. in Kay (2003, pp. 210–22)

Pratten, Cliff F. (1971), *Economies of Scale in Manufacturing Industry*, Cambridge University Press, Cambridge

(1988), *A Survey of the Economies of Scale*, Economic Papers, Commission of the European Communities, Brussels

(1991), *The Competitiveness of Small Firms*, Cambridge University Press, Cambridge

Prencipe, Andrea (1997), 'Technological competencies and product's evolutionary dynamics: a case study from the aero-engine industry', *Research Policy*, 25, pp. 1261–76

Prendergast, Canice (1999), 'The provision of incentives in firms', *Journal of Economic Literature*, 37, March, pp. 7–63

Prendergast, Renee (1992), 'Increasing returns and competitive equilibrium – the content and development of Marshall's theory', *Cambridge Journal of Economics*, 16, December, pp. 447–62

Prescott, Edward C. and Visscher, Michael (1980), 'Organization capital', *Journal of Political Economy*, 88(31), pp. 446–61

Putterman, Louis (ed.) (1986), *The Economic Nature of the Firm: A Reader*, Cambridge University Press, Cambridge

Putterman, Louis and Kroszner, Randall S. (1996a), 'The economic nature of the firm: an new introduction', in Putterman and Kroszner (1996b, pp. 1–31)

(eds.) (1996b), *The Economic Nature of the Firm: A Reader*, Cambridge University Press, Cambridge, 2nd edn. of Putterman (1986) with a selection from material published in the 1st edn. and eleven new essays

Rabin, Matthew (1998), 'Psychology and economics', *Journal of Economic Literature*, 36, March, pp. 11–46

Radner, Roy (1968), 'Competitive equilibrium under uncertainty', *Econometrica*, 36(1), pp. 31–58

(1996), 'Bounded rationality, indeterminacy and the theory of the firm', *Economic Journal*, 106(438), pp. 1360–73

(2000), 'Costly and bounded rationality in individual and team decision-making', *Industrial and Corporate Change*, 9(4), November, pp. 623–58

Raffaelli, Tiziano (2003), *Marshall's Evolutionary Economics*, Routledge, London

Rajan, Raghuram G. and Zingales, Luigi (1998), 'Power in a theory of the firm', *Quarterly Journal of Economics*, May, pp. 387–432); repr. in Foss (2000, vol. III, pp. 128–67)

Ramazzotti, Paolo (2004), 'What do firms learn? Capabilities, distribution and the division of labour', in Foster and Metcalfe (2004, pp. 38–61)

Rao, C.R. (ed.) (1964), *Essays in Econometrics and Planning*, Pergamon Press, Oxford

Research Center in Entrepreneurial History (ed.) (1949), *Change and the Entrepreneur: Postulates and Patterns for Entrepreneurial History*, Harvard University, Harvard University Press, Cambridge, MA

Ricketts, Martin (1987), *The Economics of Business Enterprises: An Introduction to Economic Organisation and the Theory of the Firm*, Edward Elgar, Cheltenham, 3rd edn. [2002]

Richardson, George B. (1972), 'The organization of industry', *Economic Journal*, 82, September, pp. 883–96; repr. in Earl (1988, vol. II, pp. 57–70); repr. in Buckley and Michie (1996, pp. 59–74); repr. in Casson (1996, pp. 618–31); part. repr. in Putterman and Kroszner [1996b, pp. 136–45]; repr. in Foss (1997b, pp. 60–72); repr. in Foss (2000, vol. IV, pp. 15–29); repr. in Langlois, Yu and Robertson 2002, vol. II, pp. 3–16; repr. in Kay (2003, pp. 883–96)

Ricottilli, Massimo (2001), 'Innovative change, search and division of labour', preliminary version, Department of Economics and Statistics, University of Trieste, pp. 1–26

Rindfleisch, Aric and Heide, Jan B. (1997), 'Transaction cost analysis: past, present and future applications', *Journal of Marketing*, 61(4), October, pp. 30–54; repr. in Ménard (2004g, pp. 539–63)

Robertson, Paul L. (ed.) (1999), *Authority and Control in Modern Industry*, Routledge, London

Robertson, Paul L. and Langlois, Richard N. (1992), 'Modularity, innovation and the firm: the case of audio components', in Scherer and Perlman (1992, pp. 321–42)

Robinson, Edward Austin Gossage (1931), *The Structure of Competitive Industry*, Cambridge University Press, Cambridge, rev. and reset edn. [1958]

Robinson, Joan (1952), *The Rate of Interest and Other Essays*, Macmillan, London

(1980), 'The time in economic theory', *Kyklos*, 33(2), pp. 219–29

Roe, Mark (2003), *Political Determinants of Corporate Governance: Political Context, Corporate Impact*, Oxford University Press, Oxford

Romer, Paul M. (1989), 'Capital accumulation in the theory of long-run growth', in Barro (1989, pp. 51–127)

(1990), 'Endogenous technical change', *Journal of Political Economy*, 98(5), pp. 72–102; repr. in Mansfield and Mansfield (1993, pp. 12–43)

(1991), 'Increasing returns and new developments in the theory of growth', in Barnett *et al.* (1991, pp. 83–110)

(1998), 'The theory behind the soft revolution', *Journal of Applied Corporate Finance*, 11(2), Summer, pp. 9–14

Rosenberg, Nathan (1965), 'Adam Smith on the division of labour: two views or one?', *Economica*, 23, May, pp. 127–39

(1969), 'The direction of technological change: inducement mechanisms and focusing devises', *Economic Development and Cultural Change*; repr. in Rosenberg [1976, pp. 108–25]

(1976), *Perspectives on Technologies*, Cambridge University Press, Cambridge

(1978), 'Progresso tecnico: l'analisi storica', in Carmignani and Vercelli (1978, II, p. 626–45), English version 'The historiography of technical progress', in Rosenberg [1982b, pp. 3–33]

(1982a), 'Learning by using', in Rosenberg (1982b, pp. 120–40); repr. in Lazaric and Lorenz (2003a, pp. 575–95)

(1982b), *Inside the Black Box: Technology and Economics*, Cambridge University Press, Cambridge, repr. [1985]

(1990), 'Why do firms do basic research (with their own money)?', *Research Policy*, 19, pp. 165–74; repr. in Stephan and Audretsch (2000, vol. II, pp. 197–206)

(1996), 'Uncertainty and technological change', in Landau, Taylor and Wright (1996, pp. 334–53)

(2002), 'America's university/industry interfaces: 1945–2000', Department of Economics, Stanford University, mimeo, May

Rosenberg, Nathan and Birdzell, L.E. (1986), *How the West Grew Rich: The Economic Transformation of the Industrial World*, I.B. Tauris, London

Rothschild, Michael and Stiglitz, Joseph E. (1976), 'Equilibrium in competitive insurance markets: an essay on the economics of imperfect information', *Quarterly Journal of Economics*, 80, pp. 629–49; repr. in Williamson (1990b, pp. 141–61)

Rubinstein, Ariel (1998), *Modeling Bounded Rationality*, MIT Press, Cambridge, MA

Rumelt, Richard P. (1994), 'Foreword', in Hamel and Heene (1994, pp. xv–xix)

(1995), 'Inertia and transformation', in Montgomery (1995, pp. 101–32)

Runde, Jochen (1998), 'Information, knowledge and agency: the information theoretic approach and the Austrians', draft, Girton College and New Hall, Cambridge

Rura-Polley, Thekla and Miner, Anne S. (2002), 'The relative standing of routines: some jobs are more equal than others', in Augier and March (2002, pp. 273–303)

References

Russell, Bertrand (1938), *Power: A New Social Analysis*, Allen & Unwin, London, 7th impression [1957]

Sabel, Charles F. and Zeitlin, Jonathan (eds.) (1997), *World of Possibilities: Flexibility and Mass Production in Western Industrialization*, Cambridge University Press, Cambridge

Sacconi, Lorenzo (1997), *Economia etica organizzazione*, Laterza, Roma–Bari; English trans. from Italian by Eulama Literary Agency, *The Social Contract of the Firm: Economics, Ethics and Organisation*, Springer-Verlag, Berlin [2000]

Sako, Mari (1992), *Prices, Quality and Trust: Inter-Firm Relations in Britain and in Japan*, Cambridge University Press, Cambridge

Salanié, Bernard (2000), *The Microeconomics of Market Failures*, MIT Press, Cambridge, MA

Sathe, Vijay (2003), *Corporate Entrepreneurshop: Top Managers and New Business Creation*, 'Foreword' by P.F. Drucker, Cambridge University Press, Cambridge

Saviotti, Pier Paolo (1996), *Technological Evolution, Variety and the Economy*, Cheltenham, Edward Elgar

(1999), 'Knowledge, information and organisational structures', in Robertson (1999, pp. 120–39)

Saviotti, Pier Paolo (ed.) (2003), *Applied Evolutionary Economics: New Empirical Methods and Simulation Techniques*, Edward Elgar, Cheltenham

Saviotti, Pier Paolo and Metcalfe, J. Stanley (eds.) (1991), *Evolutionary Theories of Economic and Technological Change: Present State and Future Prospects*, Harwood Academic Publishers, London

Scazzieri, Roberto (1993), *A Theory of Production: Tasks, Processes and Technical Practices*, Clarendon Press, Oxford

Scherer, Frederic Michael (1980), *Industrial Market Structure and Economic Performance*, 2nd edn., Rand McNally, Chicago

(2000), 'Professor Sutton's "Technology and market structure"', *Journal of Industrial Economics*, 48(2), June, pp. 215–23

Scherer, Frederic Michael and Perlman, Mark (eds.) (1992), *Entrepreneurship, Technological Innovation and Economic Growth: Studies in the Schumpeterian Tradition*, University of Michigan Press, Ann Arbor

Schulz, Martin (2002), 'Organizational Learning', in Baum (2002, pp. 415–41)

Schmalensee Richard and Willig Robert D. (eds.) (1989), *Handbook of Industrial Organization*, 2 vols., Elsevier, Amsterdam

Schumann, Dirk (1999), 'Buddenbrooks revisited: the firm and the entrepreneurial family in Germany during the nineteenth and early twentieth centuries', in Robertson (1999, pp. 221–39)

Schumpeter, Joseph Alois (1912), *Theorie der Wirtschaftlichen Entwicklung*, Dunker & Humblot, Berlin, English trans. from German by Redvers Opie, *The Theory of Economic Development: An Inquiry into Profits, Capital, Credit, Interest and the Business Cycle*, Harvard Economic Studies Series, Harvard University, Cambridge, MA, 1934, first published by Oxford University Press, New York [1961]

(1949), 'Economic theory and entrepreneurial history', in Research Center in Entrepreneurial History (1949, pp. 63–84)

Scitovsky, Tibor (1979), 'Can changing consumer tastes save resources?', in Malinvaud (1979); repr. in Scitovsky [1986, pp. 117–27]

(1986), *Human Desire and Economic Satisfaction: Essays on the Frontiers of Economics*, Harvester Wheatsheaf, New York

Screpanti, Ernesto (1995), 'Relative rationality, institutions and precautionary behaviour', in Groenewegen, Pitelis and Sjöstrand (1995, pp. 63–83)

(2001), *The Fundamental Institutions of Capitalism*, Routledge, London

Sen, Amartya (1999), *Development as Freedom*, Oxford University Press, Oxford, repr. [2001]

Shackle, George Lennox Sherman (1954), 'The complex nature of times as a concept in economics', *Economia Internazionale*, 7(4), November, pp. 743–57; repr. in Shackle [1990, pp. 3–13]

(1955), *Uncertainty in Economics and Other Reflections*, Cambridge University Press, Cambridge, repr. [1968]

(1958), *Time in Economics*, North-Holland, Amsterdam, 2nd printing [1967]

(1959), 'Time and thought', *British Journal for the Philosophy of Science*, 9(36), pp. 285–98; repr. in Shackle [1990, pp. 14–27]

(1972), *Epistemics and Economics: A Critique of Economic Doctrines*, Cambridge University Press, Cambridge

(1979), *Imagination and the Nature of Choice*, Edinburgh University Press, Edinburgh

(1990), *Time, Expectations and Uncertainty in Economics: Selected Essays of G.L.S. Shackle*, ed. James Lorne Ford, Edward Elgar, Aldershot

Shane, Scott (1994), 'The effect of national culture on the choice between licensing and direct foreign investment', *Strategic Management Journal*, 15, pp. 627–42

(2003), *A General Theory of Entrepreneurship: The Individual–Opportunity Nexus*, Edward Elgar, Cheltenham and Northampton, MA

Shapira, Zur (1997a), 'Introduction and overview', in Shapira (1997b, pp. 3–8)

(ed.) (1997b), *Organizational Decision Making*, Cambridge University Press, Cambridge

Shapiro, Carl and Varian, Hal R. (1999), *Information Rules: A Strategic Guide to the Network Economy*, Harvard Business School Press, Boston, MA

Shelanski, Howard A. and Klein, Peter G. (1995), 'Empirical research in transaction cost economics: a review and assessment', *Journal of Law, Economics & Organization*, 11(2), pp. 335–61

Shleifer, Andrei and Vishny, Robert W. (1997), 'A survey of corporate governance', *Journal of Finance*, 52(2), June, pp. 737–8

Siebert, Horst (ed.) (1995), *Trends in Business Organization: Do Participation and Cooperation Increase Competititiveness?* International Workshop, J.C.B. Mohr, Tübingen

Silverman, Brian S. (1999), 'Technological resources and the direction of corporate diversification: toward an integration of the resource-based view and transaction cost economics', *Management Science*, 45(8), August, pp. 1109–24

(2002), 'Organizational economics', in Baum (2002, pp. 467–93)

Simon, Herbert A. (1951), 'A formal theory of the employment relationship', *Econometrica*, 19, pp. 293–305; repr. in Simon (1957, pp. 183–94); repr. in Simon [1982, vol. 2, pp. 11–23]; repr. in Putterman (1986, pp. 103–10); repr. in Casson (1996, pp. 79–91); repr. in Foss (2000, vol. II, pp. 276–87)

(1955), 'A behavioral model of rational choice', *Quarterly Journal of Economics*, 69, February, repr. in Simon (1957, pp. 241–60); repr. in Simon [1982, vol. 2, pp. 239–58]

(1957), *Models of Man: Mathematical Essays on Rational Human Behavior in a Social Setting*, John Wiley, New York

(1959), 'Theories of decision-making in economics and behavioral science', *American Economic Review*, 49(3), June, pp. 253–83; repr. in Simon [1982, vol. 2, pp. 287–317], repr. in Earl (1988, vol. I, 77–107)

(1972), 'Theories of bounded rationality', in McGuire and Radner (1972, pp. 161–76); repr. in Simon [1982, vol. 2, pp. 408–23]

(1976), 'From substantive to procedural rationality', in Latsis (1976, pp. 129–48); repr. in Simon [1982, vol. 2, pp. 424–43]

(1978), 'Rationality as process and as product of thought', Richard T. Ely Lecture, *American Economic Review*, 68(2), May, pp. 1–16, repr. in Simon [1982, vol. 2, pp. 444–59]; repr. in Ménard (2004b, pp. 14–29)

(1982), *Models of Bounded Rationality, Volume Two: Behavioral Economics and Business Organization*, MIT Press, Cambridge, MA

(1987a), 'Behavioural economics', in Eatwell, Milgate and Newman (1987, vol. 1, pp. 221–5); repr. in Simon [1997a, pp. 277–90]

(1987b), 'Bounded rationality', in Eatwell, Milgate and Newman (1987, vol. 1, pp. 266–8); repr. in Simon [1997a, pp. 291–4]

(1991), 'Organizations and markets', *Journal of Economic Perspectives*, 5(2), pp. 25–44; repr. in Keasey, Thompson and Wright (1999a, pp. 67–86); repr. in Ménard (2004g, pp. 128–47)

(1992), 'Introductory Comment', in Egidi and Marris (1992, pp. 3–7)

(1997a), *Models of Bounded Rationality, Volume 3: Empirically Grounded Economic Reason*, MIT Press, Cambridge, MA

(1997b), *An Empirically Based Microeconomics*, ed. Piero Tedeschi, Raffaele Mattioli Lectures, Raffaele Mattioli Foundation, Cambridge University Press, Cambridge

Slater, Gary and Spencer, David A. (2000), 'The uncertain foundations of transaction costs economics', *Journal of Economic Issues*, 34(1), March, pp. 61–87

Smith, Adam (1776), *An Inquiry into the Nature and Causes of the Wealth of Nations*, 2 vols., Clarendon Press, Oxford [1976]

Sobrero, Maurizio and Schrader, Stefan (1998), 'Structuring inter-firm relationships: a meta-analytic approach', *Organization Studies*, 19(4), pp. 585–615

Social Accountability International (2002), 'An overview of SAI and SA8000', in http://www.cepaa.org/accreditation.htm

Spence, A. Michael (1974), *Market Signaling: Informational Transfer in Hiring and Related Screening Processes*, Harvard University Press, Cambridge, MA

Spender, John-Christopher (1989), *Industry Recipes: An Enquiry into the Nature and Sources of Managerial Judgement*, Blackwell, Oxford

(1996), 'Making knowledge the basis of a dynamic theory of the firm', *Strategic Management Journal*, 17, Winter Special Issue, pp. 45–62

Spiller, Pablo T. and Zelner, Bennet A. (1997), 'Product complementarities, capabilities and governance: a dynamic transaction cost perspective', *Industrial and Corporate Change*, 6(3), pp. 561–94

Sraffa, Piero (1925), 'Sulle relazioni tra costo e quantità prodotta', *Annali di Economia*, II, pp. 277–328; English trans. by John Eatwell and Alessandro Roncaglia, 'On the relations between cost and quantity produced' in Pasinetti (1998, pp. 323–63); repr. in Kurz and Salvadori [2003, pp. 3–43]

(1926), 'The law of returns under competitive conditions', *Economic Journal*, 36(144), December, pp. 535–50; repr. in Stigler and Boulding (1953, pp. 180–97); repr. in Kurz and Salvadori [2003, pp. 44–59]

Stalk, George, Evans, Philip and Shulman, Lawrence E. (1992), 'Competing on capabilities: the new rules of corporate strategy', *Harvard Business Review*, March–April, pp. 57–69

Stephan, Paula E. and Audretsch, David B. (eds.) (2000), *The Economics of Science and Innovation*, 2 vols., An Elgar Reference Collection, The International Library of Critical Writings in Economics, Edward Elgar, Cheltenham

Stigler, George J. and Boulding, Kenneth E. (eds.) (1953), *Readings in Price Theory*, Allen & Unwin, London, repr. [1970]

Stiglitz, Joseph E. (1989), 'Incentives, information, and organizational design', *Empirica – Austrian Economic Papers*, 16(1), pp. 3–29

Stiglitz, Joseph E. and Weiss, Andrew (1981), 'Credit rationing in markets with imperfect information', *American Economic Review*, 71(3), June, pp. 393–409

Storey, David J. (2000), *Small Business: Critical Perspectives on Business and Management*, 4 vols., Routledge, London

Sutton, John (1998), *Technology and Market Structure: Theory and History*, MIT Press, Cambridge, MA

Sylos-Labini, Paolo (1992), '*Capitalism, Socialism, and Democracy* and large-scale firms', in Scherer and Perlman (1992, pp. 55–64)

Szulanski, Gabriel (2000), 'Appropriability and the challenge of scope: Banc One routinizes replication', in Dosi, Nelson and Winter (2000b, pp. 69–97)

Takeishi, Akira (2001), 'Bridging inter- and intra-firm boundaries: management of supplier involvement in automobile product development', *Strategic Management Journal*, 22, pp. 403–33

Tang, Antony M. Westfield, Fred M. and Worley, James S. (eds.) (1976), *Evolution, Welfare and Time in Economics: Essays in Honor of Nicholas Georgescu-Roegen*, Lexington, MA and Cambridge, MA

Tani, Piero (1976), 'La rappresentazione analitica del processo di produzione: alcune premesse teoriche al problema del decentramento', *Note Economiche*, no. 4–5, new rev. version with the title 'La decomponibilità del processo produttivo', in Becattini (1987, pp. 69–92)

    (1986), *Analisi microeconomica della produzione*, La Nuova Italia Scientifica, Rome

    (1988), 'Flow, funds and sectorial interdependence in the theory of production', *Political Economy: Studies in the Surplus Approach* 4(1), pp. 3–21

Tattara, Giuseppe (ed.) (2001), *Il piccolo che nasce dal grande: le molteplici facce dei distretti industriali veneti*, F. Angeli, Milan

Teece, David J. (1998a), *Economic Performance and the Theory of the Firm: The Selected Papers of David J. Teece, Volume One*, Edward Elgar, Cheltenham

    (1998b), *Strategy, Technology and Public Policy: The Selected Papers of David J. Teece, Volume Two*, Edward Elgar, Cheltenham

Teece, David J., Pisano, Gary and Shuen, Amy (1997), 'Dynamic capabilities and strategic management', *Strategic Management Journal*, 18(7), pp. 509–33; repr. in Foss (1997b, pp. 268–86); repr. in Teece [1998b, vol. II, pp. 197–221]; repr. in Langlois, Yu and Robertson (2002, vol. II, pp. 217–41)

Teece, David J., Rumelt, Richard, Dosi, Giovanni and Winter, Sidney (1994), 'Understanding corporate coherence: theory and evidence', *Journal of Economic Behavior and Organization*, 23, pp. 1–30; repr. in Casson (1996, pp. 501–30); repr. in Teece [1998a, vol. I, pp. 187–217]; repr. in Foss (2000, vol. IV, pp. 74–101); repr. in Langlois, Yu and Robertson (2002, vol. II, pp. 368–97); repr. in Kay (2003, pp. 468–97)

Thompson, S. and Wright, M. (1995), 'Corporate governance: the role of restructuring transactions', *Economic Journal*, 105, May, 690–703

Tirole, Jean (1999), 'Incomplete contracts: where do we stand?', *Econometrica*, 67(4), July, pp. 741–81; repr. in Ménard (2004c, pp. 35–75)

Townsend, Harry (ed.) (1971), *Price Theory*, Penguin Books, London, UK 2nd edn. [1980]

Tunzelmann, G. Nick von (1998), 'Localized technological search and multi-technology companies', *Economics of Innovation and New Technology*, 6, pp. 231–55

Turvani, Margherita (2001a), 'Reading Edith Penrose's *The Theory of the Growth of the Firm* forty years on (1959–1999)', in Garrouste and Ioannides (2001, pp. 148–78)

(2001b), 'Microfoundations of knowledge dynamics within the firm', *Industry and Innovation*, 8(3), December, pp. 309–23

Tversky, Amos and Fox Craig R. (1995), 'Weighing risk and uncertainty', *Psychological Review*, 102(2), pp. 269–83; repr. in Kahneman and Tversky [2000, pp. 93–117]

Tversky, Amos and Kahneman, Daniel (1974), 'Judgment under uncertainty: heuristics and biases', *Science*, 185, pp. 1124–31; repr. in Kahneman, Slovic and Tversky [1982, pp. 3–20]

(1992), 'Advances in prospect theory: Cumulative representation of uncertainty', *Journal of Risk and Uncertainty*, 5(4), October, pp. 297–323; repr. in Hey (1997a, pp. 483–509); repr. in Kahneman and Tversky [2000, pp. 44–65]

Tylecote, Andrei and Visintin Francesca (2002), 'Financial and corporate governance systems and technological change: the incompleteness of fit of the UK and Italy', *Economia e Politica Industriale*, no. 114, pp. 81–108

Vannucci, Alberto (1997), 'Inefficienza amministrativa e corruzione', *Rivista Trimestrale di Scienza dell'Amministrazione*, no. 1, pp. 29–55

(2004), *Governare l'incertezza: scelte pubbliche e cambiamento istituzionale*, Rubbetino, Soveria Mannelli, Catanzaro

Vannucci, Alberto and della Porta, Donatella (2003), 'Corruption in policing and law enforcement: a theoretical scheme for the analysis of the Italian case', in Einstein and Amir (2003, pp. 21–52)

Vercelli, Alessandro (1995), 'From soft uncertainty to hard environmental uncertainty', *Economie Appliquée*, 48(2), pp. 251–69

(1999), 'The recent advances in decision theory under uncertainty: a non-technical introduction', in Luini (1999, pp. 237–60)

Waddington, Conrad H. (1977), *Tools for Thought*, Jonathan Cape, London

Walker, Gordon and Weber, David (1984), 'Transaction cost approach to make-or-buy decisions', *Administrative Science Quarterly*, 29, pp. 373–91

Walliser, Bernard (1989), 'Instrumental rationality and cognitive rationality', *Theory and Decision*, 27, pp. 7–36

Wernerfelt, Birger (1984), 'A resource-based view of the firm', *Strategic Management Journal*, 5, pp. 171–80; repr. in Foss (1997b, pp. 117– 30); repr. in Langlois, Yu and Robertson [2002, vol. II, pp. 59–68]

Westhead, Paul and Wright, Mike (eds.) (2000), *Advances in Entrepreneurship*, 2 vols., An Elgar Reference Collection, Edward Elgar, Cheltenham

Whelan, Robert (1999), *Involuntary Action: How Voluntary is the 'Voluntary' Sector*, IEA, Health and Welfare Unit, London

Williamson, Oliver E. (1981), 'The modern corporation: origin, evolution, attributes', *Journal of Economic Literature*, 19(4), December, pp. 1537–68; repr. in Ménard (2004e, pp. 35–66)

(1985), *The Economic Institutions of Capitalism*, Free Press, New York, repr. [1987]

(1989), 'Transaction cost economics', in Schmalensee and Willig (1989, vol. I, pp. 136–82); repr. in Williamson (1996, pp. 54–87)

(1990a), 'Chester Barnard and the incipient science of organization', in Williamson (1990c, pp. 172–206); repr. in Williamson [1996, pp. 29–53]

(ed.) (1990b), *Industrial Organization*, Edward Elgar, Aldershot

(ed.) (1990c), *Organization Theory: From Chester Barnard to the Present and Beyond*, Oxford University Press, New York

(1991), 'Comparative economic organization: the analysis of discrete structural alternatives', *Administrative Science Quarterly*, 36(2), June, pp. 269–96; repr. in Williamson [1996, pp. 93–119]; repr. in Williamson and Masten (1999, pp. 101–27); repr. in Foss (2000, vol. III, pp. 219–51); repr. in Ménard (2004d, pp. 10–37)

(1993), 'Opportunism and its critics', *Managerial and Decision Economics*, 14, pp. 97–107

(1996), *The Mechanisms of Governance*, Oxford University Press, New York and Oxford

(1997), 'Review of *The Economics of the Business Firm. Seven Critical Comments*, by Harold Demsetz, Cambridge University Press, Cambridge, 1995', *Journal of Economic Literature*, 35, March, pp. 129–30

(1999a), 'Human actors and economic organization', preliminary version, University of California, Berkeley

(1999b), 'Strategy research: governance and competence perspectives', *Strategy Management Journal*, 20(12), pp. 1087–108; repr. in Foss and Mahnke [2000, pp. 21–54]

(2002), 'Empirical microeconomics: another perspective', in Augier and March (2002, pp. 419–41)

Williamson, Oliver E. and Masten, Scott E. (eds.) (1995a), *Transaction Cost Economics, Volume I: Theory and Concepts*, An Elgar Critical Writings Reader, The International Library of Critical Writings in Economics, Edward Elgar, Aldershot

(eds.) (1995b), *Transaction Cost Economics, Volume II: Policy and Applications*, An Elgar Critical Writings Reader, The International Library of Critical Writings in Economics, Edward Elgar, Aldershot

(eds.) (1999), *The Economics of Transaction Costs*, An Elgar Critical Writings Reader, Edward Elgar, Cheltenham

Williamson, Oliver E. and Winter, Sidney G. (eds.) (1991), *The Nature of the Firm: Origins, Evolution, and Development*, Oxford University Press, Oxford

Wilson, James A. (1980), 'Adaptation to uncertainty and small numbers exchange: the New England fresh fish market', *Bell Journal of Economics*, 11(4), Autumn, pp. 491–504

Winter, Sidney G. (1967), 'Toward a neo-Schumpeterian theory of the firm', The RAND Corporation, Santa Monica, CA, draft, forthcoming *Industrial and Corporate Change*

(1988), 'On Coase, competence, and the corporation', *Journal of Law, Economics and Organization*, 4(1), pp. 163–80; repr. in Williamson and Winter [1991, pp. 179–95]; repr. in Casson (1996, pp. 483–500)

(2005), 'Towards an evolutionary theory of production', in Dopfer (2005, pp. 223–54)

Winter, Sidney G. and Szulanski, Gabriel (2001), 'Replication as strategy', *Organization Science*, 12(6), November–December, pp. 730–43

Witt, Ulrich (1998), 'Imagination and leadership – the neglected dimension of an evolutionary theory of the firm', *Journal of Economic Behavior and Organization*, 35, pp. 161–77; repr. in Langlois, Yu and Robertson (2002, vol. III, pp. 66–82)

(1999), 'Do entrepreneurs need firms? A contribution to a missing chapter in Austrian economics', *Review of Austrian Economics*, 11, pp. 99–109; repr. in Witt [2003, pp. 389–400]

(2000), 'Changing cognitive frames – changing organizational forms: an entrepreneurial theory of organizational development', *Industrial and Corporate Change*, 9(4), pp. 733–55

(2003), *The Evolving Economy: Essays on the Evolutionary Approach to Economics*, Edward Elgar, Cheltenham

(2004), 'On the proper interpretation of "evolution" in economics and its implications for production theory', *Journal of Economic Methodology*, 11(2), June, pp. 125–46

Yang, Xiaokai and Ng, Siang (1998), 'Specialization and division of labour: a survey', in Arrow, Ng and Yang (1998, pp. 3–63)

Young, David (1995), 'The meaning and role of power in economic theory' in Groenewegen, Pitelis and Sjöstrand (1995, pp. 85–100); repr. in Hodgson [2002b, pp. 48–61]

Zander, Udo and Kogut, Bruce (1995), 'Knowledge and the speed of the transfer and imitation of organizational capabilities: an empirical test', *Organization Science*, 6(1), January–February, pp. 76–92

Zenger, Todd R. (2002), 'Crafting internal hybrids: complementarities, common change initiatives, and the team-based organization', *International Journal of the Economics of Business*, 9(1), pp. 79–95

Ziman, John (ed.) (2000), *Technological Innovation as an Evolutionary Process*, Cambridge University Press, Cambridge

Zingales, Luigi (2000), 'In search of new foundations', *Journal of Finance*, 55(4), August, pp. 1623–53

Author index

347

Subject index

abilities 15, 212
incomplete, and radical
uncertainty 127–8
individual 47–55, 135–6, 158, 174,
246: and aims of firm 93;
completeness 50; and freedom 86;
and variety 71
and labour market 24
and local knowledge 121
managerial 11
and perfect-rational behaviour 114
and reserves 206
and specialisation 219
absorptive capacity 21, 29, 169, 236
accountability 197
accreditation 195
organisations 197
acquisitions and mergers 5, 241–2
adaptation 164
adaptive behaviour, see sequential
aiming
adjustment, and innovation 223
adverse selection 33, 101, 106
advocacy activities 100
AEG 72
agency relationship 83–4
and bribes 84–5
agglomeration economies 35
aims
conflicting 46
of the firm 93, 97
heterogeneous 46
identification of common 230
individual 7, 43–6, 107
see also sequential aiming
aircraft production, market
structures 253–4
Anglo-American corporate
governance, ownership
structure 93–4

anti-trust policies 86, 235
appropriability of information and
knowledge 28–32, 34–5
artisan production, and flexibility
177, 244
aspiration levels 121, 223
asset specificity 155, 158–9, 161–2
assets of the firm 15, 130
financial 134
knowledge 131–2
organisational 132–3
ownership and aims of firms 98
ownership and rights 91, 92,
95, 208
physical 134
relational 133
strategic 141
AT&T 4
authority 208–9, 210
see also control rights; hierarchy;
managerial coordination
auxiliary transformation processes 146

banks, and corporate capitalism 94
basic conditions 7, 19
definition 24
influence on decision-making
process 24
substantive uncertainty 63
behaviour
adaptive, see sequential aiming
and aims of firms 93
cognitive 214–15
inconsistency 46
behavioural regularities 215
Bell Labs, laser patent 65
Bosch 72
bounded cognition 117
bounded rationality 117–18, 155
bribes 84–5

349

organisations (*cont.*)
  and internalising activities 107
  and knowledge assets 132
  market and 1, 16–18, 37, 82–5
  regulating markets 77, 193–8
  rising costs 258–60
outsourcing 95, 202, 248–9
ownership forms 93–7
  separation from control 95
ownership structure, and
  incentives 104, 105

participation, and learning
  processes 21
partnerships 92
patents 29
path-dependence 75–7
pay policy incentives 107–8
pecuniary economies 171
penalties, and incentive contracts
  103–4
performance evaluation 107
performance feedback, and sequential
  aiming 224
performance-related pay systems 110
piece-rate compensation 107
political bodies 79
post-contractual information
  asymmetry, and moral hazard 101
poverty alleviation, and corruption 85
power 45, 99, 208–10
  and knowledge 230
  see also employment contract;
  market power
pre-contractual information
  asymmetry, and adverse
  selection 101
principal–agent relationship 83–4
  and moral hazard 103
private governments and
  hybrids 203–4
problem-solving procedures, and
  cognitive rationality 116
procedural justice 110
process organisation 132, 138
product bundling 42
product differentiation 53
product warranties 191–2
production
  competitive pressure 51–2

costs of 251, 252
  and knowledge-based economy 51
  scale and flexibility of 243–4
production costs, and economic
  indivisibility 39
production elements 38
production patterns 138
production process 5, 40, 247
  decomposition of 143, 253
  divisibility of information and
    knowledge 168
  non-saturability 168
  and replication costs 168
  and technical advance 72
  temporal dimension of 55
  see also complementarities;
    economies of scale; process
    organisation
production unit 5, 40, 43
productive capacities, range of 163
productivity, and specialisation 218
  see also incentives; teams
profits 98–100
  as residual income 98
  managerial theories of the firm 98
  maximisation and uncertainty 122–3
  perfect competition 97
property rights
  and contracts 154
  and growth of enterprises 80
  and technology 76–7
  theory of 91, 92, 182
property structure 89
  types of 92
public organisations 79

quality uncertainties 33
quasi-rents 33, 82, 83, 106, 229
QWERTY keyboard 11–12, 75

radical uncertainty 12, 14, 19, 20, 61,
  62, 73–5, 187–8
  economic process 123–4, 125
  firms' functioning and growth
    124–5, 156, 205
  and imagination 117
  and incentives 110–11
  and incomplete contracts 160–3
  increase in 78–9
  and transaction costs 161